MW00333529

The Story I Tell Myself

HAZEL E. BARNES

The Story I Tell Myself

*A Venture
in Existentialist
Autobiography*

THE UNIVERSITY OF CHICAGO PRESS
CHICAGO AND LONDON

Hazel E. Barnes taught Classics, humanities, and philosophy at the University of Colorado. Now retired, she lives
in Boulder. Her books include *An Existentialist Ethics, Sartre and
Flaubert*, and the translation of Sartre's *Being and Nothingness*.

The University of Chicago Press, Chicago 60637
The University of Chicago Press, Ltd., London
© 1997 by The University of Chicago
All rights reserved. Published 1997
Printed in the United States of America

06 05 04 03 02 01 00 99 98 97   1 2 3 4 5

Library of Congress Cataloging-in-Publication Data

Barnes, Hazel Estella.
    The story I tell myself : a venture in existentialist auto-
biography / Hazel E. Barnes.
        p.   c.m.
    Includes index.
    ISBN: 0-226-03732-0 (cloth)
    1. Barnes, Hazel Estella. 2. College teachers—United
States—Biography. 3. Feminists—United States—
Biography. 4. Existentialism. I. Title.
CT275.B4474A3   1997
305.42′092   96-29600
[B]—DC21   CIP

Parts of chapter six, "Existential Feminism," appeared
originally in *Simone de Beauvoir Studies*, volume 10, 1993, and
are reprinted by permission.

This book is printed on acid-free paper.

CONTENTS

v

Photographs follow pages 108 and 260.

RECOGNITIONS and ACKNOWLEDGMENTS

At the time when I was divided between the urgent wish to write my autobiography and hesitation as to the wisdom and feasibility of undertaking so personal a project, the support of a particular few was decisive in determining me to go forward with it. My longtime companion, Doris Schwalbe, courageously read through each section and discussed it with me before I submitted it for proper typing; to my sister, Jean Newcomer, and my brother, Paul, I sent copies of the typescript for each major section as I finished it. The responses of all three were immeasurably helpful. Almost as indispensable was the encouragement of other persons who, without having the opportunity to read the manuscript, expressed sustaining belief in the worthwhileness of the enterprise and my ability to carry it through. Among them I want to thank especially Betty Cannon, Geraldine Hammond, Marcus Edward, Stanley Konecky, and Cal Briggs.

The pattern of my narrative inevitably has highlighted certain people without naming others who for many years were significant figures in my life and responsible in large part for the pleasurable flavor of day-to-day existence. In speaking of my early days, for instance, I did not mention my twin cousins, Marvin and Melvin Barnes, six years older than I, who brightened my childhood with indulgent entertainment and remained friends throughout my adult life. I will never think of my time in Greensboro, North Carolina, without fondly remembering Charlotte Kohler and Mary Catherine Cortner, nor of my stay in Charlotte without calling to mind the embracing presence of Evelyn Baty (Christman) and Jane Miller (Crosby). My best memories of Columbus, Ohio, evoke images of Robert and Lisl Lenhert and of Jack and Jinny Radow.

My personal landscape in Colorado, especially within the University, is so heavily populated that it is all but impossible to single out fairly a small cluster of those who have contributed most importantly to the more than forty years I have lived here. From the beginning my congenial associations with the faculty of the Philosophy Department have given me intellectual stimulation. I took particular delight in arguments with fiery Joe Cohen and with Bert Morris, humanist *par excellence.* Forrest Williams, Phyllis Kenevan, Wesley Morriston, and I were bonded by our common interest in Sartre and other Continental philosophers. In the case of some of the other faculty members, they and I did not understand each other's philosophy at all; we simply liked each other. I should add here the name of another philosopher, Jane Cauvel, at Colorado College, whose friendship I have especially cherished since we became acquainted in the fifties. Most intimately interwoven in the texture of my life were those with whom I regularly shared leisured activities as well as academic concerns. I think especially of Harriet Jeffery and Dorothy Anderson, close companions in the early period; of Don Vollstedt, who lived next door; and of Ulrich and Bobra Goldsmith. Bobra considerably enlarged the view when she forsook academia to establish herself as a leading expert on the breeding and training of llamas. I would include here, too, the three men, and their wives, who made up the Classics Department when I came. Karl and Helen Hulley and Donald and Gilberte Sutherland, who, though no longer living, remain always present; John and Eleanor Hough, who, as they shaped those first years, have continued to gladden the recent ones. Still central in my life, too, are those who joined the Department just a little later: Harold and Hara Tzavella Evjen; Ernst Fredricksmeyer and his wife, Gloria, a member of the office staff; Joy King, and her husband, Edward, rostered in the Chemistry Department but a close friend of all of us.

Along with all of these are others I have known, not named here but individually remembered and appreciated, who have left their indelible mark. My story of myself would not have been what it is if I had not known them.

Coming back to the book itself, I want to add a little more in the way of acknowledgments. I owe a special debt of gratitude to Luzie Mason, who prepared the typescript with meticulous pains and accuracy. Her ability to spot errors and inadvertent ambiguity in what I had written has been immensely useful. In this, as in other projects, she has aided me greatly, professionally and as a friend.

Since this account is based on reminiscence rather than research, it stands without the array of footnotes and references that would accompany an academic text. In one instance, however, I want to recognize outside sources. In documenting my memories of specific events which occurred at the University of Colorado in the 1960s, I have drawn on information presented in three historical works: *Glory Colorado! A History of the University of Colorado, 1858–1963* by William E. Davis; *Our Own Generation: The Tumultuous Years, University of Colorado 1963–1976* by Ronald A. James; *The University of Colorado, 1876–1976: A Centennial Publication of the University of Colorado* by Frederick S. Allen et al.

Finally, this book might appropriately have been dedicated to T. David Brent, Senior Editor at the University of Chicago Press. David Brent expressed his confidence in the value of the projected work almost before I myself dared to believe in it. His perceptive and sympathetic reading of each installment that I sent to him gave me added incentive to continue. His critical suggestions significantly improved the quality of the final product. To work with him has been a joy and a privilege.

Boulder
October 1996

Living with the Century

APOLOGIA FOR AN AUTOBIOGRAPHY

> Everyone wants to write because everyone feels the
> need to be *signifying*, to *signify* what he *experiences*.
> Otherwise it all goes too fast, you have your nose to
> the ground like a pig forced to dig up truffles; there is
> nothing.
>
> Jean-Paul Sartre

I am not quite coeval with the century. I was born in 1915. But that first decade and a half hardly counts—a spillover from the nineteenth century in all but calendar time. By most reckonings, it was the advent of World War I in 1914 that began the job of turning the century into what it is. So I missed it by a year. Of course, neither I nor the century is quite finished, and either of us, with a little luck on my part, might overflow the boundary a bit as the nineteenth century did. Personally, I believe it more likely that historians will say that the twenty-first crowded the twentieth by stepping in ahead of schedule. However that may be, it is clearly time for both the century and me to ask how we made ourselves and what we think of what we have become. There is no lack of voices to sing out for the century. Each by itself is of necessity fragmentary; taken together, they are as dissonant as much of the period's music. I myself have no intention of trying to establish my credentials as one of the soloists or even to suggest what seems to me a proper refrain for the chorus. Yet, in tracing the fundamental project of my own life, I am acutely aware of my changing relation with whatever appeared to be the prevailing mood of the century in my corner of the world. At the beginning behind it, later briefly ahead of it, sometimes gloriously moving with it, I have also at times sensed myself estranged from it and wondered, seeing how much of myself was invested in the part of the century now past, if I had outlived myself.

Jean-Paul Sartre would say that I, like everyone else, am a *universel singulier*, a singular universal, or, as I prefer to put it, a unique universal. We are all products of our time and place, so much so that to ask what sort of person you would have been if you had lived in another historical and geographical setting is as meaningless as to wonder what a sunset would be like if it came at noon. Still, beneath it all, every individual is, at the start and finish, absolutely singular. Demonstrably no two of us are exactly alike. In our lived experience we feel ourselves to be selecting among the available ingredients out of which we make ourselves as well as choosing how to combine them. The coming into being of a unique universal is the subject of every (auto)biography, as it is of mine. Of course, I could have made this obvious point more simply without invoking the heavy Sartrean terminology. But it seemed to me appropriate to make reference to Sartre here at the beginning for several reasons.

One of the hallmarks of this century is our increased realization that to recount history is also to create it, that every narrative is told from a particular point of view, in varying degrees overt and covert. My own perspective is avowedly Existentialist and Sartrean. For a long time my professional life has been associated with Existentialism, since I am best known as the translator of Sartre's *Being and Nothingness* and since I was among the early ones in this country to lecture and write on the work of Sartre, Beauvoir, and Camus and to introduce Existentialism into the classroom. With my career as scholar and teacher so closely tied to a particular literary and philosophical movement, I lived, rather than observed, its changing role in the public regard. For more than four decades the content of my life has been colored by my work on Sartre. It would be impossible for me to write a record of even my earliest years which was free of his influence, or that of Simone de Beauvoir. Nor would I wish to do so.

The discovery of French Existentialism was a turning point in my intellectual life. It was not a religious conversion, not even an atheistic one. I am not modeling this account of myself on the personal testimonies I heard as a child when my parents took me to old-fashioned revival meetings; that is, this will not be the story of how I found Sartre and what he has done for me. Sartre was not my Savior. And while my admiration for him and for Beauvoir included a large measure of empathy, I cannot say that either one was ever my ego ideal. Indeed, since it was in my thirty-fourth year that I first began to read Existentialist writers (religious as well as humanistic), it might seem absurd for me to lay so much stress on this philosophy as an essential fabric of my being, still less as a unifying motif of my life. Yet, if I seek to trace the underlying patterns of my story and to make sense of my eighty years of living, the questions that arise cluster around my encounter with Existentialism. Standing before my own history as if I were presenting study questions to a class, I ask:

Why did my encounter with Sartre's philosophy come to me less as a revolution in my thought than as a revelatory validation, despite the fact that viewed from the outside, everything in my background and personal history would seem to point in the opposite direction? How did it happen that I, whose immediate and extended WASP family lived self-confined in the belief system of one of the most strictly fundamentalist sects, came to find myself at home in the thought of a radical, atheistic French philosopher? Especially, how was this possible when I had established myself in the forties as a professor of Classics, with a particular interest in ancient philosophy, one whose sole venture into broader social service had been a three-year stint of teaching in postwar Greece, under the auspices of an American missionary board? How was it that from my first introduction I felt such empathic affiliation with Parisian intellectuals whose lives—quite apart from their fame and achievements—were so unlike my own, both in external events and in intimate lifestyle? And how did this watershed event transform the life that followed? Clearly such questions are integral for me as I reflect on my past. Do they justify the writing of an autobiography?

Autobiography as a literary form has never been more popular; the majority of serious readers prefer it even above the novel. I suspect that this is partly because the traditional novel is worn out and the self-conscious experimental novels are usually too difficult to be read for relaxation. But the popularity of the form goes beyond literary preference. College courses in autobiography are common; what is new is that they offer to teach how to write it as well as how to read it. Therapists sometimes advise their clients to write down their life stories. The elderly are exhorted to do so as a constructive device to overcome boredom. Presumably the intention in this instance is also to promote self-understanding and to evoke in the elderly a sense of fulfillment as they find treasures of meaning in their lives. I have only cautious approval for this prescription. When Tolstoy's dying Ivan Ilych turned retrospective, he screamed for three days in horror at the barren waste of his past; and few persons, I think, would go on to conclude, as Ivan did, that somehow none of this mattered and all could be redeemed. At any rate, the urge to record one's life history has become so omnipresent that we are all too likely to find ourselves reading our friends' autobiographies—or listening to them on tape—with the same mixture of curiosity and embarrassed constraint we feel in looking at their home movies. There is no difficulty, particularly in our hyperconscious age, in explaining the impulse to write a book about oneself. We all want, as Sartre says, to bear witness; that is, to carve out our being in the world by giving durable, visible form to what we have done, felt, and believed. But why, save in the case of the world's "stars," should anyone want to look at another's self-portrayal? Or, more pointedly, why do I proffer mine?

I suppose the catalytic spark for me was my recognition that I had played an active part in initiating, not merely in reacting to, one of the currents tributary to the American intellectual mainstream in the mid-century. This was brought home to me especially when scholars (Ann Fulton was the first, to my knowledge) undertook to write the history of Existentialism in this country and contacted me to inquire about the influences leading to my interest and active involvement with the movement. To write of myself as a part of this history may be worthwhile and perhaps not only from the point of view of scholars interested in the by-paths of the history of ideas. There were many people, students especially but not exclusively, who responded personally and with excitement to the writing that came from postwar Paris. I think I may speak to, if not for, them.

Similarly, in my move from fundamentalism to a rejection of all formal religion, I was surely not walking a solitary path. The fundamentalism in which I was brought up resembled but, in important ways, was profoundly different from that which some believe to be gaining strength today. I should like to add my voice to the record.

Among the most influential pronouncements of the mid-century was certainly Beauvoir's assertion, in *The Second Sex*, that "one is not born but becomes a woman." It is perhaps in reflecting back on this process of becoming a woman and on my changing perceptions of what my position as a woman was in this period that I see most clearly revealed the complexity of how we insert ourselves into our own time. As a college graduate in 1937 I felt vaguely indebted to the early suffragettes and to those authors who had championed women's rights in the 1920s. If I had been asked a decade later about a movement to liberate women, I would have supported it but would probably have added that I had demonstrably liberated myself already by pursuing a university education and choosing a career rather than marriage. In truth I failed then to perceive either how different my experience was from that of most other women or how typical I was of a significant minority of women who came of age in the United States just before or during World War II. *The Second Sex* aroused me to a keener sense of my responsibility with regard to other women. The full-blown feminism that followed totally shocked my complacency. More than a challenge to my prevailing mode of thought for present and future, it thrust upon me the necessity of reinterpreting my own past. It resembled those breakthroughs in psychoanalytic annals in which the plot of a life is seen to have been quite other than it had always been taken to be. Nevertheless, some aspects of later feminism have struck me as mistaken, even retrogressive. Is this because women of my generation have built-in limitations they cannot overcome? In any case, I think that the experience of American women who chose to pursue careers in the period between Virginia Woolf and Betty Friedan has been too little explored and often misunderstood.

One thing I cannot claim is to be representative of those who have been victims of the great tragic events of the century. Compared with them, my existence has been sheltered to a degree almost abnormal. Nobody close to me died in any of the period's wars. I have known refugees from the Holocaust who lost most of their relatives because of it. I once sat at a dinner table with a group of Jewish women who had been in a concentration camp, some of whom still bore the infamous numbers tattooed on their arms. Otherwise I know of the Holocaust only from books and films. The famous Depression actually made life easier for my family. My father's low but continued salary as a high school teacher stretched farther when shops offered dresses for $8.88, and a nickel bought a giant ice-cream cone. Working for three years in Greece immediately after World War II, in Athens, while a civil war was being waged in the rural and mountain areas, considerably enlarged my parochial vision. I felt that I was caught up in historical events in a way that I had never experienced in living with the trivial inconveniences of civilian life back home in the wartime years. In the sixties I certainly believed that I was taking part in the civil rights struggle and the antiwar protest. In my teaching and my writing I committed myself. But I did not go to march in Alabama. I was never sent to jail, nor even arrested. I have been less protected from two pestilential scourges of our time: AIDS has so far stayed mostly on the periphery of my acquaintances, but cancer has devastated relatives and friends near to me, including my mother. Indeed, there was a moment in the early 1950s when the doctors thought that I might die of cancer myself. But I recovered.

Of more pleasant adventures there has been an abundance. But paradoxically, the portion of my life which I hold to be the richest, the period when I have lived most actively, have felt most keenly alive with the sense of having "found myself," is the time span which has been also the most settled—my years as a professor at the University of Colorado, where, except for a few months in the beginning, I have lived in the same house, with my friend Doris Schwalbe, since we came to Boulder together in 1953.

If I am fated to become ultimately only one of "the nameless dead" (as Sartre called them), those whose everyday actions and refusals to act make an epoch into what later generations will judge it to have been, those who are forever remembered solely in their anonymity, still it seems worthwhile to bear witness to how a particular life has made itself in our time. My friend Stan Brakhage claims that in creating the films for which he has become famous, he was guided always by the conviction that "the most personal is the most universal." This insight, it seems to me, goes beyond the obvious observation that the types of human situations and possible reactions to them are limited, that in telling of ourselves we are bound to strike a common chord with at least *some* persons. Beyond this, I think that to watch others in their solitude grappling with what comes to them, making it into themselves, and giving back to the world something which was not there before is to see the very image of what each of us is. It is to experience the least common denominator of our inwardness.

Does consistency with my basic intellectual orientation require that I attempt here an existential self-psychoanalysis? No, and yes. I do not propose to gather together the welter of mental debris of the sort people bring to their therapists. Nor is my purpose to try to demonstrate, by means of my own case history, the correctness of Sartrean psychology as opposed to that of the Freudians or the Jungians, say, or of Lacan. But since I tend to look on my inner life as characterized by a series of conversions and epiphanies, some degree of self-analysis is inevitable. Moreover, both the narrative and my interpretation of it will reflect a deep commitment to assumptions basic to existential psychoanalysis, whether in the form outlined by Sartre or as proposed by fellow travelers such as Viktor Frankl or R. D. Laing.

First of all, I accept as true the conviction that in some final and absolutely significant sense we are self-determining. I believe in the reality of the famous Existentialist freedom, not quite as it was exuberantly proclaimed by the early Sartre, who appeared almost to equate freedom with the absence of all control and conditioning, but rather in the way that Laing acknowledged its existence when he concluded that, finally, all hope of helping the mentally disturbed lies in the doctor's ability to appeal to the basic freedom of the patient. Whatever the origin of my belief in myself as a free agent, whether it is a valid perception or an illusion, I have always felt my life to be a succession of acts and of choices for which I was responsible. I could not write of it without this presupposition. In spite of all the evident constraints and particularities of my conditioning situation, my lived experience was that I was making myself. I will speak of influences rather than of causes. I will not provide explanations which make recourse to hypothetical descriptions of what may have gone on in an unconscious, personal or collective. New and deeper understanding of a past event demands a different reading of it, but does not require viewing it as having been originally a puppet show manipulated backstage.

What do I have in mind when I speak of making or even of writing about a "self"? Clearly, I do not go along with the notion, current today, that no individual subject exists within us, that our psychic core is only a set of fragmented structures imposed on us by our social environment. Or, to put it in terms still closer to accepted jargon, I do not hold that what we call the self is the product of discourse, a linguistic convention, a reflecting pool of otherness. But this does not mean that I stubbornly cling to Descartes' view of a substantial "I," clearly defined and differentiated, living like an invisible homunculus within a bodily mechanism. This is not the place for a discussion of the Sartrean theory of consciousness, ego, and self, which I do adopt and adapt. I will limit myself to saying this: I think Sartre is right in claiming that a free, prepersonal consciousness forms a self (or ego) by imposing a unity on its own experiences and reactions to them, past and present. This consciousness is never quite one with the self it has been; it never leaves off creating the self, but neither can it abandon this self, not anymore than it can wholly separate from its body; both body and ego (or self) are ever there as ground to all that a consciousness thinks, feels, and does. It is no wonder that we so often feel ourselves to be simultaneously free and yet trapped inside ourselves. In looking back at what we have been and in projecting our future selves, we continuously interpret ourselves to ourselves. As in a novel or as in a Freudian case history, we find reason to alter the meaning of many past events, and in so doing we refashion our selves. It is no exaggeration to say that my life is, that I am, the story I tell myself about myself. If my consciousness is the author, the "I" is the first-person narrator that a consciousness invents as it writes. Even if the self we take ourselves to be were as dependent and fictive a structure as Deconstructionists claim, it would still be this which differentiates us one from another. It is what we are searching for when we want to know who a person is.

I am not taking as my model either of the autobiographies by the two Existentialist writers I admire most: Sartre's *Words* and Beauvoir's four-volume work. Sartre's is an incomparable, brilliant, impressionistic portrait of the inner world of his childhood as he looks back on it, a book which tells us far more about the convictions of the adult than of the life of the child he once was. Beauvoir's realistic account, despite some deliberate censorship, remains close to the daily journals on which it is based. Where Sartre imagines, Beauvoir painstakingly records. We welcome the wealth of detail for memorable events but pay for it by having to deal with a little too much information about sites visited, persons seen, miles traveled, meals eaten. Or at least this would be true if Beauvoir were not even now so important a personage for many people that *l'appétit vient en mangeant*. I do not flatter myself that the quotidian trivia of my own life would arouse so gluttonous an appetite. On the other hand, nobody but Sartre could do the kind of thing he does in *Words*.

In writing this story of myself, I will follow a path somewhere in between Beauvoir's diachronic approach and Sartre's synchronic one. A chronological order is appropriate for the years of formation—my childhood in Pennsylvania, my education at a small liberal arts college, and graduate study at Yale—though I will be concerned with the quality and significance of each period rather than with the progression of calendar time within it. The years I spent working in Greece will stand as an interlude in the narrative as they do in my life. Writing of the rest of my adult existence seems to require a horizontal rather than a vertical progression. I will order both experiences and my reflections on them, my "life and opinions," to use the old-fashioned expression, in terms of topics: my engagements with Existentialism and with feminism, inward conversions, recollections and observations drawn from my formidable number of years as a teacher and scholar, and other commentaries on events, times, and places. In the last part of my account I will speak at some length about two things which are not wholly separable: my personal experience of aging, along with urgent concerns to which it has awakened me; and my appraisal of what my position is now with respect to what the century has become, now when it is almost over. It has been a long journey for those of us who can recall the excitement of first listening to a radio and today confront the information superhighway. The social environment has been transformed as radically as the technological one. Utopian dreams have been realized, and some nightmares, too. We change with the times, of course, as the old saying goes, but we don't necessarily keep up with them. Some sense of alienation is surely inevitable, but it is impossible for me to conclude that such feelings of estrangement are always based on inability to adapt rather than on a reasonable reluctance to do so.

My efforts to write of my life have painfully confirmed my theoretical awareness of the degree to which an autobiography is perforce a novel. It is not only that, as has so often been pointed out, words distort even as they reveal, that what is lived can never be the same as what is told. Questions of sincerity, the reliability of memory, and concern for others' feelings turn out to be far more complex than I had imagined. The problem of selectivity, which in other contexts may be purely literary, becomes more urgent; to single out *these* factors as most important in shaping a self is to mold the self presented. The most I can claim, and this I do affirm, is that the fictional character portrayed here is, at least in my eyes, a true reflection of what I reflectively see.

ONE

Being a Child

There are about five years between me and my younger sister, Jean, another four and a half between her and our brother, Paul. If my mother had not miscarried a few months before my conception, it seems doubtful that I would have been born. I have never felt guilty that my appearance on December 16, 1915, was due to the failure of the premature daughter to make it, and not smug either. Very early I somehow gathered that it was to have been either she or I; I felt obscurely that I had been lucky and that I was not the child my parents would have preferred. I was right on both counts. My father once said that I was born protesting. My mother has often described the nightmare my early years were for her—my sleeplessness as an irritable infant, my stubborn disobedience as a toddler, my continued refusal to accept No as a final answer to anything. In short, I was not the kind of child anyone would have chosen and, in the network of cause and effect, my early self-image naturally reflected such negative judgments. In light of the total picture, I tend now to play down these symptoms of the maladjusted child. But they were certainly present. Like the melancholy children wearily portrayed in many autobiographical novels, I, too, can say that I do not remember a time in my childhood when I did not assume that in the eyes of others I was the ungainly nuisance, the one who never quite understood what everyone else knew, the one who was born lacking. I looked into the mirror to discern the source of my oddity, but could find nothing to pin it down to—except that my dark hair was grimly straight and that I had holes in my cheeks. (Much later I found the holes acceptable as dimples, but for a long time I tried not to laugh too much.) Yet, while I

1

felt ill at ease and not always sure that I was loved, I was never desperate. This, I think, was because I was in fact extraordinarily fortunate in one life-saving respect: My parents and my other adult relatives always made me feel that I was important. Even my daily shortcomings were deplored as failures to live up to what I *could* be. I was an ugly duckling whose swan plumage the grownups could see already sprouting. Or, so they thought. And because they looked so hard to discover and encourage the signs of the gifted child, they inevitably found them. In this fostering atmosphere I showed myself precocious and a bit of an overachiever. Neither I nor anybody else mistook me for a genius.

For most of my existence I considered that mine had been a wretched childhood. In preparing to write about it, I was surprised to discover such a wealth of positive factors that my former judgment took on the appearance of shabby ingratitude. Obviously neither appraisal can be wholly correct. If my first set of memories was colored by my desire to enhance the distance between what I was and what I became, the later re-action was surely in part an overreaction. Only the language of dreams, in which the law of contradiction is suspended, might adequately con-vey the total paradox of those far-off days as I try now to see them as they were. For just as in a dream every figure that in bold relief stands as one thing holds nuances that say it is also something else, so my recol-lections come to me in a multicolored cluster rather than in a coherent pattern. My place in the world was privileged and restricted; I felt both loved and scorned, boxed in and tenderly nurtured. No doubt I am not unique in conjuring up this sort of medley. Still, for me it needs to be ex-plained. It undoubtedly reflects contradictions which were present in my surrounding environment of persons and places, and these I can an-alyze with some degree of objectivity—just as the waking disentangle-ment of the elements of a dream, while it distorts the dream experience itself, can sometimes reveal how it came to be and what its meanings are.

I was born in a time warp. I think the same might be said of my par-ents. Olin Barnes and May Petersen were born, raised, and married in Beach Lake (originally Beech Pond, a name that makes more sense), a small agricultural community in northeastern Pennsylvania. In 1912 my father took his first job as a teacher, in a public high school in Wilkes-Barre. He stayed there until he retired in the mid nineteen-fifties. During the months of the school year we lived in the city; we spent our sum-mers at Beach Lake. Partly this was due to the fact that my father, as a public school teacher, was free to take us all to the country for the long vacation and at very little cost since we lived there in a primitive cottage, first on my paternal grandfather's land, then on a separate lot my father purchased nearby. For my parents this was literally coming home; I believe it was also a refuge from a life that was always a bit alien to them. The residents of Beach Lake were almost exclusively the descendants of English settlers. By the time I came, the original families had so frequently intermarried that almost everyone was some sort of relative to everyone else. My mother's parents, the Petersens, were the one notable exception. They were recent immigrants from Denmark. The community received them hospitably. My grandparents adapted so rapidly that they were barely distinguishable from the others, but at least they introduced something new into the bloodstream. Still, relations continued to overlap; my mother and her sister, for instance, were also first cousins by marriage. Some decades later I was hardly surprised that my father's second marriage made me stepsister to my aunt. This was possible because my father was the second in a train of nine children and my uncle last, with a great age difference. It was my uncle's mother-in-law who married my father, no blood kin this time; I mention the fact only to underscore the degree to which the members of my extended family were interdependent within the network they had established.

On my father's side there was never any need for me to search for my roots. Documented dates of birth for his father's and mother's forebears go back to the seventeenth and eighteenth centuries in Europe. The Barnes family drifted into the vicinity of Beach Lake from Connecticut before the American Revolution; on the maternal side, the Olvers arrived in the middle of the nineteenth century, coming directly from Cornwall. I can't say that any of these ancestors was particularly illustrious. The ones from Cornwall sprang from fairly prosperous farmers, but evidently prospects for the future must have seemed brighter here. In 1957 two scions of another of the founding families, the Baldwins, took care to preserve the legends and traditions of the community by publishing a volume called *Your Heritage in Beach Lake.* (The authors were Isabel and Keturah, the last and third from last of progeny whose parents named them in alphabetical order.) The book evokes in me now, as oral accounts did earlier, a sense of near awe as I realize the courage and the heavy labor required of settlers who had to construct roads as well as to clear land for the houses they built, who struggled for years before they got postal service or easy access to public transportation.

One of the most dramatic accounts concerned my grandparents (prefixed by four "greats") on the Barnes side, William and Mary Holbert, who were captured by Indians in 1779, at the time when the British were trying to enlist the Indians as allies against the Colonists. The Indians (of course, I never heard the term "Native Americans" until decades later) came to the Holberts' farmhouse at a place now called Indian Orchard, near present day Beach Lake. They forced the wife to summon her husband from the fields. Mr. Holbert drew a gun to defend himself but realized resistance was useless. The Indians, taking his weapon from him, gave him in exchange an inferior one. (This mysterious detail is an essential part of the story, not a late embroidery, for my Uncle Earl still had in his possession what he firmly believed to be the original gun.) The pair was taken up into New York state to Fort Hancock; here they were joined by an American Tory named Kane, who paid the Indians for every white person's scalp they collected. Shortly after the Holberts' arrival the Indians presented Kane with a new set of scalps, among which he recognized the distinctive red hair of his wife. That night he secretly left the camp, taking the Holberts with him. On foot, making their way down toward Pennsylvania, the three ate only raw food at first, then when it was safe, used the old gun to shoot a pheasant. Toward the end the two men had to carry Mrs. Holbert, who was pregnant. They reached Lackawaxen in Pennsylvania, barely escaping an ambushed attack by British and Indians across the Delaware river at Minnisink, New York.

My brother and sister and I loved this tale. We were thrilled also by the doubtful tradition that among our Cornish ancestors was one Olveras, a Spaniard who had taken refuge after the defeat of the Armada. It is true that some Spanish did end up settling in Cornwall at that date and that the name Olver (without the "i") resembles "Olveras," whereas the designation of the host of Olivers does not. We children wanted to believe this tale because of hints that Olveras was a Spanish aristocrat. Our inclinations were not always so snobbish. There was a never recorded whisper that one of the Pennsylvania ancestors had got drunk, fallen into a stream, and drowned. We enjoyed repeating this item as proof that in the past there were individuals who were not models of rectitude. Almost all of our known relatives, living and dead, were excessively religious. In England they had been dissenters, and they sought out in Pennsylvania the nearest equivalent to the Chapel at home. Here, I believe, is another reason which, along with close family ties, led my parents to hold themselves aloof in Wilkes-Barre, never fully realizing the possibilities that a new circle of acquaintances might have offered them.

Beach Lake, the population of which was approximately two hundred, had two churches—Methodist and Free Methodist. My closer relatives

were all Free Methodists. On a visit to the Free Methodist Church in recent years I found the sermon banal rather than evangelistic, and I have
been told that the Church has become relatively liberal compared with
other fundamentalist denominations. In the years when I was growing
up, it was revivalistic and pietistic in the extreme. Central to its gospel
was the necessity of an emotional, personal conversion, best accomplished by "going to the altar" and "praying through," usually quite noisily. Salvation did not come about automatically; its arrival was clearly
announced. Those men and women who succeeded in being "saved"
sometimes reached such a state of exultation that they walked or ran up
and down the aisles, shouting their joy. In this they might be joined by
one or two other persons who, already "saved" on an earlier occasion,
had now "prayed through" to a higher state known as "sanctification." I
have sometimes wondered whether this two-step salvation corresponded
roughly to the distinction between the Little Satori and the Great Satori
of Zen—though with radical differences, of course. Free Methodists of
that period did not seek to "speak in tongues" nor practice foot washing
as some sects did, but they still observed the rituals of public "testimonies" and the "love feast." This last, tamer than its name suggests,
centered on the "breaking of bread." At a designated time in a special
service in the afternoon, all members of the congregation left their seats
and moved about, clutching a small chunk of bread. This they offered to
one another, eating a crumb from each, usually accompanied by an exchange of kisses on the cheek, a well-intended symbolic gesture if not a
very hygienic one. More dubious was the testimony service which followed. Although most people limited themselves to a few conventional
remarks on the goodness of the Lord and how they had been helped by
Him, some testimonies were confessions in which the newly saved took
pains to paint their former sins as black as possible, as though the greater
their wickedness the more merits in their salvation. Occasionally regret
as well as repugnance seemed to accompany renunciation. For the most
part, confessions which some might find indiscreet were not lurid but
pathetic. One of the Church's most unhealthy imperatives was its insistence that every detail of unworthy conduct must be reported—if not
publicly in testimony meetings, at least acknowledged to someone who
could serve as judge. Otherwise, unabsolved, the sin was doubled. Even
more guilt-inducing was the constant reminder of the Biblical prescription that "as a man thinketh in his heart, so is he." Shameful thoughts
were condemned as well as evil deeds and subject to the same injunction to open confession. I recall my father's comment on how painful he

found this kind of psychological pressure; yet it played its part in my own upbringing.

Both my parents and my immediate Barnes relatives, while they never overtly criticized the more vocal and emotional of the "brothers and sisters" in the Church, were more restrained in their own words and behavior. I remember being told by more than one of them that while you became a Christian by being "converted," the conversion might be an inward, gradual process. Being born again, they said, did not have to take the form of a public, dramatic event. Given this aloofness and some private modifications that my father had imposed on official doctrine, it would seem natural for my parents to have made the move away from Beach Lake the occasion for selecting a church of another denomination that they would not find so discomforting. Instead they joined the Free Methodist Church in Wilkes-Barre and, for the most part, chose their friends solely from within its membership. In so doing they were retreating from the world, and this was their intention.

The Free Methodists of my parents' youth and of my own lived by the precept, "Be in the world but not of it." Otherworldliness for them meant not only that spiritual preparation for eternity was the essential task for life here and now; it was also a requirement to differentiate oneself from the worldly by thousands of details of everyday conduct, extending even to the dress code. Drinking, card playing, smoking, and dancing were only slightly less sinful than adultery and extramarital sex. On Sunday it was wrong to buy anything; taking a walk was allowed on that day, but not swimming or roller skating. Movies were frowned on. I remember an exception was made for me with respect to *Ben Hur* and *Uncle Tom's Cabin*. Charlie Chaplin, Laurel and Hardy, and the Marx Brothers I discovered as an adult. *The Perils of Pauline* I missed forever. Strangely enough, stage plays were not prohibited, probably because the only productions available were those which had been deemed suitable for production in the local high school auditoriums. John Wesley's eighteenth-century interpretation of the Biblical warning against "gold and pearl and costly array" was taken literally. If my mother bought a hat with a feather or a flower on it, she would laboriously replace it with a handmade ribbon bow. Any sort of makeup was, of course, condemned. Jewelry was specifically forbidden, and the prohibition extended to wedding rings. At Beach Lake this was no problem since so many Free Methodist women kept their hands bare of adornment. But my mother once told me of her excruciating embarrassment when, resting on a public bench in Wilkes-Barre, she saw someone looking at her, pregnant and without a ring. She took to wearing gloves when she went outside, regardless of the temperature. Taken altogether, such restrictions did more to enforce a withdrawal from ordinary life than the Church's theological doctrines.

En route from attending a high school to teaching in one, my father left home to go to college. He went to Greenville College, in Illinois, a Free Methodist institution, which enlarged his outlook without significantly altering it. After his graduation he received some sort of fellowship which enabled him to begin graduate work at the University of Illinois in Urbana. All I know of this enterprise is that before the end of the year he discontinued his work there because of a "nervous breakdown." Knowing how scrupulously honest he was, I do not believe that this was a euphemism for academic failure. I suspect that he could not cope with the unsheltered and infinitely more sophisticated environment.

In Wilkes-Barre my parents did, to be sure, have the haven of the local church, but this was not as firmly entrenched in the community regard as it was at Beach Lake, where the members of my father's family were recognized leaders. Moreover, those who made up the congregation of the city church were mostly poorly educated, "good and well-meaning," as my parents insisted, but far from intellectual. Among the country relatives a disproportionately high number of them were teachers at various levels, with at least a college education or, at any rate, a certificate from some sort of teachers training school. To leave the world for Beach Lake was to withdraw to a sizeable enclave. My sister Jean remarked to me recently that she had hated everything about the church in Wilkes-Barre, that she could hardly bear to go to it, "but I loved the church at Beach Lake; its doctrines didn't bother me because it was where all the relatives came together." My parents were not the only ones to find the pull back to the family center irresistible. Cyrus, the youngest of my father's brothers, who became a quite distinguished professor at New York University, lived for only a few years in nearby New Jersey, then sold his home and built a house at Beach Lake so that his children might go to school there; henceforth he himself commuted weekly to New York, a distance of more than a hundred miles. My uncle's professional life was centered on the teaching of science. His extramural activities were wholly engaged in projects connected with the Free Methodist Church.

An obvious question arises: Why did these people, all of whom so highly valued education, far more than the average American, cling to a fundamentalist religion based on a literalist interpretation of the Bible, one which could be supported only by faith? Drawing on my later observations, I think they resolved the issue intellectually by invoking two ancient procedures. First, they made the distinction between scientific and religious truth. If one accepted on faith the principle that with God all things are possible, then there seemed no reason why God should not suspend His own laws to suit His own purpose. Old and New Testament miracles were no problem; they were exceptions to the rule by divine fiat. Widespread flood myths in other religions were taken to support the story of Noah's ark, rather than to refute it. The same sort of logic might be applied to such things as healing by the "laying on of hands." Oral Roberts was a fellow traveler. This attitude, however, did not extend so far as to provide room for such things as powerful old relics or most present-day visions, which were dismissed as superstition or Catholicism, which were held to be on the same level. (I do not deny that professed humility sometimes concealed considerable arrogance.) Second, a few of the Barnes group, like my father, privately accommodated by weakening the literalism just a little, allowing for a looser interpretation. My father, for instance, told me that the theory of evolution did not have to be rejected outright in order to sustain the belief in the special creation of Man. Perhaps the six days of creation reported in *Genesis* referred to six longer periods during which God's plan evolved according to His direction and provided, among other things, for the appearance at some assigned date of a creature resembling others physically but endowed with a soul. Obviously, such speculations could not be taken very far without exploding the whole structure of revealed Truth. Even as it was, those who held such slightly heretical views kept them mostly to themselves.

The question which is to me the most difficult to answer is this: Since these Barneses did not fully endorse either the letter of the Church's doctrine or the emotional exhibitionism of its revival services, why, then, did they nevertheless subscribe wholeheartedly to its otherworldliness and the narrow lifestyle the Church imposed on its members? The isolation of Beach Lake, particularly before automobiles became common and audio and visual media a part of everyday life, was certainly a factor, though it hardly seems to me to explain by itself the attempt to preserve the dissenters' ascetic way of life that the immigrants had brought with them from England. Possibly there was a certain unacknowledged satisfaction derived from feeling superior to their Methodist neighbors in their renunciation of worldly pleasures. Perhaps more simply, it was the familiar human fear that any significant change might result in a cataclysmic upheaval too great to be contemplated. More charitably, the call for self-sacrifice may have strengthened their deep sense of mission. The desire to serve others was genuine in them, wherever it came from. One of my father's sisters went as a missionary to India and died there. All of the family took it for granted that to help to make the world better was the highest form of self-fulfillment.

Politically the Church, and certainly all of my extended family, were ultraconservative. Yet, in contrast to the religious right today, these people were not out to control the world by way of forcing their own standards of behavior on others—with perhaps one exception; they were all ardent prohibitionists. As a child, I assumed that the Women's Christian Temperance Union was one of the groups initiated by our local church. The woman who later became my stepmother still wore one of the original pins the founding members had worn, a little silver axe standing for the instrument that Carrie Nation and her followers tried to use to demolish the local bars. My paternal grandfather, as a candidate for the Republican Party, succeeded in being elected to a term in the Pennsylvania Senate. I don't believe he ever addressed that body directly, but I have seen a speech he circulated to be read. It was appropriately against lifting the eighteenth amendment.

Moving back and forth from classroom to Sunday School, putting their trust simultaneously in evangelical religion and the importance of free inquiry, proud of their family heritage and egalitarian in their attitude toward others, my Beach Lake relatives lived such contradictions without recognizing them as such. Similarly, my father saw nothing inconsistent in condemning the world for its wickedness and holding steadfast to the myth of inevitable progress. When I came onto the scene, I think that I found in my contradictory situation not the crippling "double bind" of which psychologists make so much, but rather a field of contrasts that left me spaces in between for building. Or, to put it another way, my psychic environment provided both motivations for rebellions and the strength to carry them through.

THE PEOPLE IN MY WORLD

My Father

Someone said of my father in his late teens, "He looks like Abe Lincoln, and he's every damn bit as homely." Indeed, there was something of Ichabod Crane, too, in his build and in his movements. Some of the

relatives, I know, found his manner a bit odd, his behavior somewhat ec-
centric. I cannot recall any example of impropriety or of blatantly unconventional conduct on his part, but as a child I felt that he was somehow "different." He felt himself to be, and consequently was, a little
gauche socially. Much of what seemed peculiar to me then I came to
look on later as signs of his authenticity. He refused to pretend. His
likes, dislikes, and judgments were absolutely genuine, forcefully expressed, and very often contrary to what was generally expected. If he
was curious about what a stranger was doing, he inquired. If he thought
something could be done better, he pointed out how, whether to a relative, a next-door neighbor, or a public official. My father had his dark
side as well. He once confessed to me that he had seriously wondered
whether he and my mother ought to have children because they were so
"nervous." He worried so intensely about events beyond his control that
during his last years he refused to listen to news on the radio or television and would leave the room if someone else wished to do so, not that
he wanted to live under the delusion that things were going well, but because he was unbearably agitated by reports that confirmed his worst
fears or bred new anxieties.

What my mother and we children found hardest to understand was
my father's indifference toward material things, not just luxuries, but
items most of our acquaintances took for granted. My father never
owned nor learned to drive a car. We were years later than most middle-
class families in exchanging gas for electricity, a stove for a furnace, and
in acquiring such everyday things as radio, refrigerators, and toasters.
My father's reluctance to spend money went beyond the obvious need
for a high school teacher with a family to economize, but it was no ordinary miserliness. He was generous to those who needed help. When,
for example, my mother's sister died, he gladly installed her three children in our small house and supported them for a school year until their
father found himself able to look after them. One tenth of his salary
went to church and charity in obedience to the Free Methodist literal
interpretation of the Biblical command to tithe. Beyond that, he saved
for the future, vowing that he would never need to have his children
support him, never have to borrow money. (He did not even possess a
credit card.) The positive aspect of this depression psychology (before
the event) I failed to appreciate when I was growing up. Instead of being
grateful that my father owned our home, I resented living in a wretched
eight-unit row house in a poor neighborhood.

What we regarded as another manifestation of my father's oddity was the fact that he built a soundproof door for his bedroom and spent the larger part of his time at home shut up there working. (At Beach Lake he constructed for himself a cubbyhole attached to the outside of the cottage.) When he was not correcting pupils' homework or writing letters, he poured over *Barron's Financial Weekly*, studying the stock market. This pursuit was not inconsistent with his thriftiness. Despite his disdain for the things he might buy for himself and his family, he felt, for a brief period, a compulsion to accumulate wealth in order that he might do more good in the world. Possibly he had in mind the parable of the talents. He spoke to us rather of "Mr. Active and Mr. Passive." The names might have been better chosen. Unfortunately, my father's first ventures in the market were counterproductive. After losing a small but significant amount, he confined himself to theoretical speculation.

Retreat to the soundproof room still allowed time for my father to give loving attention to my siblings and me. He was thoughtful in arranging special (inexpensive) treats. Most evenings in the winter he talked with us as he cracked nuts and peeled apples for us to eat. On summer nights he took me outside to watch for shooting stars. (Jean, too small to go with us, declared that she heard one go bang.) And he made a point of telling us things about the natural world that he thought we would find interesting.

One of my early memories is of sitting in my father's lap while he told me stories. Mostly these were tales he made up, although, as I discovered years later, they often drew on narratives famous in the literary tradition. My favorite was the series featuring Cyclops and Whiskers. Each episode, richly detailed, new in its initial situation, followed the same plot line. A boy or girl was happily engaged in some pleasant activity when suddenly a bad man nicknamed Whiskers came onto the scene and began to tease or torment the child, not violently, but by taking away candy, or breaking up toys, or threatening some other equally heartbreaking act. Then, from the distance, was heard the clip-clop of footsteps, and the Cyclops appeared. This friendly giant grabbed Whiskers by the scruff of his neck or the seat of his pants and either removed him from the scene, or sent him running, or compelled him to repair the damage he had done. One way or another, the Cyclops consoled the children, leaving them better off than they had been before. I never asked my father later what had prompted him to adopt the hero and villain from Homer's *Odyssey*, radically reversing their roles. Today I wonder whether he felt some sort of empathy with the ungainly Cyclops. Or did his disapproval of the epic hero's deceitful trickery lead to degrading him to a cowardly bully? In any case, the message to the little girl listening was clear. Nasty people try to make trouble in this world, but there are also powerful forces for good, which in the end will triumph. This my father believed to be the truth, not to the point of fatuity, but "in the long run and on the whole," as William James often said.

I believe that in the stories he told to me, and later to my brother and sister, my father's chief intention was simply to give us pleasure. I do not recall that he ever gave us direct moral instruction in the form of laying down rules as to what was right and wrong, or overtly demanding obedience to his commands. But he certainly tried to instill in us attitudes which he felt to be essential to our making the most of our lives. Two occasions stand out distinctly:

One must have occurred when I was already in my teens, for my brother was present and able to understand what was said. In a spirit close to that of the old McGuffey readers and not even conceivable for the generation brought up on Sesame Street, my father told us the story of how Hamilcar, Hannibal's father, talked with his sons one day, telling them that he wanted them to be eagles. For us, too, my father said, he hoped we would become eagles, flying high above the ordinary range, distinguishing ourselves as individuals and as leaders. In a reminiscing conversation after my father's death, all three of us remembered this episode, but our adult evaluation of what it had meant to us differed radically. To me, the import was wholly positive. For while I never became what I would call an eagle, my father's words crystalized what I still regard as the most important gift of my childhood: the assumption, inbred in me, that it mattered what I did with my life, that I had both the capacity and the obligation to make it worthwhile to myself and to others. In the 1970s, reading Sartre's biography of Flaubert, I was startled to see Sartre laying down, as the duty of mother love, an imperative to develop in a child its sense of itself as a free agent, moving "like a conscious arrow" toward a destiny. A child so favored, Sartre insisted, would never feel wholly lost, whatever happened. I felt that Sartre might have been describing my father's treatment of us. My brother's judgment was negative. Granting my father's good intentions, Paul believed that the effect of such teaching was psychologically damaging, that by offering an unrealistic incentive, it tended to paralyze rather than to stimulate personal striving, to breed guilt feelings and discontent with what would normally pass for satisfying achievement. Paul regarded the message as an

obstacle he had needed to overcome. Jean did not attach much importance to the occasion that Paul and I found so significant. She concluded
that our father's great expectations of us had neither inspired nor threatened her. She had always, she said, a strong sense of her own limitations
and possibilities and lived by that, not by what he thought.

Another effort by my father to cultivate in us a resolve for self-
improvement involved only Jean and me; it must have happened when
we were both in grade school. This time he paid (or underpaid) us a dime
apiece for memorizing and reciting each day for a week a short passage
from William James. I doubt that my father had read extensively in James,
any more than he had been a serious student of Greek literature, but he
had at least read some of James's popular essays, including the one called
"Habit," from which our assigned passage came. It began with the words,

> Nothing we ever do is, in strict scientific literalness, wiped out. Of
> course this has its good side as well as its bad one. As we become
> permanent drunkards by so many separate drinks, so we become
> saints in the moral, and experts in the practical and scientific
> spheres, by so many separate acts and hours of work.

James would have had short patience with the fundamentalist religion to
which my father committed himself. Yet it seems to me that my father,
to an amazing degree, incorporated in his basic beliefs many of the ideas
we associate with James's philosophy. Or perhaps it would be more accurate to say that each one, at a different level, expressed one strand in
the Zeitgeist of the early century. There was a deliberate search for the in-
spirational, for ways to build "character," the conviction that there was a
basic goodness in humankind to which one could, with effort, find a way
to make a rational appeal.

Much of this was at odds with the Free Methodist emphasis on original sin, otherworldliness, and self-denial. Perhaps even more heretical
was my father's firm insistence that the final test for everything was
Reason. Belief in the fundamental rationality of things was an unquestioned assumption that I cherished all the way through my early adulthood. In my father's mind, the make-up of the universe and God's plan
were rational, and my father would never knowingly forsake reason even
if it seemed to turn against him. One of my most striking recollections
of my father from later years centers on one of the few occasions when
we spoke openly of our theological disagreements. The evening's discussion had been remarkably free of personal emotion despite its revelation
of cleavage. After I had gone to bed, my father came to my bedroom

door and delivered in the darkness a sort of postscript. "I did want to assure you, Hazel, that, of course, you must follow your reason in these things. If we didn't try to abide by reason—why, I don't know what would happen!" And his voice trailed off at this suggestion of the unimaginable.

A couple of years before his compulsory retirement at sixty-five, my father had to face a great upheaval. School officials suddenly discovered that for close to forty years he had been teaching accounting without being certified. Instead of granting a waiver, they decided he should teach social studies, which he was technically qualified to do, though he had never done so. This absurd decision, which my father viewed as a disaster, proved to be a great gift. He turned the course into the study of practical matters which the pupils would inevitably have to face: considerations to be made in choosing a career, household financial planning, the pros and cons of seeking a divorce, etc. He was a success. Bucknell Junior College (later Wilkes College) asked him to supervise a young girl doing her practice teaching. Their partnership was exhilarating. He found her extraordinary; she felt (or at any rate made him feel) that his guidance was invaluable. The whole experience was a triumph of sorts, though a bittersweet one, coming so late.

After his retirement, my father gave up *Barron's Financial Weekly* and turned to writing articles for *The Free Methodist* and pamphlets which he arranged to have printed at his own expense and distributed wherever he thought he might find readers. (These came out mostly in the 1960s, though they show virtually no reflection of the turmoil of that decade.) Some of them were semipolitical, e.g., "Why Communism Charms Us So," and "A Letter from America to You," which was both an apologia for the American ideal and a reproachful criticism of some aspects of the way the United States conducted itself. The most interesting to me was a fifteen-page piece, called "Keys to a Better World," that he wrote when he was eighty-one. It was a mixture of homely philosophy, sociological commentary, and psychological counseling. My sister-in-law dubbed it the ramblings of an old man. One of my colleagues to whom I showed it remarked, "I wish that at his age I might write such a love letter to the world." It was doubtless in reference to this document that the minister who spoke at my father's funeral felt it necessary to concede, along with the usual sort of eulogy, that my father's thinking was not orthodox. As for me, I found it a moving testimony, an extraordinary blend of naive style with content ranging from statement of the obvious to acute insight. In this and in the other writings, I was especially struck

with how far my father had moved from his original conservatism.
Though still distrustful of Big Government, his primary complaint now
was its susceptibility to "special interests." Much of what he advocated
resembled planks in the platform of "liberals." His view of the proper role
of his country internationally, while hardly original, was to the point,

> There are two roles of the United States in world affairs which are
> impossible and out of the question. One is to play God and to dic-
> tate terms to the world. The other is isolationism. We cannot re-
> treat from the world. We must become involved. We must relate.

He no longer conflated "true Christianity" with Free Methodism. And
while he still regarded Christianity as the "greatest social force for good,"
he modified it in the direction of an optimistic humanism. For example,

> The world *is* constantly growing wiser and better. Almighty God
> has put within humanity the power to solve practically every phys-
> ical, social, economic and political ill. We have been so busy with
> the illnesses that we have not sensed the progress.

Some of his observations might have been lifted from the pages of humanistic Existentialism: "Our whole future is mostly self-created." And,
"The 'born in sin' doctrine is violently opposed not only to reason but to
simple justice. It absolutely contradicts the idea of a loving Creator. . . .
Morality is acceptance of external ideas thrust into a child's life. External
authority decides whether an act is 'moral or not,' intrinsic morality not
being considered." And, "The real dropout from life is the one who is
just coasting." (Consider Sartre's gospel of "engaged freedom." "Not to
choose is already to have chosen.")

One statement written by my father startled me. "What we like to
call unselfishness is simply the substitution of a larger self for the old,
little self." This idea, phrased differently, was one which I had developed
in my own work. I did not remember ever having heard my father speak
of it. Had I been influenced by him more than I realized—to the point
of plagiarism? Or was there some cross-influence? I had sent my father
most of my publications, but I did not think he had done much more
than glance at them. Perhaps we had independently drawn from basic
presuppositions that we shared despite the radical contrast in our starting
points and specific commitments. I have never been sure just what was
my father's judgment on my career. I suspect it was a mingling of pride
and dismay. I am sure of our mutual love and of an understanding that
dissolved differences.

I have always felt that my father's death in 1970 at age eighty-two exemplified his strong will and validated his conviction of self-determination. When I last saw him in October 1969, he moved about as usual and seemed to me not noticeably different from what he had been the few years previously. But he insisted that he was much weaker and that he would die before the first day of spring. He overshot the mark by six days. I believe that he willed his death, not wanting to live when he could no longer take care of himself. His tiring heart gave out after less than a week in the hospital. His was a good death, one to be envied.

My Mother

I find it extraordinarily difficult to write about my mother. An objective summation of her personal traits and qualities would be comparatively easy, for she was less marked by obvious self-contradictions than was my father. But I have never plumbed the depths of ambivalence in the relation that existed between her and me, though not for lack of trying. I do not know even now exactly what she was to me or I to her. Tenderness, resentment, and pangs of guilt combine to prevent me from ever feeling that I am fair to her or to myself, whatever I may write.

My mother's parents, Walter Petersen and Elizabeth Wulff, were both Danish in origin, though the language they spoke was a form of low German. They came from the vicinity of Flensburg in the part of Schleswig-Holstein claimed by both Denmark and Prussia. My grandmother told me that when she was a child, their town kept passing back and forth between the Danes and the Germans, so that one of their neighbors kept two different national flags ready to fly as the occasion demanded. In their hometown my grandparents had resided in the same block but never really knew one another until they met by chance in New York. Walter Petersen went there by a long route. Impressed against his will into the Prussian navy, he sensibly deserted the ship at a port in South America; somehow he made his way north, married, and eventually came with his wife to Beach Lake. Nothing of this potentially rich, even romantic background interested anyone sufficiently to track it down and preserve it. The Petersens exemplified both the virtues and the defects of the Melting Pot. They undertook to learn English so quickly and so thoroughly that, to my knowledge, not one of their five children ever spoke or understood any other language. German Lebkuchen and a Danish fruit soup were my only tangible inheritance from my central European ancestors. I myself, under the spell of the longer established

Barnes-Olver relatives, never found the incentive to explore the past of my mother's family, a failure I deeply regret.

My mother was born at Beach Lake and into the Free Methodist Church. I know almost nothing of her childhood, but have reason to believe that it was not a happy one. She once confided in my sister that, while she had come to love my father after she was married to him, she had accepted his proposal chiefly to escape from life at her home. This may have been partly because she hated being forced to help with farmwork and partly that her relations with her parents were strained. She told me that her father openly favored her older sister. To her own mother she was never close. After my grandfather died, my grandmother, as was the common custom, spent a few months successively at each of her children's homes. My mother dreaded the arrival, though she made an effort to appear welcoming when the time came. The two were formally polite and considerate of one another, but the lack of warmth was noticeable. I sensed that her stint with us was painful for both of them.

Although she maintained good relations with her brothers and sisters, my mother's life was much more closely bound up with my father's family. I do not believe that they ever let her feel that she was an outsider, as might easily have happened with such different backgrounds. My mother never went to college, but she was able, in the less stringent educational structure of those days, to get a certificate that allowed her to teach in a rural grade school for a while before her marriage. With her careful use of language, her interest in reading, it never occurred to me that she was less well educated than my father and most of his siblings. I was greatly surprised to learn one day that my mother had never quite completed high school, for economic reasons. She and my father's sisters got along extremely well and worked together comfortably in summer projects ranging from picking wild berries to planning and cooking for the Fourth of July picnic. Indeed, my mother was an easy, congenial companion, cheerful, efficient, and gifted in the art of informal conversation. She was never aggressively self-assertive. In the church at Wilkes-Barre she refused to speak publicly and was reluctant to hold office, but she was a leader in getting things done. I noted that she seemed to command respect from the other women as if they accorded her a superiority she refused to see in herself.

My mother held, and I think she deliberately cultivated, a very low opinion of her own worth. Some deeply imbedded sense of inferiority she may have developed in her somber childhood, and it is possible that at least in the beginning she felt herself to be less an integrated member of the Barnes household than I realized. Perhaps also she blamed herself for not developing the potentialities she half-realized she possessed but found no opportunity to cultivate. I hold as at least partly responsible her unquestioning acceptance of church teaching, particularly its emphasis on humility and its insistence on acknowledging one's basic sinfulness and unworthiness. I felt that she, whose visible life was exemplary by Free Methodist standards, considered herself basically wicked. One result of this insecurity was her anxious concern for what others would think, an attitude which inevitably clashed with my father's social iconoclasm.

I am convinced that my mother had a capacity for happiness, which may have been somewhat lacking in my father, and which their life together only partially provided for. They were a close-knit, loving couple. I could no more have conceived of their ever divorcing than I could have imagined them capable of a crime. My father was the recognized head of the household, but he was not a strongly authoritarian figure. He gave my mother a weekly allowance, out of which she paid for her own and her children's personal expenses and routine household items. On a daily basis it was she who watched over the three of us and set the pattern for our lives. But just as my father would frequently spend time entertaining and instructing us, so on special occasions he would involve himself in household projects. I vividly remember autumn trips to the farmers' market, all of us together, my father pulling a child's wagon in which he loaded bushels of fruit, tomatoes, etc. He would help in the canning process as well. The indescribably delicious and pungent fragrance of cooking piccalilli, which on rare occasions I have happened to smell again, is for me what the madeleine was for Proust.

My parents' marriage was in many ways a partnership, and an affectionate one. (I recall, for instance, his holding her close as she sat on his lap, in our presence, a sight which—pace Freud—was not traumatic but profoundly reassuring.) Yet I cannot say that my father and mother were truly compatible. She tolerated his visionary projects for saving the world without sharing them. In truth, he demanded of her more than most women would have been willing to put up with—chiefly in the things he asked her to do without. Just one example: All of her life my mother used an old-fashioned, hand-operated wooden washing machine. But even out of a salary that peaked at about two thousand, my father's savings had accumulated so that in the year following my mother's death, he contributed a thousand dollars to buy Bibles for distribution in Japan.

While growing up, my sympathies were always with my mother in such matters, though probably out of self-interest. My mother's patience was not inexhaustible. Unfortunately, her only weapon, when she felt my father's insensitivity to everyday needs went far beyond what was reasonable or that his nonconformity was too embarrassing for her, was recourse to bitter reproaches and nagging about minor details, a practice that was occasionally effective but was always distressing, whoever was in the right or at fault.

Given the limitations of her situation, my mother was, all in all, a supportive wife and an admirable homemaker. Was she also a good mother? I am not certain, even now.

By most traditional criteria, my mother came so close to being the ideal mother that with appreciation for the care she bestowed upon me and her positive gifts, I find myself a monster of ingratitude in questioning that our uneasy relationship could be due to anything but my own shortcomings. Her children's well-being was her major concern. Her anxious care made her a bit overprotective, but not to the point of being stifling. She was eager for me to get along well with my playmates and would often arrange little parties for the neighbor children and me. Insofar as her straitened circumstances allowed, she indulged my requests for whatever was the fad of the moment—from shiny marbles to caramel lollipops—so that I could hold my own in the school yard. She and I were companions in many things. Particularly I loved going with her on her daily trips to the grocery store or "uptown." On one extraordinary day, as a rare treat, she took me into a soda fountain and, seeing my overwhelming enjoyment of an ice-cream soda, ordered a second one for each of us. Though hardly beautiful, my mother was attractive, with a good figure and abundant wavy hair. A splendid seamstress, with a good sense of design, she wore well the clothes she made for herself, well-fitted and perfectly suited for her, a trifle old-fashioned, but such was her preference. I was proud to wear the dresses, and later the full suits, she made for me, at school and occasionally even after I had finished college.

I will never cease to be thankful to my mother for her most important gift to me: it was she who instilled in me the desire to read for pleasure. Before I went to school, she read stories to me. As soon as I was able to read for myself, she arranged for me to get a card at the children's room of the public library. When I was still at the stage of *The Adventures of Buster Bear* and *The Bobbsey Twins*, she would read the books, too, so that we could talk about them together. Later we read the same popular fiction, including the serials that newspapers then featured, usually romances or detective stories. I remember specifically Christie's *The Murder of Roger Ackroyd* and Rinehart's *The Bat*. At about the time that I succeeded in getting an adult card, which a friendly librarian arranged for me before I had reached the required age, my mother began to worry that my free exploration of books was leading me into dangerous territory, but she did not impose any actual censorship. I remember only one well-intentioned but abortive attempt. Unwisely declaring that she wanted me to read something more suitable for my age than what I had selected, she presented me with a copy of *Alice in Wonderland*. Insulted at being asked to read "a child's book," I failed utterly to appreciate the wonders of Carroll's tale until I picked it up again years later.

More skillfully and to my total delight, my mother quite early put in my hands an old copy of Grimms' collection of fairy tales. This volume, with some of its yellowed pages coming loose, had no table of contents. For some reason I did not read it through consecutively but opened it at random each evening, elated when I turned to a story I had not already read. This procedure perhaps strengthened my belief that I could enter at any time into a self-contained world where everything was familiar though unrelated to my usual existence. In subsequent years I developed, and indeed still hold, the same feeling with regard to the world of Greek mythology. Today parents are often warned against giving fairy tales to children. To me this is incomprehensible. To encounter the impossible in the imaginary can be liberating. Granted, the heroes and heroines had much to endure. But neither their suffering nor the punishment of the villains was real in my everyday world. Moreover, I quickly learned that, in the tales, I could count on having everything turn out well and lead to infinite happiness for those who evoked my empathy. Above all, the stories suggested the existence of an inexhaustible treasure of possibilities, perhaps in the world itself, certainly within the covers of books. Freud wrote of the family romance, a fiction that children frequently invent and half-believe in order to give themselves parents more noble or at least different from the actual ones. My family romance was a Grimms' fairy tale. At night, as I lay in bed, I would imagine in detail the about-to-take-place transformation of our home into a palace, myself into a princess, and the splendid life we would lead. It was a safety valve, I believe. Its preposterous grandiosity prevented my seeing in it an invitation to retreat from the real world to some sort of inner imagined reality.

This rosy portrayal of my mother and me (though truthful) is not complete. It would be false to say that I did not love her, but strongly negative emotions were there as well. From the beginning our relations were troubled, and the tension between us intensified with time; it was still there beneath the surface even in later years when we consciously avoided conflict. If I were to choose a single word to describe what lay at the root of the feelings on both sides, it would be "resentment." The nature of the resentment changed over the years, but we continued to nurture it, in one another and in ourselves. Its earliest origin obviously lay in my first infancy. It is possible that some physical factor was responsible for my being such a difficult baby to care for, eliciting a negative response in my mother. I am inclined to believe instead, albeit with no evidence, that my behavior was a symptom resulting from my mother's psychological stress rather than its cause. I think she had not fully anticipated the difficulties and constraints brought on by a newborn. (Nobody was warned of postpartum depression in those days.) Exhausted to the point of desperation, she must have found me entirely a problem, not a pleasure. As an adult, I have observed instances in which a mother's sudden loss of freedom and sense of being unable to cope with the first child appeared to induce unease in the baby. At any rate, I soon took her resentment at the trouble I inflicted on her to be a rejection; I felt that she did not love me and that it was my fault. And no doubt, I, wanting to make her pay for making me feel this way, showed myself unusually willful and disobedient. The initial situation was not helped by the fact that my sister, five years later, proved to be an exceptionally easy infant to care for—a fact often pointed out to me, and not only by my mother.

One instance, which I do not remember myself but which relatives have considered worth recounting to me, may serve to illustrate the early interplay between my mother and me. As a group of us were sitting on my grandfather's front porch one Sunday afternoon, I continued to perform some annoying act until my mother said to me threateningly, "If you don't stop doing that, I'll come and make you stop." I did the same thing once more and ran, my mother pursuing. Heading for the barnyard, I picked my way through the cow plops, pausing to say, "You'd better be careful coming through here, Mother, or you'll get your shoes dirty." Evidently everyone's laughter, including my mother's, prevented any oversevere consequences. The onlookers saw as funny and slightly touching the fact that I would show concern for my mother even as I fled from her and the punishment she promised. I suspect that I spoke to discourage her from following me or perhaps to guard against my being blamed for still something more.

Rightly or wrongly, I always felt that my mother's unstinting care and attention where I was concerned were prompted by a sense of duty, not love. (Much later I noted that Sartre applies this description to Flaubert's mother. I am not trying to draw a parallel!) Upon this groundwork of resentment, as time went by, I quite unfairly established my mother as the focus of whatever objections I had to my situation. In our family my mother, for the most part, was the disciplinarian, the one who laid down the rules of everyday behavior. In particular it was she who enforced the code of conduct prescribed by the church. As this became increasingly burdensome to me, I tended to blame my mother for whatever I felt to be unduly restrictive. In contrast to my father's exaggerated ambitions for us, my mother urged us not to think too much of ourselves, to be modest in our aspiration. Pride was wicked. Her most frequent criticism of other women was that they were "stuck up." The image of myself that I was trying to form seemed to me entirely discordant with what she herself represented and with what I believed she wanted me to be.

Decades after Freud sketched out the stereotypical development of male and female attitudes toward each of their parents, feminists have shown themselves especially concerned with the story of women's relations with their mothers—the daughters' problems of overidentification and the need to see themselves as separate from the mother, new forms of the old Freudian sexual rivalry, hostility, hatred of the mother as the mirror image of the daughter's own self-dislike, and a host of other variations on this theme. Common to all of these studies and perhaps the most valuable insight has been recognition of the degree to which the basic relation between any mother and her daughter has been colored by society's attitude toward women and their place, both during the centuries of patriarchy and in the recent years of radical change, of transformations in the actual role of women and in the definitions of feminity, gender, and the like. Certainly something of this sort must have played a part in the relation between my mother and me.

If my mother ever felt dissatisfied with her status as a woman, I never suspected the fact. One memory, however, suggests to me now that I may have misread signs that were there. One day in Wilkes-Barre, when we had relatives visiting us in connection with the city's sesquicentennial celebration, my father and the other males in the group were preparing to set out for some sort of exhibit. I begged to go along. My mother forbade it, telling me, "That's the way things are. The men go out and do things. Women and girls stay home and get dinner." I could not have been more than about six at the time. It was probably my first conscious exposure to the idea that girls and boys had different pathways laid out before them. But instead of simply accepting my mother's words as a statement of fact, I was furious with her for assenting to this scheme of things and for assuming that I would go along with it. The bitterness that very probably lay behind her words escaped me entirely. Obviously I was unjust in identifying my mother with all that I wanted to reject. Nevertheless, I regarded her life as wholly unenviable and resolved that such would never be mine. To be unlike my mother became, for me, all but synonymous with realizing myself. Not that I ever clearly formulated any such resolve in so many words to myself, still less to anyone else, but there was an ongoing inward separation. I remember (this was when I was still living at home) that I did once exclaim in exasperation, "There's just too much church in our lives!" Later that morning I overheard my mother say to my father, "It's like suddenly discovering there's a stranger in the house." I was dismayed but relieved to have it out in the open.

There was never an open break between us. When I began to live away from home, I decided early on that there was nothing to be gained by flaunting the changes in my beliefs and in my way of living. I practiced no overt deceit; my parents asked few questions. Assumptions of sameness gradually became acceptance of difference. One time, shortly after my return from Greece, my mother remarked on how much greater was my breadth of experience than what she and my father had known in all their lives. I did not hear resentful envy in her words, only a sort of regret. Yet I did sometimes feel that her expressed satisfaction with my professional achievements was tempered by disappointment at my clear nonaffirmation of all that she had believed our family had stood for. She must surely have seen in this a partial rejection of herself, and it would have been natural for her to resent it.

My mother did not have an easy death. It came early, in 1950 when she was fifty-nine. She died slowly of an abdominal cancer—first surgery and radiation in the hospital, then a few months of seeming recovery, finally several weeks during which she lay in bed, much of the time half-drugged by morphine. A gratuitous, painful incident occurred shortly before the final phase. Walking alone one day, she tripped on an uneven piece of sidewalk and took a severe fall, breaking her eyeglasses. She came home slowly, crying. When my father complained to the owner of the house with the sidewalk, the man, fearful of a lawsuit, offered to make any compensation my mother deemed appropriate. She asked for money to replace the glasses and gratefully accepted twenty-five dollars as recompense for the pain she suffered after the fall. My mother died on Christmas Eve in 1950. I had spent the preceding two weeks watching over her along with my father. My parents' faith that death was a departure for the next world remained steadfast. My mother so longed for release that I found, to my distress, that I was joining in voicing the soothing reassurance that "It won't be long now," finding in this sentence the only possible consolation for her.

If I were writing a novel, I should surely want to introduce at this point a scene that would, verbally or by a symbolic act, accomplish a final reconciliation or affirmation of mutual understanding. No such scene took place. To be sure, there was neither hostility nor the frigid forbearance that marked my mother's adult relationship with my grandmother. I remember that when I told her I had found a new friend in Doris and that we hoped to share an apartment, she replied, "Good. Then you will have someone with you to help you." During the couple of years before her death, there had been a few times when we seemed to communicate more significantly than usual. Once when I had spoken to her with special sympathy, she had called me "Sweetheart," a term of endearment I had never heard her use for anyone but my father. But in these last days I felt that she had removed herself farther from me, as if no longer finding it necessary to pretend closeness, that she was leaving without saying good-bye. And I, who normally found it easy to be articulate, I was unable to break through, sitting there like an actor waiting in vain for a cue—or missing it.

I am not quite sure why I feel guilty when I think of my mother. Yes, of course there were all those problems I created for her. But I tried, too, to express appreciation on occasion. In later years I have sometimes dreamed that I was in danger, and I called out loud to her to help me. I was capable of acts of kindness toward her. I recall as a small child being praised when I had voluntarily and laboriously cracked and picked out the meat from Brazil nuts for her without eating any myself. In college, having earned some extra money, I sent her yellow roses for Mother's Day. When I got my first job and paid back to my father the small but essential sum that he had given me for my first year of graduate study, I gave my mother a fur coat at Christmas as partial return for what she had done in supporting me. Did I do these things out of love? Or did I, as I believed she did earlier, perform acts that imitated love? Or were my gifts self-evidently bids for *her* love and approval? In wondering about my mother and me, I am not sure whether I am speaking of an old scar or an open wound.

A Triad of Aunts

I have often wondered how radically different I would have been if our family had spent summers as well as winters in Wilkes-Barre. I have sometimes scoffed at the overused notion of role model. But there is no question that I had one, or—more accurately—three: my father's sisters: Ruth, Hattie, and Jennie. During the years when I was growing up, they were still unmarried; all taught in the public schools and lived at my grandparents' home in Beach Lake, at least in the vacation months. The three were so strongly differentiated that it would never have occurred to me back then to think of them collectively, and each of them appealed to, or helped to develop, a different side of me. Yet my memory of this triad of aunts tends to bring them together in a sort of composite image of concern and tenderness. I took for granted then, but have since marveled at, their extraordinary patience with me. They generously gave of themselves, never letting me feel that I was in the way, though I was constantly underfoot, asking questions, demanding help or attention in innumerable ways. Their attitude toward me was, in essence, more pedagogical than maternal. They constantly instructed me, imparting knowledge about a variety of things that they made to seem exciting; occasionally they criticized me, but always by way of reasoning discussion. Often they teased me, leading me to defend myself in argument, and they helped me to learn to laugh at myself. As time went on, each of them, to some degree, made a confidant of me, talking of her own feelings and aspirations. Perhaps I was a good listener; I can think of no other compensation they may have found for the time they bestowed on me.

Over the years, circumstances would bring me closer to one of the aunts than to the others. Indeed, now it seems to me that there was a sort of gradual progression in my own preferences. "Who do you love most?" an intrusive adult asked me when I was barely beyond the toddler stage. To which I am said to have replied, "Jesus first because you're meant to, and then Aunt Ruth." Ruth, the youngest, was the most glamorous—in appearance, in oral wit, in overall charm. Although never openly defiant of what her family held sacred, she was something of a rebel. It was thanks to her that I became aware that the 1920s marked more than a change on the calendar. Ruth was the first in the community to bob her hair and to shorten her skirts. She began discreetly to

use a touch of rouge and lipstick. She purchased sheet music of the latest popular songs and began to speak of up-to-date fads as items of interest, not just follies of the worldly. To me, in private, she hinted that
her life away from Beach Lake (for a short time she held a teaching job
in Yonkers, which she referred to as "living in the city") was quite different from her existence at home. As the guest of an Italian co-teacher,
she had actually tasted wine! Ruth took out membership in the Book-of-
the-Month Club; she first told me about, and then (as I approached high
school age) urged me to read the selections. Needless to say, my reading
reinforced the message behind Ruth's words and actions—that it would
one day be possible for me to revolt against my restrictive background.
Her example suggested that it was best to move between two worlds
rather than to forsake one wholly for the other, or to attempt to remodel
the old one. So long as my father and mother were alive, I did much as
she had done.

Ruth's own ventures proved to be little more than sightseeing excur-
sions. One year, when she and Jennie went for a summer session at Penn
State, Ruth fell in love with a fellow student, a man somewhat younger
than she and definitely not of the Free Methodist type. After a few months
this innocent romance ended unhappily, more, I understood, at his ini-
tiative than at hers; but it is possible that she, too, felt that their marriage would be unsuitable. (Ruth was not sufficiently a product of the
"roaring twenties" for any other kind of union to be conceivable.) At any
rate, it was not too long before she confided in me that she had recovered from her "passionate young love" and come to feel a deeper, more
mature attachment for one of the teachers, a Free Methodist, in the rural
high school of which she was then principal. I liked the man, and I believe the marriage was a remarkably happy one for the few years until
Ruth's untimely death from an embolism in a routine operation. The person I had so idolized seemed to me to have departed long before that.
Ruth did not continue teaching after she married, whether because her
husband's new and more lucrative position in the administration of a
large city school system in Ohio made her own work economically unnecessary, or because it was not customary for married women to work,
or both. When the pair made occasional visits to Beach Lake, I found in
place of my deliciously rebellious aunt, a woman who might well have
been a new convert to Free Methodism. I perceived that she was subtly
trying to influence me against all which she had formerly pointed out as
alluring, and I felt betrayed. Her life appeared to be centered solely on
church and home—like my mother's. I have no reason to believe that

Ruth herself was discontent with what she had become, and I am sure that her associates greatly valued her. But it seemed to me that she had forsworn herself. That the transformation in her was more than a reflection of my own changing perceptions was attested, for me, years later when I was describing to her daughter the Aunt Ruth I had once placed second only to Jesus. My cousin, who had no memories of the mother she lost so early, told me that she had heard, especially from Jennie, of the exciting young girl her mother had been and had looked in vain for signs of her in pictures taken in Ruth's later life. All she could see, she told me, was a plain, rather plump, apparently wholly conventional housewife. Truth compels me to add that I should hate to have the quality of my own personality assessed from photographs of me taken at any period.

Hattie, the middle sister, though less attractive in appearance than her sisters, was in some ways the most gifted. She confided in me more of her personal life than the others did. I alone knew that she had begun writing a novel. Nothing ever came of this, but she did win a modest success with her music. With very little in the way of training, she played the piano well enough to win local appreciation. I remember that whenever a thunderstorm threatened, my father would go to her house in the hope of hearing her. Terrified of lightning, Hattie tried to distract herself, if not to drown out the elements, by playing the piano, though the acoustics for her listeners were less than perfect. Hattie composed operettas (both words and music) for her grade school pupils to perform, and she had several of her songs published, one of which, "Pals," was formally dedicated to me. One summer, Hattie's confidences took a new turn as she talked to me of her developing romance with a young farmer from the area, whom she had met at church. Although to an outsider it seemed that the two had virtually nothing in common, their marriage lasted for the rest of Hattie's relatively long lifetime. She, like Ruth, soon gave up teaching. She submitted no more songs for publication and restricted her public performances to playing the organ at church—after the ban against the use of musical instruments was finally lifted in the 1940s. For most of the rest of her life she was a semi-invalid, almost a recluse, though, except for a late diabetes, I recall no diagnosed illness. Her famous sense of humor took on a sharper, blacker edge. I sensed that she was deeply unhappy. But the age of confidences was long past. I may be wrong in looking on her life as one of blighted potentialities. Certainly she, whose personal aspirations had been the greatest, settled for the least.

It was Jennie, the oldest of the three, whose influence upon me was most profound and long-lasting and with whom as an adult I continued to cherish a close bond of friendship. More overtly critical of me than either Ruth or Hattie, more obviously my teacher, Jennie started me on the academic path before I knew the meaning of the term. She was a little older than her siblings when she got her degree at, inevitably, Greenville College. Perhaps for that reason she entered into her studies more seriously. Her exuberance in learning spilled over to me as she introduced me, when I was of high school age and even earlier, to literary classics—Dickens, I remember especially, also George Eliot, and Willa Cather, but, above all, Shakespeare. The year after I had finished eighth grade, I read a volume of twenty of his plays, with which she provided me. At the time I enjoyed them mostly for the plots, but I developed a feeling for the language that I never lost. In a later summer, excited by her first-year course in ancient Greek, Jennie taught me the alphabet and a few verb and noun forms, then shrewdly refused to continue, telling me that I wouldn't be able to go far enough with it to count at that point and that she didn't want to spoil the luster of my future study of it if I should feel so inclined. When Jennie went on to take graduate courses in English at Penn State, she talked with me enthusiastically about the thesis she was writing on Guinevere, which her directing professor told her was potentially publishable.

Jennie's interests were not solely literary. She took me on early morning outings to watch birds, and she taught me the names and distinguishing traits of wildflowers. Occasionally we found rare varieties of plants, though the rarest of all she was never able to find for me—the yellow ladyslipper, an orchid which she herself had seen only once, deep in the woods. The little lakes and ponds and forests that Pennsylvania so abundantly offers seemed to me both paradisal and educational. As the Greek giant Antaeus renewed his strength by touching the ground (his mother, Earth), so for a long time I felt in the woodlands around Beach Lake that I was most at one with myself. During the last two and a half decades of my life, I have found the psychic equivalent at a cabin in the Rocky Mountains near Boulder.

To Jennie, who had the abilities and the interests suited to what might well have led her to become a professor and scholar, fell the lot of the unmarried daughter who stayed at home to look after her aging parents; she supported herself and them, too, in large part, on her salary as a grade school teacher in the Beach Lake school. I do not know, though it seems likely, that Jennie suppressed some inward bitterness, if not resentment. Outwardly she cheerfully developed all of the possibilities her situation offered, both in teaching creatively and in leading church-sponsored activities in the community. Reward came in an unexpected form. One day there arrived, unannounced, Thomas Shaw, originally a Quaker from Lancastershire in England, who had lived for a time in the Beach Lake area before I was born. Delighted to see him and his family, Jennie confided to me afterward that Tom seemed to her an exemplifi-cation of the type of person she most admired—a man clearly at peace with himself, gentle in manner, grateful for, rather than proud of, the modest but substantial financial success he had achieved. Without much schooling, he had developed intellectual interests, and he impressed one with the sense that here was a man of culture and wisdom. After the death of his wife a few years later, Tom made more visits to Beach Lake, and the predictable romance developed. I have known of no marriage which seemed to me happier for both parties. After my grandparents' death and Jennie's and Tom's retirements, the couple continued to live at Beach Lake, but they traveled freely; most importantly, they went to England where Tom revisited scenes from his childhood and Jennie tracked down the places in Cornwall from which the Beach Lake immi-grants had set out, even the precise farm where the Olver ancestors had lived. She established, too, a warm present bond with collateral rela-tives, whom I myself visited in the 1980s.

Marriage for Jennie was an enrichment and an expansion, not a nar-rowing. She seemed to become more fully and intensely the person I had so highly valued. Although I could not share her strong religious com-mitment and would certainly not have desired to live the life she lived, there remained always between us a level on which we communicated so deeply and with such mutual respect that it would have been misleading to speak even of tolerance and acceptance of differences. Rather, they seemed irrelevant. We never discussed directly my changing philosoph-ical and social-political views. I did send her a copy of my book *An Existentialist Ethics.* She wrote to me that she had read it and was interested to see that, in spite of everything, I still held onto a lot of the basic values that had been instilled in me as a child. Was this a sound insight? Or should it make one think rather of the grim joke that circulated some years back: "Aside from the shooting and all that, Mrs. Lincoln, how did you like the play?" I must return to this point. I have thought often that to the limited extent that one might imagine what it would have been like to have lived another's life, with all of the other's inwardness, I would be willing to have been Jennie in preference to most of the people I have known well.

My aunts were my teachers, more significantly than my instructors at school. I believe that the children who were in their classes were fortunate to have them. It is not surprising that I can never remember a time when I did not want to be a teacher myself. My aunts held up to me an image of femininity in sharp contrast to that offered by my mother. I find it interesting, though, that I never wanted to be just like any one of them. I stood aloof from their religious convictions. Their choice to marry did not lead me to make marriage my goal. I was always aware that for me the door they opened led outward.

The Three of Us in the Nest

Soon after my fifth birthday I was called to my mother's bedside. She told me to look at what I thought was a doll lying beside her. I wondered why she didn't hand it to me since obviously it was meant to be mine. Learning that this was a baby sister come to live and grow up with us, I was overcome with joy and continued to feel that somehow she was brought there for me. At that early stage I never, in the slightest degree, thought of Jean as an intruder or wished her away, as firstborn children often do when faced with a new baby. A few weeks later when she and my mother both came down with measles, I grieved to be kept apart from them and rejoiced when I broke out with spots and could be near them again. If my memories are not false, I felt in those early years neither jealousy nor resentment toward my sister, who could have been thought to usurp my place. From the start, Jean was an exemplary child—undemanding as a baby, a winsome, curly-haired toddler, a cheerful youngster who charmed everyone. Gradually I came to think it both reasonable and inevitable that my mother should love her more than me. Not that my mother ever showed favoritism overtly; both my parents were scrupulously careful to deal with us impartially, enough so that one of my cousins remarked one day on how fair everything was in our family, unlike his own. But my perception was not mistaken. My brother confirmed years later that he had always assumed that my mother preferred Jean whereas I was my father's favorite. If the latter was the case, I never realized it; in any case, it did not console me. Obviously, by then I was intensely jealous of my sister, but strangely I never turned the negative

feelings against Jean herself. If anything, my possessive love of her intensified as I saw how adorable she was in the eyes of others.

Given the five years between us, it was natural for me to take the lead
in planning our activities, telling her stories, inventing games, hunting
for new ways to entertain her, inordinately pleased when she responded
appreciatively. (Yes, I am aware that what I write sounds much like
Simone de Beauvoir's description of her early relation to her younger sister, Poupette. I was impressed with the resemblance between our experiences when I read Beauvoir's account years ago. Nothing strange here.
Perhaps we both exemplified one of the patterns sisters fall into, one of
the better ones, I think.) As Jean and I grew a little older, we simply
shared. Or so it seemed to me at the time. Now I think that I sought
subtly to dominate. In 1967, when Jean and I went on a trip to Europe
together, we talked over those childhood days. I told her that I felt that
out of my own need I had perhaps not allowed her to assert herself adequately. I was surprised at the intensity with which I found myself adding
that, if I had done so, it was for me a matter of self-preservation. Jean
acknowledged, though she did not speak reproachfully, that she had allowed me to give her the passive role. "I even let you talk for me," she said.

If Jean's manner was reassuring, the words were to me an indictment.
In her first year at high school, Jean began to have a difficulty in talking, a
problem of controlling the vocal chords so as to speak forcefully and at
the same time naturally. She was never able to overcome the impediment, though she learned to live with it and so managed that most people,
I suspect, noted only a certain hesitancy and hoarseness. This obviously
did not prevent her from achieving success, socially and professionally.
She married, had two children, and for nearly forty years held the position of director in the town library. Yet I knew that she was bothered by
the condition; she used the telephone only when necessary and refused
to speak publicly, even in a situation designed explicitly to recognize an
accomplishment of hers. In 1990, I received a letter from Jean in which
she told of running across an article that described her ailment precisely
and gave it a name—spastic dysphonia. In this and in follow-up readings
she learned that various causes had been suggested for it, genetic and
otherwise, but all of them entirely physiological, and that the condition
could be greatly and temporarily helped, it not permanently cured. Jean
decided that at the age of seventy she would not attempt any of the
fairly complicated treatments. But, although regretful over the decades
of worry and anxiety, her tone was almost jubilant in reporting how

"comforting" it was to realize that the symptom had not been caused by some psychological weakness on her part, and how relieved she felt to know that it was in no way her "fault." My own sense of release in reading her letter was a close second to hers.

I was nine and a half when my brother, Paul Edison, was born. (My father chose the names, voicing the hope that religion and science would mix. He had been responsible for my names as well, choosing "Estella" as the second because it meant "star." My mother had selected "Jean Lois" because she liked the sound.) Mother had prepared me for Paul's arrival by giving me a rudimentary, rather vague explanation of how babies came to be. Smugly in the know and with a sense of complicity, I welcomed Paul as a fascinating gift to the household. Coming so late into the family, he may have enjoyed a particular closeness to my mother, as often happens with the youngest child, especially with a boy. His arrival did not, so far as I have ever been able to perceive, upset the delicate balance of family relationships. Jean was in no way excluded. If anything, Paul's presence tended to defuse any latent rivalry between her and me. My father, toward the end of his life, once remarked to me quite matter-of-factly that "like any father" he had a "special feeling" for Paul as his son. His attitude and behavior toward us, as shown, for example, in his urging us equally to "become eagles," never revealed any gender discrimination or even differentiation.

For me Paul as a young child was a delight. When he became a bit older, but not yet fully adult, our relationship, despite or perhaps because of the age gap between us, took on a halfway romantic quality. Paul showed toward me the sort of gallantry that, in those far-off days, adolescent boys might bring into play on their first dates. I felt protectively tender toward him and privileged to share a nearness exquisitely poised between intimacy and reserve. We were proud of one another.

Paul's age put him midway in the generation subject to the draft during World War II. Like many others, he preserved his power to choose the branch of service he preferred by voluntarily enlisting in the Navy before his number came up. Among the fortunate few for whom their stint in the military provided training and education (in his case, first at Cornell and then at Dartmouth) without their ever having to serve in the field, Paul found in his Navy experience the incentive for an unexpected career choice. Earlier he had told me of his naive and touching dream that he and Jean and I might one day establish together a newspaper. Farthest from his mind then was any further involvement with the church. In the new environment he was so appalled at the lack of either meaning or moral purpose in the lives of most of his fellow sailors that he put in an effective request to join those being trained for the chaplains' corps. Though he never returned to Free Methodism, he went on after the war to take degrees in theology at McCormick Seminary and at Yale Divinity School and enjoyed a long, fulfilling career in the United Church of Christ.

The Paul I found after my return from three years in postwar Greece—a theological student, married, recently having become a father—superficially bore little relation to the adolescent I had last seen before the war was over. Our mutual determination not to admit that there could be any estrangement between us itself contributed to a certain uneasiness. Paul's explicit statement to me that, while we were no longer as close in ideas, our feelings toward one another remained the same belied what he was saying. But gradually a new kind of closeness developed and remained firm.

It is for my brother and sister, not for me, to tell their stories. But no picture of my life, either as a child or as an adult, would be fair if they were not present as part of its integral structure. I do not claim that the bond that held us together represents an extraordinary achievement on our part, or even a highly unusual one. I suppose that millions of sets of siblings might truthfully say that they have kept in constant touch over the years and distance, have extended understanding and support to each other, in short, have warmly loved each other. But just as evidently, this is not something that can be taken for granted. Why should I find more reason to love my brother, asked Montaigne, quoting Plutarch, "just because we came out of the same hole?" Little birds in the nest do not always agree. Early associations can as easily lay the foundation for hostility as for love. If I believed in Providence, I should be grateful for its putting me among the fortunate. I prefer to extend my gratitude to the other two of us and for that inexplicable, serendipitous network of circumstances we call good luck.

In 1983, after both our parents had died, chance circumstances brought us three together and by ourselves for a weekend at Jean's home. Nonstop we reminisced about our childhoods, comparing our memories, filling them out, sometimes reconstructing and reevaluating them. It was therapeutic and exhilarating. I was especially struck by two things: First, I concluded that our adult judgments on our common experience varied only slightly and for reasons easily explained. Second, I realized how greatly our individual histories differed. With the considerable span of time between each two of us, the order of our births profoundly affected the basic situations we were born into. Of course, the battles I had fought helped to clear the way for Jean and Paul in their attempts to reconcile family pressure and life outside, though whether it is psychologically better for a child to have a really clear-cut incentive to rebel, I cannot say. It is not surprising, however, that my own break with the religious teachings of my childhood was a radical rupture, whereas Jean became a member of the Presbyterian Church, without ever being deeply committed to it, and Paul ended up as a minister in the United Church of Christ. The advantage was not all on the side of my siblings. Neither of them enjoyed the special bond I had with my aunts; nor were they, as I was, privileged to accompany my Uncle Earl on local business trips and to be initiated into the wonder of eating at a restaurant. This was partly because my aunts' own situations changed as they married, and partly because it was easier to take along one child than two; they would have thought it cruel suddenly to replace one by another. And, of course, in time, the three of us became companions for each other. Games were not an important part of Beach Lake activities, but the lakes and fields and forests offered endless possibilities for recreation. At Wilkes-Barre we spent more of our time with our respective age groups, and our experiences varied consequently.

I suspect that children and adolescents today would view wholly negatively our way of life in the period when I grew up, lacking so many things that are now viewed as essential, and, at least apparently, so severely restricted in the scope of activities open to youngsters. By contemporary standards, we were all naive and unsophisticated in the extreme. The line between childhood and adulthood was more pronounced; boys and girls in their early teens were treated, for the most part, simply as older children. And that is what they were then. Clearly, it would be equally mistaken either to conclude that we lived wretchedly because we did not have what today's young ones value so highly, or to claim that, not having the kinds of stress familiar in young lives in the last decades of this century, we lived in a state of innocent bliss. Still it would be hard to exaggerate the difference, even in little things, between now and that era before plastic, styrofoam, and Kleenex. Though I cannot claim to have been born before the age of automobiles, cars were not yet, in my early years, the commonplace possessions they soon came to be. I recall streetcars before buses. I remember, though this seemed a bit unusual even then, an interminable, slow, nine-mile journey by horse and wagon from the train station in Honesdale to Beach

Lake. My very earliest memory shows that even telephones were not omnipresent: My parents and I—I in a child's stroller—set out to visit friends in another part of town. On the way we met them; they were coming to call on us. The strangeness of this coincidence impressed me indelibly; I don't know quite why. Airplanes were exotic for most people. It was after I had finished high school in 1933 that I first rode in one. A pilot had come to our area to offer short rides to customers so that they might know what it was like to be airborne. I was allowed to use a monetary graduation present to go up in the small, open-cockpit plane. My mother told me afterward that her feelings were the same as on the day she had watched me being wheeled away in the hospital for a minor operation.

Naturally, a certain relativity enters in; we have lost now some of the positive enjoyments which derived from or which compensated for our very lacks. With iceboxes instead of refrigerators and in the total absence of frozen foods to store in them, each season brought the excitement of fresh new produce, enjoyed more keenly because it was transient. We had no Pizza Hut, nor Taco Bell, nor even a close equivalent to McDonald's, but I doubt that children now find going to those places any more wonderful than our expeditions to buy ice-cream cones were to us. I feel certain that few eating adventures surpass in offered delights the occasions when our extended family made its own ice cream in an eight-quart freezer, which one man turned while another stood by with chopped ice and salt, while we children argued as to who first would get the chance to scrape off the dasher and boasted about how many dishes we had eaten the last time.

For playtime, it is problematic whether we can meaningfully speak of comparable pleasures. The change in quality of life is absolute, now that electronic entertainment permeates the lives of old and young alike. Youngsters who divide their out-of-school time between television and video games must wonder what on earth we did with ourselves. We eventually had the radio, of course, but I do not recall that in its early days my family listened to it very much except for reports of such unusual events as Lindbergh's landing in Paris. A bit later we enjoyed Jack Benny and the Amos-and-Andy show, anathematized now but universally popular then, and the Hit Parade, which I was amused, in the sixties, to discover Sartre discussing as an example of extreme other-directed conformity. But none of this held us spellbound. The neighbor children had their weekend movies. I was occasionally taken, on Sunday afternoons, to public, popular lectures delivered by naturalists or explorers or various adventurers. Perhaps for us these were roughly equivalent to the documentaries, half-entertainment, half-instructive, offered on today's National Educational TV channel.

For the most part we read library books, and we played. Some of my time I spent with a few girl friends inside the house. More often, in the years when I was in grade school, we played outside, even in the winter, boys and girls together. Some of our games were those now thought of as belonging mostly to folklore—London Bridge, the Farmer Takes a Wife, and a form of charades that for some reason we called Pennsylvania. I remember in particular a game called "Statue." One child had the task of grabbing in turn the hand of each of us others and swinging him or her until, suddenly let go, we were flung into a pose in which we were supposed to freeze, facial expression and all. Then, by prior arrangement, the swinger chose the most beautiful, the funniest, or the ugliest "statue," and that child became swinger for the next round. This rather pointless pastime fascinates me in retrospect in that it so perfectly exemplifies Sartre's concept of the judgmental Look that makes the Other into an object, like the petrifying stare of Medusa. Other games were more active, variations of tag, explorer, hide-and-seek, relievo, and even our peculiar version of baseball.

This unisex camaraderie seemed to me very natural, and none of my elders appeared to find it unusual. At Beach Lake I had been privileged to have a companion of about my age, a distant cousin, John Hicks, who was raised in my grandfather's household. John was willing on occasion to play what he considered "girls' games" with me, and I in turn rolled discarded rubber tires along with him, pretending they were cars, while he chattered on about the respective merits (imagined) of the Pierce-Arrow and the Rolls-Royce. I accompanied John on his "chores," going out to the pasture to bring in the cows, and watching while he milked them. At Wilkes-Barre the relationship of boys with girls was within the group as a whole. Gradually the custom changed. I do not recall that Jean's circle of playmates included boys. I know that Paul's experience was totally different and that his male peer group exerted a degree of pressure that neither of his sisters had felt. He once told me, for example, that the reason he had not developed the habit of reading for pleasure until quite late in his life was that his companions considered reading "sissy," only for girls.

I have no way of knowing what depths of depravity may have existed below the surface of respectability that cloaked our neighborhood. There was one occasion when my father called the police because a drunken neighbor was threatening to beat up his wife. I never saw any signs of the man's actually having done so, on that day or on any other. I heard that an unmarried young woman on our block had a baby, which was considered disgraceful; the neighbors continued to talk with her as well as about her. I never heard any discussion of pregnancy among teenagers. Child abuse, in its various forms, must surely have existed, but it was never mentioned in my hearing, nor did I see references to it when I grew old enough to read the newspapers. Granted, mine was an extremely sheltered existence. Still, it is a fact that for the lower middle class in Wilkes-Barre, children were able to be children. They could play in the streets in the early evening, just as, with occasional exceptions, adults could move about safely at any hour.

So far as racial or ethnic tensions were concerned, I lived in complacent ignorance. In Wilkes-Barre at that time an unusually high proportion of the population was made up of recent immigrants. We youngsters would ask someone, "What nationality are you?" in the same matter-of-fact way we would inquire, "What church do you go to?" Here I used to stress my Danish ancestry, feeling that the other side left me uninteresting. The city did not have many "colored people" as we would have called them then, but I think I recall (improbable as it may seem) that the elected president of the senior class in high school one year was "colored," which would indicate that our community was less prejudiced than most. This atmosphere was effective in reinforcing what I was taught at home and at school: that all people were essentially alike and deserved an equal chance. Unfortunately this belief was accompanied by the conviction that society in fact lived by this ideal. I knew vaguely that in some places (I assumed that they were in the South) "Negroes" were discriminated against, but I felt this was a temporary condition left over from the pre–Civil War period. And although I would have jumped to the defense of any one individual subjected to racial or ethnic insults, I was wholly insensitive to the group slurs blatantly present in stereotypic jokes. The fact that I had a disproportionately high number of friends who were Jewish did not prevent me from enjoying and repeating funny stories that made a Jew the butt of the humor. It would no more have occurred to me to object to the high school minstrel show than to complain that God was referred to by the masculine pronoun. I slumbered with the rest of the unawakened.

Retrospectively, I am equally impressed by the degree to which I was the product of my particular circumstances and by the absolute singularity of my conditioning and development. Our split residency at Wilkes-

Barre and Beach Lake gave to us three a perspective different from that of our peer groups at either place. In the city we felt that we were at the bottom of the barrel whereas in the country we were among the privileged leaders, though leadership in the Barnes circle did not seek to attract attention to itself. Two stories about my Uncle Earl are illustrative. A lumberman, the only affluent Barnes of that generation, he liked to manipulate benevolently behind the scenes. When a minister assigned for a limited period to the Beach Lake church proved to be intolerable to Uncle Earl, he expressed concern about the health of the man's wife and sent both of them on a month's vacation in Florida. On another occasion my uncle grew sick of the bickering of two of his workmen, one of whom claimed that he was owed a small amount of money which the other refused to pay. Uncle Earl gave the money to cover the debt to the creditor, saying that the debtor was willing to pay it on condition that he never be reminded of the fact. The debtor was told that the other man would drop the claim so long as the debtor never mentioned the matter to the creditor. The two became the best of friends.

Uncle Earl was hardly typical, even among my relatives, nor were they like the majority of the members of the Free Methodist Church, many of whom were far more grim and repressive. One of them who married into the family used to say, when laughter at the table became a bit excessive, "We're getting away from our Bibles!" I recall no such attitude at my own family's displays of hilarity. Indeed, my mother's sense of humor enabled her to defuse potential crises. I have mentioned the occasion of her pursuit of me across the barnyard. One rainy day, having caught Jean in the act of collecting water from the rainspout in her shoe, Mother exclaimed, "Don't ever let me see you doing that again!" To which Jean replied, "Well, you stay in the house then, while I do it." Laughingly my mother persuaded Jean to come inside. And once, when Paul, normally on the best of terms with my mother but this time irritated at having been denied some small request, wrote a reproachful letter (he had just learned to write), beginning "Bad Ma" and signed "Hate from Paul," her amusement and his underlying affection speedily brought reconciliation. My mother sometimes could help us to see ourselves as funny—though I never quite made that observation until this very minute.

In truth, the Free Methodists of my acquaintance did not wholly fit the stereotype of fundamentalist congregations either then or now. The hypocrisy and self-seeking greed depicted in Frederic's picture of an evangelical church in *The Damnation of Theron Ware*, for instance, were not prevalent. True, support for missionary work in Africa was usual, and social activism to improve the lot of the poor or of racial minorities at home was not. Some individuals were prejudiced against Jews and "Negroes"; the official doctrine called for equality. There was a "colored" family in our church at Wilkes-Barre, although, to be sure, they labeled themselves "South Americans" since they had come from the southern continent. I remember (but this was in later years) reading an article in *The Free Methodist* which argued that a true Christian could not legitimately oppose miscegenation. The Free Methodist Church in which I was brought up, though it in many ways resembled American Gothic, was not like the religious right of the last decades of this century.

As I try to sum it all up, I could be tempted to say that, despite some tension and narrowness of outlook, my childhood environment was a favoring one—nurturing, protective, and, partly because of its inherent contradictions, conducive to personal growth. But it could not have been idyllic. There must have been a deep flaw somewhere. I remember that I thought of myself as being basically unhappy. And when I was about ten years old, I found it necessary to adopt a strategic retreat.

FUGUE

In *Words* Sartre spoke of the deep neurosis he developed as a child. His idiosyncratic use of the term made of it almost a metaphor to symbolize his initial choice of himself as a writer, which he decided later had amounted to a preference for the imaginary over the real. I am not speaking metaphorically when I describe my own temporary neurosis, although, interestingly enough, nobody (at least in my presence) has ever referred to my odd behavior as neurotic, either at the time or since then.

Midway through the seventh grade, I developed a strange, lingering illness. It began with an ordinary case of stomach flu or something of the sort, but for many weeks I did not recover. More exactly, I no longer had any symptoms that could be observed externally, but I complained of constant nausea and of being unable to do more than to move each morning from my bed to the couch downstairs and back again at night. The doctor, unable to find any discernible cause for my ailment, prescribed rest. So I lay there, watched over anxiously, my meals served on a tray (my nausea did not altogether prevent me from eating), feeling actively miserable except for the extended periods when I lost myself in reading. With no exercise, I naturally grew steadily weaker. Then one day I developed new symptoms—fever and vomiting. Twenty-four hours later I made a swift recovery, not only from the immediate symptoms, but from all that had ailed me earlier. I sat up, I left my couch, I was cured. By now so much time had gone by that it would have been difficult for me to catch up with my class. When I seemed to be entirely well again, my parents, deciding that the fresh air of Beach Lake would be good for me, sent me to live at my grandparents' home until time for my family's arrival at Beach Lake in June.

I repeated the seventh grade with no more problems. But before the end of the second term of eighth grade, I became ill in much the same way and took to my couch again. The earlier pattern was repeated almost exactly, though for a shorter period. The siege ended when a sudden sore throat led my parents to call the doctor, a different one this time, a pediatrician with special training in what was thought of then as "nervous ailments." She urged that I must be made to sit up. Most important, she convinced me that the medicine she prescribed not only would fix up my sore throat but would make me entirely well again. Within a few days I was moving about normally. Since I had already finished the greater part of the year's work, the school authorities said that I could be promoted to high school without returning to complete the eighth grade. Once more I went to Beach Lake ahead of the rest of the family. This was the end of the matter. The remainder of my life saw no recurrence of such episodes or of anything remotely comparable to them.

Obviously the psychosomatic syndrome was the expression of some underlying strategy, whether one takes a Freudian or a Sartrean point of view. Should we speak of motives and procedures so deeply buried in an unconscious that they were totally cut off from my awareness then and largely remain so even now? Or of complex patterns in bad faith? Neither seems to me quite right. Sartre insisted that we can reflectively examine what was originally a nonreflective experience. Granted he was thinking of reactions more closely related in time. I am fully aware of the treacherous nature of memory stretched across so many decades. All the same, I believe that my recollection of the sort of feelings I had during those weeks I spent as an invalid is fairly reliable. I am certain that I was not pretending. I did not, for instance, fake illness as a way of getting myself to Beach Lake, at least not on the first occasion when I could not have foreseen such an outcome. That the hope of it might have been an additional, unacknowledged factor the second time around is, I suppose, possible; I was convinced that I was really sick. Both times I looked on what had happened as a lamentable misfortune. I felt so disgraced by the fact that I would have to repeat the seventh grade that for years whenever I was asked where I was in the school system, I felt compelled to explain that though I had been kept back a year, I had skipped the second grade—so that now I was just where I "should be." (Can I conceivably still be doing this!) I was not happy. Yet curiously I recall no feeling of anything like despair, not even severe anxiety about my situation. I did not particularly worry (though I am sure that my parents did) over the fact that the doctor could not arrive at any diagnosis of my condition. I took it for granted that I would one day recover. In short, I felt obscurely that there was something wrong but that it was not serious, an intuition that proved to be correct. What *was* wrong? Why did I feel vaguely guilty as if I were not quite ill enough to have to be confined to the couch, yet at the same time physically incapable of functioning away from it? And what, in each instance, prompted my sudden recovery?

The last question seems to me comparatively easy to answer. Each period of invalidism was initiated and was concluded by the onset of one of the ordinary ailments that all children are subject to—stomach and intestinal upsets or a form of "grippe" as we used to call it. Without claiming to understand all of the physiological and psychological mechanisms involved, I believe that what happened was basically this: The easily diagnosed physical symptoms, which really did, I am inclined to think, derive from some external, hostile invasion of the organism, acted as catalytic signals to induce a different psychic orientation, marking the beginning and the end of a fugue-like retreat. Body language expressed, more clearly than any words could have done, my profound distaste for my existence and the feeling that I did not know how to cope with it. I believe that when the initiating illness had run its course, I perceived that the expected return to normal health did not dramatically reveal a state of well-being. I suspect that in fact I did not feel much different physiologically these first days than I had before the onset of the illness. But my awareness of a basic malaise was intensified. As I tried to explain my malady to myself and to others, I could not do better than to say that I was "sick to my stomach." I was not lying, but undoubtedly my imagination exaggerated the stomach discomfort.

I find it highly significant that my specific complaint was of nausea. I am convinced that the feeling I was trying to describe was a variant of the nausea that has figured so strikingly in the literary and philosophical contexts I discovered years later. It was certainly kin to the "bad taste in the mouth" that troubled Ivan Ilych in the early days of his illness, a symptom which he gradually came to identify with a revulsion against his whole way of life. Surely it must have been related to the nausea that swept over Sartre's Roquentin, the hero of Sartre's novel titled *Nausea*, and revealed to him, as it had to Nietzsche before him, the basic meaningless contingency of existence as a whole. In *Being and Nothingness* Sartre claimed that "a dull and inescapable nausea perpetually reveals my body to my consciousness." I take it that he had in mind especially those infrequent occasions when, not caught up in any absorbing activity, we try to grasp directly just what we are as self-conscious creatures, to pin down the taste of ourselves. At any rate, I think that to examine too closely one's physical state at a given moment, independent of particular stimuli, is likely to be as unreassuring as it is to look at one's face in the mirror—at least for most of us.

It is not hard for me to see how I confused psychic uneasiness with failure to recover physically. Why did my concluding illness, on both occasions, have the opposite effect from the initiating one and trigger my recovery? My guess is that the sudden contrast between the specific new pains and my familiar vague nausea conveyed this time a sense of progress in healing, suggesting that it was indeed possible to get well. Somehow I must have been ready now—either because some strengthening change had actually been accomplished or because of an unformulated decision that the retreat to the couch was not, or was no longer, helping.

Nothing in my childhood history suggests that a purely physiological cause was responsible for this bizarre conduct. A couple of years earlier our doctor had diagnosed a slight murmur in my overslow heartbeat, a temporary condition if indeed it ever did exist (I have sometimes wondered about the medical skill of our kindly family physician). This would not in itself have caused my mysterious illness, though it is possible that the doctor's pronouncement instilled in me a tendency to look on my state of health as precarious. My family evidently felt there was a link here; Jean told me that she had always assumed that I was suffering from "heart trouble." If I was, it was metaphorically.

When I ask myself now what inner psychological needs my psychosomatic behavior was satisfying, I find an array of possible explanations, some of them contradictory, none of them adequate. One might ask first of all whether my withdrawal may have been a masochistic punishment, a jail sentence from which I was released when I had served my term. The popular Freudian depiction of guilt stemming from repressed jealousy of a more favored sister might possibly have some application here, but somehow I doubt it. I recognized the mingling of my proprietary love for Jean and resentment at my mother's preference for her. I did not repress such awareness. Was then my neurotic behavior not a punishment but a device to gain more manifestations of attention and love from my parents, and especially from my mother? This hypothesis seems to me more reasonable, but it is not entirely satisfactory either. I could not properly be said to have been an underloved child. Even my mother did not overtly treat me unfairly. It was I, more than either Jean or Paul, who was the center of attention of the beloved Beach Lake relatives and, to some extent, at least in my siblings' judgment, of my father.

An obvious question to be asked is whether my conduct could be explained simply as a device (one involving elaborate self-deception, of course) to avoid going to school. Nothing in my own recollections or in what I have learned from others supports this view. I was not noticeably popular with my peers, but I never felt excluded. A few sharp-tongued teachers kept me in terror of their possible public reproof; others showed great kindness. My grades were always high, except for penmanship and drawing; I was distinctly deficient in these skills, but my parents let me feel that inferiority here was unimportant and not my fault. I do not find any reason to believe that I resorted to drastic procedure in order to escape the classroom or the school yard.

It may be more profitable to search for other remembered traits or habits, things which, while not neurotic in themselves, might be indicative of what was in back of the overt abnormal reactions. A couple of memories are of particular interest and possible relevance.

Although I never invented a distinctly defined imaginary companion as some children do, I recall that when I was playing alone or engaged in any activity by myself, I habitually carried on an internal conversation, more monologue than dialogue, with someone I vaguely thought of as another aspect of myself, to whom I explained what I was doing and how I felt about things. Very often, though not always, it was a sort of self-justification, an enterprise to impose on this other a favorable image of myself. Today, considering this practice, I view it as being an all but literal exemplification of something that Sartre says we all do less obviously most of the time; that is, our active consciousness is perpetually unifying and ordering its experiences into an ego, making a self, fashioning it in varying degrees of good and bad faith. What was distinctive about my procedure was the degree to which I felt impelled to defend this self.

A more complex variation of this practice was a secret game I sometimes played with myself. At night in bed, with the covers pulled over my head, I pretended to be presiding over a set of little creatures ("people" would be putting it too strongly). Each one represented some aspect of my life and was held responsible for what had happened during the day just gone by. Some were embodiments of my own behavior; I scolded or praised them according to whether, for example, I had performed well or poorly in class, had been selfish or unselfish toward my playmates, had been nice enough to my little sister. Others represented hopes and fears that were dependent on other people. In particular I remember commending or reprimanding one of these imagined beings for how my mother had behaved toward me. It seems to me that at the time I found a certain satisfaction in thus summing up and evaluating the hours just lived through, and, of course, instructing these self-projections to be firm in their resolution to produce a better accounting on the next night. The procedure may have served as a safety valve, if not a self-clarification. Yet it suggests to me now that it was undoubtedly to some degree also an expression of an underlying neurosis. To an exaggerated degree, I was possessed by the feeling that I must always measure myself against some ill-defined perfection, and inevitably I had a sense of failure and guilt in not living up to it. A contributing factor may have been my father's expressed confidence in my stellar future. A more obvious source was my constant exposure to the church teaching crystalized in the frequently quoted imperative, "Be ye therefore perfect as your Father in Heaven is perfect." The idea of a Day of Judgment at the end of my life—or at the end of the world's life, as some fundamentalists imagined it—never seemed quite real to me. Perhaps a remark of my father's to the effect that he did not believe God would deal more harshly than a loving human father would with his child may have guarded me against the fear of a literal Hell awaiting me. I did not have a clear-cut sense of sin as the church would have had me do. But the sense that I lived under a Look of Judgment was always with me. I suppose one might say that I represented a classic case of a child who had developed a mammoth superego, though Freud would have been surprised to see this phenomenon in a female. At any event, one way or another I lived my days in competition with myself, making up my daily report card.

Erich Fromm, in *Man for Himself*, claims that psychological (and even physical) malaise may result from the common habit of judging ourselves overtly by an authoritarian ethics, instilled by others, while repressing our guilt at contravening what our own authentic conscience is trying to tell us. I had not then even begun to work out a coherent value system of my own. But perhaps there was one in embryo. One illustrative example that I recall clearly shows that I was at least aware of conflicts in my own judgments. In the first grade I was caught one day talking at my seat when we were supposed to be silent. I was punished by the teacher's hitting my hand with a ruler (not very hard). Since this had happened to others in the class, I felt proud rather than humiliated. But for years afterward I felt a deep and painful guilt, a real sense of sin, not on account of the punishment itself, but because I never confessed it to my parents.

With my Existentialist orientation, I find it natural to see parallels (and differences, too, of course) between this childhood experience of mine and three "encapsulated" neuroses (or, in one case, psychosis) discussed by Sartre and R. D. Laing. The first that comes to mind is Sartre's theoretical explanation of Flaubert's dramatic *crise de nerfs*, his collapse into a catatonic state from which after several succeeding minor attacks he completely recovered. Sartre's hypothesis that this behavior was a hysterical, psychosomatic, passive strategy to frustrate the elder Flaubert's plans for his son's career and to give Gustave the opportunity to become a writer seems more convincing than the traditional diagnosis of epilepsy, especially in view of the fact that the first attack occurred just when Flaubert was going to have to retake his law exam and the last one shortly before his father's death. My less dramatic illness is not as clear in its end-to-be-achieved, but is comparable in the transposition of physical and psychic elements and in its sharply delineated time span. Sartre reported an experience of his own that is further removed from mine but not entirely irrelevant. Initiated by an experiment with mescaline but prolonged for months when the physical effects were no longer operative, visual illusions of menacing marine creatures tormented Sartre, figures which he knew to be hallucinations but which he was unable to dispel. Sartre feared that he was suffering the first stages of a full-blown psychosis. According to Beauvoir's and his own account, this disturbed state was a manifestation of his underlying discouragement and doubt of his capacity to realize his literary ambitions, to make himself into the great writer of his childhood dreams. Sartre maintained that finally he banished the unwelcome images by a simple act of will. In all probability, I believe, he found himself able to do so after he had managed to deal with the inward problems they signified.

Laing's example, which at first might appear much too extreme for meaningful comparison, I find the most richly suggestive. I refer to his analysis, in *The Politics of Experience*, of the temporary severe psychosis suffered by one of his patients. Laing insisted that this fugue, as he named it, was equivalent to a period of self-discovery, of renewal, a rebirth. Laing went so far as to claim that such retreats into the abnormal were sometimes (emphatically not always) positive experiences contributing

ultimately to the subject's psychic well-being. Joanne Greenberg, the author of *I Never Promised You a Rose Garden*, told me that this pronouncement
by Laing made her unwilling to give serious consideration to the rest of
his work because he spoke so lightly and seemingly without full understanding of the intolerable suffering inherent in psychosis. I agree that a
psychotic episode of the kind Laing described is too high a price to pay,
particularly since it must be paid in part by the anguish of those near to
the patient. Nevertheless, Laing's contention that abnormal behavior may
sometimes be the external expression of a constructive struggle to solve
problems rather than signs of mental deterioration strikes me as valid.

Whatever may have been the causes and motives of my own neurotic
fugue, I think that it performed the same service for me as the psychotic
fugue Laing had in mind. To put it most simply, I believe that I did not
know how to deal with the contradictions (conflicts may be too strong a
word) in my world: the ambivalence and emotional tensions in my immediate family; my desire to be enfolded in the tender cocoon at Beach
Lake, balanced against my determination (felt especially at Wilkes-Barre)
that one day I would make myself at home in the larger, "worldly" world.
Perhaps also my habit of constantly searching for and trying to correct
my imperfections led me to feel that the gap between my extraordinary
expectations and demonstrable ordinariness was insurmountable. The
one thing of which I feel certain is that my retreat resulted from an obscure sense of helplessness; when it was over, I remember that I felt
strong, even exhilarated, at the thought that I would soon be launching
into the promising challenge of high school. I did not repress the memory of the bad period, but I put it completely behind me. In fact, it never
seemed important to me until fairly recently when I began to think of it
as a challenging intellectual puzzle.

A history like the one I have recounted would be inconceivable today. Parents or school counselors or both would put a child like that immediately into the hands of a psychotherapist. Would I have been better
or worse off if this had happened to me? Fortunately or unfortunately, I
would not at that time, as commonly happens now, have been diagnosed
as suffering from a depression that could be cured or helped by drugs. I
think I am glad of this, for, at best, improvement would have been only
symptomatic. Psychoanalysis might well have prolonged the difficult
period and even have left me psychologically damaged. Other psycho-
therapeutic treatment perhaps would have shortened the period and
would have illuminated and resolved my inner conflicts. One cannot
be sure. What is entirely too probable is that I would have formed the

habit of running to a therapist whenever I found myself in a stressful situation instead of coping with it on my own and discovering the truth of Aeschylus' claim that by suffering we can gain in self-understanding and knowledge. As for the wear and tear on my father and mother, I suspect that, in the cultural climate of those days, it would have troubled them more to feel that their daughter was mentally ill than to worry over her inexplicable physical ailments.

The irrefutable fact is that before the end of that spring of 1929 I was entirely and lastingly cured of my debilitating symptoms. This is not to say that since then I have been any more free of neurotic traits than the average person. Undoubtedly I have come to cherish them as inextricably part of the fabric of the self I have continued to create. Anyone is free to argue that with expert counseling I might have become a better-adjusted, happier individual and achieved greater things. Theoretically this is possible, as is the opposite conclusion. Speaking for myself, I cannot, of course, declare that I am wholly satisfied with everything that I have done and been. But I can go this far: I have often thought that a test as to whether a person felt his/her life to be fulfilling would be whether at a given moment in full adulthood, he/she could truthfully affirm, "I do not want to die tomorrow, there are too many things I want to do. But if I knew that I had to do so, I would not feel that I had a right to complain that I have been shortchanged, or that I had not lived significantly." Not arrogantly but with gratitude, I can truthfully say this today, and I would have been able to say so for several decades now. I have more content than regret with "my self, that incomparable monster preferable to all others," as Sartre liked to say, quoting Malraux.

TWO

Being Educated

PUBLIC SCHOOLS

Franklin Grade School

O ne day recently I watched a news report covering the return to the classroom by Denver teachers after a weeklong strike. In what must have been one of the middle grades, the youngsters streamed in happily, exchanging mutually welcoming hugs with their teacher. In light of the constant liturgy of negative reports on today's schools, the sight was greatly reassuring. Granted the selectivity of the news camera, I can't believe that the scenes were rigged. Surely *these* children must have been learning something and enjoying it, since they were so clearly glad to be back. At the same time, I thought with amusement of the contrast with my own daily entrance into our grade school (eight grades together, no division into elementary, middle, and junior high school). At the stroke of the bell, gathering in the school yard before the door, we first saluted the flag and recited the Pledge of Allegiance. I realized that I was promising loyalty to my country; this was O.K. with me since ours was the best one, though for a long time I was puzzled as to what the "lejance" was that I was committing myself to deliver. Our oath taken, we marched to our respective rooms, class by class, in four/four time to the accompaniment of Sousa's marches. (At least we usually had Sousa; when I took a turn at tending the windup phonograph, I found a record labeled "Tea for Two" at the bottom of the pile and put it on as something new. At first, seeing the general smiles, I thought everyone was pleased, but I was quickly relieved of my post.) A somewhat formidable formality prevailed, symbolized by the straight rows of fixed desks in which we sat arranged alphabetically. We were expected to raise our hands before speaking; a special finger signal asked permission to go to the lavatory—

one at a time, of course, and we knew that the teacher would note how long we were out. I do not recall that I disliked school, but it seems to me now that I lived with a slight undercurrent of fear, even in the presence of teachers I liked.

For the most part, I am unable to revive with any trustworthiness the inner quality of my grade school years. Two exceptions, insignificant as they seem to me now, I recall keenly enough to be able still to feel again the acute discomfort they gave me. In the early grades each September we were asked to volunteer reports of what we did in the vacation. It never occurred to me that my summer at Beach Lake was anything to talk about. What seemed to count as worthy of narration was trips to Atlantic City or Coney Island. I listened to these tediously detailed descriptions of each day's venture with equal mixtures of envy, resentment, and boredom, also with a sense that it was not right for the rest of us to be forced to listen. Whenever feasible, I raised my fingers in the need-to-go-to-bathroom position. If what gnawed at me was a feeling of inferiority, this figured even more strongly in my continual distress over my inability in drawing periods. That they were called this and not art classes is significant, for we were expected to draw or paint only faithful representations of whatever was our model for the day. My zinnias were indistinguishable from my trees. Paint never stayed within my outline. On the rare occasions when we were allowed to select our own subjects (but always real objects), I fared no better. To this day I cannot "doodle" a facial profile as most people can. If we had been allowed the creative scope open to children and adults alike in today's world, I might have been able better to disguise my deficiency with blobs of colored pigment, but I would have known I was cheating. Perhaps it was salutary for me to recognize my limitations; I can remember only the misery of it. The worst of it was that somehow I felt that my awkward ineptness was what I really *was* and that the accomplishments that won me praise were only things I *did*—a curious reversal of what I later discovered to be Sartre's position. Your acts are what you *are*, as Inez tells Garcin in *No Exit*.

If these negative moments loom disproportionately heavy in my emotional retasting of early school years, the opposite is true in my adult appraisal of the positive things that the eight grades gave us in those days. I am profoundly grateful that already in the first grade we learned to read phonetically. (What fun it was to sound the short *a* by saying "baa" like lambs at play, and to bring hard *c* and *k* alive as we pretended to have a fish bone stuck in our throats!) I can now make small mistakes in spelling and pronunciation as readily as anyone, but within a framework of probabilities. I have wondered, faced with the formless clump of misplaced consonants and vowels assembled by college students trying to write, say, "Telemachus," how they could read at all. Speaking of that young hero reminds me that in the third grade our reading text gave us a simplified, condensed version of the Homeric epics. Impatiently I read far ahead of our assignment. Apparently others found it exciting as well, for I remember that at one recess we spontaneously had a tug of war between the Greeks and the Trojans. I was one of the few preferring to be on the side of the Greeks. I forget who won, but I see why I have the feeling of always having known about the Greek gods. Judaeo-Christian stories were not included, which was unfortunate, though I myself was steeped in them outside of school. To any who might be upset by this focus on the Western tradition, I can say only that traditional tales from other cultures would have added to our fun.

Retrospectively again, one other factor impresses me. At least some of our texts for various subject matters came in a series, carefully progressing from one year to the next, so that we were aware of advancing in what we learned. Indeed, we amassed considerable information. It is not the system's fault if I do not know today the chief exports of Brazil and am at a loss at how to calculate compound interest. Admittedly this last skill was taught to us in what would now be called junior high school, but I could have recited the capitals of each of our states and of the principal foreign countries years before that—and have not forgotten them all. And at no time did I find reason to believe that I was among a few leading the class with the majority left behind us.

Two specific recollections lead me to believe that we were not asked to grasp more than what was reasonable to expect of us. I think I can recall the very year when a new policy began to take over. In the fall of seventh grade, our spelling book was changed mid-semester. Whereas we had been learning to know and to spell exciting new terms like "fricassee" and "assassin," we now had to work repetitively at the common words of everyday language—"baby stuff." I felt like an advanced skier suddenly restricted to a beginners' slope. The other memory concerns a curious episode; I still cannot account for my behavior. Toward the end of sixth grade, our teacher told us we would stop our usual activities and write down everything we had learned in English during that school year. I seem to recall that we spent a prolonged period of a couple of days at the task; I suspect it was in reality one or even a half day. I decided that in that particular year the only absolutely new thing I had learned was the parts of speech, which I had enjoyed, but that looking back on the past months, everything else seemed to me a repetition. So I quickly wrote at the top of a sheet of paper, "I have learned the parts of speech." The rest of the time until we turned our papers in I sat there, doing nothing, fearful but determined, rehearsing to myself what I would say when challenged. To my relief and intense disappointment, nothing ever happened. My paper was not graded or returned; it was never even mentioned. Nor did my report card that month reflect anything unusual. So totally abortive a revolt was discouraging.

It was in that same spring that my imaginative life first took a romantic turn. Even without today's barrage of sexual imagery, explicit and implicit, we girls talked together as if knowingly about love, which we viewed as something magical, overwhelming, transforming, incomprehensible, and glamorous—except in the case of a few of our somewhat older acquaintances who unworthily acted a bit foolishly under its influence. Gradually I began to be aware that one of my classmates, Leonard Freeman, a good-looking, dark-haired Jewish boy, was ideally suited for the role of lover. I gave him a lilac, which he accepted, looking puzzled. I overheard him telling another boy that he wondered why I would do that, but I was not troubled. My act meant that I was "in love." At ten years old, I saw a cleavage in my life. Henceforth I could attach a name to the shadowy person I sang popular love songs to, in my head, and a focus for the mysterious longings that swept over me when I gazed at the full moon. "Leonard," I murmured. I was perhaps the silliest girl in Wilkes-Barre.

Coughlin High School

High school did not bring about the logical next chapter in my sentimental education; that is, I did not become involved in a close romantic relationship of even the most innocent sort with any of my new schoolmates. This may have been partly because, despite my imaginings, I was not really ready for it; mostly the setting did not foster it. Our school life had nothing remotely resembling the social patterns of the fifties, let alone the conduct that has prevailed since the sexual revolution and the new permissiveness. Aside from the senior prom, there was a little dating, though more often in small groups than individually. A few boys and girls were known to be "going together," thought of as couples, but they were the exceptions, not the rule. Austere and artificial, perhaps intolerable from the point of view of most present teenagers, this situation did not seem repressive to us. Certainly not to me, and I honestly do not believe that I was unusual in this respect, at least among the girls, who

were far more likely to cherish a crush on a movie star than on the boy
sitting in the next row. This state of affairs might well elicit a sigh of envy
from today's teachers. Pregnancies, if there were any, were extremely
rare and effectively hushed up. No girl would have openly admitted to·
having had sexual relations with anyone or would have dared to accuse
another of it to her face. At most I heard whispers that one of our companions "went too far with boys," though I'm not sure exactly what that
meant to us. In other respects, too, we lived in a different world from
that in the second half of the century. Smoking was officially prohibited
in or near the school, though some of the boys occasionally sneaked a
cigarette in the lavatory. I never saw or heard of any pupil with a gun.
Drugs were unthought of. In my senior year, it was rumored that a few
of my classmates had imbibed alcohol at a weekend party, though nobody reported ever having seen someone drunk. Teachers' authority was
virtually unquestioned. At most a pupil was reproved for "talking back"
or being "saucy." This is not to say that outside school hours adolescents
were never caught up in anything unsavory, or that problems of which I
was unaware may not have existed within the school. I am sure that I do
not exaggerate the comparative serenity of the overall picture. Yet ours
was a typical public school for Pennsylvania, not even one that drew primarily from affluent sections of the city.

For me the four years were a period of equilibrium. Since my father
taught at Coughlin High School, I was not entering uncharted territory.
His presence was not intrusive, and both my parents were sympathetic
listeners as I monopolized the dinner conversation with accounts of
what had happened each day at school (truthful reports, if not always
quite complete). It was a time of growth within established perimeters. I
was happily busy with a variety of projects. I loved having a part in the
Christmas play. I enjoyed working on the staff of the school journal. I
had several close girlfriends who gave me glimpses into home lifestyles
different from my own. With them I attended, and voluntarily, more
sports events than I have witnessed in my entire life since then.

I will not attempt any detailed comparative evaluation of the academic side of things in secondary education then and now. In its own
way the contrast in curricular matters is perhaps as vast as in the social
sphere and even more complex. We were incomparably behind in technological training. We possessed a minimum of the special offerings currently under attack in some circles as nonessential—we had nothing in
art, for instance, either creative or historical. We did have once a week
for one term instruction in the rudiments of music. And surprisingly we

had a comparable course in public speaking, in which I learned skills that have stayed with me all my life. No honors courses were provided, no classes designed either for the gifted or for those who might need remedial work. Yet from the first day we were divided in a pattern both practically useful and vicious. We enrolled—or our parents enrolled us— in one of three sharply differentiated programs—the "college preparatory course" for persons with hopes of going to college, the "commercial course" for those who wanted to become accountants, stenographers, etc., and the "general course" for whoever found neither of the others appealing. This last pathway was less demanding in its requirements; the numbers taking it increased gradually as pupils found themselves unable to keep up with one of the two others. A minimum of choice was allowed within each of the three. In the college preparatory, which I took, I remember that we were free to choose between three years of German and three of French; for one semester, between physics and trigonometry.

On the surface our core program was impressively substantial, heavy on math and science with history, Latin, and English studied throughout the four years. Given my school-oriented background and my desire to excel, it was natural that my grades were among the top. This fact in itself makes me suspect that the quality of my education was not as good as my description of it might suggest. I never took to science courses and was hopelessly clumsy in what little laboratory work was required. I regarded assignments in math as difficult and unrewarding. I recall sitting in a class in plane geometry memorizing twelve sonnets from the copy of Edna St. Vincent Millay's *Fatal Interview*, which I held on my lap and looked down at surreptitiously. Thanks to an unusually good memory, as mine was then, and mostly, I am sure, because of the generally low level of expectations, I more than held my own. There may have been another factor as well. I learned later from my father that my physics teacher had said that he always gave girls an "A" if they even tried, since he believed that physics was no fit subject for them anyway.

English, foreign languages, and history were my forte. Most of our history classes involved mere rote memory and recitation. The exception was Miss Steiger's class in American history and civics. She scolded us from time to time for not raising questions about what we read and for not trying to think for ourselves. Inwardly I felt justly rebuked; outwardly, as a coward, I voiced agreement with classmates who called her too strict and mean. But she was one of the two or three teachers I went back to see in later years. Studying foreign languages was fascinating but unexpectedly frustrating. With a naivete hard to credit, I had always imagined that learning a new language would mean mastering a sort of code which would transform one language into another in the way that a key unlocks a cryptogram. As I began freshman Latin, I was dismayed to realize that no table of correspondence existed and that I must learn from scratch as a baby would. It was not until college that I grasped the full arbitrariness of linguistic signs; this revelation came when I took Hebrew and discovered that human speech did not universally conform to the pattern of Indo-European inflections. My second frustration, of an entirely different nature, was associated with French, and this, more than anything else that I recall, testifies to the backwardness of American education then, at least at my school. French was taught to us almost exactly as Latin was. We learned the rules of grammar, memorized vocabulary, and translated, with a bare minimum of attention paid to our ability to pronounce words correctly. As a result, none of us could speak French effectively, not even conceive of thinking in it. A year of college French could not compensate me for the dearth in the first three years, a serious handicap to me in my later career when I became known as a Sartre scholar. On the other hand, my facility in translating may have been enhanced by this faulty approach. All is grist to the mill.

English was my greatest joy, both reading and composition. Here I believe that I am on solid ground in declaring that our instruction was superior to most of what high schools have offered in recent years. (This is certainly true if I may judge on the basis of my experience with college freshmen in humanities.) We did not read contemporary novels or plays, and I can understand the arguments on both sides with respect to the position that they ought to have been included. Instead we had an assortment of the standard classics of English literature. I recall specifically Dickens's *A Tale of Two Cities*, Arnold's miniature epic, "Sohrab and Rustum," and Eliot's *The Mill on the Floss*, an interesting choice in light of today's concern with gender bias. Each year, too, we studied one of Shakespeare's plays. Miss Austin worked out with us an analysis of the dramatic structure of *Hamlet* that would not have been out of place in a college classroom.

We were required to write an abundance of themes, each one of which was carefully corrected and handed back to us. One of the assigned topics, I remember, was an imaginary interview with our future famous selves. I portrayed myself as a novelist, still wearing glasses but elegantly dressed, living by myself in a luxurious apartment. In answer to the journalist's query as to why I had never married, I answered to the effect that

I really didn't know, that somehow I had just never wanted to be married. All I can say now about that singularly unilluminating response is that it accurately reflected my attitude then—neither conformist nor overtly rebellious, curiously sanguine.

In my free time I read voraciously. My teachers referred me to current best-sellers. On my own I discovered and devoured the works of Alexandre Dumas and Victor Hugo, feeling a strangely empathic, if imaginary, familiarity with the worlds they described. Of course, I was reading beyond my level of full comprehension, emotionally as well as intellectually, but my inner life, I think, was enriched rather than deluded. At that time I read also more poetry than at any other stage in my existence. Mostly it was contemporary poets. My favorites were certain women poets—Edna St. Vincent Millay, Amy Lowell, Sara Teasdale, Elinor Wylie, but I was fond also of Carl Sandburg, Robert Frost, Conrad Aiken, and Langston Hughes.

My reading of poetry and my mistaken persuasion that I could write it were encouraged by the woman who taught me freshman English— Edna L. Smith. Three of us girls proclaimed ourselves worshipers of Miss Smith, but mine was the most consuming devotion, lasting for the rest of my time in high school. I measured the quality of every school day by whether I did or did not see her. This kind of common schoolgirl crush is usually passed over lightly as either a faint prefiguration of adult sexuality or a female variety of simple hero worship. My love for Miss Smith was not sexual save possibly in the vague sense that both Freud and Sartre claim that all human relations are sexual. I did not try to imitate her in the way that some apostles copy the mannerisms of their idols. One small episode is illustrative here. In those days, even outside Free Methodist circles, many people held that nice women did not smoke. One day a friend told me, with shocked dismay, that Edna Smith had been seen smoking. For the rest of the day I felt physically ill. By the next morning I had decided that if Miss Smith used cigarettes, smoking could not be wrong, that it must be rather the mark of women's growing independence. I did not resolve that someday I would take up smoking myself. Miss Smith offered me no message, no mission. I think that basically I knew that she possessed no extraordinary gifts. On the several occasions when I visited her in later years, my feelings had changed, but I felt no sense of disillusion. She was, as she had always been, personable, attractive but not beautiful, warm and outgoing, interested in literature and the arts, one who possessed a zest for living, a woman who fortunately was not atypical of the high school teachers I have known over the years.

Miss Smith's treatment of me was exemplary. Though she surely was aware of my adoration, she never alluded to it, nor sought in any way to exploit it. But she was sensitive to it and careful to make me feel welcome when I approached her, to praise and all too rarely criticize my poetic effort, to build my self-confidence by subtly communicating that she liked me, that I mattered. Neither she nor I ever attempted to bridge the natural distance between teacher and student. Indeed to do so would have destroyed the essential quality of the relationship. Above all, she was the center for the imaginative side of my affective life, for every nuance of hope and despair, each fluctuation of the heart (my own, of course), all imagined outpourings of idealized devotion. Poised somewhere between my earlier mooning over Leonard and the revelatory response of the youthful Dante to his meeting with Beatrice, perhaps there was present, too, despite the obvious differences, an element of the complex of real and imagined emotions the troubadour entertained toward his poeticized mistress.

In retrospect, my close to four years of preoccupation with Miss Smith (I more or less took time off during summer vacations at Beach Lake) appears to me exaggerated, a bit ridiculous, but not downright unhealthy or damaging. At worst it fostered my tendency to lead my life as if it were literature, but I was never seriously tempted to trade in the real for the imaginary. Her own positive outlook was good for me. I remember that once when I presented her with a tome of melancholy reveries, she said, brusquely, "No, don't be like that!" I do not believe that I tried to make her into a mother figure, as some psychologists might suggest. But it goes without saying that the old Freudian notion of sublimation is entirely relevant. Too inhibited, too sheltered, too ignorant to court or to allow the development of any sexual relation of the kind so commonplace among present-day adolescents, either heterosexual or lesbian, what might have been expressed as erotic desire was transformed into a romantic, lived dream in which playacting and genuine passion were inextricably intermingled. Even in recent years Miss Smith occasionally shows up in my dreams—never, in any discernible sense, substituting for another person, neither threatening nor lifesaving, most often in a situation in which I am trying to find her.

Although it had always been assumed that I would go to college, the question of which one was not brought up until the spring of my senior year (1933). In this respect, of course, I was already more fortunate than many of my classmates. My high school attendance coincided in time with the financial crash of fall 1929 and the worst years of the Great Depression. For many of the brightest, college was out of the question, and there was no assurance of a decent job. Still, for me there was never a question of going to the college of my choice. What was possible? I found to my dismay that my mother assumed I would go to the same Free Methodist college that most of my relatives had attended, and this I resolved that I absolutely would not do. The only visible alternative was to live at home and enroll in a junior college, a branch of Bucknell University, which had recently been opened in Wilkes-Barre. This seemed to me only slightly less undesirable.

Then one day my father talked with our school principal about what I might do. Mr. Super informed him that scholarships were available for persons like me and that he would be on the outlook for such possibilities. A few days later a serendipity occurred so consequential for me that even now I regard it as providential, though not the work of a Providence. Mr. Super received notification of a magnificent opportunity which seemed designed for me. Wilson College, which had just received the vast Curran estate, announced that it would award twenty Curran Scholarships for the next year. The account read like a fairy tale. Dr. William Curran was a nineteenth-century physician in Philadelphia who believed in the importance of giving to women the same kind of education men enjoyed. Dying in 1880, he left a will directing that the sum of money he was leaving should be held in investment until it reached the amount at which interest could be used each year to support young women's college education. He did not name the institution which was to receive the inheritance but specified that it must be a woman's college with Presbyterian affiliation. The awardees were to be chosen on the basis of competitive examinations. They would be required to study two years of Greek, two of Latin, one of Hebrew, and they must, before they graduated, prove their ability to recite the Westminster Shorter Catechism. Except for the last item, these requirements were not significantly different from what would have been asked of young men in higher education in that period. In this country, as in England, colleges and universities still reflected to some degree the curriculum originally intended primarily to train future clergy. When the Curran money was finally ready for distribution in 1927, a legal dispute inevitably arose as to which institution best met the criteria. Lawsuits dragged on until Wilson College in Chambersburg, Pennsylvania, just barely within the prescribed hundred-mile radius of Philadelphia, was designated the re-

cipient. I will add parenthetically that the near miraculous quality of the
first awarding of the Curran Scholarship in the very year that I finished
high school increases when I consider its subsequent history. Already
before I had graduated, awardees were asked to settle for the amount of
money for which they could demonstrate actual need. Only a few years
later I learned that an admixture of unwise investments and unforesee-
able financial mishaps had virtually exhausted the estate.

With hubristic confidence that I would win in the college board examinations, my father had me send in my application and made no alternative plans. His assurance was somewhat shaken when in the couple
of weeks between the end of the school year and the date of the tests,
he personally undertook to prepare me for the examination in math.
"Hazel, you must be tired, or you're not as bright as I thought you were,"
he exclaimed one day. Either the other applicants also demonstrated the
accuracy of the prevailing belief that girls were ill suited to mathematics
(a situation which dominant cultural patterns had made to be true) or
I did well enough in the other tests, English, Latin, and scholastic ap-
titude, to compensate. I was awarded one of the twenty Curran Scholarships; it would pay for tuition, board, room, even my books, for all
four years.

While I was in high school, my way of life had changed externally
only a little—a bit more freedom to spend time at my girlfriends' homes,
permission to see a wider selection of films and plays that my parents
deemed suitable. Inwardly, I felt that I was no longer the same person as
the child who had entered there. I recall a revealing incident. An older,
well-intentioned woman, who served as a dean for girls, took me aside
one day to talk with me about how I might find things when I went on
to college. As tactfully as she could, she enjoined me to seek a kind of
breadth which might be out of harmony with my family training. I listened with two strongly contradictory reactions. I resented her obvious
effort to undermine my parents, and I regarded her advice as unnecessary. I considered that in my heart I had already broken away from even
what she herself would have approved. No, I do not remember just what
sort of wickedness I had in mind.

Commencement day found me simultaneously sad and happy. I felt
that it was time to leave, and yet I was reluctant. Some of my Beach Lake
relatives came for the occasion. Miss Smith presented me with a book
of poetry (by Frances Frost) with a dedication signed with only her first
name, Edna. My entry for the class song had been selected for first
place, and we sang it together to the tune of "Farewell to Arms," taken

from the current popular movie. This text, remarkable for the number of clichés it managed to include, stayed with me for a long time. Many years later in Toledo, Ohio, it served as a salutary reminder. As I walked away from the last "fatal interview" of still another failed romance, I suddenly realized that the lines from the song were singing themselves in my head. And I perceived, to add still another cliché, that I had no reason to be deeply unhappy that this chapter, too, had ended.

WILSON COLLEGE

At a welcoming party for freshmen, I was presented to the elderly president of Wilson College, Dr. Warfield, who surprised me by recognizing my name. He informed me, with slight amusement, that my father had written to him to inquire if Wilson's religious orientation were sufficiently orthodox (*i.e.*, fundamentalist) for his daughter to be entrusted there. Dr. Warfield said that he had sent back his assurance that my father need not worry. It must have been a reversal of role for him inasmuch as to most people the president represented an ultraconservative view of an almost vanished generation. It was in order not to offend him that no mention of smoking appeared in the college's printed rules and students were informed by discreetly placed notices that they might smoke in designated rooms. It was he also who was said to be responsible for our having to wear old-fashioned, all-covering black gym clothes— bloomers and long stockings.

How typical living patterns at Wilson College were compared with those of other women's colleges of the period I do not know. In a few respects the institution still smacked of the ladies' seminary or finishing school. We were expected to wear dresses and hose (not pants) for dinner, long gowns for the occasional evening concerts and lectures. Some of the students found these requirements irksome. I quite took to the custom myself. I confess that I have never lost my pleasure in clothes. I did not feel it necessary to wear jeans and a tank top in support of Civil Rights and feminism in its early days. Except at weekends we sat at tables for eight, our places assigned by lot at regular intervals. At the head of each table a faculty member presided. I should say, a woman faculty member. Married men ate at home. I do not recall that there were any single men or married women on the faculty. Meals must have been an endurance test for our hostesses. I have often wondered why they never rose up in revolt. Even at the time I regarded their presence as a privilege granted to us. Those long-suffering women talked with us of cur-

rent events, recent books and films, new trends in art, their own travels;
in short, they contributed immensely to our extraclassroom education
in what was going on in the world.

Having spent the last thirty-eight years of my career teaching at
large public universities, I no longer favor single sex education. I believe
that one cannot legitimately argue that for all undergraduates either a
university or a small college is better. Some persons are allergic to apples,
and others fare better with them than with oranges. I know that for me
Wilson was in truth the ideal alma mater, the fostering mother. Although
not overtly feminist, our professors took it for granted that we should all
prepare seriously for a career because it was intrinsically rewarding, not
just as a practical recourse to fall back on until one got married or in
case of unexpected need. Academically, though it did not enjoy the prestige of the seven "sister colleges," Wilson (with some six hundred students) held its own among a group of small Eastern women's liberal arts
colleges known for their academic excellence. Moreover, I came there at
a propitious moment.

The Curran bequest added immeasurably to the administration's optimistic expansiveness. We had a large proportion of extraordinarily fine
faculty members, most of them women. This was not due entirely to the
increased endowment. Small women's colleges in the thirties were able
to attract and to hold a surprisingly large number of excellent female
scholar-teachers—for two reasons, I think: because the comparatively
few women who won their Ph.D.s in those years were of necessity
gifted and dedicated, and because few state or private top quality universities were willing to hire women. Not quite typical but illustrative
was the case of Cora Lutz, professor of Classics. Of all my professors
she was the one who did the most in advancing me in my own career.
Herself a Classics Ph.D. from Yale, she persuaded me that I should apply
for admission to her old department, where I was accepted. Later she
arranged for me to come back to Wilson for a lecture visit, and it was
she, I am sure, who initiated the college's decision to give me an honorary degree in 1965. (I was at least able to dedicate one of my books to
her while she was still alive.) But her own story is of more interest than
the account of her concern for a student.

Cora Lutz had so distinguished herself as a scholar in medieval Latin
that, when she retired, Yale offered her a full-time position working with
manuscripts in its Beineke Library; she was also invited to teach a course
in medieval Latin. She turned down the offer of teaching and accepted
only a half-time appointment at Beineke, her reason being that she

wanted to devote more time to research. Until ill health at last brought on total retirement, she published a series of articles, some of them on medieval scholars, others on local historical figures whose papers were in the Yale archives. I prolong this digression on Cora Lutz to add an anecdote that shows how truly remarkable she was. She once told me in confidence that, while she was still at Wilson, she had been offered the chairmanship of a department at a wealthy, distinguished university. Although her salary would have been increased by several thousands of dollars, she refused the offer. She explained to me why: She would have been appointed over the head of the man who had been expecting to be chair, a situation she felt promised only trouble. But more decisive, the dean who interviewed her, in an attempt to show the institution's recent advancement, kept telling her that he had been able to buy so-and-so as chair for one department, to buy an eminent scholar in order to put another department on the map, and so on. Cora Lutz decided that she did not want to be bought, and she stayed at Wilson.

I had come to college expecting to major in English and, in my sophomore year, had gone so far as to take Anglo-Saxon, which was required of English majors. I did not exactly become disenchanted with English, though I was beginning to be just a bit impatient with it. Much as I admired the critical skill of my instructors, I naively felt that studying English literature was perhaps better as an avocation that I could easily pursue by myself. The rich complexity of the background needed to appreciate the Greek and Roman writers seemed to promise infinitely more. In any case, Beowulf was no match for Homer, whom I was reading in Greek that semester. I decided to major in Classics. This decision did not delight my parents, though they made no effort to dissuade me. My father viewed it as impractical. My mother thought I was motivated by the desire to show myself superior in a field too esoteric for most people. In truth I had simply fallen in love with the ancient world, especially the Greek part of it—its language, its literature, and later its philosophy. I was not totally blind to the two great flaws of Hellenism—its slavery and the abject situation of women. If I was too willing to overlook them, it was partly because such injustices were apparently a part of all past history and mostly because, like most of my and earlier generations of women, I had cultivated what I would have defended then as an impersonal, universal reader's view. Later feminists, of course, correctly pointed out that we were reading empathically as men.

I have never regretted my choice of Classics, though as a Sartre scholar I theoretically should have been better served by studying more

of French and/or philosophy. It was only much later in my life that I
felt I had to defend what might be seen as a retreat from engagement
in the contemporary world. But by then, just when I felt the need of
them, I found alternatives—first by engaging myself in work in postwar
Greece, and later on, when I had made myself ready for it, by taking up
Existentialism.

I did not live solely for the classroom. It is hard for me now to recall
just what the activities were that seemed so absorbing to us, but I remember that our days were pleasantly full. For the first few weeks I was
caught up in a loosely knit group that seemed to have formed itself fortuitously rather than because of specific, common interests. Then, toward the end of the first semester, the pattern was decisively altered.
Professor Knowles, my teacher in English composition, who had been
intrigued as well as appalled by my choosing as the topic for my first
theme, "Man's Interest in the Abstract from Plato to Freud," had succeeded in disciplining my efforts. She still found me odd enough to be
interesting. One day in conference, she told me that in a different class
she had another unusual student, a girl I knew only from a distance, and
she thought we would like to read each other's papers. Through Miss
Knowles we did so and arranged to meet.

Evelyn Wiltshire came into my existence in much the same way that
Zaza arrived on the scene for Simone de Beauvoir (in the early days of
their friendship, that is, not at all in the sequel of the story). In social development Evelyn and I were at opposite ends of the spectrum. Whereas
for me Wilson was a liberation, Evelyn found it so foolishly restrictive
that she recklessly broke many of its rules—with impunity, it seemed. In
high school she had been surrounded by boyfriends. At home, on vacations from Wilson, during the entire four years, she followed an established pattern of going out in regular succession, scarcely missing an
evening, with three men. Without any significant return on her part, each
of them, anxious to marry her, fully aware of the other two yet willing
to hang on hopefully, provided dinners, shows, dancing, and at least after the lifting of prohibition, occasional imbibing. All of this struck me
as ultrasophisticated and glamorous. (I did not consider it from the point
of view of the men.) Evelyn was far ahead of me in intellectual rebellion.
While she was as naive as I in serious political understanding, she could
boast of having a friend who was a Marxist. Immensely self-confident,
she professed herself open to questioning not only prevailing shibbo-
leths, but the most basic social structures. Dos Passos was her newly discovered favorite author. Evelyn had not been brought up in a religious

background. Not only did she resent Wilson's insistence on church attendance, she did not even consider herself a Christian. Coming from Pittsburgh, in contrast with Wilkes-Barre, she was familiar with museums
and could speak knowingly (if not deeply knowledgeably) of the avant-
garde. The poems and essays she wrote were perhaps not in substance
beyond the level of mine, but they had a certain flare, an air of worldly
wisdom that mine lacked. At first simply bowled over by Evelyn, grateful but puzzled that she wanted my company, I fairly quickly ceased to
be a mere follower. Just what Evelyn saw in me, I am not sure. She herself has said that along with interests we genuinely shared, she appreciated in me a certain seriousness of purpose and integrity. Be that as it
may, our intense friendship proved to be a lasting one, still binding today.

What struck me as remarkable about Evelyn's disdain for established
religion was that she showed it was possible to reject the whole body
of Christian doctrine quite casually and without any sense of guilt. Her
position was not determining for me in settling the question of my own
belief. My process of total deconversion was gradual and extended over
many years. But Evelyn's attitude influenced me in a more positive direction. While hardly a model of rectitude, she did introduce me to a new
kind of authenticity. She refused to judge herself by others' expectations. She gave me courage to think more boldly for myself. After a
while guilt was no longer my constant companion. It was easy for me to
break away from the superficial regulations Free Methodism had imposed
on my conduct inasmuch as I had always inwardly rebelled against
them. I learned to dance or to think I could (many of my later partners
may have wished that I had not). In Evelyn's company I tried my first
cigarette and tasted my first cocktail (the latter on a visit to Pittsburgh,
not within the environs of Wilson). My immediate and intense dislike of
smoking was such that I can take no credit when friends today struggle
to break the habit and tell me how wise I was not to take it up. Alcohol
was different. From the start I found it an enhancement, occasionally a
consolation, never (I recognize that I am one of the lucky ones) a problem.

Evelyn's contempt for college regulations eventually caught up with
her. I had gradually prevailed upon her to recognize that needless non-
conformance was not worth the risk. But soon after the beginning of the
second term of freshman year, Evelyn's roommate (with what motivation
I do not know) suddenly came forth with charges that several months
earlier Evelyn had falsely reported her times of arrival and departure on
dates away from campus, had pretended to have been present at required
events when she had not been, etc. The truth came out, and Evelyn was

suspended for a month, the question of expulsion left hanging in the air as a real possibility. Making an appointment with the registrar-dean, I pled with her that Evelyn did not deserve so severe a punishment for what anyone might have done. "But you would never have lied as she did," said Miss Disert. I recklessly declared that I could have done so. "I do not believe you," she replied. But she seemed impressed by my staunch support. Evelyn was allowed to return after the month's suspension. (Ironically, she, too, is one of the few alumnae to whom Wilson has since awarded an honorary degree.)

During Evelyn's absence I kept her informed each day of class assignments, and she speedily caught up with her work. She was a bit embittered, more careful, but not really chastened. Miss Knowles, who had originally brought us together, not only invited us to visit her occasionally, but treated Evelyn as a heroine. She once remarked to me, "You would never have done anything like that. *You* will never disgrace your parents." I felt subtly shamed and rebuked. But she was right.

Evelyn and I roomed together for the remaining three years. Soon we formed a close bond with another classmate, Agnes Gross. Others dubbed us tritely "the Three Musketeers." We have remained friends, keeping in close contact with each other throughout our professional careers and since our retirements. Agnes Raymond (her first husband's surname) became a professor of French at the University of Massachusetts. Among other things, she prepared the Pléiade edition of Giraudoux. Evelyn, under the influence of her first husband, Erwin Goodenough, exchanged the field of English, in which she had taken an M.A. at Yale, for that of psychology, writing on the subject of sex differences exhibited in the behavior of young children. As Evelyn Pitcher (taking the name of her second husband), she was honored by Tufts University when she retired from there, by having a building named after her.

We three had friendly acquaintances among the other students and occasionally moved within wider circles. For the most part we kept to ourselves. We tended to dip into extracurricular activities rather than to become truly involved with them. For required gymnasium work we rejected team sports in favor of individually scheduled hours in tennis, swimming, and canoeing on the little stream which flowed poetically through a wooded area at the edge of the campus. Evelyn and I both worked on the college literary journal, named *Pharetra* after the Greek word for quiver, of which I was editor and Evelyn associate editor in our senior year. We all three watched but did not participate in the pageant at the May Queen festivities. We were a bit disdainful of such things as the daisy chains and "stepsings" that were features at women's colleges at that period. But in December we joined the groups singing carols in French and in Latin outside faculty homes and consumed our share of the offered cocoa and cookies.

I think it was William James who said, "Joy is conscious growth." I suppose that is why the three of us (Evelyn after an initial rebellion) found our lives in Wilson's sheltered environment so exhilarating. To be sure, we remained apolitical. Wilson had no trace of the social ferment that, in some large city universities, sometimes led young men to become socialists or short-term Communists. Perhaps it was the very absence of heated debate on sociopolitical issues that left room for the intense intellectual fervor that our traditional studies evoked in us, that and the enthusiasm for knowledge and learning our professors genuinely felt and were able to communicate to us. Agnes, Evelyn, and I took enough courses in each other's respective majors in French, English, and Classics to be able both to argue happily over problems raised in what we studied together and to share in the excitement of our separate discoveries, as Evelyn, for example, attempted to convey to us the powers of Virginia Woolf, Agnes the awesome achievement of Proust, I the wonders of Plato. As my critical ability developed, I wisely abandoned my aspiration to write poetry, replacing it with a lasting commitment to interpretative criticism and scholarship. We lived with ideas, passionately engaged while at the same time priding ourselves on our objectivity.

For me, scholarly pursuits were never wholly separated from my personal search for answers with respect to religious and philosophical questions. I will reserve discussion of these matters until I am ready to report more fully on a series of conversions and intellectual revelations that I experienced over a longer period. For the moment I will say only that in spite of sharp differences in the meaning intended, I could apply to my position at the time I left Wilson, the statement Sartre made about himself at an even earlier age: I had lost my belief in God, but I still held on to the Holy Ghost.

My four professors in Greek and Latin, delighted to find in me a convert to classical antiquity, gave me excellent guidance, insisting, for instance, that I must take German in order to be able later to carry on scholarly research in graduate school. But would I be going to graduate school? The head of the department, without my knowing it, had written to my father a letter urging that he look favorably on the idea. When he spoke to me of her letter, he expressed pleasure at her appraisal of my abilities; he said nothing to disabuse me of the belief that finan-

cial circumstances, except in the unlikely event of my being offered a
fellowship—would require me to seek a job as a high school teacher.
Indeed, my program at Wilson had been designed with this in mind, in
spite of my indulgence in four years of Greek, and I had taken the education courses requisite for teaching Latin in the Pennsylvania secondary
school system.

I did my practice teaching in the Chambersburg high school. This
experience, by the way, was the most inauspicious introduction to a
teaching career that can be imagined. I was assigned to a class in sec-
ond-year Latin (Caesar's Gallic Wars, of course). My mentor was Miss
Huber, the oldest of the school's teachers, not particularly amiable. She
said little to me, but we seemed to get along well enough, and I enjoyed
the teaching itself. I took pains to make Caesar interesting to the pupils
by telling them just a little of the historical context, and I endeavored to
explain the vagaries of Latin case usage by constant reference to comparable or contrasting English usage. Toward the end of the term and
without warning, the sword descended. The head of the Education
Department at the college called me in to tell me that Miss Huber had
declared my teaching barely acceptable, charging that I had taught the
class ancient history instead of Caesar, and English grammar in place of
Latin. Still today I find these charges absurd. The real reason in back of
Miss Huber's disapproval of me emerged later. The fault was mine. In
what I had regarded as just a friendly exchange, I had trustingly confided in one of the other teachers my hope of one day going to graduate
school. This was interpreted as a haughty announcement that what I
really wanted was to get a Ph.D., that I wasn't interested in high school
teaching and, by implication, that I looked on myself as superior to those
who chose it as their career. Given my admiration for my aunts, not to
mention my father, who had worked in primary and secondary schools,
the accusation could hardly have been true. But, obviously, I had been
tactless, insensitive to how my words might be taken by others, and in
that I was culpable. Fortunately for me, the chair of Classics, who had
visited my class, grasped the situation and smoothed things over, changing
Miss Huber's proposed C to an undistinguished but more acceptable B.

Evelyn and I happened to have a couple of days free between our last
exams and Commencement, a kind of magical interlude. I remember us
as spending most of the time lying in the sun or drifting in a canoe on
the Conococheague, and talking over what was past in our joint experience and what was about to come. Poised ready to leave college, we
looked back on the four years, reflectively ordering the experience, and

finding it richly good. It was as though we possessed in those few days a crystalization of happiness. As for the future, we knew that openings for teachers were scarce. Neither of us had been offered a graduate fellowship. I had been named as an alternate at Bryn Mawr, but I did not learn of it until later, and it was not something to be counted on. We did not believe that our fathers would or could provide funds for our continued education without outside financial aid. Yet, optimistically, we expected everything to work out well. We were convinced that there would be opportunities to do interesting and worthwhile things and that we would find our lives to be not a fairy tale, to be sure, but basically what we wished them to be. The remarkable fact is that we were right, though I fully recognize, in my own case, how much of this has been thanks to other people and to simple good fortune rather than to my own endeavors.

Marriage did not enter into our speculations. Evelyn certainly did not intend to marry any one of the three men she still continued to see when she was at home. I suspect that the probability of eventually marrying may have been more a part of her expectations than of mine, but I may be judging in the light of what happened later. If I thought of marriage at all, it was as an unlikely but possible complication to be confronted when the occasion arose. In fact, I had already rejected the possibility once, though so many factors were involved that I can hardly say that this was a clear-cut choice between marriage and a career. My life at Wilson did not bring about any significant encounters with young men, appropriate or otherwise. But at Beach Lake, in the summer after my freshman year (at long last, I imagine someone saying today), I drifted into a romantic involvement with a distant cousin. Herbert Olver, a few months my junior, embodied all of the ideals and best hopes of the community at Beach Lake. Bright, personable, well behaved, he had already announced his commitment to becoming a Free Methodist minister. He and I shared only a common background and a strong sexual attraction. That was enough for the few delirious weeks left in the vacation. No, "delirious" makes it an overstatement. There were strict, unwritten rules as to what was and was not allowed for courting (or "sparking") couples, and we stayed within them, barely. Moreover, on the first occasion when Herbert, assuming that we would marry rather than formally proposing, referred to something he would do for me in the farther future, I felt a shiver of apprehension. I took it for granted that I was truly in love. How else to explain the deliciousness of our being together? But I could not envision a prolongation of the relationship. When I tried to do so, I saw only what I would be giving up of my past expectations, not what I would be gaining instead. I realized that Herbert knew nothing of the person I was in my own eyes, or to others who knew me. To be fair, I did not make an effort to comprehend what lay more deeply in him. Once back at Wilson, the sense of irreconcilable differences quickly translated itself into the perception that after all I was not in love with Herbert. I gradually stopped writing to him. At Christmastime I deliberately stayed at home when my father and Jean made a visit to Beach Lake. Then I wrote a letter formally breaking things off. Wanting to spare Herbert's feelings (it never occurred to me that he, too, might have had second thoughts), I tried to give the impression that my decision was firm but reluctant, implying that it was not due to my feelings having changed.

I found myself trapped by this half-lie the next summer when I once talked with Herbert alone. My infinitely delicate approach was halted midway when, with sudden realization, I exclaimed, "But you're not still in love with me, are you?" Confessing that he was not, he managed to convey that he was persuaded that my own resolve had been one of courageous self-renunciation and that even now he believed I still felt the same. I was too embarrassed to set him straight. Afterward I laughed aloud to and at myself, but it would have been better if I had admitted the truth and laughed along with him. I wonder whether discomfort at the false position I had put myself in prompted me over the next few years, in occasional meetings with Herbert, to stress overmuch things that would accentuate the differences in our outlooks, an unworthy impulse *épater le bourgeois*. This, too, passed. Herbert married one of my childhood friends, a woman who was in every respect a working partner with him in his work as a minister, both within the church and in social welfare projects supported by the State of New York, where they lived. In 1989, when I made a lecture visit to Hartwick College in Oneonta, Herbert phoned me to say that he and his wife had seen an announcement of my talk and hoped we could get together. Finding common ground, the three of us conversed for two hours, both about people at Beach Lake and about our adult lives away from there. At the end, Herbert spoke with affectionate amusement of our teenage idyll. Amidst good-bye hugs, we agreed that it had helped to prepare each of us for later, more mature relationships. The morning was a remarkably satisfying closure.

To return to the transitional summer of 1937: Agnes wrote that she had landed a position in a high school in southern Pennsylvania. She stayed there for a couple of years before going on to graduate work. Nothing had come through for Evelyn or for me. I dutifully wrote a few letters and went for an interview with the superintendent of public schools in Wilkes-Barre. My father did not urge me to do more; much later he told me that he believed he and I together could have located something if we had tried harder. I believe that he had in mind all along that he would enable me to go to graduate school if I did not find a high school position. Then, when the summer was nearly over, several things happened within two days. Bryn Mawr wrote that the person designated ahead of me had accepted the fellowship; I was no longer in the running. But my father told me that, since he had not had to contribute to my education at Wilson, he was willing and able to advance the money so that I could go to Bryn Mawr anyway. Then came a telegram from Evelyn: Her parents were sending her to Yale. My mother was reluctant for me to substitute Yale for Bryn Mawr, suspecting that all manner of perils lurked in the big university in New Haven, but she could see the advantage of my going in the company of a friend. It was Yale that I myself preferred. So Yale it was to be.

YALE UNIVERSITY

If my memories of Wilson tend to assume the likeness of an impressionist painting, a joyous blend of light and color, those of Yale are heavily chiaroscuro, strong patterns of dark and light on both the personal and the academic sides. All but literally, I set foot in the outside world for the first time. Residing in a dormitory, I had known Chambersburg only as a setting for the college, and, indeed, save for its picturesque location and its history of having been on the fringes of action in the Civil War, it offered little to be experienced, and still less to be remembered. At Yale, Evelyn and I roomed in a house reserved for graduate women; we lived in New Haven. We came to know its grocery stores, its markets, and its surprisingly large number of excellent restaurants, which even on our slender means were accessible for special occasions. I still think that in some absolute sense food prices were disproportionately low in those years when we could buy a pork chop at the grocer's for less than ten cents, or a full meal at Child's for under a dollar. Even allowing for the vast difference between my allowance then and my income now, it seems to me that I paid with more ease for a lobster dinner on New Year's Day at the stately Taft Hotel than when I confront the astronomical bill at the more moderate of upscale restaurants in the nineties. New Haven was

smaller then, and safer. We never had reason to fear walking alone at
night, and nobody warned us to stay out of certain sections. If ethnic
tensions existed, we were unaware of them. We all knew of the large
Italian community. It was there that I first ate pizza, served on newspapers
spread out on wooden tables with, of course, carafes of chianti.

It was exciting to feel so close to the center of the world of entertainment and the arts. New York exerted over most of us the kind of drawing
power which would-be starlets have felt for Hollywood. I managed to
go there several times and stopped, whenever possible, on my trips from
and to Wilkes-Barre. But New Haven, quite independently of Yale, had
much to offer. Friends and I took full advantage of the Schubert Theatre,
at which plays and musicals often opened before their Broadway productions. I did not find the city beautiful, but it had a certain charm
with its colonial church on the central green, its elm-lined streets (this
was before the elm blight). Strangely enough, though I was acquainted
with its wharves, I never thought of New Haven as a port. For me what
dominated it topographically was its two great rocks, East and West, and
the ridge stretching from one to the other. Many times, with a single
companion or in a group, I climbed up to East Rock, less often to the
western end, and once I walked the long miles between them.

In coming from Wilson to Yale, I had moved from a sphere of mostly
women to a man's world. In this connection especially I realize the singularity of each person's experience in the midst of what seems the same
set of conditions. Women constituted a small minority in the graduate
school. There were no undergraduate women in Yale College, and no
women faculty members except possibly in some special schools such as
Music and Nursing. Only a negligible minimum of formal restrictions
applied to us as women. If I was aware of being forbidden to dine at
males-only Morey's, I was not bothered by being excluded. My impecu-
nious male graduate companions did not go there either. One annoy-
ance was Linonia and Brothers Library, an attractive reading lounge on
the first floor of Sterling Library which housed a special collection of
books, including a series in demand by Classics students. We women
were permitted to step inside the door and ask for books, which we
could take out, but we were not allowed to sit down in the room or to
examine the shelves. The official reason was that the lounge was intended for undergraduates, but male graduate students were never asked
to identify their status. A similar rule produced an absurd episode in
which I played a central part. I sought and was given permission to audit
a low-level reading course in Italian. The class was meant for graduate

students but met in a building designated for undergraduates. Because of my presence, the sole woman, the class had to move to the School of Graduate Studies. At least the professor chose to move the class rather than to remove me.

On another occasion some of us graduate students asked if we might sit in on a series of lectures a visiting professor in Classics was to give to an undergraduate class. My male companions were all admitted. I was refused, not because of any university regulation, but because Professor A. M. Harmon, the head of the Classics Department, did not consider that the subject matter of the lectures, the comedies of Aristophanes, would be appropriate for me as a young women to hear discussed in male company. Unawakened as I was to any serious feminism, I found this decision preposterous and was angered by it.

This infringement on my academic freedom was as nothing compared with reports I heard from Evelyn and other women doing graduate work in English. Here a couple of professors were known deliberately to exclude all females from their seminars. There was the tale (I do not believe it was apocryphal) about the one of them who evaded the official rule for open admission by limiting the class to three or four students and personally selecting the favored ones on the basis of written application. Once, fooled by an apparently masculine first name, he found himself confronted on opening day with a woman holding proof of admission. After some argument he allowed her to stay. Without question, individual women from several departments had good reason to complain of unfair treatment, despite the university's avowed policy. By contrast, except for the Aristophanes skirmish, I found the Classics faculty exemplary. Neither personally nor by hearsay did I ever perceive the slightest hint of injustice or condescension or differentiation in the attitude of the professors toward female as compared with male students where academic matters were concerned. Given all that I have observed and read in the decades since that time, I find it remarkable and a tribute to the men involved.

Among the complaints that I heard of professional bias from women in other departments, there was virtually no mention of sexual harassment in the form of offensive personal conduct of the kind so often reported today. I cannot believe that Yale men were a breed apart. Was it simply that no woman was willing, or else felt it unwise, to report that she had been harassed? Was every initial charge effectively repressed? I do not think that the professors found them so freakish as not to look on them as women. It is barely possible that the fact that women were so few led the professors to consider them as exceptions to be treated with special care. I wish it were possible to know.

Inevitably ours was an entirely male education. For that matter, my training at Wilson had been only slightly less so if regarded from the point of view of present-day feminists. If the goal had been openly proclaimed to be the development of a "male mind" in both sexes, any of us who protested would have objected to the term rather than to the reality. Insofar as we rebelled against prevailing concepts of women's roles, it was because we wanted to show that we could indeed think like men, hence deserved the respect and the opportunities available to men. Tradition we recognized as sexist, but we subscribed absolutely to the principle that knowledge was gender neutral. In this assumption we were at one with those faculty who were not hostile to women.

My entrance into a predominantly male sphere was more revolutionary in my social than in my academic life. The graduate students in Classics were a closely knit group; almost immediately I felt drawn into the inner circle. Some of us practically took up residence in the Classics library on the top floor of Phelps Hall. All of us and a few of the younger faculty joined in a social hour over tea every afternoon. The names of many of my associates would become familiar to classical scholars over the next decades—Lionel Pearson, Frank Gilliam, Howard Porter, George Dimock, William Willis, to list a few who come first to mind. One with whom I cherished a particularly close Platonic friendship was Stephen Keeler, the son of an Episcopalian bishop in Cleveland. Of all the group, he struck me as the most irreverent, the one most bent on living the life of an Epicurean (in today's sense of the word, not the ancient). It turned out that he spent his career teaching at Robert College, an American school near Istanbul (it later grew and was transformed into the University of the Bosporus), making a useful contribution to society instead of seeking fame or affluence. One of the things of lasting value I learned at Yale was the possibility of warm friendship between men and women, a relation in which the sexual is not denied but bracketed.

Much as I enjoyed the collegiality, it strikes me now that we led a strange sort of existence—not decadent precisely, but inbred and self-absorbed. Along with much gossiping, there was some talk about our academic work and enthusiasms. I recall that one spring some of us (the number dwindled to two) read *Daphnis and Chloe*, the Greek pastoral romance, in the Botanical Gardens. The latest popular novels and plays and whatever had appeared in the last *New Yorker* figured regularly in our conversation. We rarely spoke of politics or social problems and never save in the most superficial terms. Nobody showed any sense that as privileged academics we had a mission or responsibility beyond our individual careers. I must take back this blanket assertion; there was one exception. For a year we had in our midst a special student (not enrolled in the regular degree program), a Canadian who openly acknowledged that he was a "card-carrying Communist." I saw quite a bit of him. He spoke to me quite freely of how being a member of the Communist Party determined even his personal life, but he never tried to convert me, or any of the other students, probably because he considered us hopeless. Our political apathy is particularly hard to explain since the years concerned were fall 1937 till spring 1941. Of course, I do not mean to say that we were not at all concerned about the war overseas, but we did not allow it to impinge greatly on our thoughts or plans for the future. The best I can say of us is that in later years some proved themselves capable of action in ways that could not have been predicted. One thing which did have an impact on us was the sudden influx of refugee scholars from Europe, and students, too. Among the latter were two bright young men who went on to distinguish themselves in the world of Classics, Heinrich Immerwahr and Heinrich Hoenigswalt ("Henry" each became later). I did not question them about the pressures that had forced them to leave their country, but this was out of a diffident discretion rather than from lack of interest. Instead, others and I concentrated on making the newcomers feel at home with us. Among other trifling memories, I recall introducing the two to the process of popping corn in a fireplace; I watched with pleasure the expressions of pleased amazement on their faces as they exclaimed, "It opens!"

Off campus, throughout the four years, with companions from Phelps Hall or with acquaintances Evelyn had made or with persons I met in chance encounters, I played. I think that at no other time in my life have I quite so relentlessly pursued the goal of having a good time. Some movies and theater, an occasional concert, but mostly an assortment of purely recreational activities—ice-skating, square dancing, scheduled evenings of folk dancing, ordinary ballroom dancing (though seldom in a ballroom), and parties, parties, parties. I find no reason to apologize. To be sure, our play was not quite like the games I knew as a child on our block on Wright Street. But neither was it comparable to the life depicted in literary portrayals of life in the "flaming twenties." We drank a lot, of course, occasionally a little more than was good for us, but not in the way that too many on college campuses abuse alcohol today. If we lived by any sort of sexual code, and I suppose we must have, it would be difficult to formulate it precisely. Casual sex was certainly not the rule. One did not take it for granted that going to bed together would be the natural conclusion to a first date, or even that it would necessarily happen after several dates. Lip service, at least, was paid to the ideal that governed most of the Hollywood movies of the period: Rosalind Russell, Ginger Rogers, et al. were presumed to be virginal at the start of the film. Passionate embraces were a sure sign that the pair had found their true loves and would marry after the inevitable obstacles and misunderstandings were overcome. The audience was never shown scenes of sexual consummation, which one assumed would follow after the wedding. In the unusual instances in which liaisons were formed outside marriage, there was always some unassailable reason why this had to be the case; most often the story ended in noble renunciation or tragedy. The *sine qua non* was the requirement that sexual passion be inextricably linked with love or an overpowering infatuation mistaken for love. I do not say that the average woman—still less the average man—at Yale during my time there would have accepted this formulation in so many words, or that they actually lived by it. But the implied standard was sufficiently prevalent to have two results among the graduate women to which I can attest with reasonable certainty: First, it was virtually unheard of for a woman to have a large number of sexual partners. If it was unheard of simply because none would have admitted to such promiscuity, that brings me to my second point. Among the graduate women (I exclude here those women who married the men they met at Yale) there were very few—if I may judge by what I learned directly or by the grapevine—who held themselves aloof from any sexual liaison; but, by convention, any illicit affair (and it would definitely have been so regarded) must be cloaked in secrecy. And secrecy frequently, if not inevitably, bred guilt feelings, at least an uneasy sense of having transgressed a recognized social norm. Even if conventional expectations were in themselves hypocritical, those who did not conform to them were led to adopt a certain hypocrisy in turn. It was an unhappy state of affairs, and an unhealthy one. The current situation, a take-it-for-granted near-promiscuity, does not seem to me ideal either. But at least now one is free to work out one's individual code and openly live by it. At any rate, this is so for adults, perhaps not for the very young.

And what of myself at Yale? How did I handle the erotic dimension? I muffed it. My social relations with men were of two kinds: There were the friends with whom I joined chiefly in group activities, and the friends with whom I went out on individual "dates." For the most part neither offered any serious problem, and this overall pattern continued for my entire time in New Haven, regardless of the emotional turmoil resulting when the inevitable disruption occurred.

Predictably, in the spring of my first year, one of the friendships suddenly took a new turn. On the basis of a few kisses and some tender phrases, implying more than they promised, I decided that I had found the one and only man I could love. But this was May, and we would be separated until September. I dreamed away the summer. In one of the few letters I received from him, I read the strange sentence, "Everything is the same here except that now it is August." I was right in taking it as a warning. When we met a month later, in the wake of one of New Haven's devastating hurricanes, I learned that all was over, if in truth anything had ever been. Why do I mention so trivial a happening? Because, in my folly, I allowed this unhappy love to cloud over the whole Yale experience. That he and I, in the everyday flow of events, were often brought together enabled but did not cause me to keep the wound from healing, to hope unrealistically that things might change again, to try to find ways to make it do so. Even yet I can recapture all too keenly the taste of that morbidity; explaining it is more difficult.

At different periods in my later life, I developed two hypotheses to account for my behavior. Not long after leaving Yale, when I had decisively realized that I was not by nature a self-tormenting type, I decided that my earlier conduct must be labeled neurotic. Although I had not had a recurrence of the psychosomatic affliction that had disturbed my childhood, I had never quite got rid of the idea that somewhere, buried deeply within me, was a secret melancholy, a hidden wound such as Flaubert alluded to in himself and Sartre spent hundreds of pages trying to analyze. I could not then, nor can I now, describe it precisely or pin down its origin. It may have been nothing more than the memory of the earlier neurosis never quite resolved. The habit of living with a suffering barely covered over, though almost wornout, had never altogether left me. It was convenient to replace the feeling with an identifiable, ill-fated passion and to look upon my daily life as a brave attempt to find happiness in spite of it. Stupid, of course. But I am not trying to deny that I was a fool, only to explain how I managed it. I still think there is some truth in this hypothesis. I remember that one of the things I felt attracted to in the man involved was that I thought I perceived that there was in him, too, an underlying *Weltschmerz* and ultrasensitivity to the difficulties inherent in what I would in the future learn to call our "existential condition."

Still later, when I had occasion to rethink how I had lived my own "feminine condition," I decided that what I had taken to be a purely neurotic response was instead, or also, a self-protective device, equally misguided perhaps but at least based on a positive impulse to preserve what was most important to me. Even in that first summer when I pictured a happy reunion to come, my imagination confined itself to the environs of Yale and New Haven. I never considered that I might abandon my academic ambitions nor posed to myself the question of how they might be fitted into the scheme of another person's life, a man's. My subsequent adoption of the myth of a blighted passion insured that I would not become seriously involved in any other attachment. Being already "in love," I could not "fall in love" with anyone else, and I could not have conceived of wanting to marry for any other reason. Thus I effectively guaranteed that I would not be tempted to exchange the library for the kitchen. Why I should have felt that this was a necessary either/or I reserve for another context.

Nothing ever works out entirely neatly. Eventually I had a very brief affair with an undergraduate; neither of us pretended it was love. I was prompted by curiosity as much as by desire and by the feeling that it did not matter much anyway. I had the sense not to confuse disappointment with remorse.

I had not come to graduate school for love affairs and parties, no matter how all absorbing they threatened to become at times; my resolve to pursue a career as a teacher and scholar at a college or university remained firm as ever. But here also things did not go altogether according to expectations. Academically, in the first months I found graduate work a letdown. I may have fallen into the slump experienced by many first-year students. Undergraduate courses feature the essentials but also the high points; we lived on the peaks, as it were. Now we seemed to move chiefly in the underbrush, and I had not yet discovered the joy of clearing out and cultivating a small plot of my own. I think there was another factor. Classical scholarship at that period was itself restricted in a way that it is not now. When not concerned with the establishment of texts and purely historical questions, it too often concentrated on minutiae, on ringing one more change on wornout topics already over-debated. Naturally it could not provide the kind of excitement, enrichment, and opening up that the field has enjoyed—and suffered—in response to the recent challenge of feminist classicists, Deconstructionists, and other iconoclasts. But American classicists then (certainly at Yale, and I believe this was usually true elsewhere) mostly looked on psychological interpretation and on literary criticism as suspicious—"subjective," not scholarly. The ideal was the pure *Wissenschaft* of German universities.

Our classes were of two sorts: In small seminars we were assigned topics and took turns in reading our written reports with critical remarks from the professor which might or might not be illuminating. My extreme example of dreariness is a course for which I had enrolled with high hopes—a study of the choral odes of Aeschylus. Just two of us took it; Bill Willis was my fellow sufferer. Mr. Harmon gave to each of us the task of examining a particular metrical pattern and testing a theory he had about Aeschylus' metrics. I have long forgotten what we were hunting for, but I remember that at the end, Bill and I both concluded that what Mr. Harmon suspected to be the case proved not to be true. This result he took with good grace and only slight embarrassment, pointing out the value of disproving an untested theory. This I was willing to grant; in my eyes his fault was one of omission. During all of those weekly sessions, in which we laboriously labeled every metric foot in each one of the Aeschylean choruses, never once did we consider the connection of the prosody with the poetic quality of the ode, either in sound or in meaning. The songs might as well have been inventory lists. Our procedure might have been compared with that of the man inside John Searle's famous Chinese computer room, who carries out instructions by handling objects as directed but without the slightest knowledge or interest in what the process is all about.

In the reading courses, part of the time we students were asked to translate, and the professor commented; now and then we were given something resembling an informal lecture. On the whole, I did not find these classes as exciting as those I had enjoyed at Wilson. Perhaps, in truth, they were not greatly different; possibly I had wearied of this approach or had outgrown it. There were certainly some bright spots. In his course on late classical and early Christian authors, Edmund Silk's sensitive portrayal of the conflicts in the young Augustine was extraordinarily moving; his analysis of this transitional period as both a new birth and a putting of old wine in new bottles was masterly. I appreciated the dry humor of Arthur Hubbell, the trenchant wit of Alfred Bellinger. I reminded myself that it was a privilege to study with outstanding scholars. Still, it did seem that a concerted effort was made to keep us away from what might have fully engaged us. When, for example, we

studied Cicero's orations against the scoundrelly Verres, Professor Bellinger clearly had all the relevant facts in hand. But the topics he gave us
for our papers concerned neither Cicero's oratorical style nor the nature
of provincial Roman government. Instead we were asked to concentrate
on the kind of objects that Verres stole from the Sicilians. It fell to me to
track down information and illustrations for small items—jewelry, lamp-
holders, and, I remember specifically, soup ladles. Truth compels me,
however, to confess that I found this research rather interesting, and
possibly it was worthwhile for us to delve into such everyday matters.

I realize that part of the trouble lay in the fact that my own interests
did not lead me to take full advantage of some of the unique opportunities that Yale made available. We literally lived in the midst of rarities. I
recall carrying home from the library copies of the original Aldine editions of obscure late Latin writers not at that time available in modern
printings. Had I been so inclined, I might have asked to engage in textual
studies of early manuscripts in Yale's rich collection. It was my responsibility if my initial excitement at being admitted to a class in which we
worked with unread or not yet fully deciphered papyri dissipated when
I tried to piece together tattered bits of business contracts or administrative regulations. On the top two floors of Phelps Hall, we were surrounded by original sculptures and inscriptions, most of them from Yale's
archaeological excavations at Dura-Europus, a Hellenistic city (later
taken over by the Romans) on the Euphrates River.

Unexpectedly, Dura-Europus played a part in the two developments
that transformed my graduate career. Professor Michael Rostovtzeff, pre-
eminent among even the most famous of ancient historians, offered a
seminar titled simply "Dura-Europus." I took it because he was teaching
it; fortunately, as it turned out, for this was the last graduate class which
he handled wholly by himself. A man of tremendous breadth and profundity, Rostovtzeff was quintessentially what every teacher of graduate
students might hope or strive to be. Instinctively he knew how to guide
without controlling, how to make our individual reports a meaningful
part of the experience of every member of the class. With him I realized
the promise of the rewards of individual research, to which I recognize
now my undergraduate teachers had only barely introduced me. The
yearlong seminar was divided into two distinct parts. During the fall we
studied the cultural environment of Dura-Europus at the time when it
rose to power and developed its distinctive character. I reported on the
literature with emphasis on its reflections of domestic life and attitudes.

I proudly brought in, as an extra bit of supporting data, a piece of an
original papyrus, a marriage contract. Afterward Rostovtzeff said to me
privately, "Your synthesis of the literary scene was brilliant, brilliant. But
why did you waste time with the papyrus? All that it showed was that
the institution of marriage existed, and we already knew that." I perceived
that originality was not measured by the presence of genuine artifacts.
All of this was preparation for the second term, in which we worked
with very specific problems arising from the finds at Dura-Europus and
not hitherto discussed. From a list of suggestions we chose our own subjects. I took as my challenge the goddess Artemis-Azzanathconah, who
had a temple at Dura-Europus. Obviously the Greek Artemis had been
superimposed on the figure of a local deity, or deities. In tracing down
the roots of her new name, I quickly learned that "anath" and "conah"
stood respectively for "queen" and "creator," epithets applied to many
goddesses in Asia Minor. The prefix "Azza" was apparently more regional—in short, a puzzle. I do not recall that I arrived at any definitive
conclusion beyond establishing that we had here one more example of
how the chaste huntress goddess of mainland Greece, the virginal Diana
of later European poetry, held for the Greeks in Asia Minor a strongly
sexual aspect, linking her with a multitude of mother goddess types in
cults throughout Asia Minor and Mesopotamia. I never followed through
on Rostovtzeff's suggestion that I undertake an extended study for eventual publication, in part because for once I recognized my limitations.
The very magnitude of the project at once excited and deterred me.
Even within the confines of my particular investigation, I discovered
infinite ramifications. In tracking down Semitic linguistic roots, I was
able to make a little practical use of what Hebrew I was able to remember
from what I had learned at Wilson, but it did not go very far. Of the
other languages in the Near East I was wholly ignorant. I did not have a
specialist's training in ancient Near East history nor in comparative religion. But I learned to grasp and to be fascinated by the syncretism of religious beliefs in the Hellenistic world, the interplay of common themes
and individual variations, the interpenetrability of religions. In this instance the historical approach had been profoundly illuminating.

Another turn in my academic career was still more consequential for
me. One of the things I especially appreciated about my department
was the personal interest our professors took in our academic progress,
whether or not we were at the moment enrolled in a class with them.
One morning, in a chance encounter, Bradford Welles, my papyrology

professor, questioned me about my plans for the dissertation. I explained that I had committed myself to writing on the problem of the origin and development of the Greek essay, which I had been working on in Mr. Harmon's seminar on Lucian, a more fruitful venture than the one on Aeschylus. I added, really to my own surprise, that I wasn't much excited about it and that what most interested me was ancient religion and philosophy. "Then change your topic," he said. "I don't think the subject you have now will ever work out anyway. It's much too large and too vague. If philosophy is what you want, go over to see Erwin Goodenough and ask him to steer you to something you'd like to do." Without hesitation I did so.

Thus I went to see academically the man whom, unbeknown to Welles, I had been watching in a private drama of his own. Our second year at Yale, Evelyn had been given a work project by the office for student aid. She was assigned to do typing for Erwin Goodenough, just launched on the study of the wall paintings of the third-century Jewish synagogue at Dura-Europus. Iconic representation in synagogues was something hitherto unknown. On the basis of the prohibition against graven images, it had been supposed that religious sculpture or painting would simply not exist in synagogues. Opposing those who held that the scenes depicted solely episodes of Jewish history, Goodenough argued that they expressed religious significance, utilizing symbols common to many of the religions and religious philosophies of the Mediterranean world. Some of the symbols, he thought, had primarily sexual implications, and Goodenough's interpretation, at first influenced more by Jung's theory of archetypes, increasingly took on a Freudian cast. His research in the ancient symbols, for Erwin and Evelyn, took on the same role that the story of Lancelot and Guinevere played for Dante's Paolo and Francesca. It was indeed explosive material for a middle-aged professor with four children and a young woman whom virtually every man she met had found seductive in personality as well as in appearance. For the first time Evelyn found a man who offered more than flattery, amusement, and diversion. In the very beginning she may have fallen in love with his ideas and the image of herself that he proffered her, more than with the man himself. Erwin inevitably found in Evelyn the embodiment of all that was expressed by the symbols of numinous femaleness in Hellenistic religion. In his mind, his relation with her apparently did not so much unite as identify passionate Freudian libido with the anagogical love Plato described in the *Symposium*. Sex, like Platonic love, could bring one to the verge of the ultimate *mysterium*. One may smile at this. All the same, it was closer to the truth of their relationship than the cynical view of some of the critics among the Yale faculty, who dismissed the relation as just one more instance of the familiar pair—a victim of male menopause in pursuit of an ambitious woman. Their marriage (in 1941) and the reciprocal understanding on which it was based lasted for over twenty years.

I return now to the morning when Mr. Welles suggested that I go to consult Goodenough, who was rostered in the Department of Classics as well as in Philosophy and History. Knocking on his office door, I felt exultantly that now at last I would be embarking on the project I had been waiting for without knowing it. Erwin, as I had learned to call him, received me kindly, but he at first refused to take me on as a student on the ground that his research was so consuming that he could not add anything more to his teaching load. I confess with shame that I cried. Unable to stand tears, Erwin consented to take me on for consultations. He stipulated that I must carry the weight of the undertaking. He would suggest readings. I might come in at fixed intervals to ask him questions. Presumably, proceeding chronologically, I would thus fill in any gaps in my background in Greek philosophy and would find a dissertation subject. The plan was speedily modified. Whatever tentative question I brought up on whatever subject, Erwin was inevitably reminded of his latest discoveries in the symbols of ancient religion. Our discussion periods became a series of reports by Erwin on his own research, and I was pleased with this since his syncretistic approach correlated with my work for Rostovtzeff's course.

Before starting on his thirteen-volume work *Jewish Symbols in the Greco-Roman Period*, Goodenough had published a comprehensive study of the writings of Philo Judaeus (c. 20 B.C.–c. 50 A.D.), a Jewish philosopher writing in Greek, something of a mystic, who sought to establish a connection between the Old Testament and Greek philosophy. Although in some respects Erwin's new interests were in sharp contrast with Philo's emphasis on ascetic rationality, Philo's method of allegorical interpretation relied heavily on symbolic meanings. It almost surely must have strengthened Erwin's predisposition to find religious significance in the paintings in the Dura-Europus synagogue. One day he suggested to me that in the *Enneades* of Plotinus, a third-century Greek Neoplatonist philosopher, I would find a different but comparable attempt to harness philosophy in the service of mysticism. He suggested that I investigate it.

In spite of its unprepossessing title (*Enneades* or "Ninths" because the work is divided into six parts, each with nine treatises), the book was a thrilling discovery for me. The culmination of Greek thought, pushing

Plato to the point of all but betraying him, seminal for Christian theology yet resistant to any personalizing of the divine, it leads one to dizzying speculation as to what Western Christianity would have become if Plotinus' considerable influence on Augustine and his contemporaries had been still greater or much less. I knew at once that here was the field of my doctoral dissertation; with a bit of guidance from Erwin, I focused on the topic "Philosophy as Katharsis in the *Enneades* of Plotinus." The notion that the practice of philosophy is itself the pathway to purification of the soul and the grasp of eternal Truth was already present in Plato. With Plotinus it was expanded and made far more complex in a monistic conceptual scheme that is in significant respects closer to Eastern thinkers than to Plato.

I was utterly enthralled by Plotinus, whom I still believe to be, at least among Western philosophers, the thinker who has most successfully blended rationality and mysticism. If one is willing to go along with the basic premise that all of reality, including ourselves, is permeated by an eternal spiritual force, hence is essentially one, then the rest of the Plotinian system is impeccably consistent and enormously attractive. It offers a point of view closely akin to what I have come to think of as the temptation of Eastern philosophy, to which so many Westerners have succumbed. What I particularly marveled at in Plotinus was his conviction that the sole path to the reality that was beyond reason was reason itself. Only after exerting our intellectual powers to the utmost and seeking all knowledge possible, could one arrive at the "very crest of the wave of intellect" from which one might be lifted up and absorbed in unity with the One. My admiration for Plotinus was tempered, however, by a curious reluctance. I never quite became a believer. I think that both my empathic reading of him and the final resistance were related to my early exposure to Free Methodism. For years I was haunted by the claims of special knowing in the conversion experience, even though I was repelled by the paltry nature of what led up to and followed from it. The Plotinian "flight of the alone to the alone" transcended the material world; it confirmed the intellect even as it went beyond it. But I had fought too long against the life-denying aspects of religious fundamentalism to be attracted now to any form of asceticism. While Plotinus did not advocate the radical renunciation of a Simeon Stylites or a Hindu *sannyasi,* the contemplation he called for entailed a denigration of the other goods of this world. "To know yourself is to know your source," he said. Perhaps. But even if it could be proved that there is a spark of the divine fire at our heart, is it better to contract and to restore this to its parent flame or to create an expanded self intermeshed with the visible world around us?

In the 1940s, I came across a passage in Camus's *The Plague*, in which Dr. Rieux asks whether even if God does exist, it would not be best for Him if, instead of looking toward the sky where He sits, we would struggle against the power of death in this world. At first I took this to be a criticism of traditional Christianity. Then, when I learned that when Camus was at the University of Algiers, he had submitted a thesis titled *Christian Metaphysics and Neoplatonism* with a long chapter on Plotinus, I wondered whether he had Plotinus' philosophy in mind instead. I looked up the thesis, published in the Pléiade edition of Camus's works. I was disappointed at how little of his personal evaluation he had included, but there was some. Like me, Camus had marveled at the aesthetic quality of Plotinus, of whom Camus said that he thought as an artist and felt as a philosopher. He noted that Plotinian intelligence was not mathematical reason but rather a thinking cloaked in emotion that expressed itself in images rather than in concepts. Camus expressed approval of Plotinus' appreciation for the natural beauties of the physical world, a theme found later in Camus's lyrical essays, which hold a hint of natural mysticism almost (never quite) at variance with his professed atheism. I can only wonder as to whether Camus, like me, found the richness and self-completeness of Plotinus' comprehensive system so compelling that he felt it must be either embraced or rejected *in toto*. Certainly his humanistic Existentialism is the antithesis of Neoplatonism.

Looking back, I find another odd link with what came afterward. A central theme in Plotinus' philosophy is nothingness. Evil is the absence of good, matter is unreal because it is at best a shadow, the lack of what is ultimately the only reality. Even the One is defined privatively. It transcends all things because it is not any thing. Plotinus' view of it is perfectly represented by the Eastern parable of the man who is directed to seek for Brahma by peeling a fruit, then its seed, then the inner kernel, and is told that the nothing that is left when all else is stripped away, "*That* is Brahma." The nothingness in Sartre's *Being and Nothingness* is more dissimilar than it is comparable to Plotinian nothingness. But both philosophers demand of their readers the ability to conceive of negation as an active force without making it into a something.

I held in the background of my thought a reserved space for the Plotinian complex of ideas as if they were put aside, waiting to be put into use. When Eastern philosophy began to offer itself as a viable option in the postwar culture of this country, I was intellectually interested, enough to go to the University of Hawaii in the summer of 1951 for postdoctoral courses in Indian philosophy. I can imagine a scenario in which, with my predisposition for it, I might easily have become a convert. But by then I had undergone another sort of conversion and was immune.

One of the marked differences between graduate school then and now was the fact that we were generally expected—and many of us actually did—finish our work within four years instead of prolonging it to the point of making of it a mini-career in itself as it so often is now. One of the reasons was that the practice of using graduate students as teaching associates was far less prevalent. As a woman, I would not have been allowed to teach at Yale in any case. I held fellowships all but my first year, once an alumna fellowship from Wilson, twice grants from Yale. Thus except for a small amount of time spent in grading papers for extra cash, I was a full-time student. All the same, the last semester was a great rush. I began the actual writing of my dissertation after Christmas, submitted it in early May. I had a minimum of supervision, which may have helped to speed things up. Goodenough was away, traveling in the western states, including Nevada, partly to recover from a "nervous breakdown" brought on by the stress of his impending divorce, partly as a practical step to speed up the legal proceedings. Some of the time I did not have even an address for him. I did succeed in getting from him a long letter in which he expressed approval of my most essential chapters, and I had one helpful interview with him when he visited New Haven for a few days in April. He was off again before the day of my oral defense of the dissertation, and a second reader, Professor Calhoun from the Divinity School, took his place. All went well. A week later I took my general written examinations. (The Yale Classics Department modified this mad schedule a short time afterward.) I had not had adequate time to study for these. I have always believed that I passed them chiefly on the basis of my excellent undergraduate training at Wilson.

Sally O'Neill, the wife of Eugene O'Neill Jr., the son of the dramatist, and an instructor at Yale, did the final typing of my dissertation for me. The O'Neills had made of me a sort of protégé my last term. (They quickly dropped me a bit later, which seems to have been their habit with protégés.) I treasured every one of Gene's occasional references to Eugene O'Neill Senior. On the whole, however, he discouraged my questions about his father and preferred to regale his listeners with tales of the battles Gene had fought with his two former wives. By his own admission he had been most passionately in love with his first wife, though I gathered from his description of their stormy relationship that they spent a large part of their time throwing plates and other objects at one another. Gene and Sally at this later period seemed to have anchored snugly in harbor. They were extraordinarily kind to me. When my parents came for my graduation, the O'Neills joined us for an evening of tea and lemonade in my room. With exquisite tact they made appropriate small talk, Sally only once slightly startling my mother, with reference to the kidneys in port wine which she had served me for breakfast. The presence of those four people in the same room seemed to me a miracle. It helped to reassure me that I need not be rent apart inwardly even though I lived my life in two spheres.

After commencement, I spent a week at Chocorua in New Hampshire at a lodge managed jointly by Yale University and Smith College. I have ungratefully forgotten the name of the man who made it possible. The story went that a philanthropist visiting Yale one summer was appalled to see women graduate students sweltering in New Haven's heat (before air-conditioning, of course) as they labored over dissertations or prepared for examinations. His gift to Yale provided an expense-free retreat in the fresh coolness of the mountains. Why Yale decided to make Smith a partner in the program, I do not know. Perhaps there were not enough graduate women at Yale to take full advantage of the privilege. I do not believe the donor would have begrudged my going there for refreshment after the grueling semester rather than when I was still doing my research. At any rate, I felt greatly revitalized by my stay. (But I wish I had known then that William James had once had a summer home at Chocorua!) I was with two friends from Yale. One was Doris Anderson, in Classics. She taught at various colleges after taking her degree, but died when still young. The other was Eleanor Bustin (later Mattes), a good friend of Evelyn's and mine who was doing graduate work in Yale's English Department. Eleanor ended her career teaching at Wilson College, further strengthening the bond among the three of us. Most recently she has written a biography of Erwin Goodenough. In our small group at Chocorua the majority came from Smith College, two of them faculty members. Mary Ellen Chase was there, professor of English and author of a best-selling novel, *Mary Peters*. She entertained us delightfully, primarily with a running commentary on the difficulties she was

having reading contemporary poets, whose work she found both challenging and exasperating.

The interlude at Chocorua resembles in my memory the closing,
vacation-like days that Evelyn and I spent at Wilson, though the contrasts are as significant as the similarities. At Wilson I had recalled my
experience there with unalloyed pleasure, but I was eager for the next
stage. I had immense confidence in the farther future, though the pathway to it was still obscure. Trying to get a balanced perspective on my
years at Yale, I could not overlook the unhappiness, gratuitous though it
may have been. I had been slow to realize the unique scholarly opportunities that were there for the taking, and I felt that I might have done
more with them than I did. At the same time, the intensity of life on all
sides and the intellectual excitement of the work I had done first in Hellenistic religion, then with Plotinus—all this, plus the wealth of scholarly resources, made me feel that to leave Yale must be to descend into a
lesser sphere. I could somehow not imagine what my life would be next.
As I went for the last time to the New Haven train station, after a brief
stop on the way back from New Hampshire, I felt that I was saying
good-bye to myself.

The rest of the summer I spent with my family at Beach Lake, waiting
for a job to be offered to me. I mean that literally. At the present time
graduate students send out dozens (if not hundreds) of copies of formal
applications and resumés. Nationwide announcements of posts available
appear in the publications of professional organizations of the various
academic disciplines. And there are the famous "slave markets" at the national meetings of the American Philological Association, the American
Philosophical Association, the Modern Language Association, and their
kin, at which candidates and departmental representatives confront each
other in brief interviews decisive for their respective futures. In 1941, no
faculty member suggested to any of us that we should do more than to
register with Yale's placement office. This was not because openings were
plentiful; they were not, although qualified candidates were relatively
few as compared with the multitudes today. In the spring I had had one
interview with the president of Russell Sage College, who came to New
Haven. So, at another hour on the same day, did Robert Fink, who had
come to the end of his nontenured appointment in Yale's Classics Department. Understandably, he was the one selected.

By late August not a single possibility had come up for me. Meanwhile we had a visit from Erwin and Evelyn Goodenough, now married
but without publicly announcing the fact. My father asked Erwin if he

could not do something to help me find a teaching position. "I never promise to find jobs for women or Jews," he replied. My father was outraged but continued to maintain that a Ph.D. degree from Yale would surely produce something. His naive faith was vindicated. Walter Allen, one of the instructors I had known at Yale, wrote me from his present position at Chapel Hill in North Carolina that he had heard there was a newly opened vacancy at the Woman's College of the University of North Carolina at Greensboro. A young man who had agreed to go there had unexpectedly received a better offer and had asked to be released. I wrote at once to apply, and I think Walter Allen sent in my name as well. The department chair, who was traveling in the North with his wife, arranged to meet me at a hotel in Wilkes-Barre. After a quite brief conversation, he offered me the job on the spot; I accepted it almost before he ceased speaking. My father came to meet me halfway up the block. The elation and joy of all of us was unrestrained. I had been appointed as instructor of Classics at thirteen hundred dollars a year. The salary was low even for that time and place. I learned later that the money had been intended for an assistantship of some kind. But the chair had boasted, "I bet that in these days I can get an Ivy League Ph.D. for that." He did—two, if you count the young man from Princeton who so fortuitously made way for me.

THREE

Conversions and Epiphanies

I am interrupting the chronology of my narrative to go, first back in my story, and then a little ahead of it. Long before I knew that Sartre had done so, I was accustomed to think of my life as marked by a series of conversions. In my case, there were epiphanies of sorts, ranging from sudden intellectual or emotional insights to revelatory dreams and experiences verging on the mystical—at least as some might see them. All were manifestations of an ongoing search for meaning in which the personal and the philosophical were intertwined. I am speaking of the years before I knew of Existentialism. Very roughly, for too sharp a division would be misleading, I look back, in terms of this narrative, to record my gradual break with the doctrine of traditional Christianity, forward to speak of my attempts to arrive at more far-reaching resolutions.

Sartre used the word "conversion" to denote progressive changes in one's basic orientation, in one's way of being-in-the-world, both with respect to his life history and in his philosophy. In a general way, I will be doing so as well. For a long time, however, "conversion" held for me a denotation and connotations quite foreign to anything in Sartre. The closest parallel I have found to it in literature is in James Baldwin's *Go Tell It on the Mountain*, though the conclusions for his hero and for me were radically opposed. Once again the scene is the church which so dominated the landscape of my childhood and early adolescence.

BREAKING OUT

When evangelists came for revival services, they regularly issued the "altar call." We members of the congregation were exhorted, coaxed, pleaded with to come kneel at the altar, to give ourselves to the Lord, to be saved. This invitation followed immediately after the preaching of the gospel. I have never doubted the sincerity of the deliverers of these impassioned sermons. But what a marvelously crafted sales pitch! Descriptions of the perils of the Day of Judgment and of the horrors of Hell were lurid enough, but these were gross and obvious, as were the images of Jesus and Satan knocking at our hearts: the one clad in white, sorrowfully pleading, longing to forgive (loving parent with wayward child); the other clothed in red or black, alternately blustering and softly insinuating. More subtle manipulative psychological devices skillfully exploited everyone's latent insecurities and uncertainties. Look inside yourselves, we were commanded, and answer honestly whether you are wholly at peace with yourself. Have you nothing to hide? Are you not guilty? Of course we were guilty! Who could boast of a life in which there was absolutely nothing to be regretted or ashamed of, especially since we had been led to believe that a thought suppressed, a wish rejected was as a deed performed? "As a man thinketh in his heart, so is he." If we did not have the firm assurance that we belonged to Jesus, then we had rejected him. And if we waited, it might be too late. (By tomorrow, as the salesman says, the car may have been sold, and in any case, the price will go up.) Our immortal soul was at stake. My soul as a material entity was so real to me in my childhood that I visualized it as an oval organ located somewhere between my heart and my liver. It was not until my father one day confessed his inability to pin down its location more precisely that I began to realize that its physical existence was not demonstrably a fact.

If it was vaguely flattering to think that cosmic powers were competing for our souls, it was clear also that our souls would not remain our own. The imperative was not self-affirmation but self-surrender, subjection of heart and mind to the Divine Will. What was promised was not just a far-off Paradise but the rewards available to us in this life if we would but reach out to take them. "Perfect submission, perfect delight," sang the hymn. The "peace that passes understanding" would be ours. We would be assured that all our guilt was washed away as though it had never been. Our hearts would know no more conflict. No longer would we be tired or weary. Where now there were darkness and turmoil, there would be certain assurance. Most powerful of all, perhaps, was the claim that only those who had personally experienced conversion and rebirth could know; otherwise we were like the foolish who declined to try a delicious food they had never tasted. Thus even our reason was implicitly appealed to: Who would be so rash as to decide without testing?

To the minister's pleas were now added the interjections and prayers of a few sanctified elders who might go to the side of the various seekers as they, one by one, went to kneel at the altar rail, joined gradually by some of the already saved who wanted to renew or to reaffirm their commitment to the Lord. Meanwhile, those members of the congregation who remained at their seats continued to sing the gospel hymns, not now the vigorous calls to action such as "Rescue the Perishing" or "Bringing in the Sheaves," but the spiritually seductive ones with languorous melodies: "Softly and tenderly Jesus is calling." Or "Come unto me, all you who labor and are heavy laden, and I will give you rest." For years, I sat, uncomfortable, glued to my seat and wished it were over. I did not go to the altar—except once, and this brought me an unexpected deliverance. What was different about this time, I do not know. Perhaps I was unusually tired and longed for the promised rest. At any rate, I decided to take the dare, to go up front and kneel at the altar and see if anything happened. Then I would *know*. So I went. I did not "pray through." As I recall, I did not pray at all. I suddenly realized that I had made a mistake. The altar was no different from the pew. There was nothing I wanted there and nothing to be found. I felt slightly ashamed of having "gone forward," but I knew that I had settled something. This was not my path. I was tempted no longer.

All the same, a recollection from my very early days at Wilson suggests to me that the process of breaking out had not been quite so clean-cut as I had thought, or else that my emotions had not quite kept pace with my mind. A small group of evangelically inclined students met ten minutes before noon on class days for a brief religious service before lunch. Occasionally I went to these; once I gave one of the five-minute presentations. I am appalled to remember that I actually delivered the kernel of Free Methodist doctrine: that the God we knew as Father now would one day confront us as the Judge, that this was an entirely reasonable arrangement and we should take it to account in ordering our lives. I cannot now comprehend this action or its motivation. Was I doing it because I thought it would please my parents if they knew? I had no sense of being hypocritical. Yet I recall feeling uneasily that I was forcing myself beyond my inclination. This phase soon ended, and for the first time in my life I began to attempt to reason things out from scratch.

The college required that we attend church on Sunday morning, but we were permitted to choose where we would go. There being no Free Methodist church in Chambersburg, I was relieved of family expectations and free to shop around. Comparable fundamentalist services held no allure, and I found myself increasingly bored with the bland rituals of other Protestant denominations. (I have forgotten whether the city had no Catholic church or whether it simply never occurred to me to go there.) Before leaving Wilson, I had come to resent the required religious services and was careful to take advantage of every allowed "cut." This outward pattern but dimly reflected the private search I was undertaking. I find it amusing that in my intellectual pursuit, I followed the path set down by the Western tradition: My faith (what there was of it, for I think it was less personal conviction than the habit of obedience) was challenged first by classical humanism, then by evolutionary science, finally by studies in comparative religion. Ontogeny repeated phylogeny.

With an enthusiasm matched only by my naivete, I relived the ancient enterprise of discovering the highest good—in the Pre-Socratics, in Plato and Aristotle, in the Stoics and the Epicureans. And after all this, the decisive work for me was Lucretius' poem, *De rerum natura*, which I studied in a senior-year Latin course. "The evangelist of atheism," our teacher, Dr. Franklin, called him, and I was his convert. Lucretius' powerful attack against the crimes committed in the name of religion, his nearly thirty proposed proofs against the possibility of human immortality, his impassioned persuasion that power lies within ourselves to find serene happiness even in this world where "something bitter always rises up amidst the flowers," his claim that life is sweeter for the very reason that death is a nothingness and that no God will promise or threaten or in any way interfere—all this combined with Lucretius' immense compassion for the human species was irresistible. I went to Dr. Franklin and told her that I was beginning to think that "Lucretius was right." Caught between her pleasure in my admiration for the poet whose work she had been teaching us and her own religious commitment, she counseled me to counterbalance Lucretius' "partial" view with Virgil's deeper and fuller grasp of the divine working in human affairs. It was to no purpose.

I realized even then, of course, that the bulwark of Lucretius' theory, Leucippus' and Democritus' view of a universe made up of atoms moving randomly in empty space, was hardly the same as contemporary scientific hypotheses about the nature of material reality. But I took it as a metaphorical equivalent. All that remained was for me to attach this to Darwinian evolution, with its scheme of a purposeless universe governed by chance. The groundwork, I suppose, was laid in my year of biology, but what chiefly influenced me was popular treatments I ran across in which various writers, scientists, or mere journalists, in layperson's terms, discussed the contradictions between Darwinism and traditional theological beliefs. It was typical of me that the apocalyptic moment came with my reading of a novel, Homer Smith's evolutionary parable centered on the lungfish, *Kamongo*. I recall finishing the book as I sat, the only one in the room, in the library's browsing section, on a late Sunday afternoon. Closing the book, after a few minutes of thought, I said aloud to myself, "No, I really *don't* believe in God." If what I felt at that moment was not "the peace that passes understanding," it was at any rate a liberation born of understanding. That afternoon in the library was conclusive. I think I can truthfully say that I was never again even slightly moved to return to Christianity, neither in one of its traditional norms nor in any of its later dilutions.

In preparing to write of this moment, I hunted up and reread *Kamongo*. After nearly six decades, the novel inevitably had lost much of its power so far as I was concerned. Now I find its view of the human species needlessly reductionist. I can conceive of some readers responding more sympathetically to the listening Padre than to the self-assured scientist. What strikes me most forcefully about my earlier reaction is that I regarded the portrayal of a universe without inherent meaning or goal as liberating; not a reason for despair, but a summons to action. A prolepsis of my later response to Sartre's "Man is a useless passion"?

Yet even on the intellectual level there remained a suggestion of another task to be confronted, a path not yet sufficiently explored to see whether it led upward or to a dead end. Lucretius was not the only one of the classical writers to open a door for me. There was also Plato. Three hours a week in my sophomore year, one other student and I read Plato with Charlotte Goodfellow. Although she herself was not deeply interested in philosophy, she conscientiously made sure that we situated Plato in his philosophical environment so as to understand what he was reacting to as well as what he was saying that was new. Thus, I suppose that it was thanks to her that I took the first step toward eventually becoming, if not a philosopher, at least a teacher of philosophy.

Under Miss Goodfellow's direction, I actually met not Plato but Socrates, on trial, defending his way of life, in the *Apology*; refusing the offer to escape from prison, in the *Crito*; drinking hemlock in the *Phaedo*. Like most readers, I still find in him one of the supreme examples of human courage and integrity. Yet I felt back then, as I do now, that there was something as preposterous as it was impressive in Socrates' decision that since, as he believed, nothing evil could happen to a man wholly devoted to pursuing what was good, therefore death, to which the Athenians condemned him, must be a good thing. I did not at that date make the distinction I would draw now between Socrates and Antigone as archetypes for conscientious objectors: Socrates scorning, almost welcoming death; Antigone, desperately wanting to live, confronting death as an undeniable evil but nevertheless choosing it in preference to what she regarded as duty both to kin and to divine will. Antigone is perhaps peculiarly, though not exclusively, a woman's exemplar.

Our Plato text included a brief section taken from Plato's *Symposium*: Alcibiades' description of Socrates' fortitude while on military service, the mystic trance that came over him while the army rested in camp, his self-control. I determined to read the entire dialogue in English. On a warm spring day, I carried the book to a secluded grassy spot on the edge of campus. Lying on my stomach, in the sun, flowers and birds pouring their scent and song into the air around me, in this idyllic setting I perused what must surely be the most poetic of all philosophical works. I could scarcely credit what I was reading. So this, too, was philosophy— this drama, half comic, half tragic, wholly poetic, with its psychologically penetrating insight into love's universal yearning. The fusion of emotion and intellect overwhelmed me. Diotima's description of the ascent from the first impulses of erotic love for another's bodily beauty to the vision of eternal and absolute beauty and truth commanded all the powers of my imagination. I was dazzled, half-blinded. If I related it at all to the Christian concept of the eternal, it was solely by way of contrast. The idea that there might be another reality to be reached by some special mental ascesis was, I am sure, nourished at its roots by my childhood exposure to the possibility of mystic insight into what William James called the "something more." But Plato seemed to me to call for the expansion of the self, not for self-abasement. I did not give to Plato's vision my full reasoning consent, as I did to Lucretius. Still, the sense that there might be a spiritual quest which I had chosen not to explore stayed with me, implicitly, if not wholly acknowledged.

I spoke earlier of my graduate student research in Hellenistic religion and Neoplatonism. The former gave me further support for the view that Christianity was one answer, but not the answer. Under Goodenough's influence, I developed an intense interest in the psychology of religion. Plotinus' mysticism fascinated and challenged me. But all of this I kept on the intellectual level, at a distance. Despite the ferment of mental activity, I did not, during that period, experience any decisive self-revelations or epiphanies, positive or negative. These were to come in the four years that immediately followed.

BREAKING THROUGH

North Carolina, while not the Promised Land, proved to be far from the place of exile my Yale provincialism had led me to expect. After two years at the Woman's College in Greensboro, I taught for two more at Queens College in Charlotte, a smaller college for women, with less academic prestige. I went there because I was offered an increase in rank to associate professor, several hundred dollars more in salary, and the opportunity to teach a bit of philosophy as well as Classics. Not having the feeling that I had found my permanent niche, I did not put down roots. In both cities I lived in a small room in a private home. (As an illustration of economic relativism, I note that in Greensboro I paid thirty-five dollars a month for a room in a private home; this included breakfasts and dinners, which set for me a standard of excellence for southern cooking which I have not seen equaled since.) The extraordinary friendliness extended to me and the lack of pressure gave me breathing space. I was provisionally content and found my time there a period of personal growth. Philosophical enlightenments are generally thought to lead to a feeling of greater harmony with oneself. In my case the resolution of psychological tensions and the cutting of intellectual knots worked hand in hand, but the personal adjustment was well underway before I achieved what I thought of as a final resolution of my philosophical pursuit.

Without dwelling on them, I may point to several significant factors, both social and private, that led me to effect a much needed self-improvement. Most obvious was the war, first the increasing probability that the country could not escape being drawn in, and then our sudden plunge into the midst of it. An almost more violent awakening was my introduction to southern racial patterns. Everything in me rebelled against them. Many of my new acquaintances, of course, were accustomed to live with this blind spot in their otherwise kindly, even altruistic attitude toward their fellow humans. Others of my close associates, native southerners as well as northern visitors like me, were appalled at the situation. We discussed endlessly what should and might ultimately be done. Meantime, while we were no heroes, we tried in small ways to resist the prevailing current. Gradually, I became politically committed to a strongly liberal point of view, though not remotely an activist. At least, and this was new for me, my hopes and my fears, my fervent interests were directed outward, beyond myself and my immediate circle.

Most decisive of all, I was teaching. I had always assumed that to be a teacher was my vocation, but I had never thought of teaching as a mission, nor deeply questioned myself as to why I wanted to teach. In the course of doing it for forty-five years, I have accumulated a mass of reflections on what teaching has come to mean for me. Already in that early stage, without much in the way of self-reflection, I found it an exciting challenge to awaken students' interest and to satisfy it. I savored the gladness of watching another's delight in mastering a skill or in seeing new vistas, an experience in which giving and receiving are indistinguishable. The positive response of my classes bolstered my self-confidence. More importantly, I began to realize that I had knowledge and even a certain wisdom worth sharing. Both in the classroom and in my greater involvement with the world outside, I began to feel that I was acting, whereas in the past I had been chiefly reacting. I think the change in me was illustrating the truth of two seemingly opposed axioms of psychology: I recall that Karen Horney remarked that the neurotic or maladjusted person literally cannot be fully concerned about others when all psychic energy is of necessity directed inward. But that other truism applied, too: it is only by engagement with others that one's own self is nourished. I trod a healing, not a vicious circle.

What primarily concerns me here, however, is not the details of an overdue and quite ordinary process of maturation, but rather the series of not so usual revelations and self-revelations that culminated in what I think deserves to be called a conversion. The first of these was so low-keyed as barely to qualify for its inclusion as an epiphany, but I think of it as such because of its suddenness and its lasting results. It was certainly a moment of self-revelation. In Greensboro, some weeks after my arrival, I walked out alone one evening in a country-like section near the edge of town and stopped at a bridge over a small rivulet. Have you ever, as I have, marveled at how many literary self-confrontations take place on bridges? Is it only because if the bridge is high enough and the river deep enough, the possibility of suicide suggests itself? Or is there an elusive truth in the ancient use of the river as a philosophical metaphor? On this evening I was emphatically not indulging in any reflections of that kind. I believe I was hardly thinking at all, merely delighting in the exquisite pastel tints of the after-sunset glow, the light on the browned grasses, and the utter peace of the quietness. All at once it was as if something spoke inside me and said, "I am happy, really happy." The self-reflection that followed was not a rational appraisal, but rather a revelation that gradually formed itself into words. I saw that I was finally freed of the unhappy love that had burdened me; it was gone. But this was a minor detail. I had the sense of exchanging a distorting mirror for an open window. In the past, I had viewed myself as a melancholiac, a "sick soul" as I would have said if I had been as familiar with James then as I am now. In words I remember as being approximately these, I exclaimed, "But I'm not like that at all! The kind of people I admire are not the negative ones but the positive, and I have been one of them without knowing it!" Relieved of some hidden pressure, I went on to say aloud (and this I remember exactly), "I am able to think again." But this basic optimism that I discovered within me, and which has stayed with me, is more emotional than rational. It is quite separate from any objective assessment I may make of any given situation, my own or our society's or the probable future of the human species. It has become part of my temperament, whatever and whenever its origin.

Strangely enough, this wholly positive, waking transformation occurred just a month or two before I had the only full-fledged mystic experience I have known, and this one was wholly, terrifyingly negative. Having to go to the hospital for minor surgery, I was given nitrous oxide. This "laughing gas," as it is sometimes called, is famous for inducing out-of-the-ordinary experiences of a kind familiar in the literature of mysticism. In *The Varieties of Religious Experience*, James draws on several such reports. Indeed, there is a tale (though it may be apocryphal) that James himself once asked to have nitrous oxide administered to him in the hope of achieving some kind of mystic revelation. Unfortunately, as the story goes, he remembered nothing of what he had experienced, and his only reported words were, "God, what a stink!" Without any expectations, I fared either better or worse than James, depending on the point of view, and there were consequences. After losing awareness of my immediate surroundings, I had the feeling of being suspended on the narrowest of edges over gulfs of emptiness, on "The Razor's Edge," as Maugham's novel of that title expressed it. Strained to the utmost, with an anguish half mental and half physical, I exclaimed, "There's nothing there. No matter what I may ever say in the future, there is nothing, absolutely nothing." The words I can remember verbatim; I doubt that I will ever forget them. The inarticulate sensation of pained desolation I can recall now only abstractly. But for a long time afterward it would recur as I lay in bed waiting to sleep. Sometimes I would deliberately keep myself awake for a while, afraid of what might come if I let go of everyday consciousness. This episode, negative though it was, fit perfectly the four requirements James laid down as characteristic of all mystic experience: *passive* it was to an extreme, and *transient, ineffable* as well, for I would not have been capable of describing it precisely even on first awakening. It was also indisputably *noetic*. Its revelatory aspect was so overwhelming as to impel me to declare that whatever I might come to think in the future, *then* at that moment I *knew*. As I reflected on it afterward, it was obvious that my encounter with nothingness under the anesthetic was connected somehow with the concept of nothingness I had met in the pages of Plotinus; but in that context, nothingness was cloaked with radiant promise, not desolate emptiness. In sober thought I did not believe that this pain at the heart of reality was a revealed ultimate truth, but the compelling force of what I remembered was disquieting. This happened in the winter of 1941–42. It was not until the summer of 1944 that my uneasiness was finally dispelled.

Meanwhile, a couple of years later when I was at Queens College in Charlotte, I had a series of three exceptional dreams, all indicating that my neuroses were either dissipating or assuming a more congenial form. The dreams were so vivid, so clear, and so evidently signifying that by constant repetition of them in my mind then and since that time, I think that I have a reasonably trustworthy recollection of them today. Naturally I am aware that there is a collection of cautionary precepts to be observed. I may have distorted the dream when I first told it to myself, and still more in retellings during the decades that followed. Psychotherapists could and almost certainly would see other meanings in the dreams than those I discovered. Yet, I can speak with assurance about what I took the dreams to be when I first asked myself what they meant and what now they seem to me to have signified. In short, I am recording the place of the dreams in my life as I lived its unfolding.

The first of the dreams was so made-to-order that it might have been written by a clumsy novelist. I am almost ashamed to introduce it here. I dreamed that in an unidentified countryside I was observing a cocoon on the verge of being opened. This was something I had done frequently in waking life, always with a sense of wonder. But this cocoon was enormous. Rapidly, accompanied by a burst of music, the creature inside began to emerge. Amazed, I beheld, not a giant moth but a bevy of angels flying outward and upward. As I watched them ascend toward a great light, I realized that they were not angels after all, but my students. I felt a great joy that stayed with me as I awoke. This banal creation is too obvious to need interpretation. Would I have dreamed it if I had not read

Plato? I recognized immediately a crude picture replica of his statement that while many persons seek to extend themselves in flesh-and-blood offspring, others prefer "children of the mind."

The second dream was centered literally on a secret recess to be opened up. This time I dreamed that I (my adult self) was in my bedroom in my childhood home. Somehow I was responsible for supervising the work of tearing down the walls. As they fell, a secret chamber was revealed. In it was a Negro (to use the term current at that date). He was a fugitive from the law, and I was told that I would receive a large reward for leading to his arrest. My reaction to this news was the most significant element of the dream. At first, when the room and its occupant were revealed, I felt joyously triumphant. Then, when I was notified of the reward, I was overwhelmed with sorrow and guilt. I felt that it was dishonorable and wrong for me to accept money in return for delivering up the man to punishment. (I woke up before learning whether my dream self refused the money or decided to accept it along with the guilt.) For some reason this dream appeared so important to me that I immediately set about fixing it in my mind and trying to figure out what it signified. The hidden room was easy to explain. As a girl, I read voraciously the books of Augusta Huiell Seaman and others, in which the heroine solved mysteries by discovering secret passages, etc. I was so entranced by the idea that I hopefully tapped along the walls of my grandfather's house, which was sufficiently large and ramshackle to render the notion unlikely rather than insane. My imaginary uncovering of a hidden chamber in my bedroom pointed to some sort of self-fulfillment and resolution of a problem. But why a Negro, and whence the mixed reactions?

I finally came up with what I think is a likely explanation. At that time I was increasingly disturbed by the surrounding racial oppression and by my own discomfort at following the established guidelines of segregation with respect to where I ate, where I sat on the bus, etc. Had I done anything about it? Mostly only in words voiced to my like-minded companions. But I had taken a couple of baby steps. While in Charlotte, for example, I had accompanied as faculty sponsor some students to attend a conference on race relations, held at Bennett College, a Negro college in Greensboro. At Queens, another faculty member and I arranged with a student group to hold a reception and discussion to which we invited students from Johnson C. Smith, a Negro college in Charlotte. All went well, and we congratulated ourselves on having made a breakthrough.

When the Queens girls returned from their spring vacation visits with their families, we proposed a follow-up program. Politely we were told that one such occasion had been fine, but they thought it would be better now to move on to some new social concern. I believe that my dream reflected all of this in two ways: On the one hand, it expressed my growing realization that looking outward was essential to self-development. From this point of view, the discovery of the fugitive Negro was positive, virtually an admonition. On another level, I believe it was a rebuke for a certain self-congratulatory tendency on my part. I have always distrusted the kind of "do-gooders," whether missionary or liberal, whose social service seemed to offer a little too much nourishment to their own self-image. I recall, in particular, a couple who undeniably did much to help others, but who seemed actually to enjoy painting the horrible details of the suffering of those whose case they were pleading. Intellectually convinced of the justice of their cause, they loved their mission more than they empathized with the victims. The feeling of shame that swept over my dream self warned me against this kind of psychological exploitation.

The last of the dreams was the most consequential and the one that most baffled me at the time that it occurred. It seemed that I was in a house located vaguely near a woods. I was in great distress because someone had just informed me that I was going to have to stay and live there. I would be sharing the house with a woman named Kay, but in the dream her presence seemed of no particular significance. The important point was that I was to be forced to remain in such a remote place, far from everything of interest to me. Then, abruptly, with no transition at all, I was holding in my hands a golden orchid. With overwhelming delight, I shouted out that now everything was all right, that since I had the flower I could stay there and be happy. Awaking, I felt psychically refreshed, deeply content, at peace, and fulfilled—as profoundly and reassuringly as in any of my real-life peak experiences, of which I have known a significant number. The feeling continued, not only for that day, but recurring at intervals for some weeks—a sort of counterpart to my earlier anesthesia-induced trauma of desolation. I could not explain that dream. In particular, what or whom did "Kay" stand for? The dream Kay was superficially identifiable as one of my casual acquaintances at Queens College, but I had never taken much interest in her, nor did she represent any specific point of view which might have figured significantly. Perhaps she was a stand-in for someone else, a Catherine who was a close friend, a woman I admired but one who held views with which I was in strong disagreement. But this hypothesis did not lead anywhere. Today I believe that, in her very indifference, Kay represented my immediate surroundings, which I felt to be mostly unstimulating, but which had nevertheless fostered personal growth. What was most mysterious, however, was the golden orchid. Quite obviously it stood for psychic adjustment of some sort, or a clue to self-understanding. My gradual discovery of why my imagination had selected precisely this as its symbol came far to outweigh the significance of the dream itself. (I should probably add that I am fully aware that any Freudian would take the orchid as a symbol of masculine sex. At the time I did not know this, nor the etymology of the word "orchid." In any case, I do not believe that the Freudian implication was the effective interpretive key, but rather something else which I learned later.)

This dream came to me in the late spring of 1944. That summer, I took two graduate courses in philosophy at Columbia University. Each class was, in its own way, a landmark for me. One was with Donald Piatt—from U.C.L.A., I think. I have forgotten the title of the course; it was concerned with Pragmatism, at least in part, but what interested the professor most was the question of the nature and mission of philosophy. I have often quoted Piatt's definition, which he adapted from Ducasse: "Philosophy is the exploration of scientific meanings for values in living." With slight modifications of my own, I think I have taken this as a basic assumption in philosophy classes I have taught ever since.

The other course, taught by a Professor Bowman from Union Theological Seminary, was called "Philosophy of Religion," or something of the sort. Here it was not the professor himself but what he required of us that had important consequences for me, both in my scholarly work and in my personal evolvement. First, the reading list included James's *The Varieties of Religious Experience.* Throughout the book, but especially in the chapters on conversion and mysticism, James gives accounts, in their own words, of persons who had known a variety of mystic states, conversions, and revelations that passed for special knowledge or Truth— from Protestant Christians, Catholic saints, Vedantists, Buddhists, and others, examined and commented on by a philosopher-psychologist, at once objective and sympathetic. Two points that James made impressed me especially. The first was his clear-cut distinction between the powerful reality of the experience as such and the explanation given of it by the subject who reported it. In most instances, the "revelation" was taken to be tightly bound to, if not the proof of, the religion or teaching dominant in the seer's immediate circumstances. A coincidental happening drove home this point for me. In connection with the course, we students were encouraged to visit some of the religious centers unfamiliar to us. At a Sufi meeting place, a woman spoke to us of her own conversion to Buddhism. As she told her story, she, a Caucasian with a nominal Christian background, had gone, on an impulse, into an empty Buddhist temple. Kneeling there, she had achieved, in a mystic, wholly emotional way, the sense of a rebirth. In her case, return to normal everydayness was followed directly by a talk given by a Buddhist priest. She recognized in all that he said the explanation of what she had undergone. She was "reborn" into Buddhism. Had she chanced to enter a different place of worship on that day, very likely another sect would have added a convert. James's insistence that a mystic experience held validity for the subject, but gave him/her no authority to dictate the behavior of others was eminently sound.

It was another of James's statements that affected me most profoundly. James discussed, at length, the way in which comparable positive, dynamic, expansive, self-fulfilling or self-transcending states occurred in diverse settings and with varying consequences in the lives of the converts and mystics. Almost parenthetically he added the observation that not all of the reports were like this—that a minority of them testified to devastating experiences of desolation or despair. Indeed, James had given a famous account of a negative one of his own. Within me, simultaneously two barriers gave way. I perceived that my terrifying insight under the anesthetic and others' claims of miraculous salvation were on exactly the same level. Neither could justly lay claim to ultimate truth. I need not fear the threat nor feel that I had failed to turn the one and only key.

Professor Bowman's course started me on a second series of personal discoveries. Carl Jung was also on our reading list. While at Yale, I had attended a public lecture that Jung gave. Aside from a sense of awe at being in the same room with so famous a person, I had not been particularly impressed, partly because his heavy accent made understanding difficult, mostly because I was unfamiliar with his work, without the necessary background requisite for intelligent listening. As I read him that summer at Columbia, two things happened. Struck with a certain resemblance between Jungian theory and aspects of the philosophy of Plotinus, I chose this parallel as the subject of my required paper, and suggested Gnosticism as the probable link and common influence. Later the paper was published in *Philosophical Review* (1945). In light of what is known today of Jung, what I wrote at that early date is superficial and inadequate, but I take a certain pride in having anticipated a conclusion which others' research after Jung's death corroborated. More important to me personally was my discovery that Jung had written a book called *The Secret of the Golden Flower.* In this he documented the discovery that not only in the dreams of his patients, but in myths and in various writings drawn from an overwhelming expanse of space and time, the golden flower, like the four-part mandala figure, symbolized the attainment of a balanced harmony of psychic forces within an individual, essential for self-understanding and self-realization. My own dream of the golden orchid might have been inserted amidst these accounts, adding still more evidence, but attracting no particular attention. Seeing it as part of a universal pattern was exhilarating. For a time, it seemed to me to guarantee the truth of Jung's psychology. Yet I did not finally become a Jungian. Even at the peak of my excited discovery I was bothered by the notion of a Collective Unconscious inhabited by archetypal figures, which seemed to me less a scientific hypothesis than a supernatural fantasy, at best a metaphor. But, if all these symbolic golden flowers did not spring from a Collective Unconscious, where *did* they come from?

I asked myself again why, or out of what part of my past, my dream self had selected this particular image for its message. And I found that I knew. I remembered my Aunt Jennie's telling me of her having found the rare yellow lady slipper (the popular name for a wild orchid) deep in the woods at Beach Lake; I recalled how we had hoped, but looked in vain, for another one. This never discovered treasure I finally grasped years later in an imaginary setting in North Carolina. No wonder it was precious. It was something I had been searching for since I was a child. Yet, if I could account for the symbolism of my dream flower in terms of my individual history, was it pure coincidence that all those other people, with no Aunt Jennie and a Pennsylvania forest, had chosen a golden flower as an image with the same basic meaning? I finally solved this puzzle to my own satisfaction—undramatically and, I think, by a sound reasoning.

I decided that the golden flower belongs to the great collection of natural symbols—like the earth as mother, like the vine as ever-renewing life, like the pillar as the male organ, like the lion as the incarnation of fierce strength, like the butterfly as a symbol of rebirth, like what is perhaps the most universal and self-evident of all natural symbols, the snake. The snake is especially interesting in showing how the same object can hold multiple meanings, all linked with what it intrinsically is. How easy it is to understand how the snake, which goes in and out of holes in the ground, which can lie stretched prone on the ground but suddenly stiffen and strike, which sheds its old skin for a new one, should, in widely separated regions, stand variously for the soul of a dead person, for the phallus, for spiritual transformation and immortality. So, among the snake, the butterfly, the pillar, et al., I would place the golden flower. The beauty and relative rarity of the metal gold colors the flower with preciousness. The flower has become so trite a metaphor for the full realization of what was promised in the bud that its obvious universality is readily apparent.

I was once asked what the difference is between calling something a natural symbol and naming it an archetype. Perhaps there is none at all if by archetype one simply means an observed pattern derived in part from natural resemblance and in part from linguistic tropes. But between the natural symbol and the archetype, as most Jungians take it, lies the whole weight of mysteriously functioning unconscious forces, and I have never been able to see either the evidence or the need for this clumsy machinery. Later I encountered an elaborate theory of the "material meanings" of things—in Sartre's description of slime and holes in *Being and Nothingness*. I make no claim to having anticipated this sophisticated "psychoanalysis of things," as Sartre called it, borrowing the term from Bachelard, but it has the notion of natural symbols at its core. Nobody, to my knowledge, has attempted seriously to employ it as an alternative and less fanciful approach to the sorts of parallels Jung attributes to psychic archetypes. I think there is room for such a procedure. Perhaps it would be worthwhile to do a phenomenological research into the existential meaning of bridges and rivers.

I have spoken of this inward odyssey as leading to a conversion. But was it, strictly speaking, a conversion? Or was it, in essence, no more than a deconversion? And if it was, indeed, a conversion, then a conversion to what? If one may use the term for a significant psychological transformation, then a conversion it certainly was. Philosophically, the answer is less clear. I suppose my position could have been loosely defined as a form of naturalism, combined with social liberalism. In Fromm's language, I had achieved "freedom from . . .," and even, with my resolve to find means of constructive action, a degree of "freedom to . . ." I had not built or borrowed any firm philosophical underpinnings for my overall outlook. Still, for quite a long time I moved comfortably, without feeling any pressing need to investigate further.

As I write today, the question arises as to how I might view the things I have described if I looked at them from a Sartrean perspective. For Sartre, conversions meant primarily a radical shift in point of view. He held that each person's "fundamental project," his/her basic orientation or way of being-in-the-world, can be thrown into question and radically altered, since we are always uneasily aware that it is our own invention and *could* be different. Sartre mentions religious conversions as examples of this happening. His philosophy does not allow for any influx of the supernatural; it does provide room for the meaningful or revelatory dream. But instead of having recourse to the Unconscious, he holds that in a dream, a consciousness has put itself into the imaginary mode. Just as the body in a dream is an imaginary body, so the consciousness that acts and reacts in a dream is an imaginary consciousness. Apropos of my tortured realization that "there is nothing," Sartre might see in it a reflection of what he would hold to be two truths of our being-in-the-world: First, the Universe has no purpose or meaning beyond what humans put into it. Second, consciousness itself is nothing substantial—only the pure activity of assuming a point of view on something, that is, it is consciousness of objects and simultaneously a self-consciousness. To be aware of an object is also to be aware that the awareness is *not* the object. Fifty years later and irrespective of Sartre, I see in my encounter with pure negativity one other possibility. At that date I was still under the influence of Plotinian philosophy though beginning to drift away from it. Today I suspect that the "revelation" may have derived from my unclarified feeling that after all the "nothingness" of which Plotinus made so much was purely verbal, that in fact it was nothing at all. Ironically, some critics have made the same observation concerning Sartre's concept of nothingness, but I am convinced that this is due to failure to understand what he meant.

POSTSCRIPT

This postscript is not quite an anachronistic digression. I had intended to restrict myself in this chapter to the period ending with my years in North Carolina. Unless I were to call my discovery of Existentialism a conversion, which for various reasons I hesitate to do, the summer of 1944 marked the end of my history of personal epiphanies of the sort I have been describing. There was a time in the sixties, however, when it seemed that perhaps old questions should be reopened. I will speak briefly of two episodes that I introduce partly so as not to have in my own mind any sense of leaving behind items of unfinished business, and partly because I think they are intrinsically of interest as an ironic reflection of life in the sixties as led by some of us in areas quite off the beaten track.

The addictive drugs that some in the new counterculture were touting held no appeal for me. I was curious about marijuana, which was said to be nonaddictive, but quite apart from any question of its illegality, I never wanted to try it since it appeared to promise only a transitory sensation of euphoria at the price of loss of control, if not also the possibility of lasting physical or psychological damage. The philosophical and psychological claims by those who experimented with LSD, mescaline, and hallucinogenic mushrooms left me skeptical, but they posed a challenge. In the mid-sixties I was engaged in writing my book *An Existentialist Ethics*. It was obligatory for me to determine how Sartre's theory of consciousness could accommodate, or stand up against, claims which threatened to undermine its validity. In the book, I discussed at length my conclusions with respect to the mystic and psychic insights brought on by drug-induced experiences, including a comparative examination of Huxley's and Sartre's reports of their respective engagements with mescaline. I will not repeat here, save to say that I still hold (1) that the truth revealed in these abnormal states is that of the perceiver, not that of the perceived, and (2) that Sartre's view of consciousness provides, in my opinion, a way of accounting for "oceanic feelings," the sense of being absorbed into the cosmos, and the like, that is satisfying to me, though probably not to most mystics. Intellectually, I felt content with my chapter "The Temptation of Eastern Philosophy," and I still feel so, insofar as my conclusions are concerned, though later writers have gone much beyond me in studies of Eastern thought in relation to Existential phenomenology. I was troubled, however, by the fact that I was presuming to evaluate such experiences while never having experimented with them myself. The thought of LSD frightened me. I refused to follow Timothy Leary's advice to "play Russian roulette with [my] brain." I decided to wet my toes by trying peyote.

My fling with peyote, while intended as an honest investigation to find out what would and could happen, strikes me now as not quite

unauthentic but comically academic. You risk nothing with peyote—
beyond intense nausea, wherein I fully lived up to expectation. I procured the little hard cactus buttons from Omar Stewart, a professor of
anthropology at the University of Colorado, who gave them to me on
condition that as part of an experiment he was conducting I fill out a
questionnaire on their effects. This mild escapade was not illegal. I persuaded a colleague to experiment along with me. So there the two of us
sat in the living room in two comfortable chairs before the fireplace,
with my housemate, Doris, and another friend hovering in the background, awaiting our reports of fantastic visions. Naturally we never had
any. If any formation in the fire began to emerge, I asked myself anxiously if this was a real hallucination or only my imagination. The only
"real one" was an olfactory one, which my overreflective tendencies had
not anticipated. The scent of a verbena candle was so extraordinarily
powerful that I was falsely persuaded that the room was permeated with
the smell of fudge being cooked. Except for this, and other than being
first nauseated and then as if paralyzed, about the only unusual thing I
noticed was the distortion of time. The night did not seem long. Yet
having, as it seemed to me, told the story of a large portion of my life to
my companion, I noted by my watch that only five minutes had passed.
In the morning, although neither of us had slept, we did not feel tired.
The next day a painfully stiff neck, caused by sitting so long in the same
position, sent me to my osteopath.

After this unsatisfactory attempt, I was only mildly interested when
Professor Stewart asked if Doris and I would like to attend a Native
American ceremony using peyote, one which an Apache couple would
be holding in a remote spot south of Denver. We accepted, curious to
observe the ritual, rather than to share in the peyote. Indeed, Doris came
along chiefly to watch over me and the graduate student in anthropology who accompanied us. She recalled the nausea and the semiparalysis
I had felt on the other evening; bodily conditions, incidentally, which
made me laugh when I found on Stewart's questionnaire the inquiry,
"Did you feel any aphrodisiac effects?" It was an unusually wet June; the
field where the tepee was pitched was up to our ankles in mud. We approached just before sunset, by a series of small ridges and gullies.
Obviously, we were not going to be able to leave before the sun rose
again. At the start I was puzzled and a bit disappointed. The delicately
built Apache couple delayed the ceremony long enough to show and
try to sell us some of their pottery, which they said was featured in

Goldwater's department store in Arizona. I have seen much of the cheap junk that tourists have bought, mixed in with the magnificent offerings of the southwest Native Americans. I had never seen anything quite so awful as this. The group was anything but a typical assembly of Native Americans. Of the dozen or so of us present, only the Apache pair and two burly Sioux, men who happened to be visiting in the area, were non-Caucasian. Ruth Underhill from the University of Denver, the anthropologist scholar of Native American culture, was there; also a reporter from the *Denver Post*. This ceremony, I decided, must be something which for some reason the Native Americans had decided to put on in order to inform and perhaps instruct outsiders. I could only hope that for this very reason it would be scrupulously authentic. The Apache man was the "driver," who explained about the "road," recited the prayers, etc. His wife distributed the peyote buttons, and the cups of peyote tea. Stuck as we were in this remote spot, I partook very sparingly, enough to evoke in me a feeling which the attitude of the others suggested that they shared, an unusual gentleness, a nonerotic closeness and tender consideration of each other—a communal peacefulness. Even Doris, who had not taken any of the peyote, felt it—possibly owing to the smoke from the fire on which a bit of peyote had been scattered. I can recall virtually nothing of the ritual itself. It was mostly verbal, and the words were unremarkable. Morning came at last; we shared some simple food, and the group broke up. On the way home, the anthropology student, who had talked with the two Sioux, said that although the "driver" had stressed that hallucinations were incidental and not the essential goal of this religious service, they themselves took the peyote in the hope of being given visions. Also they complained that the Apache's words and gestures had shown him to be insufficiently trained.

Within a couple of weeks a Sunday feature article in the *Denver Post* described the occasion, playing up its exotic aspects, such as they were, making no judgment as to its significance. Months later I gave a detailed report of it to my friend Ferris Takahashi. She and her husband had developed a close relation with members of the Taos Pueblo. I hoped that with her greater acquaintance with Native American culture, she might help me put the episode into clearer perspective. She listened without comment until I had finished, then burst into indignant laughter. She knew all about that pair, she said. They were not Native Americans at all. They had come from Brooklyn and were trying to pass themselves off as Apaches in order to help sell their atrocious pottery. The peyote

ceremony was a part of the "come-on." At least with our group, their effort had been wasted. Nobody had bought anything.

Thus my last search ended "not with a bang," but a snicker. Perhaps
there are lessons that might be derived from it, ranging from "Don't
wear academic regalia when hunting for wild mushrooms" to "Watch for
traces of a Brooklyn accent when dealing with Apache entrepreneurs."
But I prefer just to put a period to it.

Pl. 1. Olin and May Petersen Barnes. Wedding picture, August 1911.

Pl. 2. Hazel at two years and six months, on grandfather's farm
at Beach Lake, Pennsylvania.

Pl. 3. Hazel at time of her sixth birthday, with sister Jean (eleven months).

Pl. 4. Hazel (center) with Agnes Gross (left) and Evelyn Wiltshire (right), at Wilson College class festival.

Pl. 5. Hazel and Evelyn Wiltshire at Wilson College graduation.

Pl. 6. During her last year at Yale.

Pl. 7. With Harry in Thessaloniki, Greece, in 1946.

Pl. 8. Hazel, with Christine Osborne, setting out on trip
through Greek islands, 1947.

FOUR

Interlude

Paradoxically, that fateful summer of 1944 in New York led to my making a commitment which, on the surface, appeared shockingly inconsistent with my recent, hard-won conclusions. I became an unbaptized missionary.

In the spring my longing to do something out of the ordinary at this time of world crisis became acute. I had contributed nothing to the war effort; perhaps I could help in the rebuilding that must come afterward. Having read with particular distress and sympathy of the bravery and the suffering of the Greeks, I resolved to try to work in postwar Greece. Letters to UNRRA and other organizations that were already being set up brought only rejections. Medical personnel and social workers were needed, not untrained enthusiasts like me—even if I *had* started to study modern Greek. In New York I went to the Greek consulate. I gained nothing there except for the suggestion that I go to see the person in charge of the office of the Dodecanese National Council, who "might have some ideas." I wish I could remember the name of the man there, for he gave me excellent advice. He urged me to forget about social work and do what I was trained to do—teach. Greece would have a great need of people who could teach English, he said, and it was as a teacher that I could best help the country. He added that his secretary had already heard of an opportunity. Talking with her, I learned that Pierce College, an American school for girls, was looking for teachers. The pay would be low, barely maintenance level, for this was an institution run by the American Board of Commissioners for Foreign Missions, of the

Congregational Christian Churches. The secretary added that the missionary connection did not entail the preaching or teaching of religion.

Fearful that I would have to choose between being a hypocrite and
staying home, I nevertheless got in touch with the American Board and
was quickly reassured. The man who interviewed me was visibly relieved
that I was *not* bent on proselytizing. This was only partly because Pierce
College was in Greece, which was officially a Christian state. The presence of the college there was something of an anomaly. Located originally (under a different name) in Izmir, it had been shut down after the
expulsion of the Greeks and Armenians from Turkey in the early 1920s. It
was reestablished in Greece in response to the urgent pleas of its alumnae and teachers, many of whom were Greeks, and thanks to the phil-
anthropy of a Mr. Pierce, who contributed the necessary funds on condition that the college be named for his wife, Orlinda Childs Pierce. Even
in the Muslim Near East, the purpose of such schools was never the indoctrination of Christian teachings. The intent was to offer an American
liberal education of high quality with special emphasis on skill in English. Undoubtedly, the sponsors cherished the hope that by a sort of
osmosis, American ideals would be imparted as well; and insofar as these
could be identified with the Judaeo-Christian outlook, I suppose the
work of the Board could be said to be Christian. But in this sense, I, too,
was a Christian, as were most American and European intellectuals.
However one may view the initial motivation, the results were wholly
commendable. I have continued to admire and marvel at the extent to
which the American Board institutions have contributed constructively
to the cultural life of the countries in which they are situated and, incidentally, have fostered good will toward the United States in counterbalance to the many negative interactions with us.

Things moved as speedily as international events allowed. On May 8,
1945, "V-E Day," when Nazi Germany formally surrendered, a phone
call from Boston confirmed my appointment for a three-year term and
directed me to be prepared to leave for Europe within the next few
months. On August 28, two weeks after "V-J Day," I sailed from New
York on the *Gripsholm*, the first ship after the war to carry passengers to
Europe for purely civilian purposes. A twenty-four-hour stop at Naples
gave us our first sight of war-ravaged Europe. From the deck we saw the
sunken ships, the bombed-out buildings, the empty windows in what few
walls were left standing, the absence of all but Allied military vehicles
around the harbor. The *Gripsholm* had brought a large number of Italian
and Greek deportees, a few of them charged with criminal offenses,

many of them persons who had been living peacefully but illegally in the United States until they were caught in the surveillance connected with draft registration, ration cards, etc. On shipboard, we had liked some of them with whom we talked individually. The night before, when their voices had filled the soft Mediterranean air with romantic melodies, we had loved them all collectively. At landing, the Italian deportees were herded together on shore; nobody had made any provision for them. All night they sat with their bags under a sort of shed, inadequately protected against the pouring rain. They were still there when we left. This forlorn group of the uprooted presaged for me the omnipresent postwar misery as painfully as the bombing scars.

In Greece, which had been liberated by the Allies in the fall of 1944, there were everywhere reminders also of its civil war. This had broken out full-scale in December when the British clashed with the EAM-ELAS forces, a Communist-dominated coalition of leftist groups who, after joining the Allies in fighting the Germans, refused to lay down their arms at British command. (Incidentally, an American acquaintance of mine, by no means a Communist, who happened to be at the edge of Constitution Square when hostilities opened there, told me that she was certain the British had fired the first shot.) Since February there had been an apparently stable truce. It lasted until 1946 when ELAS revolutionaries gradually started to fight a guerrilla war, confined to the mountain areas, now solely Greek against Greek, which was not settled until a year after my departure from Greece in June 1948.

Arriving at Peiraeus with me was another appointee for Pierce College, Eilene Donner, a high school teacher with an M.A. in history and a special interest in ancient Greece, who was as ardently eager as I was to learn to know the present-day country and its people. Intelligent, perceptive, adaptable, able to savor the ridiculous in situations others found only frustrating, Eilene contributed immeasurably to my overall enjoyment of the Greek experience; she was an ideal comrade in arms in the vicissitudes of the first few weeks. A journal I kept during the first year and a half shows that I lived in a perpetual state of exultation in being where I was, no matter what difficulties arose, and of these there were many.

I hesitate to speak of hardship for us in view of the horrors our Greek associates had recently witnessed and the privations that still made survival problematic for many. We knew that the American Board would provide a safety net for us in any serious emergency. Otherwise our daily life was like that of our Greek colleagues. Water came on for only a few hours three times a week; people had to store it in bathtubs, pails, jars, anything however small that could be spared to hold it. Social engagements took the water into account; it was not unusual for someone to break off a conversation in order to hurry home in time to fill the containers. Due to worn-out machinery, electricity was rationed; we were without it three nights a week regularly, but frequently it failed unpredictably. Once, when I was teaching a late afternoon class in a basement room, we were suddenly plunged into darkness. Unable to see each other, we went on discussing the assignment until at last someone arrived with a candle. Fuel was inadequate for all of that first winter. Buildings in the Mediterranean world, I discovered, were designed to keep heat out rather than in. I wore my warmest outdoor coat while teaching, and sometimes, between classes, I would sit in the sun on the fire escape steps to warm up. Clothes of good quality were all but nonexistent in the shops, and by now everybody needed them. I remember one of my Greek colleagues crocheting a pair of stockings since she had no others. Occasionally, women were able to get hold of synthetic materials from old parachutes and make clothing from it. "Nylon" became a slang term to label any product "supremely good." One day I heard a street vendor call out, "Cherries, good cherries, excellent cherries, nylon cherries!" Some American items of the rummage sale variety were sold for high prices from vendors' carts. Gradually, as packages began to come from the United States, from relatives or via relief agencies, the appearance of the general population improved. But there were anomalies; for example, since children's clothes for special occasions are most often discarded before being worn out, I sometimes saw little girls barefoot and wearing velveteen dresses. Scarcity and galloping inflation worked hand in hand. The value of the drachma moved officially from five hundred to five thousand to the dollar between September and February. Prices changed overnight, always upward. One man reported that the price of his drink changed between his first and second order. At the bank, when Eilene and I wanted to cash traveler's checks, a kindly official refused, telling us we would do much better on the black market. Food, of course, was more available than in the war days, but it, too, was dreadfully expensive. Living with Greek families, but subsidized by the American Board, Eilene and I were in no danger of starvation. But on our maintenance salaries and (until several months later) without access to the American PX or other special privileges, we had no money for anything but essentials—bus fare, etc.

For the most part, the two of us found our material limitations at first an exciting challenge, then something taken for granted. One day, however, soon after our arrival, hungry between lunch and the late dinner hour, we scraped together enough to get a roll and a glass of water for each of us in a restaurant so that we could sit and talk over our first serious cause for dismay. We had been gradually realizing how extensive a task of reconstruction lay before us; now it seemed that we would have no tools. We had just learned that the textbooks ordered from the United States had not arrived and could not be expected for several weeks. We would face our first class in a couple of days. Greatly agitated, we declared the situation hopeless. Then, after a bit, nibbling on our rolls, Eilene and I solemnly decided that somehow we would meet the test. If our education was worth anything, Eilene observed, some of it must have remained in our heads instead of resting in books. We would find out how much we actually knew. I suppose we were a little comic as well as pathetic. At any rate, we felt better as we left the restaurant.

This particular problem found a solution of sorts. Fortunately, it was only the gymnasium (the European lycée, roughly equivalent to our junior high and high school, though somewhat more advanced in its offerings) that was to open immediately; the college division in which we were to teach all but one of our courses would begin a little later. Bookstores in Athens were able to furnish texts by Greek authors that we could use for teaching English grammar. What were we to do for reading? Our president, Kathryn McElroy, appealed to the United States Information Service in Athens, which generously agreed to give to us free whatever we could use from their selection of books—an odd assortment that included a few literary works along with volumes of information about the U.S. My class was allotted Saroyan's *The Human Comedy* and Fast's *Citizen Tom Paine.* Nobody ever complained of Howard Fast's radicalism, but some of the Greek teachers objected to the smart-alecky remarks of the school children in Saroyan's novel, thinking this portrayal no fit model for the Pierce girls.

Pierce College had been forced to close under the German occupation. Its buildings at Elleniko, next to the small airport, had been badly damaged. When I first visited it, the British had partially restored one of the buildings and were using it as a hospital. The rest were uninhabitable. The Germans had removed all metal, even nails, from the walls. The auditorium, which was better preserved than most parts, still bore a large, painted German eagle and swastika over the stage. Private houses in the surrounding village were in even worse shape: no roofs, walls partly fallen, bare ground where floors had been. And in many of these broken shells, we saw families living, huddled by a charcoal brazier; these were not the owners but squatters, otherwise homeless people. Coiled barbed wire was everywhere, and we were warned not to stray from paths because of old land mines. Some months later a young boy was killed by a mine while he was playing in a corner of the college property.

Reopening now, Pierce held its classes in four separate, rented buildings in central Athens. We teachers walked the considerable distance from one to another as our schedules demanded. The library was not yet available, since there was no place to bring together the books that Greek faculty members had saved by storing them in their homes. If today I feel that my teaching at Pierce was as satisfying to me as any I have done, it was not because of propitious educational facilities or the opportunity to offer specialized courses in a well-planned curriculum. The gymnasium, except for extra training in English, had to follow the program of study laid down by the Greek government. The pupils took an enormous number of courses; only a genius with a Renaissance mind could have mastered them thoroughly. The college program, which President McElroy was especially interested in developing, was designed to resemble an American junior college. Much later, after I had left, Pierce concentrated instead on two post-gymnasium programs to train students for social work or for business, which have become greatly respected. *Our* aim was too vast and too diffuse to make sense, though, in fact, some of our graduates succeeded in being accepted as sophomores or even juniors in American liberal arts colleges, and they did very well. To be sure, we had some excellent, university-trained Greek professors. Eilene and I were soon joined by two other Americans who stayed with us for the rest of the three years, and there were a few visiting American professors who came for a more limited stay. (There were never more than ten of us Americans at any one time.) We did a lot of pinch-hitting. I taught a history of philosophy course, which was a good learning experience for me, also a rudimentary introduction to psychology; texts for the latter had shown up in the early parcels, and the other American teachers were even less well qualified than I. Primarily I was in charge of developing a curriculum for English language and literature. My major achievement was to initiate the writing of footnoted term papers, a practice that at first aroused open resistance among our Greek teachers of English, who had not attempted anything of the sort themselves. Ultimately they said, at least, that they were grateful we had done it.

The sense of rebuilding (or, in some cases, building from scratch) was exhilarating; and, of course, in this we reflected what was going on in Greece as a whole, despite political uncertainties, shortages, and the like. It was the students themselves who gave us our greatest reward. For all of them their education had been interrupted; those at the college level had not been able to attend any classes whatsoever during the Occupation. A bit older now and knowing what they had been denied, they came ready to make the most of whatever was offered them. One never had to resort to provocative statements or to any of the devices teachers sometimes use to keep a class alert. Our chief task was to put order into the excited questioning and debates. I have never known more openly appreciative classes. On later visits, I learned that a surprisingly large number of those young women had gone on to hold positions of importance in Greece in widely varied areas of the country's economic and cultural life.

In a tradition of hospitality which they held to be unbroken since Homer, our Greek colleagues welcomed us—inviting us to their homes, introducing us to new acquaintances outside the work place, and, above all, insuring that we learn everything we could about their country, its legends and traditions as well as all that it could offer us in the present. Until late November I boarded at the home of Evangelia Athanassiadou, the widowed sister of Korali Krokodeilou, who was a mainstay of Pierce College, perhaps the most colorful and talented of all the regular Greek faculty, a woman whose ability at instantaneous Greek/English translation might have well served the United Nations. Korali lived in the house, too, as did Evangelia's teen-age son, Kostas, and daughter, Eirene. (Eilene lodged in an adjacent house but joined us for meals.) Kostas and Eirene personally escorted us on our first trip to the Acropolis and to other of Athens' ancient sites. Korali took charge of present-day cultural activities. If during her life (she is now in her nineties) Korali has missed any significant aesthetic or academic event in Athens, it must have been because two were in conflict. On the evening of my first day in Athens she took me to the meeting place of a group that sang madrigals. As the first postwar season got under way, we attended each symphony concert, opera, play, or whatever. I found it strange to hear Shakespeare's *Much Ado about Nothing* in Greek, but it was still Shakespeare to me as well as highly satisfying to the audience as a whole. The climax of the season, so far as I was concerned, came at the end of October. On October 28, we witnessed the making of a holiday. This was the anniversary of the day in 1940 when the Greeks said "No" to the Italians who formally asked for permission to invade. "Ochi (no) Day" launched a three-day celebration. One of the chief events was the first postwar production of an ancient Greek drama, put on by the reopening Greek National Theatre. It was not by chance that the play selected was Aeschylus' *The Persians*, which related the triumph in 480 B.C. of the Greeks over the huge fleet sent against them by Xerxes. This affirmation of historical continuity took my breath away. I found the production illuminating also from another point of view. In performances of Greek tragedies I had seen at home, the Chorus had always been something of an impediment, an unintelligible recital in unison by characters standing stiffly in unnatural poses. And, while I knew that originally the Chorus danced as it sang and was accompanied by music, I never was quite able to envision old men, in *The Persians*, for instance, as being anything but ridiculous prancing around and singing. Now I saw how it could have been done. Choreographed in a stately walk, dividing so as to form changing visual patterns, bodily movements echoing the chanting (not quite speaking, and not quite singing, but clearly enunciated), the twelve actors followed the rhythm of the music, enhancing the emotional impact of the words as customarily happens in opera and in musical comedies. This was but a hint of what I have seen on later visits. Greek directors and producers have led the way in showing the world that these revered ancient texts of the past, as inspiring as they are, should be viewed as being, to some extent, comparable to the libretto for an opera.

Even in the first difficult months, our Greek friends managed to dine out occasionally. They introduced us to the taverna. More social than a restaurant, less sophisticated than a night club, the taverna was a gathering place to spend the evening. A few of the newer ones in Athens offered a floor show put on by professionals, but these were the exception. Often there were musicians, but mostly the guests entertained themselves. In the earlier evening, there were family parties with children. Couples came to hold hands at secluded tables. Noisy groups celebrated with impromptu speeches. And people sang, not always in tune and sometimes not with everyone singing the same song, but with marvelous spontaneity and palpable enjoyment. Tavernas came in all shapes and sizes. I especially loved the little ones we stumbled on in the tiny, winding streets of Plaka, just below the Acropolis. Here it would often happen that guests would leave their several tables to join one of the traditional

Greek dances. Or a man might give an individual performance, beginning with a solo dance, then moving on to acrobatic stunts such as picking up a glass of wine from the floor with his mouth and drinking from it without touching it with his hands. Eilene and I never attempted anything quite so difficult as this, but we sometimes accepted an invitation to attempt to follow the intricate steps of the wavering dances. Evidently it was in these tavernas that the Greek gods felt most at home. There is a popular song that tells how they still visit this spot where the ancient city stood, how they drink freely of the retsina, and go back to the Parthenon, not steadily but staggering "from column to column."

As food became easier to obtain, a few people ventured to give parties at their homes. A Greek party, then at least, was seldom, if ever, the gathering of persons in the same age group; the entire family was present, from children to grandparents; the guest list, too, mixed age levels. Frequently the eating and drinking went on all night, though I seldom saw anyone drunk. Once, when Eilene and I, the first ones to depart, said at 2:00 A.M. that we must go, our hostess, distressed that we were leaving before the end of the meal, urged us to stay just a bit longer; she said she would "serve the dessert early."

One of these parties is indelible in my memory, since it produced my most embarrassing experience, not just in Greece but anywhere. I had been told of the carnival season in prewar Greece when masquerades would be held throughout the pre-lenten season, festivals of a kind common in many Catholic countries, still observed here in New Orleans. In 1946, a few tavernas threw out strings of confetti, but that was all. Then one day a student invited Eilene and me to a "masquerade party" at her home. Some of the guests, she said, would "wear costumes." If we wished to do so, we could either come already dressed or bring with us what we would wear and change at her house. Rising to the occasion, Eilene rigged up an outfit to make her look like Uncle Sam; I emerged as a cross between a Cossack and a pirate. Having been told to come unusually early, at five o'clock, we boarded the tram when it was still daylight—in costume, since we thought that if masquerade parties were being given, the public would understand. There were some puzzled glances, but nothing to disturb us until we arrived at Neli's home. Some of the women were wearing long dresses; all the guests were in party clothes. Our student's invitation had been in English. When she said, "masquerade party," she had intended "carnival party" as one might say "Christmas party"; by "costume" she meant "evening gown." For a long time Eilene and I sat like wilting flowers, listening to our hostess explain

that there was a difference between American and Greek customs. Nobody laughed until, finally, we broke the tension ourselves as the very
outrageousness of our transgression struck us as genuinely comic. When
we reported the episode to President McElroy the next morning, she,
too, found it funny, though her manner suggested that it was somehow
what she would have expected of us.

I have let myself get a bit ahead of my story. A decisive change had
taken place in November. Kathryn McElroy, finding it too expensive to
continue our lodging and food subsidies, made arrangements for Eilene
and me to move to the British YWCA, which housed women working
for the British military or other government services. Though our meals
did not improve in quality (I remember chiefly the too frequent presence
of Spam and canned corned beef), our existence suddenly took on an
additional, interesting dimension. Our fellow residents, who had come
from all corners of the British Empire, had fascinating tales to tell us of
their countries and their experiences in wartime and postwar work.
Often men from the British armed forces came to the YWCA, by individual invitation or for evenings of group entertainment—both officers
and enlisted men. A few of them I disliked because of their condescending attitude toward the Greeks—inferior natives, as far as they
were concerned. Others were delighted to have us as guides both to ancient sites and to our favorite tavernas or to meet with our close Greek
friends. Eilene became particularly attached to one English soldier whose
first name was Johnson; they introduced me to his best friend, Harry.
Soon we were a foursome, seeing each other almost every evening.

Johnson was prone to pranks that the rest of us sometimes enjoyed,
but not always. We did become happy co-conspirators in his most elaborate undertaking. The Athenian authorities had a habit of frequently
changing street names as the occasion arose to honor some popular
figure; e.g., the replacement that year of "University," "Academy," and
"Stadium" by "Roosevelt," "Churchill," and "Venezelos." One of us having
expressed the wish that we might name a street after ourselves, Johnson
hunted up a properly sized board and painted on it in Greek letters a hy-
brid of our four names—"Odos (Street) Hazentzonsarri," not exactly a
Greek form but one not much more peculiar than other Hellenized versions of foreign names that we had seen. Finding a somewhat isolated
corner of a street called "Pericles," we replaced the existing sign with
ours. For two weeks it stayed up there, and we wondered if nearby residents would start using the new address. It might have remained longer
had we not gathered there the night before Johnson and Harry were

transferred to Thessaloniki. Drinking a farewell toast beneath our sign, we broke the glasses rather noisily. Next morning the sign was gone. "Pericles" did not reappear until weeks later. I have sometimes tried to feel ashamed of this episode but never quite succeeded.

In April, at the time of our spring break, Eilene and I managed, for a small payment and after much negotiation, to fly to Thessaloniki on a British transport plane; we sat on wooden benches lined up against the wall. Thessaloniki (Salonica), at that date still resembling a small town, was wholly caught up in celebrating Easter, an observance covering most of the preceding week and the following Monday. The ceremonies connected with it were as much a reenactment as a commemorative—from the public funeral procession with simulated coffin on Friday evening to the tumultuous shouting and firecrackers that greeted the priest's proclamation after the Saturday night mass and precisely at midnight, "Christos anesti" (Christ has risen). At least in the Greece of that period I noticed that even nonbelievers took part in the preliminary fasting and did not look on Easter as just another holiday. When I questioned them, I was told that the religious aspect was inseparable from respect for Greece as their nation. This I could understand, for during the centuries of Turkish control, religion and language were all that truly set the Greeks apart and made them a people—in Asia Minor as well as in Greece itself. My friend Hara Tzavella (Evjen) favors another theory—that fasting has a universal psychological and physiological root, the feeling that there must at intervals be a rite of cleansing. The four of us happily celebrating our being together in Thessaloniki were primarily detached observers, but I think that the mingling of mourning and rejoicing in the rituals perhaps affected and certainly suited our mood. These delightful few days would be our last ones together. Neither couple expected any further reunions. We had learned, separately and together, that a relation could be tender and exciting, comfortable and wholly trusting even without a future; it could rightly be called love, and one did not say good-bye to it without pain.

By September of 1946 the British had closed down the hospital at Elleniko, and two of our college buildings had been sufficiently repaired to be usable for administrative offices and classrooms. Students were bused in every day, since boarding facilities were not yet ready. Most of our American personnel, however, moved into rooms on the second floor of another building only partially restored; the ground floor had no glass in the windows, though we carefully locked the doors each night. Situated close to the sea with Mt. Hymettus behind us, we were not yet disturbed by the low-flying planes entering and leaving the airport next door. (In the 1960s, air traffic had increased so greatly that the airport took over the campus and the college was forced to leave its lovely spot and move inland.) A year after my arrival, although the physical signs of war were gradually disappearing, things were still far from normal. Almost none of the neighboring bombed houses had been touched. When we went swimming, we walked out on the German-built landing piers. A field nearby was filled with parts of abandoned tanks. Not far from the college entrance gate stood an old pill box, now converted into a comical-looking little bar. Each morning the students, walking from the buses to their classrooms, passed German war prisoners who had been brought to help with the cleaning up and rebuilding; their headquarters for the day was one of the old army huts that still cluttered the campus.

Ten of us, plus an infant, lived in close community that year. Six were Americans: Julie Hodges, originally from England, was another American Board recruit who had arrived a little after Eilene and me; she had been with us for most of the previous year. Christine Osborne came now for two years, by special arrangement with Scripps College, from which she had just graduated. The two years stretched into an indefinite stay for her that still continues. She married Alcibiades Kalopothakis, editor of one of Athens' leading newspapers. Gertrude Ford officially worked with an organization sponsored by the American Friends, but she taught a little at Pierce on the side; she exemplified all that I have come to admire as characteristic of Quakers. Jean Davis, a one-year visiting professor of sociology from Wells College was more easily upset by the uncertainties of Greek life than the rest of us; she surpassed us all in the concrete benefits she bestowed, arranging for scholarships, etc., to enable some of our students to continue their education in America. Of the four Greek adults two were faculty members: Marika Pikramenou, who taught chemistry, and Sophia Meria, in English. Sophia had obtained permission to bring with her to live in the college her husband, their tiny daughter, and a woman who looked after the baby while her parents were at work. Sophia, who had been born in Turkey, inevitably announced that Stamos, the only man, was "our husband" and the rest of us his harem. Stamos, the soul of propriety, went along with the joke. In truth, their presence somehow cemented us as a family. Henceforth, even though employed at an American school, I never had the feeling, as I sometimes did at the British YWCA, of living in an enclave.

In the spring of 1947, I happened to meet in Athens the editor of *Ethnikos Keryx* (the *National Herald*), a newspaper published in New York for Greek Americans. He asked if I would like to do a weekly column for the paper's English section. I wrote thirty-three of these, at which point I asked to be released from the commitment because of the pressure of other activities and because I felt I was running out of inspiration. In my column, "From Week to Week in Greece," taking a different topic each time, I recorded rather lightheartedly my reflective impressions of the life around me. The articles are, in many respects, period pieces, and not only because of echoes of the recent war. The Athens of that date, when traffic was more likely to be blocked by a donkey cart than by sheer congestion, would be entirely unfamiliar to a present-day Athenian. One week I presented ideas some of us had as to how Greece might develop its virtually untapped tourist resources, a hope that has been overfulfilled.

In reading today my yellowed copy of these pieces, I am struck by several things: Most obvious was my intense love for this country and its people. Naively I expressed the wish that as my readers in the U.S. were Greek Americans, I wanted to think of myself as an American Greek. Naturally I could not be enthusiastic about everyone and everything. I encountered a fair number of civil servants whose sole mission seemed to be to obstruct. Bureaucratic red tape rivaled, perhaps even surpassed, what I had known at home. I could not approve of the endless civil conflict. Nor of the situation of women. Patriarchal patterns were deeply entrenched. Although women could vote in local elections, they could not vote in the national, parliamentary ones. (Full suffrage for women did not come until 1952.) Male jokesters liked to tell me the worn-out story of how a former government had considered a law allowing women to vote but rejected it. The reason supposedly was that it would grant the privilege only to women over thirty and no woman would admit to being qualified. On the other hand, a few women's associations were already working for equal voting rights, and many women held worthwhile jobs, sometimes out of economic need, but often because they found the work rewarding in itself. In most respects I admired—or, at the very least, found intensely interesting—the life around me.

Avid to know and to understand, I sought to pin down characteristics that were distinctively Greek; I delighted in every detail of local color. Even the most everyday things were fascinating. For illustration, choosing almost at random, I will quote here from one of my newspaper reports called "Riding the Suburban Buses."

Leaving Athens is fairly easy since the Greeks use the queue system most democratically; but coming into Athens is quite a gamble.
The driver may stop and he may not. It depends on how many
people are already on the bus and how many are waiting. . . . All
drivers seem to have a particular aversion to people carrying suitcases, and I have known them to refuse to allow travelers to get on
thus laden. I don't know why since suitcases seem to be the only
things which cause objection. Many times I have scratched my
legs climbing over huge market baskets. Once I stood on top of a
folding bed. I have had my face brushed by a bouquet of roses and
by an armload of leeks. At Easter time there were countless people
on board with a lamb. . . . My own private ambition is to ride from
Peiraeus some day with a freshly caught octopus dangling from
one arm. . . . There are many little things which may happen to
vary the trip. Recently there was a man carrying a bouquet of
flowers. The conductor proceeded to remove enough to give one
blossom to everyone on the bus. The customer at first protested,
then smiled and accepted thanks as though he first had thought of
the idea. . . . Most of the buses are of pre-war vintage. During the
war they were used to transport troops to the Albanian front and
to bring the wounded back to Athens. Considering the state of the
mountain roads over which they traveled, I wonder that they can
hold together at all now. As a rule, they have either no glass in the
windows or broken panes, and the roof is too low for a person
more than five-feet-two to stand comfortably. . . . Even with my
scant Greek I enjoy the friendly willingness of everyone to talk
with me. When other passengers hear me with my false accent
giving the name of my destination, they immediately take a personal interest in seeing that I get off at the right place. Once when
a friend and I protested because the bus was not going to the place
named in the sign outside, the whole busload joined in our spirited complaint and demand for reform. . . . When I met someone
who came from the same village as the Greek who married my
third cousin in America, the bond we formed was unbreakable!

The motif most often repeated in these articles was my appreciative
awareness of the degree to which ancient Greece still lived in the present. Geography was the most obvious link, reinforced by nature. I can
attest for a fact that the frogs in rural Greece say "brekekekex koax," as
Aristophanes represented them, not "chug-a-rum" or whatever it is that

frogs croak in the United States. My sense of continuity sprang from more than topography. I was not so idiotic as to believe that every Greek was linked by blood to those of the classical era, a view no more sustainable than the opposing declaration by a leader of Yugoslavian Macedonia that living residents of Greece are *not* descended from the ancient ones. Before going there, I had read of the seeming endless incursions of tribes out of the north from the time when the country was part of the Roman Empire, the later temporary occupations by invaders from Italy and elsewhere in western Europe, and the centuries of total domination by the Turks. There is no history of an uninterrupted cultural tradition in Greece any more than of a distinct racial inheritance. One must be careful, though, not to assume a total cleavage between ancient and modern Greeks. In the monasteries, in the Medieval period, there were still some efforts to preserve ancient knowledge as well as precious manuscripts. Our contemporary scholars have begun to recognize the modest but significant contributions to Renaissance learning that came from Greeks in the Eastern half of the Mediterranean world. During all those centuries, there was never a time when there did not exist a large group of people, in Asia Minor as well as on the Greek mainland, who considered themselves Greeks, held together by their language, by their common religion, and by the fact that they inhabited an area they believed to be the land of their ancestors.

It was with this kind of continuity in mind that, from the beginning, I felt that ancient Greece was figuratively a backdrop to the modern scene as the Acropolis was literally. Unlike some Hellenophiles, I never made the mistake of looking at contemporary Greeks solely in terms of their relation to the past, either sentimentally as if they were incarnations of the ancients or disdainfully as latecomers who had nothing of their own to offer. I recall, from a subsequent visit, how angry I was with Edith Hamilton on the occasion when she was publicly presented with the symbolic key to Athens. Speaking emotionally of her awe at being made a citizen of the city so splendid in history, she said not a word in acknowledgment of the modern nation, nothing about its cultural achievements, not even a formal expression of appreciation for its having undertaken to produce the ancient dramas in the restored outdoor theater in which she was standing. I myself worked hard to become acquainted with modern Greek authors, and the results were rewarding. I was interested also in the folk arts and traditional songs and national dances that the Greeks were intent on preserving. But two things combined to insure that my experience was constantly colored by awareness of the past in the present. One was the simple fact that I *was* a classicist, always on the lookout for what still existed from the remote past, whether a material object, a linguistic pattern, a religious practice, or an intangible attitude that would pass by unnoticed by nonclassicist visitors. The other factor was the attitude of the Greeks themselves. Whatever may have been the attitude of the average Greek toward the ancient heritage in the long period of darkness, modern Greeks have an acute sense of themselves as heirs of a tradition going back to mythological times. This is true not only of the highly educated. The anthropologist Ernestine Friedl, in a study of a comparatively isolated community, *Vasilika: A Village in Modern Greece*, comments on the tremendous pride the villagers took in being Greek. Not only did they take for granted a historical continuity that linked them directly with antiquity. They believed firmly in the existence of definite ethnic traits they shared with the ancients, and they took delight in pointing out links between themselves and characters in Homer's *Odyssey*. However unscientific and unhistorical such claims may be, the convictions were deeply entrenched. What Friedl describes for a rural settlement in the mid-fifties I discovered, with variations, ten years earlier. Not many of my Greek friends would have insisted on anything resembling an inherited national "character." All cherished a feeling of enjoying a special link with the historically famous Greeks of the past. They and those of my American friends who shared my special interest in ancient Greek civilization took pleasure in discovering actual carryovers, when they were demonstrably there and, on occasion, playing whimsically with resemblances that could equally well be real or purely fanciful.

Trivial but interesting was the obvious sameness of proper names; I delighted in having my class list filled with such names as Athena, Aphrodite, Demeter, Andromache, Iphigenia (no Clytemnestra, as I recall). As a classicist, I was fascinated by what had happened to the Greek language. Despite many words borrowed or changed in meaning and the radical alteration in what scholars believe to have been the original pronunciation, it is hardly an exaggeration to say that modern Greek is essentially a modified and greatly simplified version of ancient Greek. Even new syntactical usage, such as replacing the infinitive by *na* (from "*hina*," "in order to") with the subjunctive, is a recognizable change. Although I could never claim to be really fluent in modern Greek, I found it much easier to deal with the language than my nonclassicist associates did. Frequently, when at a loss for the correct word, I used an ancient one; sometimes evoking amusement, I was usually understood.

One interesting phenomenon was the coexistence of old and new forms in strictly defined usage. Thus the suffix *poleion* (from the ancient word for "sell") appeared on shops, attached to the classical name of the product, although the product itself was popularly designated only by the new term. We ate *psomi* (bread), but bought it from an *artopoleion,* got our *krasi* (wine) from an *oinopoleion,* and tried on *papoutsia* (shoes) at an *hypo-dematopoleion.*

Modern Greek regularly uses the plural form to designate a language (because a language is a collection of letters, I wonder?). In the case of Greek, the present custom may be said to reflect reality. When I was there (this is still true in some contexts), there was a sharp cleavage be-tween the popular language, Demotiki, and Katharevousa ("purified" Greek). The latter was the result of an official action taken by the Greek government in the nineteenth century to attempt to halt the "deterio-ration" of Greek by fixing the limit at which natural change was ac-ceptable. Theoretically, Katharevousa remained the written language of official documents and scholarly writing, and Demotiki the language spoken or sung. Novelists and poets worked in a no man's land, bor-rowing from both and recombining into new forms. By the time I came to Greece, the issue had become highly politicized. In my column, I pondered,

> Do the conservative politicians tend to think more in Kathare-vousa, or does using Katharevousa for official papers make them more conservative? In any case, it must be a tremendous choice for a Greek parent. "Shall I teach my child Katharevousa and have him read only Rightist papers or Demotiki and have him read only Leftist? Or shall I teach him both and run the risk of confusing him at an early age by the discovery that he can't believe every-thing he sees in print?"

When the conservative government of that time endeavored to enlarge the sphere of Katharevousa, the officers of our college student govern-ment resigned rather than be forced to use the possessive form auto-dik*iseos* instead of the popular autodik*isis.* Standing apart from their po-litical views, many critics hoped and believed that writers would gradually blend the vivid simplicity of Demotiki with the wider vocabu-lary and syntactical possibility of Katharevousa, creating a language they claimed would be unparalleled in its expressiveness. Meanwhile, I took pride in ceasing to confuse such words as *marouli* (lettuce) and *moulari* (mule).

Almost as obvious as the continuity in the language were the carryovers in religion, visibly evident in a lintel or column from an ancient
temple embedded in a Byzantine church standing on the same site. The
village priest came with incense to purify our college buildings in a ritual reminiscent of purificatory ceremonies thousands of years old. In
shrines or churches dedicated to a Christian saint, grateful worshipers
left metal representations of a healed limb or other organ, just as clay
replicas of bodily parts had been dedicated to Asclepius, the Divine
Physician, or Apollo the Healer. And a host of other examples have
been cited by historians of religions.

I wondered, half-seriously, whether the old custom of consulting an
oracle still remained; this was when Jean Davis's sociology students used
money from their class treasury to consult a fortune-teller the day before their final examination. Since the woman knew no English, she said
she was unable to read the typed questions that her inner eye could see,
but she indicated with her hands the parts of the text from which they
were drawn. Girls who concentrated on these sections claimed to have
benefited. When I suggested that my students take a test under the conditions of an honor system, there was an outcry of protest, not because
personal honesty was not a virtue, but because the ethical imperative to
help one's friend had priority. It would be far-fetched to hint at the
influence of Odysseus. Still . . .

This was "the best and the worst of times" for viewing the archaeological treasures. None of the great museums was open yet to the public;
in fact, most of the portable, priceless art objects stayed in their hiding
places until after the civil conflict was ended, after I had left Greece.
But, to compensate, there were no crowds. A few visitors walked on the
Acropolis, but there were no protective barriers, no scaffolding. In other
spots, I and whoever was with me were frequently by ourselves. Often
we entered by an unlocked gate; sometimes we climbed over the fence.
Only once were we accosted inside. This was when a guard unexpectedly
wandered by the Queen's megaron at the Palace of Knossos on Crete.
Smiling, he told us to call him when we were ready to leave so that he
could unlock the gate for us. At Epidaurus, Eilene and I spent a whole
day, seeing of other living creatures only a flock of turkeys that strayed
into the theater. Our group of Americans had a proclivity for indulging
in activities that seemed to us appropriate to the setting. In Kerameikos,
the historic cemetery, one of us read aloud from Thucydides' report of
Pericles' funeral oration, standing near the spot where tradition says the
newly fallen warriors were buried. We put on an impromptu pageant

to celebrate the Mysteries at Eleusis. In whatever appropriate place we found ourselves, we raced in the stadium, recited in the theater. We were not so absurd as to costume ourselves—except once. This was when Ralph Harlow, a retired visiting professor from Smith College, insisted that Eilene and I don sheets at Delphi and pretend to be officials judging the races—for the benefit of Ralph's movie camera. We got our own back. Ralph lived in hope of picking up one of the ancient *ostraka*, the clay shards that the Athenians used to vote to exile a politician. Finding, in the Agora, a small fragment of pottery (there were dozens lying around), we scratched on it the Greek letters for Ralph's name and quietly placed the shard, half buried, near where he was standing. He spotted it and, for a moment, thought he actually held an ancient ballot.

To explore in this fashion the famous sites now so formally enclosed and restricted (necessarily, of course) was an incomparable privilege. And, in spite of any seeming lightness in speaking of it, I was reverentially appreciative of what I was seeing. On my first visit to Delphi, a few of us arrived at night and stayed at the house where French archaeologists had formerly lived. The caretaker showed us the deserted sanctuary by moonlight. As I looked out afterward from my window, I said to myself in Greek, "My heart is at its home." The feeling was genuine though my expressing it aloud may have been a bit histrionic.

In Greece it was possible then (and still is, if one is lucky enough to have a Greek archaeologist as a friend) to go to out-of-the-way solitary sites that are especially privileged windows onto the past. I will speak of just one of these, which I visited in 1947 and described in one of my newspaper reports—Plato's cave. My friend Ero Nikolaidou and two of her sisters took me for a picnic near an unmarked cave high up in the mountains above Varkiza, on the coast south of Athens. This cave still held remains of archaic statues and inscriptions, one of which stated that the cave was sacred to Apollo and the nymphs. Was it really connected with Plato? As I wrote in my column,

This cave is a very special one inasmuch as some people think it is the one Plato knew. The story is that his parents took him as a child to this shrine and that the Muses, meeting them, placed Hymettos honey on his lips so that afterward he had the gift of sweet and melodious language. Later, runs the tale, Plato visited the cave, and the shape of it inspired him to write in the seventh book of *The Republic* the famous comparison between the prisoners in the cave and people who are bound by false belief or opinion. It

is true that the descent to this cave is steep and rough, as Plato
said, and its shape does suggest the idea of a low wall back of the
prisoners with a light above and behind.

Thinking of the ancient Greeks who used to come here believing the
cave to be the haunt of divine beings,

> I walked from the lighter entrance into the darker section. Sud-
> denly my head began to swim and my scientific outlook almost col-
> lapsed as I beheld coming toward me a nymph-like figure wearing
> a white dress of ancient cut and carrying a lighted torch. In the
> half-light and flickering shadows, it was a long minute before I
> convinced myself that it could *not* be. Then, of course, I realized
> that it was my friend Ero who, sympathizing with my desire to re-
> capture the spirit of another age, had decided to aid in strength-
> ening the illusion. . . . I have too much interest in modern Greece
> and hope for the future one for me ever to waste time lamenting
> the passing of earlier splendor. Just the same, it is a good thing oc-
> casionally to live in two ages at the same time.

The truth is that in those years I lived simultaneously in the two worlds
most of the time.

When I began my third academic year at the college, although the
main dormitory was still not ready for use, a few students came to
stay with us as boarders, most of them girls whose homes were away
from Athens. This was but one of many signs of returning normality.
Our situation was, in fact, paradoxical. Life in the cities was the easiest it
had been since the outbreak of World War II; many of the mountain areas were in the hands of guerrillas, Communist-controlled and aided by
the governments of Albania, Yugoslavia, and Bulgaria (so at least it was
charged). The last piece I wrote for the *National Herald* (December 1947)
expressed a feeling quite in contrast with the self-confident optimism of
earlier days.

> When I first came here in 1945, people were just beginning to add
> mountain village names [places of outstanding heroic action or ca-
> lamity in World War II] to the long list of Marathon . . . Thermo-
> pylae . . . Mesolonghi. Some spoke proudly, "The list is concluded
> now. We have peace." Others remarked, "We have come to the
> end of another chapter." Now we have begun the next chapter.
> Here in Athens we do not see the big events—only the everyday

accumulation of little signs to remind us that we are at war. Police permission is required if we are to go away from Athens and its immediate vicinity. The inflation is worse than at any other time since the occupation, and prices are higher. One is allowed to buy only restricted amounts of food at tavernas, and this time the law is really enforced. Places of entertainment must close early. In the emergency an antistrike law has been passed. Certain newspapers have been banned, their offices closed. Workers have been asked to contribute one day's salary to a fund for soldiers' families and refugees from war areas. A person going to the theatre is offered a slip along with his ticket. He pays a few hundred drachmas extra, proceeds for war victims. Solicitors for another campaign knock on the doors to ask for money for woolen goods for soldiers. School children have been given wool and asked to knit it into socks and sweaters. It is all a pattern bitterly familiar even without the deeper notes of sadness—news of relatives fighting, lost, captive, killed. Anxiety in hearts everywhere. And too many people feel that there is no hope that a solution will ever be found.

The last sentence is the most significant. I think that very few, if any, of my Greek acquaintances wanted the insurgents to win. But most of them had nothing good to say of the Royalist government (established in 1946), which they considered oppressive and fascist.

When Eilene and I arrived in Athens, we were determined that together we would learn to understand the political situation; we might as well have hoped for an interview with the goddess Athena. Still we tried. We read, we asked questions, we watched popular demonstrations. In those days, just after the war and even before the Truman Doctrine had gone into effect, the United States was very popular. On one occasion, however, we attended a demonstration, supported by all except the extreme Left, that was protesting against the Allies, believed by the Greeks at that point to be inclining toward the Albanian Chatza who, the Greeks feared, might lead a movement to take over north Epirus. The crowd was amazingly good-humored, even in its earnestness. Eilene and I joined in with the rest in shouting the Greek words for "Justice," "north Epirus," and, finally, "Shame on the Allies!" That was going a bit far. But then, I do not intend to run for President.

Strongly influenced by liberal publications in the United States, Eilene and I had both expected to find that popular sympathy would lie decisively with the recently defeated rebels. We quickly learned that we were mistaken. At least among the persons we met, no matter how liberal their theoretical commitments might have been, almost all condemned the leftist forces for the many atrocities of which they had been guilty. The personal accounts we heard of relatives gratuitously killed on both sides were many and horrifying. On the other hand, the majority of our acquaintances resisted the renewed polarization. A number of them pinned their hopes, vainly as it turned out, on the possibility that out of the proliferation of political parties there might emerge an effective coalition of the Centrists and the non-Communist Left. In our search for knowledge, Eilene and I brazenly went to a couple of offices and asked for information. One of these was the headquarters of a group that distributed an English language publication (propaganda sheet, if you prefer) in places where British and Americans were gathered (such as the British YWCA). Highly critical of governmental actions but not actually subversive, this seemed to the two of us, one-sided as it was, to be a useful second voice that foreigners ought to hear if not to heed. At the editorial office we found a group of attractive, idealistic young people who insisted they were against Communism but opposed the fascistic tendencies they saw all around them. For a short time we sent them suggestions for improving the translation of their material into English, for which they thanked us. I do not believe this group was a Communist front, but I will never know. I was reminded of them here at home by some of my students in the 1960s.

Although the hyperactive phase of our quest ("Diogenes with no lantern," Eilene called it) subsided into interested but passive observation, irruption of the political into our everyday lives was constant. As an example, the first winter in Athens several of us returning home one night saw two men with clubs chasing a third man. Two Greek men from our group ran to the rescue. They reported that the pursued claimed to be an innocent citizen, threatened by Royalists who disagreed with anti-Royalist sentiments. The attackers said that he was a Communist out on a nefarious mission. Whether either, neither, or both of these claims was the truth I could not tell. It was a first-hand encounter with the sort of thing we had heard was happening every night.

After the 1946 elections and plebiscite brought in first a rightist government and then the restored monarchy, life became more restricted. To an extent this was the natural consequence of the renewed fighting in the mountains and countryside. We realized how close this remote war had come to us when the police one day canceled the permission that had been granted us the day before to have a class picnic at a spot a little beyond the thirty-mile limit within which we could move freely. There had been a battle there the night before we were to go. Nobody could complain of this sort of protective prohibition. Other measures that were intended specifically to limit freedom of expression and even of thought were clearly oppressive.

Two instances touched us at Pierce College. A pupil in our gymnasium, the eleven-year-old daughter of one of our Greek teachers (the mother herself was not involved), was arrested for distributing antigovernment propaganda literature. She was held in a prison with convicted prostitutes and other women hardly appropriate as companions of a girl not yet in her teens. Eilene and I, with two of our Greek colleagues, requested an audience with Queen Frederika to ask for clemency. Eventually someone phoned from the Palace to say that we might come the next day and to give instructions as to how we should conduct ourselves in the presence of royalty. We practiced our curtsies and rounded up hats. Gloves were a problem, since we couldn't find a matched pair for Pitsa Poumbera. Finally, since we had been told to carry one glove so as to leave the right hand bare, Pitsa made do with two left-hand gloves of approximately the same color. The Queen received us graciously and quite democratically, advancing to shake our hands, not giving us time to curtsy. Queen Frederika, who was herself German by birth, not Greek, spoke excellent English. So informal was her manner that after an initial, clumsy attempt to use the third-person "Your Majesty," I (as did my companions) relapsed into "You." I am quite sure that we forgot to walk backward in withdrawing from the royal presence. Like most Americans, my commitment to democracy does not prevent my being impressed by the glamour of royalty and high aristocratic titles, perhaps for the very reason that they seem to belong to another age. From this point of view, my visit to the Palace was a great occasion, if not quite a peak experience. In terms of its purpose, it was a failure. After listening to us, the Queen said firmly that no child of eleven could have responsible political opinions, that the girl must have been a pawn for someone else, and she, Frederika, would look into the matter. Then, in what sounded like a prepared speech addressed primarily to the two Americans, she spoke of her wish to establish an equivalent of Boys Town in Greece and of her hope to get United States funds to help support it. Some time later we learned that the Palace had sent down to the prison an inquiry concerning Mrs. Economou's daughter, but that nothing further had happened. Eventually the political prisoners were housed together, and the mother told me that the children there were being well educated by some of the best professors in Athens, also prisoners. I left Greece without having heard anything more of the matter.

A second episode involved two of our faculty. In the late spring and early summer of 1947, I served as acting president of the college for two months while Kathryn McElroy was in the United States. After the term had ended, I was suddenly wakened one day at 5:00 A.M. and told that police had come to arrest two faculty members (a husband and wife), who happened to be staying temporarily on the college grounds. There was no specific charge against them. When I begged that at least the woman be allowed to ride in the front of the truck since she was pregnant, I was asked scornfully whether I thought the Communists would show any concern for her comfort. We soon learned that on this same morning several thousands of persons suspected of leftist leanings had been rounded up. Without trial they were taken to be confined on an island, the majority on Ikaria. Gradually, during the summer, individuals came up for trial and most of them, our teachers among them, returned to Athens.

The episode in which I personally and wholly innocently came under suspicion had its serious moments, but I remember it chiefly for its comic aspects. In this same summer, Christine Osborne and I took a trip through the Aegean Sea on our own, staying for two or more days on each of nine islands. Number eight was Santorini (ancient Thera), whose history probably gave rise to Plato's myth of the lost Atlantis. Later archaeological excavations conducted by Professor Marinatos in the late 1960s uncovered remains of a flourishing civilization comparable to, but significantly different from, that of Crete in the mid second millennium B.C. The volcanic eruption that destroyed it left standing only pieces of the outer crescent of the original island; they look down on the deep harbor in the center of which a queer black deposit shows where the cone of the volcano once was. Our arrival at Santorini was appropriate to this bizarre place. Scheduled to arrive at eight the previous evening, our ship, already late, inexplicably put in at Ios, an hour and a half away, a tiny island inhabited but without electricity, and stayed there at anchor until 3:00 A.M. Arriving at our destination at dawn, tired and a bit bewildered, Christine and I arranged to get ourselves and our light luggage up the long ascent with the aid of a driver with two donkeys and a mule. We checked in at the first hotel we saw. Attempting to get some sleep, we found ourselves being eaten by bedbugs, my only such experience ever at a hotel in Greece. So we moved to another, and somewhat better one, called the Vulcan. Long afterward I read in Beauvoir's autobiography that she and Sartre and Bost had stayed there in 1937. Today Santorini is second only to Mykonos in the throngs of tourists it attracts. A funicular has replaced the donkeys for utility purposes. (Sensation seekers can still ride the animals for fun, if they are so misguided.) When Christine and I were there, the barren island supported only a tiny population, and that not very well. Arriving a bit late for lunch one day, we found the only open restaurant in the state of Mother Hubbard's cupboard, literally with nothing left, not a piece of bread, not an egg, not an olive. The owner informed us that we must let him know ahead of time if we planned to eat there so that he could get in the food necessary.

That first day, not knowing quite what to do with ourselves, we walked down the long set of steps to the beach for a swim. There we saw a number of people idly enjoying themselves. Two young men, Athenians, introduced themselves and offered to show us the classical ruins at the other end of the island. We spent a delightful day with them, though Christine always referred to our walk of several hours with no food and in a wind so strong it blew my glasses over the cliff, as the Bataan Death March. We were somewhat startled when our companions informed us that they were exiled leftist officers (not Communists, we were assured), confined to Santorini. (A remote island can easily be made a prison without bars.) Back at our hotel we found a written order for us to come at once to police headquarters. We had, in fact, broken the law. In the confusion of our delayed arrival, we had totally forgotten to sign in with the police as we had faithfully done on every other island. Though annoyed, the official seemed to accept our apologetic explanation and asked us if we knew that our new friends were among a group of captives on the island. We assured him that we had just been so informed. The Fates conspired against us. Ships called only occasionally, and ours failed to show up on the day scheduled so that we had to stay several days longer than we had planned. Meanwhile, since we had not been told not to associate with the Athenians and since none of the local residents made overtures to us (as they had done on the other islands), we continued to spend time with the two of them. One evening we went with them to the house where they stayed, listening to records on an old windup phonograph. (Improbable though it may sound, so far as conduct was concerned, we might have been on a double date on the Wilson

College campus.) A few of the other exiles made friendly approaches to us, sending glasses of wine to our table, buying us a sweet, or sitting a while just to talk. On our last evening we expressed our gratitude by inviting these several men to be our guests at the taverna. Suddenly the chief of police and his assistant looked in on us. We offered each of them a glass of wine and proposed a toast to Greece and all friends of Greece. The police drank, the others did not. Our departure from Santorini was marked by a landslide that injured the man who had invited us to accompany him in the descent to the harbor. Fortunately for us, we had thought he was going too early. Christine exclaimed, as she had on several occasions during our adventurous island hopping, "O Lord, for what worse disasters hast thou preserved us this time?"

Sailing away, we thought that this was the end of the Santorini stay, but there were two or three more paragraphs. When the time came for all of us American teachers to renew our work permits, Christine and I were summoned to a police office in Athens and closely interrogated (Why, out of the dozens of Greek islands, did we choose to go to Santorini? Why didn't we travel in the Ionian Sea instead of the Aegean?) and scolded (as foreigners we must be careful to associate with the honorable members of Greek society, not seek out the worst). Our permits were renewed, but grudgingly. This was but a prelude.

When Stella, one of our student boarders, invited me to spend Easter weekend at her home in Larissa, in central Greece, I went to the police office near Elleniko for the required permission to travel. Here, asked to sit in a chair facing a strong light, I was subjected to a truly rigorous questioning as my interrogator set forth the full case against me: At Santorini I had used Greek, in the Athens station only English. Did I know Greek better than I pretended? (This, at least, was flattering.) Everything indicated that Christine and I were probably Communist agents. We had come into the village without signing in with the police, and we had moved from one hotel to another one, where we took a room next to an exiled colonel (this was news to me). On the first day we had made contact with two enemies of the State, had spent a day in their company away from all witnesses and an evening at their lodgings. We had talked with several other exiles. The policeman concluded by saying that the Santorini report stated that the police there were unable to decide whether Christine and I were Communist agents or prostitutes. My attempt to suggest a third alternative was brushed aside; it had to be either/or. Although I refused to accept one or the other of the two labels,

the fact that I finally received the travel permit suggests that the policeman settled for the nonpolitical one. I have never added that briefly held
professional status to my resume.

My stay at Larissa brought an ironic conclusion. Anxious to comply
with every letter of the law, I told Stella's father at the airport that I must
report at once to the police. No rush, he said, he would take my papers
down to his friend the next day and have him sign my exit permit as
well so that I would not have to bother later. On Easter Sunday I went
with Stella and her family to a picnic dinner given by the commander of
the local military headquarters. As we ate our spitted lamb and enjoyed
the national dances, led by the commander, some recently captured
guerrillas looked on from behind their wire enclosure, occasionally engaging in good-natured banter with the guests. I could have spoken with
them myself, if I had so desired. But I had no wish to do so and nothing
to communicate.

I have never felt more personally caught up in the movement of history
than during those critical years in Greece. If, however, I have given
the impression that I lived in the spatial equivalent of a time warp, that
is only partially true. In Greece I did, indeed, put on cultural blinders
with regard to most of what was happening in the rest of the world. But
on two occasions, once in each of our long summer vacations, I left the
country.

In June 1946, Eilene and I embarked on a trip of over two months
through the Near and Middle East. It began in not quite the way we had
planned. On the *Gripsholm* Eilene and I had met Walton Hart, vice-consul
at the American Embassy. He remembered us with many kindly acts,
helping us with our mail before we had regular delivery, and inviting us
to various Embassy receptions. At one of these, beholding our greedy
amazement at the variety and abundance of the delicacies on the table,
he took us behind closed doors and packed bags of food for us to take
back with us to our living quarters. Now, just after the end of our school
term, he presented us with his greatest gift, arranging a free ride on a
plane that was to take some military and State Department personnel to
Ankara. We had already intended to go to Turkey just then, as representatives from Pierce to a conference of American Board missionaries to
be held at the American Academy for Girls, at Scutari, on the Asiatic
coast opposite Istanbul. Ankara is an overnight train ride from Istanbul,
but that was an attractive alternative to the several days of bus and train

travel we were planning to Thessaloniki (our British friends were no longer there) and overland to Istanbul. The nine weeks we spent in and between Turkey and Egypt deserve a separate chapter; I restrict myself to a few remarks.

Turkey, unscarred by war and with endless fields of lush green, seemed to us at first vastly more prosperous than Greece. Closer observation in the rural areas showed conditions closer to those associated with the poorer parts of the Third World. On the outskirts of Tarsus, for example, the home of Saul/Paul, and for us the convenient location of another American Board school, were many people living in clay huts. In the stream that flowed through the village, people drew drinking water, bathed, scrubbed kitchen pots, and washed clothes; children swam, and domestic animals drank at the edge. It was at Tarsus, incidentally, that I heard an amusing piece of information. Contractors were putting notices in the paper, promising to pay for any remains of Roman pipe that anyone could find and bring in. These would be used in putting in a new water system. They were preferred to new ones because they were cheaper and would last longer. In Turkey, women did not wear the veil. Many worked in the fields, sometimes by themselves, sometimes along with the men. I noticed one odd couple walking along the road, he standing unencumbered, she bent C-shape by a load of wood she carried on her back.

Eilene and I were thrilled to see in Turkey the remains of civilizations older than Greek, as well as the great mosques, palaces, and treasures of the Turkish Sultanate. We did not forget the Greek sites. Troy was off-limits because it was located in a military zone. Other sites were much as we had found them in Greece, hard to get to, solitary, but open to our explorations. Ironically, I found Ephesus disappointing because there was so little to see, much still unexcavated, and the rest largely overgrown with weeds. On a visit in 1988, my companions and I saw an entire ancient city laid out before us, filled with visitors. Lest we lose each other, we agreed to meet in an hour at the library.

Travel conditions were often difficult, but it never occurred to us that it might be dangerous for two young women to be wandering around alone. Mostly we stayed at American schools, but occasionally we stopped at a hotel. At one in Bergama, we were startled to realize that a policeman had been sitting outside our room all night. A fellow guest, a Scotsman who was working in the area, told us that the man was probably there for our protection, adding that the Turkish police felt a great responsibility for foreign women travelers and that the local chief of police would probably be greatly relieved at our departure. This unobtrusive observation manifested itself on one other occasion, a time when, in order to change trains, we found ourselves spending the night in a small waiting room so dense with travelers that literally we could neither move nor sit (on the floor) without stepping on someone, or being trod on. At our train's arrival, we tried helplessly to push our way through. Suddenly two young men appeared and picked up our bags. "Follow us," they ordered, led us to our train seats, and left without uttering another word or seeming to understand our effusive thanks.

Lebanon I remember chiefly for the magnificent Roman temples at Balbek and for Beirut, which seemed to us then the closest equivalent to a thriving, peaceful American city we had seen since leaving home. In Syria, the museum at Aleppo overwhelmed us with its wealth of Sumerian, Hittite, and Assyrian finds. On the edge of the city we were delighted by the unexpected spectacle of a camel corps in from the desert and practicing formations for an upcoming review. In Damascus I at last saw the paintings from the synagogue at Dura-Europus. As we looked at them, we were approached by Professor Krölling from Yale, the scholar who had opposed Goodenough by arguing that the scenes depicted were wholly historical. We discussed the disagreement good-naturedly. (I believe that later scholarship has tended to blur the interpretative either/or.)

This being the year before the state of Israel came into being, we found Palestine under the uneasy control of the British, with Jerusalem in particular very like an armed camp. In Jerusalem, through our missionary connections, we stayed at the residence of a fundamentalist group, which each evening held a prayer service; everyone was asked to recite a verse from the Bible. From my childhood I recalled, "Behold, he that watcheth over Israel shall neither slumber nor sleep." This I recited with feeling, seeing in the verse something quite different from simple reassurance.

Besides delighting in visits to spots familiar to our imaginations since childhood—Jericho, the Sea of Galilee, Nazareth, Bethlehem, as well as Solomon's quarries and the traditional holy places in Jerusalem itself— Eilene and I were eager to learn all we could about the present situation. Under the influence of Ralph Harlow in Athens, we had become ardent pro-Zionists and came bearing introductions to some of Ralph's acquaintances who were working in Jerusalem. They received us kindly, showed us projects of sociological interest, talked of plans that might be put into effect if Israel should, indeed, become a state. Among other things, they took us to one of the Jewish collective settlements. The kibbutz that we visited was one of the more radically communitarian. I recall that I was favorably impressed by what was being attempted but reflected that my strong individualism would prevent my being happy in such an environment.

At one point, Eilene and I came close to being caught up in the conflict in Palestine—in the most innocent way possible. On an excursion to the Dead Sea, we stopped, like all tourists, to take a picture of the Jordan River, not realizing, however, that we were parked near to the Allenby Bridge, which had recently been the target of Jewish terrorists. Suddenly we were accosted by angry Arabs who accused us of being American spies, sent there by local Zionists. For a few minutes we fully expected to be arrested or, at the very least, to have our cameras confiscated. Luckily, our Arab driver persuaded the would-be arresters that we were only the harmless sightseers we claimed to be.

Ralph Harlow and the persons we met through him often referred to statements (and showed us copies of the papers containing them) in which the British and others of the Allies had definitely promised that land would be given to the Jews for what would become Israel. (I regret not being able to recall exactly which documents they were.) A little later, in Cairo, I invoked these sources in an argument with an American reporter I met there. To prove his claim that Arabs, not Jews, had a right to at least a large portion of the territory in question, he persuaded someone at the American Embassy to let him remove temporarily (and secretly) a copy of another official document, this one spelling out promises made by the British to the Arabs. Without question the two papers were incompatible. We gloomily concluded that empty promises had been given to both sides.

Providence was a little negligent in watching over Eilene and me as we tried to enter Egypt. On the train an official checking our passports told us that the visas we had obtained in Athens were outdated. The Egyptian consul in Athens had carelessly put in the wrong dates (in Arabic) so that we were about to arrive on the day indicated for our departure. At first we were told that we would be put off the train at the next stop and sent back to Jerusalem. Eventually this sentence was modified so that we got off at Kantarah, located close to the Suez Canal. There we spent the night in a locked waiting room, we trying to sleep on one bench, an Egyptian guard with a red fez on another. In the morning we obtained telephoned permission from Cairo to proceed. We both spat into the canal as we crossed it.

Egypt, still under King Farouk, showed extremes of wealth and poverty beyond what I had ever seen. At the American University, nearly empty in the summer, we had a room free except for twenty-five cents apiece to pay the servant who cleaned it and made our beds. We ate well at a nearby pension for well under ten dollars a day. A foreigner could live luxuriously for very little. The obvious poverty of great masses of people, many of them living in the streets, made even the inhabitants of the village at Tarsus seem enviable. Here women wearing veils were everywhere. Through one of the university teachers we met persons, some of them Egyptian, who told us of the unrest beneath the surface and of hopes for a social revolution. (This goal was, at least partially, achieved by the coming to power of Nasser in the 1950s.) Though we had been in other Muslim countries, it was in Cairo that I first became aware of how inextricably religion and politics were intertwined in the Middle East. As an example, a young Egyptian, a Copt with the famous name of Rameses, told me that he was going to change his name to a Mohammedan one and convert to Islam, not as a matter of faith, but because it was only as a Muslim that he could hope to play any effective part in Egyptian politics.

Needless to say, Eilene and I were excited by the remains of Egypt's past glory. Even in New York I had spent a disproportionately long time in the Egyptian section of the Metropolitan Museum. Here the riches seemed infinite. If any one experience reached a greater height than the others, I think it was our visit to Karnak, near Luxor. In the afternoon, Eilene and I, alone save for a guide, explored the temples and the surrounding grounds. After sunset the guide led us up onto the roof of the Great Temple of Amon, where we sat and watched the rise of the full moon that, once in the sky, seemed to be covered with a green phosphorescence. Nearby, Venus was encircled by a yellow corona. After we descended and were walking through the moonlit temple, my hand accidentally touched the arm of the statue of the seated god, still warm from the sun. For a moment I felt that I had an eery flesh-and-blood contact.

Eilene and I left Egypt feeling that we understood why Herodotus and his Greek contemporaries stood so in awe of Egypt, which they looked on as the source of both scientific knowledge and secret mysteries. We felt that we were ourselves increased in wisdom after the

weeks of travel. We looked different, too. Our friends exclaimed that
our skin was now pure yellow—from the Atabrine tablets we had taken
to ward off malaria.

With my second trip outside of Greece the next summer I just
missed my "appointment in Samarra." My years in Greece (1945–
48) saw the explosion of Existentialism in Paris. I knew nothing of it. I
cannot lay the blame on the cultural backwardness of Athens. Undoubtedly, if I had been interested, I might have found persons and articles to inform me of what was going on in other capitals of Europe. It
was I myself who chose to be wholly absorbed in things Greek. The
previous summer in the Near and Middle East had found me similarly
concentrated on the possibilities of my immediate environment. One
specific, unrecognized opportunity I had already passed by. One of the
first Americans I met in Greece was a friend of President McElroy, Mary
Coolidge, a philosophy professor from Smith College. In 1950 she published an influential article on Existentialism, relating it directly to James's
Pragmatism. While I do not know whether five years earlier she had already been reading Sartre, the possibility remains that I might, in the
course of that first fall, have become interested in what I heard of him
and moved to read his work, had Miss Coolidge and I conversed on any
subject save our immediately exciting environment. (It was she, by the
way, who told me that the British had fired the first shot in Constitution
Square.) I think also that Kathryn McElroy at one point mentioned that
she was reading something by Kierkegaard, but that she spoke of him as
merely an interesting, recent Christian theologian. The all but unbeliev-
able fact is that I was actually in Paris in late August/early September of
1947, where I spent two weeks with a friend from Northern Ireland
whom I had known while I lived at the British YWCA. We went to the
opera twice, haunted the museums, wandered around the Left Bank, visited Chartres and Versailles, even went to the Folies-Bergère. Neither
of us had any reason to inquire if something by Sartre or Camus was
playing at one of the theaters. Nor did we order a pernod at Les Deux
Magots. I traveled on to Switzerland and to Italy, then back to Greece,
without having seen or heard the word "Existentialism."

I have called the three-year period I spent chiefly in Greece an interlude. Its intrinsic value to me I cannot overestimate. I would go so far
as to say that if, out of all the years of my life, I were to choose three
consecutive years to be relived exactly as they had been, with no super-

imposed reflective insight, the stretch of time beginning with August 1945 is what I would choose. That is not the same, of course, as saying that these years are the ones in my life I would most want not to have missed. I recognize that this was not the most formative period for me, nor had I yet made the definitive move toward the outlook that has dominated the major portion of my already long life. I did not seek to renew my contract with the American Board. Pierce College did not offer quite the kind of academic career that I wanted, and I decided that I did not wish, on a permanent basis, to live as an expatriate. I knew that Greece would be forever my second country, but it was time to go home. And, still unknown to me, it was more than time to overtake my missed rendezvous.

FIVE

Engagement with Existentialism

A FLOURISH NOT OF TRUMPETS

I have always found a certain charm in the scholarly practice of using the Latin word *floruit* to say of someone whose precise birth and death dates are unknown that he/she "flourished" in, say, the middle of the second century; that is, this was the time when the person is known to have done whatever most distinctively defined that person's life. If I were to assign to myself a "flourishing," I would extend it over a long stretch of thirty-eight years—to be exact, from the fall of 1948 to my retirement in 1986. While this period did not lack important changes, it seems to me, at least retrospectively, to have been a unified and coherent whole. These were my Existentialist years, of course. (In this respect, 1986 does not mark an ending.) It was the time during which I most fully developed the potentialities I possessed both as teacher and as scholar-writer. Throughout, I felt that personally and professionally my life was integrated, without conflict and painful dilemmas. I was not an enemy to myself; I could face the inevitable external problems without self-created inner turmoil. I suppose that I should modify this claim just a bit. I was neither quite so exemplary a model of psychological adjustment nor so obnoxiously complacent as my words may have suggested. Between the peaks and midway in the high plateaus, there were even a few sloughs of despond. But, taking everything into account, it was a bona fide flourishing.

This time span, the heart of my career, does not fall naturally into temporal subdivisions. Although I do not intend to abandon narrative or to substitute ideas for events and people, still, a topical or thematic approach seems better suited to the complexity of what I am trying to re-create. Yet, even as I write this, I note once again that no scheme for recollection ever works out entirely neatly. Deciding to begin with the most overarching and integrative theme, my involvement with Existentialism, I realize at once that the story of my initial encounter and engagement with it is inextricably bound up with events of my professional and personal life in the first five years after I returned from Greece. Some of these, in turn, have implications and future developments more far-reaching than their tangential bearing on my discovery of a new philosophy. They will appear in this first account much like the subjects stated in the exposition of a musical composition, to be developed later. So I will begin with a chronological narrative and then depart from it.

This is enough of a fanfare. The scene is laid in Toledo, Ohio; the action begins, appropriately for a teacher, with a student's question.

ENCOUNTER AND ENGAGEMENT

In 1948, university teaching positions were more plentiful than they had been seven years earlier. I was able to choose among several possibilities. I selected the University of Toledo, primarily because my schedule would be half in Classics, half in philosophy. Normal teaching loads in those days were such that I taught as many courses in each of the two departments as would now be considered full-time in one. Each of my middle-aged chairmen was kind to me and resented, on my behalf, any attempt by the other to demand too much of me. (The two men hated one another as the result of a love rivalry back in the far past.) It was the philosopher, Gardner Williams, who played a decisive role in opening up new opportunities for me.

In an introductory course in philosophy, early in the second semester of my first year, just as the class was getting under way, a student, a woman whose name I no longer remember, asked me, "What is this Existentialism everybody is talking about?" I confessed uncomfortably that I did not know much about it but that, on the basis of what little I had read, it seemed to me to be a somewhat sensational attitude toward life and a philosophy of defeatism and despair. Afterward I felt ashamed, and not just because of having had to admit to ignorance. (*That* was an experience with which I was all too familiar.) For some reason I suspected that I was transmitting others' judgments, which might very well be false, and I sensed obscurely that I had failed to look into something which might be important to me. At once I went first to the library, then to the bookstore, and I began by reading whatever was available in

English. I can best describe my response with an old Quaker expression: The Existentialist writers, Sartre most of all, even at the start, "spoke to my condition."

I mentioned my new interest to Gardner Williams, with whom it seemed I never ceased talking philosophy. Perceiving my sense of happy discovery, he said, "Since you think that this new philosophical movement is so important, would you like to work on it this summer and fall and then offer a course on it next year?" I believe that the course I taught in the spring semester of 1950 was the first of its kind to be offered by a philosophy department in this country. The course itself was both terrible and wonderful. I realize today how dreadfully superficial my treatment of the subject was, how much of it derived from secondhand sources. I am sure that I would blush now if I were so unfortunate as to remember the specific inaccuracies of which I was certainly guilty. But the handful of students who took it evidently shared my excited sense of discovering a new and satisfying way of looking at the difficulties, the possibilities, and the responsibilities of the human condition. It was for all of us an awakening.

For the course, insofar as was possible in so limited time, I tried to introduce my students to both religious and humanistic Existentialism. (At this time, Sartre publicly linked himself with Heidegger as representative of the "atheistic" branch.) Very quickly I zeroed in on the three Parisians: Sartre, Beauvoir, and Camus. Just why did they, and Sartre in particular, speak to me so directly and forcefully? As I look back now, my response then seems both improbable and inevitable. On the surface, my family background, my professional training, my career as a Classicist would seem to point in the opposite direction. Looked at more closely, my previous history held all the threads necessary for weaving into this new pattern.

I was brought up on Jesus and William James. The latter had been instrumental in my deconversion, though not in the way James himself would have thought probable. But my interest in him had led me to read more extensively in Pragmatism, in the work of Dewey as well as of James. Other scholars, as well as I, have commented on the affinities of Pragmatism and Existentialism, though they have differed among themselves in their interpretation of the precise influence of the former on the reception of the latter in the United States. It has been argued both that Pragmatism prepared the American reading public for Existentialism and that philosophers here resisted Existentialism because they had ready at hand a more cheerful version of it. To mention only the most obvious points of resemblance, I was already familiar, thanks to James or Dewey or both, with the notion of relative truth, of truths "made" in a process of verification; I had been attracted also to the way that the Pragmatists, while sternly rejecting the existence of any discernible plan in human or cosmic history, placed a heavy emphasis on voluntarism and the need to work for social improvement—without either supernatural or self-evident natural support for its absolute rightness. If Pragmatism served as an intellectual preconditioning, the religious fundamentalism worked both positively and negatively. Humanistic Existentialism (my term) served as an antidote to the narrow irrationalism of evangelical Christianity while demanding even more in the way of self-responsibility. My inbred conviction that life is difficult and that I was accountable for what I made of my life remained intact; also the imperative that my actions should accord with what I authentically believed. I may add that Sartre's propensity for utilizing the old theological concepts and metaphors, even as he assigned new meanings to them, reinforced my sense that he was recasting my childhood teaching in an acceptable form. Certainly his insistence that we must create our own values came to me as a message of liberation, not a counsel of despair. I saw it as an optimistic challenge to action. I suppose, too, that my practice of viewing my life as marked by a series of conversions aided in my willingness to move in a new direction.

My having taken a Ph.D. in Classics is perhaps harder to fit in. Some of my acquaintances have marveled that as a classicist I could ever come to feel at home with Existentialism. But as Sartre pointed out, we ourselves designate (if we do not invent) the particular causes and motives that prompt our actions. If I consider my classical training as *predisposing* me to being receptive to Sartre, Beauvoir, and Camus, I find several points relevant: Most obviously, though maybe not of primary importance, these three writers all had the sort of education that led them to use classical images and to sprinkle throughout their work a wealth of references to Greek figures; e.g., Sisyphus, Prometheus, the House of Atreus, Medusa, Pyrrhus, and Cineas. As I mentioned earlier, Camus and I both wrote dissertations on Plotinus. More subtly, I think that the Greeks' concept of philosophy itself was not foreign to the way the French writers viewed it. In their own way they were equally trying to describe our existential condition and to define the authentic life. Even the high value the Greek philosophers placed on reason unites more than it separates them from the French Existentialists. Sartre's dialectical reason differs radically from Plato's and Aristotle's contemplative reason, but Sartre himself has pointed out—and criticized—the excessive rationality of *Being and Nothingness.* Camus paradoxically tried to establish a "logic of the absurd." Finally, my classical orientation had accustomed me to disregard or to downplay the distinction between philosophy and literature and to see how they often worked together. And with Sartre, just as with Plato and Aristotle, the line between philosophy and psychology, if it exists, never serves as a barrier.

There was a new factor as well. Gardner Williams was writing his book, *Humanistic Ethics.* He may have exaggerated in stating in the "Acknowledgments" that he owed to me "a very special debt for the final, indispensable, and drastic revision of the entire manuscript." We did indeed discuss it all in detail. While we disagreed about some things, I accepted his basic premise: that one could write meaningfully about ethics without appealing to metaphysical certainties or any kind of absolute values, and about social responsibilities and community even if assuming individual self-interest as a starting point. (I could not quite stomach Williams's term "egoistic hedonism.") Williams neither challenged Freud nor made much of him, mentioning him only twice: once to question the assumption that love and sex are similarly expressions of the same libido, once to observe that if we are to live happily, we should seek to know as much about the subconscious as possible. Williams undoubtedly helped me to sharpen my own thought in areas where we were in basic agreement. What I felt was missing in his book was a view of consciousness that would support the responsible freedom on which his position depended. The nature of the self and the status of what we glibly call self-knowledge were what primarily interested me. Dissatisfied with Freud and Jung, I still saw no way to get around them. When I came across Sartre's description of consciousness, I welcomed the theory as being exactly what I had been groping toward, though, I hasten to add, I am under no illusion that I would in time have succeeded in formulating it.

Sartre, in particular and specifically, spoke to my condition by providing a philosophical theory that gave foundational support to convictions that I had held without being able to justify them except in the way one subjectively takes certain values to be self-evident. Most of all, he appealed to my strong individualism, especially to my reliance on the notion of self-determination, both as starting point and as goal. His view that the ego is the product of consciousness and not part of its structure came to me not only as the solution to an intellectual puzzle but as an enlightening explanation of the peculiar sense I had of my own personal reality. I had always felt that I carried around with me a self-structure that was a burden without being a recourse. It was liberating to me to think of consciousness as distanced from its own creation, capable of assuming a new point of view on it and of altering it. Sartre's concept of the self made sense to me. It had never seemed to me that self-realization was a matter of discovering and fostering a true self that lay buried inside, like the oak in the acorn. I had never liked the idea either; I found it to be just one more version of determinism. That we make ourselves by our own pattern struck me as descriptively correct. The notion that the self belongs to an ego which consciousness creates is, of course, complex and controversial. I will return to this point in a later context.

What are usually considered the negative aspects of Sartre's ontology—our epiphenomenal upsurge in a universe incommensurate with our human desire for purpose and meaning, the lack of any external absolutes to guarantee the rightness of our actions—these corroborated what I already believed. I especially liked Sartre's denial of a determining human nature, something which his description of consciousness made it possible for me to accept. All of these things, far from diminishing the dignity of the human individual, in my eyes, enhanced it.

Two consequences of Sartre's claims that consciousness is self-creating activity were of particular significance in my response. Ethical concerns are implied in all of his work. Most specifically in his lecture *Existentialism Is a Humanism*, he developed the idea (or, if "developed" is too strong a word, he suggested it) that if we want to live authentically—i.e., consistently with the truth of our human condition—we must individually create our own ethics, that since we are responsible for the selves we have made and are making, we must answer for them, at least to ourselves. Less clearly expressed but implicit in his declaration that in choosing for ourselves, we choose for humankind, I heard the plea for the need to develop collectively an ethics appropriate to all of humanity that would not violate individuals' freedom to establish their own value systems. A humanistic ethics I would have called it then, despite Sartre's sometimes sarcastic comments about traditional humanism. If Sartre ever succeeded in this attempt to develop a collective ethics, it was posthumously. I made my own feeble effort in the sixties, in *An Existentialist Ethics*, a work that glaringly demonstrates the gap between intention and achievement.

A second consequence of Sartre's ontology was probably the most meaningful for me personally: the absolute equality of all self-making individuals. Farther down the line I would become aware of the difficulties attendant on a politics of equality. In the forties, Sartre's concept

problem of dualism/
Kantian choice?

of a free, self-determining for-itself gave the lie to all claims of a natural superiority or inferiority based on race or sex. My ultraliberalism abhorred all racism. While I had succeeded in establishing myself as a professional woman in a man's world, I resented both the objective limitations imposed on women's aspirations and the attitude that as a woman I must either conform to prevailing patterns of "femininity" or be considered deficient for failing to fit them. My embryonic feminism found its justification in Sartre's ontology. More than that, Sartre's insistence that traditional value systems and social prescriptions were purely human inventions and, most important of all, his claim that by our collective actions men and women themselves define what "humanity" is and will be seemed to clear the way for a truly open future and, among other things, for the total transformation of the field of possibilities for women. That I was guilty of a certain naivete I do not deny, but this is how it seemed to me then. Greatly as I admired Beauvoir's *The Second Sex* and much as I learned from it, the book did not come to me as a revelation. I found in it rather the logical, expected corollary to *Being and Nothingness*. (I am speaking only of my initial reaction and do not mean this statement as my final judgment on the worth of Beauvoir's contribution.)

If, instead of stressing the way in which my personal outlook made me receptive to Sartre's philosophy, I were to point to those ideas of his which appealed to me strictly intellectually, I suspect that my list would not greatly differ from that of most Sartrean scholars. But along with such obvious matters as his acute analysis of the mechanism of "bad faith" (the lie to oneself), the infernal aspect of human relations, the role of the imaginary, and the magical nature of emotional behavior, what attracted me especially was a certain underlying coherent unity in Sartre's thought. Though it was years before I felt that I adequately grasped the interconnections of the various parts of his philosophy, I sensed the presence of a unifying motif from the beginning. I refer to the constant interplay of the subjective and the objective in our ambivalent existence as both being and nothingness—as it is seen in the relations of consciousness to the ego, in the tension between facticity and transcendence in bad faith, in the subject-object conflict in human relations, even in the three dimensions of the body. But I am getting too far from my account of my early encounter with Existentialism and of the circumstances surrounding and leading to my undertaking to translate Sartre's *Being and Nothingness*, the decisive turning point in my career. It is time to return to my narrative.

I begin with a seeming digression. One of the members of the class in

Existentialism was Doris Schwalbe, a graduate student who had returned to the University of Toledo, from which she had taken her B.A. in English a few years earlier. After a stint in the Navy, in World War II, she had taken on a couple of odd jobs in California; she had worked as a clerk in the Orange County assessor's office and also, as she likes to boast, as a packer of oranges. Now she was studying for a degree in education to qualify her to teach in the public schools. With room in her schedule for electives, she chose to take first-year Greek, which I was teaching, and in the following spring, the philosophy course. I had not seen more of her than of other students until the end of that term. At a weekend party on the shore of Lake Erie, to which another of my students had invited both of us, Doris and I came to know one another much better. In the summer we met frequently as friends and developed a close relationship that is still central in our lives. I have brought Doris in at this point because she, as well as Gardner Williams, was influential in urging me to continue my research in Existentialism and to write about it. With their active encouragement, I took the first step.

In April 1951, at Earlham College in Richmond, Indiana, at a joint meeting of the Ohio and Indiana Philosophical Associations, I read a paper called "Existentialism: Positive Characteristics." The title rightly indicates its superficiality. No matter. My presentation came first on the program; it dominated the discussion that day and the next. Whether favorably disposed or hostile, those present were evidently ready to take Existentialism seriously as a significant challenge to philosophical thought.

I am sure that it was at least in part owing to my contribution at this conference that I was offered for the following year an assistant professorship in the Philosophy Department at Ohio State University. I was overjoyed to accept, inasmuch as there had been unfortunate changes at Toledo. A new president of the university found it financially expedient to curtail existing programs. Among other cuts, the university would no longer offer any Classics courses; Williams henceforth would handle philosophy by himself. Some of my faculty supporters persuaded the president to keep me on in another capacity; I could have stayed as director of the evening school, a purely administrative job that I did not want. At OSU I would be wholly in philosophy. I joined the department in September.

That fall, I decided that I was far enough along to think of writing a book on Existentialism. In a letter to Philosophical Library, which held the copyright for many of the relevant books hitherto published in this country, I described my project. I cannot recall today exactly what my proposal was, but it must have focused primarily on Sartre, and perhaps on Beauvoir. And I think I was planning to emphasize matters relevant to ethics. As things turned out, it made no difference. In explaining what I had in mind, I felt that I had to establish my credentials. I said that I had been working with things available only in French and that with my training in translating Greek and Latin, I found it easy to translate this material. Rose Morse at Philosophical Library wrote back in essence, "When you have finished your book, we will be glad to have you send it to us. Meanwhile, you sound like precisely the sort of person we have been looking for to translate Sartre's *L'Être et le néant*. Would you be willing to do it? The royalty will be one percent." I must say that the last sentence was extremely misleading. I assumed that it meant one percent gross. When the first reckoning was made, I was informed that it was one percent net. I never did receive any significant amount from that publisher, and, I learned later, neither did Sartre. The most important return I received from Philosophical Library was written permission to quote *in perpetuum* from *Being and Nothingness*. Philosophical Library was not a respectable publishing firm, but it had the acumen to lead the way in publishing new texts in Continental philosophy. Fortunately, the prospect of monetary reward played no part in my decision. I knew that no sum I might get would compensate for the amount of work involved. I wanted to do the job because I thought it would be useful to others, and because I felt that I was not quite ready to write my own book and that to translate Sartre's major work would be the best possible way to understand it. I was quite casual about it all, never for a moment thinking of it as the step which would transform my entire academic career. Nor did I ask myself whether with only three years of badly taught high school French and one yearlong course in college, and with a bare minimum of background in philosophy, I was qualified to do the task. Had I raised the question, I might have had the good sense to say No. But without taking time to consider, I wrote immediately to say that I would be glad to translate *L'Être et le néant*. And I set to work.

This was, as I have said, the fall semester of 1951. As nearly as I can reconstruct the sequence, I completed the rough draft in the summer of 1954, spent the next year checking and revising it, then proofreading the typescript prepared by a local typist. ("It never did make any sense to me," she told me later.) I wrote my Introduction in fall 1955 and began reading galley proof early that winter. *Being and Nothingness* came out in June 1956. Philosophical Library very quickly put it on the remainder list in order to sell it at a more moderate price, not because there had been no demand for it, as some misinformed persons have claimed.

Four and a half years from the invitation letter to the day of publication might have been reasonable for the project if I had been free to devote myself to it full time. But these turned out to be, in many respects, the most unpropitious years possible. Except for the summer quarter of 1953, when I took leave without pay for health reasons, I was teaching a full schedule. Why did I never try to get a grant? Out of a combination of ignorance and stupidity. I had not been at any one university long enough to have earned a sabbatical; a program of faculty fellowships of the kind I enjoyed in later years at the University of Colorado was not yet available. It simply never occurred to me to apply to any of the national foundations. In the academic year 1952–53, two near disasters threatened to bring my work to a halt, if not to a full stop.

The first year at Ohio State had gone smoothly. For most of the fall quarter of 1952 I felt that life could not have been better. Doris, who had exchanged her teaching job in Toledo for one in Columbus, shared an apartment with me, and we had together found ourselves in the midst of a particularly stimulating and supportive circle of friends, both within and outside of the university. I had reason to believe that my teaching was recognized as being quite a bit above average. The translation was progressing steadily. And I had the exciting opportunity to air my views to the public in the state at large. The university radio station, WOSU, had an arrangement with the Philosophy Department by which one faculty member each quarter offered twice a week a fifteen-minute program designed to appeal to any listeners interested in philosophy. I called my program "Philosophy and Yourself"; for all practical purposes, it was an introduction to Existentialism. The public response to my talks was highly gratifying; it confirmed my feeling that I was onto something of more than strictly academic interest, and it gave me still more incentive for translating *Being and Nothingness*. Then, when I had just one week left to go, I suddenly had to see a doctor because of uncontrollable bleeding. Tests revealed that I had cancer of the uterus, that it had reached the stage when it would be foolhardy to postpone hospitalization. I canceled the remaining talks, arranged to have others take over my class work, and went into the hospital for several days of treatment with radioactive cobalt. The radiation left me too sick to do anything but suffer for a week. Doris was heroic. Besides taking care of me, she read my final examinations aloud to me and recorded the grades we managed to work out together.

Compared with the experiences of many cancer victims, even among the fortunate ones who have not tragically succumbed, my story was not very traumatic. The following quarter, although for several weeks I had to have debilitating X-ray treatments, I taught my classes as scheduled. (There was one day when I fainted in class and had to be driven home ignominiously by one of my students, but that was only because on that morning, on top of an X-ray treatment, I had badly pinched a finger in the car door.) The succeeding quarter, which I had free in any case, I had the follow-up surgery, and I recovered fairly quickly. All of this, though unpleasant, would have been tolerable if a quite different consuming anxiety had not come along in the midst of it.

It was not fear of death. Once again, if I were writing fiction instead of the arranged truth we call autobiography, I would link my close encounter causally with my philosophical commitment. One of the common motifs in Existentialism is, after all, the consequences of the sudden realization of one's mortality. But the timing was all wrong. With me cause and effect were reversed. One night, earlier in Toledo, in what was probably a preliminary manifestation of the condition that became cancer, I suffered severe hemorrhaging to the point of losing half my blood. Alone in the house, fainting when I tried to rise from the floor, I suddenly realized I was about to die. With no philosophical speculation at all, instead of seeing my past life pass before my consciousness as popularly one is supposed to do, I felt a sudden surge of empowering anger. How stupid it would be, I thought, to die simply because I could not get to the telephone. By force of will, I got there. Later, when I heard the diagnosis of cancer, accompanied by the doctor's assurance that I had a good chance of survival, I was distressed by the thought of all that I would have to go through, but I never at any time doubted that I would make it. My reaction may have been simply the usual unenlightened one, or perhaps I was less intelligent than others in refusing to entertain the notion of defeat. I am neither so naive nor so crass as to hold that one can overcome a disease by willing not to give into it. But insofar as a strong will to continue an existence one finds positive is a contributing factor to recovery, I had everything in my favor. It is ironic that one source of my increased zest for living was my work with the philosophy I had once carelessly labeled a gospel of despair.

What I did perceive to be a serious threat to my well-being was something unrelated to the state of my health. This was the notice I received in January, soon after my return to teaching, that I was without a job for the next academic year. When hiring me, the departmental chairman, Albert Avey, had said that I could expect tenure if my performance proved satisfactory (academic life then was still remarkably casual). Everett Nelson, who came in as chairman a year later to replace the retiring Professor Avey, told the three of us nontenured faculty that we must leave. To me he said that I had not published enough. Since I had not done the usual sort of academic research while I was in Greece, my list was indeed slim—four articles and four reviews, but I mentioned my current work on *Being and Nothingness* as perhaps significant. "That's only a translation," Nelson said. In any case, the interview was a charade. Nelson told senior faculty members, who pled that I might stay, that he had made it a condition for his coming to OSU that he should be allowed to replace all nontenured faculty in the department with analytic philosophers of his own choosing. I was angry but helpless. Some years later, when Albert Avey and his wife visited me in Colorado, over the breakfast table he made a most surprising statement, one that threw a new light on the whole situation. He told me that at the time when he first wrote to me, he had been directed by the dean to consider himself a caretaker chairman who would simply make what provisional arrangements he thought would most benefit the department until the new chairman took over. Proudly Avey said to me, "I thought then that the best thing I could do for the department was to hire people worthy of staying permanently." Fortunately, by July of the same year in which I was fired at OSU, I received an appointment at the University of Colorado. Now I look on the earlier loss as an example of what Doris and I like to call an "obligatory benefit," an unwelcome obstacle that turns out to have been a good thing.

Health problems, losing one job and moving to another, while no help to my translation enterprise, did not, in the long run, create as much difficulty as my publisher, Philosophical Library, did from start to finish. Rose Morse and Dagobert Runes, director or owner (I never quite knew which), rushed me relentlessly. When I was still in the early part of *Being and Nothingness*, Morse and Runes decided to bring out the chapters on "Bad Faith" and "Existential Psychoanalysis" in a preliminary volume with the title *Existential Psychoanalysis*. These sections I hurried through, out of sequence, before I had adequately established my terminology for the book as a whole. I wrote for it a popular sort of introduction. Doris and I typed this volume ourselves, on two different machines, and the publisher and printer accepted without demur what must surely have been the most unsightly manuscript ever submitted to them. It appeared in the fall of 1953. (I made some revisions in the translation before incorporating it in *Being and Nothingness*.) The pressure continued. The manuscript of *Being and Nothingness* never had any copyediting. The publishers were in such a hurry that by the time the last installment of galley proof arrived, straight from the printers, no editorial checking whatsoever had been done. A graduate student, Lynn Martin, read to me from my typescript while I looked at the proof. There was no time to check again with the French except when something sounded so very wrong to me that I looked it up. It is a wonder that the published work did not have more errors than it did. I do not know today whether I should call this undertaking a *tour de force* or a *folie à tous*.

During these years I never questioned the worthwhileness of the project nor wished that I had not committed myself to it. I had read only some sections of *Being and Nothingness* before starting to translate it. My slow movement through Sartre's ontology convinced me still more firmly of its validity. The chapters on "Bad Faith," "Concrete Human Relations," and "Existential Psychoanalysis" were refreshing oases where Sartre, in his examples, opened the door to everyday human beings more than in other parts of the book. And I gloated over those frequent extraordinary pronouncements, occasionally somber, sometimes preposterously funny: "Nothingness lies coiled in the heart of Being—like a worm." And "Man is a useless passion." But also, "Water skiing is the ideal limit of aquatic sports." "Slime is the agony of water." And "A good part of our lives is spent in plugging up holes." The sexist overtones evoked in Sartre's discussion of slime and of holes amused rather than irritated me, probably because, as I have indicated, I felt that his philosophy made feminism a natural consequence.

I had not corresponded with Sartre while I worked on the translation. When I finished it, I wrote to tell him of the fact and received a sort of "thank you" indirectly through his secretary, Jean Cau. In 1957 I sent a letter to Sartre, asking if I might see him in July when I planned to be in Paris. Cau wrote, giving me the dates for the time period when I might come for an interview. As it turned out, the dates were wrong. When I phoned, I was told by Cau that Sartre was just about to leave for Italy. I prefer to blame Cau rather than Sartre, but the fact is that I had sent a letter immediately on my arrival in Paris a few days earlier, which should have made a meeting possible. I never tried again, partly because I realized that neither Sartre's English nor my oral French was adequate for the kind of conversation I really wanted. Sartre was kind to me subsequently, however. He granted me unrestricted permission to quote from his work and to use passages from his plays and novels when I was making a television series, and he allowed me to have, and to quote from, a copy of his notes for the never written fourth volume of *The Family Idiot*. Simone de Beauvoir, whom I finally met in 1984, told me that she and Sartre both appreciated what I had done for them. (I will speak more of Beauvoir later.)

Now, forty years later, I ask myself, "Was it a good thing that I accepted the invitation to translate *L'Être et le néant?*" From my own point of view, the question is hardly meaningful. If I had not done so, I would now be an Other in a way far exceeding Rimbaud's and Sartre's "*Je* est un autre." My scholarly career was virtually re-created. To be sure, I could have written on humanistic Existentialism without doing the translation of *Being and Nothingness*, but not with quite the same authority, in the eyes of the public or in my own eyes. Yes, for myself my decision to translate it was certainly a good thing. I am grateful for the sequence of chance events that led to my being offered the opportunity.

I have tried to answer for myself, as objectively as possible, the harder question: Was it a good thing in itself? Would it have been better, in the long run and for others, if I had never written the letter to Philosophical Library and if *L'Être et le néant* had waited for someone else to translate it? Obviously, if Philosophical Library had found a person or persons better qualified than I, and if he, she, or they had completed and published a more accurate and readable version in June 1956, this would have been a far better thing. But I doubt that it would have been possible to produce a relatively perfect version in that time span unless, which is unlikely, the translator(s) had absolutely nothing else to do during those years. Of course, someone else (or I myself, for that matter) could have done a better job if given a few more years, which would have allowed for more consultation and collaborative checking. But would it have been better to have a superior *Being and Nothingness* come out in the sixties or seventies? My feeling today is that even a five-year delay would have resulted in the book's just missing the critical moment at which interest in Sartre's literary work and curiosity about French humanistic Existentialism had created a receptive public and that it might have deterred potential scholars. In any case, should I assume that someone else's translation, whenever it appeared, would necessarily have been preferable? Some translations of other works by Sartre I admire greatly, but I have seen some that are worse than mine.

Really, it all comes down to what I think of the work as it stands, and there my judgment is inevitably mixed. I certainly should not have included that ridiculous "Key to Terminology," which is inadequate when it is not misleading. I have not read my Introduction for many years, and I do not intend to reread it now. My feeling is that while it is not what I would write in the nineties, it was appropriate when it came out and is at least noninjurious to students. (I never assigned it to my own classes.) And the text itself? Most reviewers praised its clarity and readability. The *Times Literary Supplement* reviewer said I had failed to take the opportunity to rewrite the work so as to make it more accessible to English-speaking readers. This I took as a compliment. It was never my intention to rewrite Sartre. I did try to make his discussion clearer by breaking up some of his overlong paragraphs and overloaded sentences. I took particular pains with pronouns. I avoided using "it" in places where Sartre's masculine or feminine form identified the reference but English "it" would not. Sometimes Sartre's pronoun could have referred to more than one word. When I was certain what he meant, I repeated the appropriate noun. On the rare occasions when there was any doubt, I deliberately left the ambiguous "it" so that readers could decide for themselves.

Above all, I tried very hard to make the whole thing readable, as it is in French despite the difficult content. Basically, I think I succeeded in this. I take pride, too, in having established the English forms of Sartre's terminology; the result for the most part has withstood the test of time. Walter Kaufmann wanted to change "bad faith" to "self-deception," but this seems to me simply perverse. It makes it impossible to follow Sartre's play on the relation of bad faith to faith as such and to belief; it suggests that bad faith is identical with already familiar concepts of self-deception rather than a specific phenomenon, the explanation of which is inseparable from Sartre's ontology. I am more or less neutral with regard to the suggestion that instead of rendering *mobile* and *motif* respectively as "motive" and "cause," I should have paired, in English, "motive" with "reason." It is true that "cause" carries undesirable overtones of natural determinism. But "reason" seems to me to hold an implication of something's being rationally correct, which is equally inappropriate here. Of course, I should have used "intend" for *viser à* instead of the literal "aim at," a rather important slip on my part. Nobody, so far as I know, has commented on my changing the subtitle between the hardback and paperback editions from "An Essay on Phenomenological Ontology" to "A Phenomenological Essay on Ontology." For some forgotten reason I momentarily decided that the second was a better description, but I should have stuck with the first version. Today I think I would write, "An Essay *in* Phenomenological Ontology" and hope that the reader would

hear a fuller echo of the French *essai* as "attempt," which English "essay"
has mostly lost.

All this avoids the real issue. The first printing of *Being and Nothingness*
contains a number of errors. Many of these were due to the printer's
slipups and to inadequate proofreading; others were of my own making.
I later corrected the most obvious of these. The 1972 printing is the
most accurate to date, but Simon and Schuster, who took over the paperback, never responded to a dozen or so corrections I sent after that. And
every time I have used the book in teaching, I have made for my students
a few more corrections or modifications. All the same, I was devastated
when in March 1988 Peter Caws informed me that in the previous year
Timothy O'Hagan and Jean-Pierre Boulé had published a forty-page
booklet called *A Checklist of Errors in Hazel Barnes' English Translation of Jean-
Paul Sartre,* L'Être et le Néant. The editors had never got in touch with
me; in the booklet they formally invited everybody to send in notice of
additional errors which might be found—everybody but me, I guess, for
they never sent me a copy. The document itself does indeed list actual
mistakes, some of which I myself had already discovered, others not.
Many so-called corrections are trivial or captious, involving simply a
preference for another word or phrase. In other instances I would defend my own version. I note, by the way, that *viser à* is rendered as "focus
on," which is no closer to "intend" than my "aim at." The errors for which
I accept responsibility were mostly not due to my ignorance of idiom-
atic usage, obscure grammatical practices, etc. Occasionally I simply had
read too quickly and was careless. In a few instances I did the equivalent
of misspeaking. Sometimes I made the same sort of mistake I frequently
do in proofreading my own writing in English; that is, having inadver-
tently put down a different word from the one I intended. I see it as what
I meant, not as what actually stands there. I like to think that more time
for checking would have corrected most of such things, though probably not all. In any case, I think that if I had been asked to cooperate, the
Checklist would have been much better, as well as more gracious. In 1994,
Gramercy Books brought out a new edition of *Being and Nothingness,* one
which reproduced the original printing exactly. Thus another opportunity for improving the text was lost. I was not told anything of this
enterprise, either, discovering the new volume quite accidentally.

So, in light of all this, should I regret that I decided to undertake the
translation? We are brought back to the questions of when someone
else's would have appeared, and whether in fact it would have been significantly closer to perfect, and how the answers to these two questions

should be balanced against one another. No wholly objective judgment
is possible. Speaking for myself and with full consideration of everything, I confess that if I had it to do over again, I would do it.

MAKING IT MY OWN

While it would not be accurate to say that the translation of *Being and
Nothingness* was for me a means to an end, I have always regarded it as a
stepping-stone to doing my own writing about what I found so promising in Existentialist philosophy. Three years after *Being and Nothingness*
appeared, I published my first book—*The Literature of Possibility: A Study in
Humanistic Existentialism*. (For the paperback edition the publisher reversed
the order in the title, believing that *Humanistic Existentialism: The Literature
of Possibility* would attract more readers.) Before writing it I had got in
touch with the University of Nebraska Press, for no particular reason except that a friend of mine was pleased with what that press had done
with a book of his. Along with a letter stating very generally what I
planned to do, I sent copies of the talks I had given over the Ohio State
University radio station years before, to give an idea of the sort of questions that continued to interest me and to show that I could write about
them in terms intelligible to nonspecialists. In replying, Emily Schoss-
berger, who was then the editor-in-chief, devoted her letter chiefly to
pointing out that the talks could not be published in their present form,
something I had not even imagined, but added that if I were willing to
turn them into a book, the chances were "good that it would reach publication." Later, after I had sent her the first few sections so that she
might be in a better position to judge, she wrote that she would soon
have occasion to drive through Boulder and would then discuss the matter. Over lunch on our patio she informed me that she herself was about
to move to the University of Chicago Press and would like to take the
book with her. At the same time she so stressed the difficulties it would
be likely to meet at Chicago that she left me feeling that its acceptance
was most unlikely. Instead of asking her to proceed with the plan, I consulted my friend Gerald Busby, a sales representative from Knopf. He
talked with one of the editors of that press, who said that no matter how
good the book might be, they were overcommitted on their quota for
academic books for the near future. At this moment of total discouragement, I unexpectedly received a letter from the new editor at Nebraska, Virginia Faulkner, asking me almost reproachfully why the press
had heard nothing further from me concerning what it regarded as a

"commissioned book." By chance, the three presses involved were the ones which ultimately published most of my books, each bringing out at least two. The treatment I received from all of them was the antithesis of what I had experienced with Philosophical Library.

If for no other reason, I would be glad that I began with Nebraska since it gave me the opportunity to become acquainted with Virginia Faulkner. Having published her first novel at age twenty, Virginia worked briefly in Hollywood (a bit of her dialogue survived in the film *Camille*) and for the old *Vanity Fair*. Her greatest claim to behind-the-scenes fame was that of being the ghostwriter of Polly Adler's *A House Is Not a Home*. She told me of evenings at Adler's living quarters, spent playing cards or conversing while Polly frequently stopped to arrange appointments for girls in the house. Now back in her hometown in Lincoln, Virginia's efforts to expand the press's offerings in areas outside regional history were appreciated and supported by the university, which realized what a treasure it had in her. Although she and I had little in common except for some literary enthusiasms, we became fast friends. With neither background nor much interest in philosophy, Virginia grasped appreciatively what I was trying to do and gave guidance where it was needed. Mostly she sent me letters of encouragement, accompanied by such witty commentary that I felt her correspondence merited publication as much as what I was producing.

Writing *The Literature of Possibility* was a joy. My primary intention was to introduce readers to the philosophy of Existentialism through the literary works of Sartre, Beauvoir, and Camus. Though some notable critical studies of each of them had appeared, there were not many. I could feel that I was pioneering rather than struggling to find something new to say in a field cluttered with secondary material. I was not exactly original in grouping the three French writers together, but nobody before me had examined closely the way in which they could be seen as complementing each other's work so as to offer a coherent new way of looking at existential problems. Of course, I had to deal with serious divergences. Sartre's and Camus's famous quarrel had already taken place. And I felt uneasy about treating Camus as an Existentialist since I knew he had disavowed the term. As soon as my book was published, I wrote to him saying that I was sending him a copy. I added the following:

> I realize that you have stated time and again that you are not an existentialist. My intention is certainly not to try to prove that in spite of yourself you must be made into one. It is my belief that

when you see the way in which I have defined and expanded the term "humanistic existentialism," you will not be offended that I have presented a study of your writing in a book with this title.

The truth of the matter is this: Originally I had meant my book to be primarily a discussion of the literature of Jean-Paul Sartre and Simone de Beauvoir. (It is I who did the American translation of Sartre's *L'Être et le Néant*.) Then as I wrote, it seemed to me that the picture of man which they have presented is incomplete. In many instances I felt that it was you who had developed more fully themes which they suggested, you who have on occasion provided answers to their questions. For this reason I have presumed to include the three of you (certain other writers too, but only you three extensively). I have not, however, tried to pretend that you yourself are in full agreement in even the most important respects with Mlle de Beauvoir and M. Sartre. What I have attempted is rather to show that you have been occupied with similar problems and that the results of this concern on your part and on theirs may be significantly compared and contrasted.

It has been a great pleasure and a profoundly meaningful experience for me to spend these years in living so closely with your work. I should be deeply distressed if what I have written should in any way disturb or displease you. Please know that the book (in all sections where your ideas are presented) is at least intended to be a tribute to you.

Camus replied in a letter dated October 14, 1959. He wrote (in translation),

I have not yet received your work, but I look forward to reading it. I understand that you could see in me what I should prefer to call an existential writer rather than an existentialist writer. I simply insist on being precise. For many years now I have not believed in either the premises or the conclusions of existentialist philosophy, or of what has been called that in intending to refer to Sartre's philosophy. In fact, Pascal, Kierkegaard and Nietzsche are existentialist thinkers and Sartre is not one. But since we must use the terminology and the vocabulary of our time, even when they are false or unintelligent, it is better to say that if Sartre is an existentialist, Pascal, Nietzsche, and Kierkegaard are not. These nuances will explain to you that I understand very well your point of view, that

I am not offended by it and that I am simply and sincerely grateful for the interest and sympathy that you wish to show me.

Camus died in early January of the following year. I do not know whether he ever read my book. Even in light of his response, as puzzling as it is enlightening, I think that time has vindicated me. Especially when contrasted with later intellectual movements in France, the works written by these three, if they do not speak in unison, at least make a well-blended trio.

Though Sartre's philosophy was pivotal, he did not dominate the volume. Strangely enough, as a person (if I may say that of one I knew only in print), he was to me less appealing than either of the other two, partly because of a certain abrasiveness in him; partly because, in spite of Sartre's specific plea for the necessity of putting persons before ideas, his concern for others seemed to me more abstract, less emphatically compassionate than the somehow more personal understanding I found expressed in Beauvoir's and Camus's writing.

Camus I admired for his ability to convey the existential anguish of our human condition, as he does so splendidly in *The Myth of Sisyphus*, beginning with the statement that the only truly serious philosophical problem is suicide. When I was asked one time, along with a few other persons, to read on a public occasion a ten-minute passage that I had personally found of greatest significance, I chose the closing pages of this essay, voicing Sisyphus' (and Camus's) glorious affirmation of the value of our human enterprise in the face of an absurd universe, as Sisyphus discovers that "the rock is his thing." Especially in his fiction, Camus moved me by his understanding of the painful tensions suffered both by those trying to cling to religious faith in an existence filled with evil and suffering, and by those who sought for ethical certainties in a world without God. I liked, too, his notion of "calculated culpability," developed in *The Rebel*, the idea that in recognizing the necessity of choosing the lesser evil, we must acknowledge that it is nevertheless evil and cannot be dissolved in the good. And I appreciated his careful balance between the sentimentalization and the condemnation of humankind. I think of how, at the end of *The Plague*, Dr. Rieux, despite his pessimistic observation that the germs of pestilence will always be there to threaten us, concludes that there is more in humankind to admire than to despise. And Camus himself, in commenting on the antihero of his novella *The Fall*, condemns the cynicism that would demoralize and prevent us from living our lives with our own "just measure of meanness and magnificence."

Beauvoir, of course, took on special and increasing importance for me as I myself became more caught up in feminism. In *The Literature of Possibility*, I made use of *The Second Sex*, but chiefly within the broader contexts of human relations in good and bad faith and of responsibility for self-determination. Already I appreciated in Beauvoir's writing her willingness to examine more closely the implications of problems passed over rather carelessly by Sartre, and to test an abstract principle by putting it into a concrete setting either real or imagined. At that time I thought of Sartre and Beauvoir as co-workers, he marking out the path, she making major contributions in special areas. I did not have the prescience to foresee the degree to which her defense of Sartreanism and her seemingly marginal modifications of it would radically influence the social philosophy set forth in Sartre's *Critique of Dialectical Reason* (1960). Neither, so far as I know, did anyone else—unless it was Sartre and Beauvoir.

Reviews of my book were mostly very favorable, none really bad. One critic, at a later date, referred to it as monumental. I felt that this was a bit inappropriate for a work so basically unassuming, but I suppose that anything is monumental if it marks a certain stage. Considering the date of its publication (1959), I still find it something I am glad to have written. The weakest section is my discussion of Sartre's work on Jean Genet. Without Sartre's as yet unpublished *Critique*, I failed to grasp the extent to which he had added a new dimension to his social philosophy; I concentrated instead on the individual psychology and the role of literature. My treatment of what Sartre was doing in that biographical study was seriously incomplete. What pleased me most in the book's reception was the many letters I received from readers who responded to my secondary, unstated purpose, which was to communicate to others the philosophical and psychological insights I had found personally valuable. This meant that at times I had done more than to explain and to interpret; I had added commentary of my own to underscore or to extend, never, I believe, to distort what I had found in the works I discussed. I strongly emphasized the optimistic aspects of Existentialism, though I took pains not to overlook what many persons saw as its dark side. Even Nicola Abbagnano, the Italian Existentialist, whose declaration, "Freedom is possibility," I quoted on the opening page, seemed to me to make things a bit too easy—as though "possibility" were a synonym for the "positive." I did not want to make Existentialism sound like the gospel of Norman Vincent Peale!

Within the confines of my first book, except for occasional references, I spoke of humanistic Existentialism solely as it appeared in the work of the selected three. In other contexts, written and spoken, I was far more inclusive. I recall that in an introductory lecture on Existentialism, I used as my basic structure Paul Tillich's triad, the three ways in which our human Being is threatened by Nonbeing (from *The Courage to Be*) and found it equally adaptable to religious and to humanistic Existentialism. In my class in Existentialist literature, both in the late fifties and over the years, I included works of religious Existentialists—Miguel de Unamuno, Walker Percy, Graham Greene (who was at least enough of an Existentialist to make some in the Catholic Church uneasy). All of these the students and I alike enjoyed. Several times I used Kierkegaard's *Fear and Trembling*, but although I myself have found it exciting, very few of my students shared my enthusiasm. I was dismayed at the willingness of most of them to consider Kierkegaard of interest only as a case study in abnormal psychology. To me, his powerful, impassioned reaffirmation of the ancient "Credo quia absurdum" compelled reverential respect, even though I had emphatically rejected such a choice for myself. In another class that I taught, the students and I examined Sartre's psychology and his suggestions for an "Existential psychoanalysis" in relation to other philosophical/psychological systems—as contrasted with the positions of Freud and Jung, as fellow traveler with Viktor Frankl and R. D. Laing, and in a delicate balance of parallel and divergence, in comparison with the humanistic psychologists, particularly Erich Fromm and Abraham Maslow.

Obviously I could not make myself an expert on all Existentialist thinkers. I never worked seriously with Marcel or Jaspers. I read somewhat more in Merleau-Ponty but made only limited use of him. My perhaps indefensible omission was my all but complete neglect of Heidegger. I did discuss him superficially and one-sidedly in a short chapter in *An Existentialist Ethics*, but that is all. The truth is that I had—I won't call it a blind spot with regard to him but rather a serious mental block against him. I reacted most negatively to Heidegger's use of his own philosophy in welcoming Nazism, which was evident long before revelations since his death have shown the full extent of his involvement with the Nazi party. I objected to his ahistorical, idiosyncratic interpretations of the Pre-Socratic philosophers, though I admit that I am moving against the prevailing tide in this respect. And I felt that the peculiar twist of his philosophical language, whether intentional or not, obscured clarity of thought rather than expressing nuances more precisely. I am afraid that my feeling regarding Heidegger was like my attitude toward playing bridge: I did not play it well enough to enjoy it or like it sufficiently to want to learn to play it properly. I have read enough by and about Heidegger to realize that I am almost certainly at fault and have doubtless failed to take advantage of what might have benefited me. But I have chosen to regard the situation as one that can no longer be remedied.

Even before *The Literature of Possibility* had come out, I had been invited to speak about Existentialism to various groups, on campus and off, in the Boulder-Denver area. After its publication, invitations came to me from a great many places across the country (and ultimately even outside it) in a sort of crescendo, diminishing after I retired but never entirely giving out. This kind of thing happens naturally with any scholar or writer, and I do not claim that I was among those most in demand. (I certainly was not among the highest paid.) What was, if not unique, distinctive in my case was the wide variation in my audiences. Everyone, it seemed, wanted to hear about Existentialism and at all levels, each demanding a lecture appropriate to its particular background and interest. This diversity derived partly from the nature of Existentialism itself, which, at least as it manifested itself in Paris, had been simultaneously an austere philosophy (and psychology), a literary movement, and a popular fad. In my book, addressed to the educated, general reader, I had tried to integrate the literary, philosophical, and psychological aspects. Now I focused more specifically on one or the other as occasion demanded. Rather than feeling torn apart and fragmented, I felt that it was all to my own benefit. It was as though I were asked to develop many different sides of myself and to share them with others.

In a college or university I might meet with a philosophy seminar or colloquium; usually there was a public lecture for which I was expected to rise to the challenge of speaking intelligibly to students and interested lay persons while still offering something of interest to the philosophy faculty. Occasionally I gave talks to high school classes, to church organizations, to women's clubs, to office groups that wanted to be instructed over lunch once a month, and to loosely formed associations of persons who combined social evenings with the desire to learn something of what was going on outside their own fields. There is something endearing in the American public's desire for self-improvement, though regrettably nowadays it seems to be expressed mostly in health pursuits. There was also what I thought of as "applied Existentialism." Would I, please, speak "from the Existentialist perspective" on teaching, on psy-

chological counseling, on drugs, on suicide, and—a bit later—on feminism, and on aging.

I entertained particularly congenial relations with two groups—or,
perhaps more accurately—subgroups. The first was with religious workers, usually those of a liberal cast or sympathetic with the New Theologians. With Bishop James Pike, who came once to Boulder, I got along
so well that we agreed to keep in touch with one another; unfortunately
it was not long before he died tragically, lost in the desert in Israel.
Somewhat surprisingly, also, communication was easy and rewarding
with Catholic philosophers, who invited me to speak at a meeting of
their national association. I attribute this partly to the scholastic tradition, which has strongly encouraged genuine debate, and partly to their
respect for anyone who takes seriously moral questions and matters of
ultimate belief. Most fruitful for me personally were my sessions with
psychologists. Not so much with classroom professors of psychology,
and emphatically not with behaviorists. In the sterile, repetitive arguments, always on the issue of freedom versus determinism, we could never
find common ground even for discussion. With psychotherapists and
psychological counselors, even with some psychoanalysts, in spite of
basic disagreement with regard to the teachings of Freud, I felt that they
were open to further exploration. Perhaps because their overriding concern was to help people, they were interested in hearing about anything
that might work. Once, by invitation, I conducted a workshop for a
group of clinical psychologists in Los Angeles. It had been arranged by
Douglas Corey and Jeannette Maas. These two together had been developing and extending, in practice and in print, the possibilities of the
"reverse therapy" proposed by Viktor Frankl, a psychiatrist whose work
is considered by most to be a form of existential psychoanalysis though
he himself preferred the term "logotherapy." Corey and Maas had recently discovered *Being and Nothingness* and wanted me to discuss with
them and the others Sartrean ideas that would be useful in psychotherapy. The inappropriateness of my role soon ceased to embarrass me,
and I found the experience exhilarating. By the time I left, I felt reassured
not only about the relevance of Sartre to the practice of psychotherapy,
but also about what was going on in these circles in California.

I found it tremendously exciting to be caught up in all of these activities. I suppose I became in my own way a sort of preacher after all,
though not a Free Methodist one. I do not deny or apologize for the fact
that to some degree I worked with what Thomas Flynn has disdainfully

labeled "popular Existentialism," though he has never accused me personally of doing so. I have always believed that where it is appropriate, one can simplify without distorting—in somewhat the same way that classicists use original Greek and Latin texts in their classes when they can and teach from an English translation when this is the only thing possible. There was no serious danger of my becoming nothing but a popularizer. In classes in which I taught only Sartre and in lectures and colloquia within my own university and elsewhere in the academic world, I discussed the more difficult aspects of Sartre's ontology and began developing my own point of view on the problems and possibilities arising from it. I recognized that in my enthusiasm for Sartre there was the risk of becoming too much an uncritical disciple. I tried to guard against this by taking pains to point out statements of his that seemed to me to need questioning. With my students I took special care to avoid proselytizing; I feel no guilt in this respect. More generally, I suspect that I could not defend myself against the charge of having been more a proponent than a critic of Existentialism, but I see nothing dishonorable in that.

One of the most interesting by-products of my philosophical commitment was a proposal from people at KRMA, the Denver affiliate of National Public Educational Television, that I work with them on a series of ten half-hour shows for the national network. These would be concerned with Existentialism. I would be host and discussant and would select illustrative material for filming. After viewing our pilot tape, the national office approved and granted us funding. I called the series "Self-Encounter." For each program I chose a basic theme, which I developed in informal lecture with accompanying visual presentations. Sometimes the visual material served as background to add emotional connotations to an idea, or to enhance a mood. More often we interpolated dramatic scenes taken from plays and from dialogues in novels. Our actors were chiefly students from the University of Colorado at Boulder and from the University of Denver. For a most obvious example to highlight Sartre's negative view of human relations in bad faith, I chose the scene from Sartre's No Exit in which Garcin declares, "Hell is Others." It was balanced by Hélène's discovery (from Beauvoir's The Blood of Others) that "Others are there" and that one is responsible for them. In comparing Sartre's and Camus's political positions we set Hoederer's conversation with Hugo (in Dirty Hands), the one in which the party leader defends the practice of justifying the end by the means, against Camus's scene with the three terrorists (in *The Just Assassins*) where Dora tries to convince the other two that "there are limits." I did not restrict myself to works by my favored trio. We had already taped an excerpt from T. S. Eliot's *The Cocktail Party*, a play in which I had always found Existentialist themes and which its author had expressly declared to have been written in part "contre Sartre." In the face of Eliot's publisher's adamant refusal to let us use anything from it, we had to do over again a major portion of the show. I changed my comments to make a quite different point so as to accommodate a passage from Richard Wright's *Native Son*. One of our most effective scenes was a dramatic adaptation from Unamuno's story "The Madness of Doctor Montarco." It was in the program dealing with Existentialist attitudes toward the meaning of death, and I have extremely painful reason for remembering it clearly. A young actor from the University of Denver played the role of the Doctor, who valiantly proclaimed his defiance of the power of death and our right to believe in our personal immortality. Between that day and the morning when we taped the next show, this man was killed; he was accidentally electrocuted when he tried to rescue a kitten stranded on a telephone wire. The tragic gratuitousness of the event and the bitter irony of its timing cast a long shadow over all of us.

"Self-Encounter" was telecast on the national network in 1962, repeated later on some of the stations. The public's reception was most gratifying, greatly exceeding the expectations of the local producer, John Parkinson, and the director, James Case, as they confessed to me. I think they had both been a bit skeptical about the project, even as they gave it their best effort. (Jim used to refer to the selections I took from Beauvoir's *The Mandarins* as our soap opera.) Appreciative letters streamed in. Some argued with me over specific points; others asked questions. So many correspondents wanted to have suggestions for further reading that I was asked to prepare a reading list that could be sent out on request. The most negative response was from someone who knew me. Nettie Sue Tillett, my friend and colleague at the Woman's College in Greensboro, wrote to say frankly that she found the subject matter distasteful and wished that I had stayed with Classics.

I loved both the process of making the programs and the enjoyable flurry that they evoked. I was never under any illusion that I might have a further career in television. Along with being decidedly nonphotogenic, I never felt entirely comfortable in performing for a faceless audience whose reactions I could not perceive. (On the radio at WOSU, I at least had enjoyed the benefit of getting reactions from listeners between broadcasts.) A few of my friends and former students said they found me on television a bit lifeless and cold in contrast to the person they knew. This may well have been the case. It was hard to be spontaneous when I was wondering whether or not my comments would fit into the time allotted me, calculated down to the second. By an unkind coincidence locally, the half-hour program before mine offered Alan Watts presenting Zen Buddhism. Where Watts was a charismatic guru, I was a professor strayed from the classroom. But the public was charitable. A large number of people wrote in to ask if tapes could be purchased for private or for group use. (It is startling to realize how short a time home-recording of TV programs has been possible.) I don't know what the national office, to whom I referred everyone, responded. In the years following the telecasts, I received enough requests so that I myself made an inquiry, only to learn that the tapes had by then been destroyed. Obviously I should have anticipated this possibility and sought to buy them myself. This kind of thing has happened to me so often that I belatedly conclude I am lacking in some of the rudiments of self-protection.

By the 1960s things had changed within the Existentialist movement and in the public's attitude toward it. But while no longer an object of curiosity, it had won a secure place in college curricula and had by no means become a dead option for persons thoughtful enough or naive enough to be seeking a philosophy to live by. For myself I think of *An Existentialist Ethics* (1967) as the culmination and closure, in my writing, of the concerns that had dominated my work with Existentialism for almost two decades. (I sent this book to Knopf, for whom I had done a translation of a short work by Sartre.) The title I chose very carefully. As it indicates, I was not attempting to write *the* Existentialist ethics, but rather to work out what I believed to be the logical consequences for an ethics if I started from a Sartrean position. (At one point I had the ill-conceived idea of calling it "An Existentialist's Ethics.") Apropos of this use of the term, my friend Glenn Gray, at Colorado College in Colorado Springs, a Heideggerian who was entrusted by Heidegger with the responsibility for all final translations of his work in the United States, complained to me that my implied definition of "Existentialism" was one that could be properly applied only to me and to Walter Kaufmann, the Princeton professor who, among other things, brought out an early anthology of Existentialist writers. Gray had a point, and perhaps Kaufmann might have wanted to distance himself as well. Although I do not believe that I was quite so idiosyncratic, this was certainly the most personal of my books—up till now.

In this volume, as in most of the things I had written up until the end of the sixties, the reading audience I had in mind was not strictly an academic one. I wanted to appeal as well to nonspecialists, inside and outside the university, who had become interested in Existentialism and wondered (as a number of persons in so many words said to me), "If I accept this position as a premise, then what?" I cannot say with certainty that I succeeded in striking the proper balance. Some may have felt that I tripped and fell between two stools. I do not regret the decision. Excerpts have appeared in philosophy textbooks, and appreciative letters have come from philosophy professors and students as well as from people outside Academe. *An Existentialist Ethics* was one of a hundred books, out of those published in 1967, selected to be sent to the White House library. I have never received a letter indicating that anyone there had read it. A most surprising statement I heard not long ago from a professor of philosophy who had initiated my being invited to give a colloquium for his department. He told me that *An Existentialist Ethics* was the first philosophy book he had ever read. As I listened prepared to be highly complimented, he added, "I was still in high school." I took refuge in the thought that he must have been a very unusual high school pupil.

One criticism that was made of the book was that in stressing the heavy responsibilities of freedom, the necessity of self-scrutiny in order to escape bad faith, the habit of "thinking against oneself," as Sartre put it, I paid too little attention to the joyous side of liberation and the enjoyment of the expanding self. Although such was not my intention, I think it may have been a fair observation. Perhaps that is why my Aunt Jennie felt that I had not gone as far from my roots as I believed I had.

An Existentialist Ethics did not develop quite as I had originally intended. Somewhere in the process of writing it, I decided to include my reactions to certain competing voices in the contemporary scene. As a result, a special appeal that the book had when it appeared makes parts of it seem outdated today—or else of purely historical interest. (One basically friendly reader remarked to me recently that I must surely be the last, if not the only, philosopher to have written seriously about Norman Mailer and Ayn Rand.) But, as Sartre once said, "We write for our own time!" That the bulk of the volume remained relevant was attested

by the decision of the University of Chicago Press to reprint the paperback in 1978. It stayed in print until 1994, and a trickle of letters and
phone calls continues to tell me of persons who have found it meaningful.

As everybody knows, the avant-garde is eventually transformed by
passersby into the rear guard. If you ride the crest of the wave, you
go down when it does. But you don't necessarily drown. Three separate
factors worked to influence and to alter somewhat the way in which I
continued to adapt Existentialism to my own interests: Sartre's turn in
the direction of Marxism; the hostile takeover by the Deconstructionists; the new feminism.

In the early 1950s, Sartre's political pronouncements and activities
proclaimed him as a fellow traveler with the Communists; he decisively
broke with them in 1956, following the shameful behavior (as he and
most of the world saw it) of the Soviet Union with regard to Hungary.
In an essay first published in 1957, later included in his *Critique of Dialectical Reason* (1960), Sartre referred to Existentialism as a parasitic ide-
ology living on the margin of Marxism; he asserted that after originally
opposing Marxism, Existentialism now sought to be integrated into it.
On first encounter with the *Critique,* many critics and scholars thought
that it represented a radical renunciation of the philosophy of *Being and
Nothingness.* By now, I think, most would probably agree with what I
thought at the time: that despite much that is totally new and unexpected, earlier positions have been modified, not abandoned; the *Critique*
still rests on the ontology of *Being and Nothingness.* One of the results of
Sartre's new stance was that his individual influence was extended. Now
it was sociologists and political theorists to whom his new work especially appealed. Sartre himself, of course, did not stand still. As the student revolution got under way in France in 1968, Sartre embraced it
with open arms. In another of his publicly proclaimed conversions, he
announced that henceforth he would stand apart from any and all parties in favor of issue-oriented politics and confrontational activism. His
love for the young militants was not altogether reciprocated. Some still
sought his assistance; others insisted on seeing him as a member of the
hated Establishment. On one occasion an anonymous note instructed
him not to be so long-winded. It may have been partly due to this ambivalence that while Sartre continued to join in protests and demonstrations and to lend his name to leftist publications, even when he did not
wholly agree with their views, he concentrated, in his writing, on *The*

Family Idiot (1971–72), a choice which he himself acknowledged to be a retreat and evasion.

Where was I in all this? I did not convert with Sartre at each new stage of his thought. I was disturbed by his close rapprochement with the Communists in the 1950s and relieved when he broke with them. My reaction to the *Critique* was quite different. I read it soon after it was published and, at Blanche Knopf's request, translated its prefatory essay, which was published as *Search for a Method* (1963). (The title of the English edition, *The Problem of Method,* is a more exact translation, though I like mine better.) Sartre's thought in the *Critique* is so individually his that its validity or nonvalidity is not inextricably tied to theoretical Marxism, still less to Marxism as it has been historically applied. Over the years, particularly in working with it in a graduate course, I have increasingly appreciated the profundity of the work. But although I have used a modicum of it in *An Existentialist Ethics* and in several articles, I have not integrated it into my own work to the degree that I did with the earlier Sartre. What I did do was to write a small volume, titled simply *Sartre,* for a series edited by Walter Kaufmann and published by Lippincott in 1973. In this, the least personal of my books, I traced to my own satisfaction the unity of Sartre's philosophy that held firm despite all the surface conversions. Then, following Sartre, I, too, turned to Flaubert.

But between the writing and the publication of my *Sartre and Flaubert,* I had an unexpected opportunity to get involved in an enterprise that came close to being an example of applied Sartreanism, one directly dependent on the *Critique.* In the summer of 1980, I received a phone call from Haim Gordon, a Jewish professor in the Department of Education at Ben Gurion University of the Negeb at Beersheba in Israel. His getting in touch with me was the result of a series of encounters in a network of chance. He was a friend of my former student and friend Betty Cannon; she had already put him in touch with another former student of mine, Jan Demarest, now a sociologist with a Ph.D., whom he had persuaded to go to Ben Gurion and work with him on a project called "Education for Peace." From a German foundation Haim Gordon had received a grant for three years. Its purpose was to support a study group to be composed equally of Jews and Arabs (all Israelis), half of whom would be students at Ben Gurion, half from schools in the Beersheba area. Gordon wanted me to come for a couple of weeks as an official observer who would report to the sponsoring agency and as semiparticipant. His selection of me made sense as he explained what he had already done in the first year and hoped further to accomplish. I was astounded to hear of the plan and I endorsed it enthusiastically. On the basis of his study of Martin Buber, Gordon proposed that the group explore the possibilities of the I-Thou relationship between individuals, extending it to establish this kind of trusting relationship between Jews and Arabs as individual members of the group. During the first stage there would be no discussion of the Jew-Arab political conflict but an attempt to demonstrate the possibility of understanding and trust between persons of contrasting cultures. Afterward they would study the nature of the conflict itself; Gordon hoped that it would help prepare Jews and Arabs to work together as leaders trying to resolve it. By the time he phoned me, he had decided on his own that a social philosophy was needed to supplement Buber's views on personal relations, and he believed he had found it in Sartre's *Critique*, especially in Sartre's discussion of the emergent "We" in the group-in-fusion. His bold idea was to wed Buber's intimate I-Thou with the collective action of a group based on trust. Though I was not without reservations as to the practicality of this Utopian goal, the proposal seemed to me a step in the right direction. Philosophically I was elated. Sartre himself, in a late interview (*Hope Now*), had remarked that the political struggle against oppression could not be finally effective unless it were based on our developed capacity to feel meaningfully our unity in a common humanity. I myself had long maintained that relations in good faith could be sustained by realizing the other two dimensions in Sartre's metaphor of the Look—not the objectifying hostile stare, on which he focused in *Being and Nothingness*, but the Look-as-an-exchange and Looking-at-the-world-together, precisely the two steps to be taken in the "Education for Peace" project. In late May of the next year (1981), I went to Israel. Doris came with me as traveling companion; we were met at the airport by Haim Gordon and Jan Demarest, who was already settled in and amazingly well advanced in Hebrew.

I found much that was good in the venture, which was now finishing its first year. Aside from the few occasions when I myself lectured or led the discussion, I mostly sat and listened while someone, from time to time, murmured in my ear a translation of what was being said in Hebrew, not a very satisfactory procedure. More enlightening were my conversations outside the formal meetings with some of the participants, the majority of whom knew English. Here I was indeed impressed by their own estimate of how far they had advanced in their sympathetic comprehension of each other's problems. Haim Gordon and I had occasional disagreements. He noted in me a lack of enthusiasm for what I thought of as extracurricular sensitivity sessions. I accused him to his face of assuming too much the role of authoritarian guru. But our frankness was an expression of our mutual respect. I have come to admire him still more as we have kept in touch and have met on his occasional visits to the United States.

At Beersheba I visited a kibbutz again, where one of the Jewish women students was living, also an Arab high school, and the home of one of the Arab students in the group. The kibbutz, in its physical appearance, was considerably upgraded since my visit in the forties. The material standard of living was noticeably higher than in the Arab village, though the house in which we were entertained there was pleasant enough. The contrast between the position of Jewish and Arab women was marked, of course, but in my particular experience, I was struck by an ironical juxtaposition. Jewish women in the group complained to me that after an initial thrust toward equality, patterns of work responsibility in the kibbutz had tended to fall into the traditional gender-determined structures; they felt that the women's movement in Israel was fifteen years behind that in the United States, a judgment with which Jan Demarest concurred. When I visited an Arab high school, itself a radical innovation for a traditionally nomadic people, the principal proudly pointed out that this year for the first time girls had been admitted. At the home of our young Arab host, his mother did not join Jan and Doris and me for the meal. We ate with the men of the family. Talking with us afterward, she told us that each of her six sons on graduating from the university had received a gold sovereign. The seventh child, a daughter, was just finishing a secondary school. "She, too, will go to the university," the mother said and showed us the sovereign she was wearing on a chain around her neck until the day the young woman would graduate. Another lesson in the relativity of human aspirations and the danger of rash generalizations.

The "Education for Peace" project was short-lived. When Israel entered into the war in Lebanon, the group was dissolved, and Gordon voluntarily went to fight with the Israeli army. Ever since his return, however, he and his wife, Rivca, have worked continuously on several fronts to promote peace and justice in the relations between Jews and Arabs in Israel; among other things, they edit an English-language newsletter to keep people informed of what is happening on the scene and behind it. In publications in this country, Haim has continued to write articles on Sartre, especially as his views can be made relevant to problems in Israel.

During the weeks that I was in Israel (Doris and I prolonged our stay for a bit of tourism), my own emotions were in constant conflict. Seeing the many ways in which my early Zionist hopes for the country had been abundantly realized, I was filled with marveling admiration; but like so many other well-wishers, I could not reconcile myself to the degree to which the government had gradually taken on the unwelcome role of oppressor. Still, owing to the particular associates with whom I spent most of my time, I felt an optimism which later events belied. Only recently (1996) does it show signs of bearing fruit, and there is still the ever present danger of a killing frost. My sole venture in applied social philosophy proved to be rewarding to me. I cannot say that it was very useful to anyone else.

My departure from Israel brought in a variation on a theme. At the airport I, unlike the rest of the passengers, was delayed for a considerable time while my luggage was meticulously scrutinized and I was subjected to close questioning as to what I was doing at Beersheba, what my credentials were, etc. Obviously my association with the "Education for Peace" project rendered me suspicious as an Arab sympathizer. I remembered but did not mention that on my former visit, I had been nearly arrested by Arabs as a presumed Jewish saboteur. It balanced out.

The fall of this same year (1981) saw the publication of my *Sartre and Flaubert*, which I had begun to write four years earlier. It was a request from a graduate philosophy student that transformed into an immediate enterprise my resolve to tackle Sartre's three-volume study of Flaubert as soon as I had time. (Directly or indirectly, a surprisingly large proportion of my scholarly work has been sparked by students' questions or expressed interest.) In spring 1976, Joel Peterson, whose French excelled that of most of our students who had technically passed the foreign language examinations, asked me if I would do an "independent study" course with him on the first volume of Sartre's hitherto untranslated *L'Idiot de la famille*. I gladly consented. We set ourselves a weekly quota of a hundred fine-printed pages out of the eleven hundred and discussed each assignment for most of a morning. Although I did this on top of my usual class schedule, it was one of many times in my career when I realized how fortunate I was to be paid for doing what I most wanted to do. Joel's dissertation on Sartre took him in another direction. I do not know whether he ever read the other two volumes or not. I felt compelled, not only to finish them, but to write my own critical study of the work. Serendipitously, I received just then a call from Allen Fitchen at the University of Chicago Press, inquiring whether I would like to undertake the translation of *L'Idiot de la famille*. When I declined, saying that I preferred to concentrate on my own study of it, Mr. Fitchen said that the press would be interested in that. Very shortly I had a contract.

The auspicious quality of this beginning seemed to stay with me as I wrote the book. Enormous as the task was—to bring into some coherent form a critical appraisal of Sartre's sprawling, nearly three-thousand-page opus—I found that the very fact of its being a cumulating synthesis of Sartre's wide-ranging thought over four decades gave me a manageable avenue of approach. *The Family Idiot*, if it is not the most fundamental and influential of his works, is certainly the richest. In examining Gustave Flaubert's interaction with his family and with the wider social sphere, with the "Objective Spirit" of his culture, as Sartre liked to say, using Hegel's term, the work reconciled the idea of the individual as a self-maker (understood in terms of the fundamental project set forth in the chapter on "Existential Psychoanalysis" in *Being and Nothingness*) and the process of social conditioning described in the *Critique*. In exploring the nature of Flaubert's choice to work in the imaginary, Sartre picked up for astonishing development both the psychological and the aesthetic insights of his two early books on imagination. He inserts, almost as digressive essays, exciting discussions of the psychology of the actor, the status of the work of art as "a real and permanent center of de-realization," and the nihilistic aspects of much mid-nineteenth-century French poetry. There are vignettes on the underlying significance of the restrictive clothing worn by Flaubert's contemporaries, who distrusted the "natural man"; on the practical joke as a device to deal with a universe "allergic to man"; and on a lapdog, fascinatingly if not altogether convincingly depicted by Sartre as initiated by its owners into boredom and frustrated by just missing the attainment of full self-consciousness. A special reward to me was the fact that in order to comprehend the distinctive nature of Sartre's "Flaubert," it was necessary for me to read Flaubert himself. (This was to reread in the case of the major works, but I had never before looked at the juvenilia or at the letters.) Similarly, I had to consult what had been written by at least the most influential of Flaubert biographers and critics—e.g., Jean Bruneau, Victor Brombert,

Benjamin Bart, Enid Starkie, and Francis Steegmuller. Thus I had the feeling of opening up a new field for myself as well as working with a still expanding Sartre. The whole process of writing was extraordinarily revitalizing. When the University of Chicago Press accepted the manuscript of *Sartre and Flaubert*, none of which I had submitted earlier, and asked for no revisions and only a bare minimum of copyediting, I was ecstatic.

Plans for the formal announcement of the book increased my pleasure. The press and the University of Chicago sponsored a conference on Sartre, to accompany the appearance of Carol Cosman's translation of the first volume of *The Family Idiot*, Paul Schilpp's volume of essays on Sartre and his response to them in the Library of Living Philosophers series, and my book. I myself read a paper on "Beauvoir's Autobiography as a Biography of Sartre," which led to my having stimulating discussions afterward with Margaret Simons and Deirdre Bair, with whom I have been friends ever since. Outstanding Sartre scholars, most of whom I had known personally or in their books, gave papers on various aspects of Sartre's work. Enjoyable as all this was, I had an unexpected sense of uneasiness. Benny Lévy presented a view of Sartre's philosophy that seemed to me to do violence to him. Yet some of the people present, whose opinion I respected, were willing to go along with Lévy, at least part way. This, of course, was but a faint echo of the split among Sartre supporters in Paris, some of whom, including Beauvoir, claimed that Lévy had distorted Sartre's views in the 1980 series of published interviews that Lévy had had with him, while others (among them Sartre's adopted daughter, Arlette Elkaïm) argued that the first group was merely unwilling to grant that Sartre might have significantly altered his positions in his last year, as he had done on earlier occasions.

Still more important to me was another observation. I was struck by the number of papers that approached Sartre's writings from a Deconstructionist perspective, something I had so far seen only in non-Sartrean contexts. Feeling alienated rather than stimulated by this new method of questioning a text, I felt that in these discussions I was sitting on the sidelines. It took a little longer for me to realize more fully how radically my position had been changed in relation to the prevailing academic *Zeitgeist.*

Reviews of *Sartre and Flaubert* were reassuring, some of them quite laudatory. I was especially pleased that some commended me for being at home in Flaubert scholarship as well as in Sartrean philosophy. But I was disappointed that the book did not seem to be selling as well as my others had. Then one day, a very late review enlightened me, pointing out what I should have realized on my own. The reviewer, after remarking condescendingly that what I had done was fine as an example of nineteenth-century criticism, said I had failed entirely by Deconstructionist criteria. In particular he attacked me for being concerned with the question of whether the portrait of Flaubert that Sartre produced by such painstaking analysis was consistent with what we know of Flaubert from his own writing and from what his contemporaries said of him. Since *The Family Idiot* was, and could be, only a literary creation, the reviewer wrote, he could not understand why I should have raised the question of verisimilitude. Illuminated as much as dismayed, I realized that success or failure in accomplishing what I had set out to do was considered irrelevant. I was comforted by the thought that while Sartre himself had said that in some respects *The Family Idiot* was "a true novel," he had explicitly stated that his original purpose in writing it had been to answer, by his study of Flaubert, the question, "What can we know of a man today?" But with the Deconstructionists, of course, any mention of the author's intention is taboo.

I have to admit that the growing dominance of Deconstruction in academic circles threatened my confidence that I could continue writing what others would find worth reading, in a way that realizing Existentialism was no longer in vogue never did. So far as the latter was concerned, I had long since abandoned my role of expositor and missionary and was happy to be a co-worker with the many Sartrean scholars who had come on the scene. For while Sartre was no longer a scandal, he was here to stay in the academic curriculum and was a still lively subject of discussion at philosophy conferences. But Deconstruction, in its fundamental principles, seemed to challenge the validity of all that I had been doing.

I never was (and am not now) wholly hostile, nor without appreciation for the significant contributions that proponents of Deconstruction have offered. Structuralism, its close ally and immediate predecessor, I had welcomed in my other field, Classics, as a supplementary approach to the search for the meanings underlying religious ritual and myth. In my classes I had introduced work done by the American anthropologist Terence S. Turner and by the British classicist G. S. Kirk. With respect to Deconstruction, initially I was greatly and favorably impressed with the impetus it gave to feminist reinterpretations of literature and to the re-evaluation of women writers. And who could possibly object to the careful scrutiny that brought to light the subtexts beneath the texts and the hitherto unsuspected possibilities of intertextuality? In *Sartre and Flaubert* I had found it helpful to discuss Jonathan Culler's reading of Flaubert in *The Uses of Uncertainty,* a very early book of his. But the excesses of many of those writing as Deconstructionists appalled me. I am not only unconvinced but outraged at attempts to demonstrate that Euripides' *Bacchae* and Sophocles' *Electra* are not to be read as serious explorations of human problems but as the self-conscious reflection by the Greek trage- dians on the process of playwriting—as if they were contemporaries of Robbe-Grillet. (What, I ask myself, has happened here to the sacred principle of not meddling with the author's intention?)

Naturally, as a Sartrean I was dismayed by the overall tendency of Deconstruction to depersonalize, to reduce the person to modes of dis- course, to view individuals as only reflections of the input of others. Neither could I accept the idea, underscored by Lacan, that we are "spo- ken by language," its servants rather than its creators and users. And quite independently of my Existentialist precommitments, I—like many others—resisted the notion that since in interpreting literature absolute truth is unobtainable in most instances, the only alternative is a relativ- ity that would put all meanings on the same level. In my view, to claim that the strongest reading of a text is the most mind-stretching (I be- lieve this was said by Stanley Fish), or that any sentence can be made to mean anything, is to reduce interpretive criticism to an empty game, one in which nothing can be gained because nothing can be lost. Either that, or one must agree with the conclusion I once heard voiced by an unhappy member of an audience, that there are no longer great writers, only great critics.

Whether it was wise or merely cowardly on my part, I never at- tempted to confront Deconstruction directly. Instead, in later articles I focused on that aspect of Sartre's philosophy that was the chief object of Deconstructionist attacks on him—his view of consciousness and the ego. Working with posthumous material (Sartre's *War Diaries* and *Note- books for an Ethics*) as well as taking a new look at what was published in his lifetime, I undertook to defend him against the old charge of being a Cartesian in new dress and, in particular, I tried to develop more posi- tively the possibilities for psychology that are implicit in his view of the ego. I don't think that I ever went over the line into revisionism. When asked one time how I thought Sartre would react to what I was presenting, I replied truthfully that I could not be sure. He might reply, "I once said that I never learned anything from those who wrote about my work, and I am not about to change my mind now!" But equally well he could say, "Of course, Hazel, it's all true, but it's so obvious. Why make such a fuss about it?" In any case, I have derived much personal satisfaction in writing these papers.

I pointed out earlier that along with Sartre's shift toward what he (not many other people) considered to be neo-Marxism and the emergence of Deconstruction, the new feminism compelled me to see my own work as differently situated. With the English translation (1952) of *The Second Sex*, Beauvoir became a major figure for vast numbers of people who had no interest in Existentialism as such. For a time, the book may have led some persons to look into both her and Sartre's philosophical work in order to understand her position better. Gradually, as the feminist movement developed, some of its leaders began to attack Beauvoir, primarily for what they considered to be detrimental dependency on a male-oriented philosophy. Consequently, after years of presenting Beauvoir's position as quintessential liberating feminism, I found myself writing of her defensively. But the story of my relation to Beauvoir's and other feminism overflows the account of my engagement with Existentialism, and I will keep it for the next chapter.

It is perhaps debatable whether it is better or worse to commit oneself so fully to a particular philosophical position as I have done. Without much effort, I could see myself as a sort of caricature. Particularly in relation to Sartre, there is something a bit ludicrous in my having followed in his wake, like a puppy or an assiduous attendant, picking up each book as he wrote it and tossed it behind him, then considering what use I could make of it, or writing my own commentary on it. I myself have never felt this commitment to be an imprisonment but rather something that gave me a footing, a base on which to stand as I looked outward. Of course, I did not abandon the interests I had pursued in the decades before that day when my student asked what this thing called Existentialism was all about. Paradoxically, I might as easily be charged with spreading myself too thin as of having focused too narrowly. Most often my diverse interests worked together harmoniously. One of my most successful and enjoyable ventures in effecting a synthesis of my diverse scholarly concerns was the writing of my book *The Meddling Gods: Four Essays on Classical Themes* (1974), in which my Existentialist orientation gave me a fresh outlook on classical motifs, ranging from the investigation of the Gorgon to Eliot's adaptation of Euripides. Whether it is self-delusion or not, I like to think that what I have done in relation to Sartre is to have adopted a basic framework for my thought; if I have kept this structure as my dwelling place, I have at least gone outside to design my own garden in its environs.

SIX

Existential Feminism

THE CAT AND THE QUEEN

In 1984, a little less than two years before her death, I asked for and was granted an interview with Simone de Beauvoir. I had received a couple of letters from her earlier in response to my sending her my first book and to my asking permission to use her work on my television programs; they were gracious replies, but not significant. This time was different. Determined that there should be no miscarriage of plans, I wrote ahead to ask when she would be in Paris that summer and whether I might count on seeing her. Along with my letter I sent a manuscript copy of an article, "The Forms of Farewell," destined for later publication in *Philosophy and Literature;* it dealt with Beauvoir's account of the closing decades of Sartre's life (*A Farewell to Sartre*), and with some of her fictional anticipatory encounters with aging. In the paper, as delicately as I could, I had commented on possible meanings in back of some of Sartre's behavior, on the pattern of her life with Sartre at that period, the rift with Benny Lévy, etc. Any fears that I had that she might take offense proved groundless. She wrote,

> I have read with immense interest your article on "The Forms of Farewell." I was moved by its sympathy, its understanding; I admire its profundity and its subtlety. It has made me reflect much, for it poses a number of pertinent questions. This is the first time that a commentary on my book has truly enriched me.

She went on to say that she would be at home in June and would be very happy (she used the masculine form of the adjective, *heureux!*) to meet me. And she gave me her telephone number.

I went to her apartment without a tape recorder, with no intention of coming away with an interview that might be published. Mostly I wanted to experience for a moment the real presence of someone with whom for many years my thoughts and imagination had been in constant contact. It was a bit of a pilgrimage as well, and I had brought along as a visible sign of tribute a small present, a Zuni silver and turquoise necklace, carefully selected so as to be significant but not so expensive as to be in bad taste.

When Simone de Beauvoir received me, I was struck by how small and old and fragile she appeared, an impression dispelled by the firmness of her voice and handshake. She was elegantly but strangely dressed—in a dark blue dressing gown over gold pajamas (clearly for display, not for sleeping) and a red turban that concealed her hair. The turban caused a bit of trouble when she slipped the necklace over it without unfastening the clasp; fortunately it did not break. The gift seemed genuinely to please her; she frequently looked down at the pendant and fingered it during the hour or so that we talked—mostly in English, but with an admixture of French on both sides.

Since she left it to me to structure our conversation, I began by saying that I had just seen *The Blood of Others,* a film (starring Jodie Foster) based on Beauvoir's novel, and I wondered what she thought of it. In a somewhat angry tone, she replied that she had not seen it and did not intend to see it. She told me that after she had initially objected to some of the plans that had been shown to her, she had not been consulted at all. Shockingly (my word, not hers), she had not even been invited to its formal presentation showing. What primarily disturbed her when she heard a friend's report of the movie was not the foolish melodramatic action that had been imposed on the plot, but the fact that whereas in the book a peripheral character was responsible for making the heroine pregnant and leaving her to confront the subsequent abortion alone, the film ascribed this role to Jean, the hero; he, she protested indignantly, could not possibly have behaved so irresponsibly. This interplay of celebrity and neglect came out more strongly when Simone de Beauvoir spoke of the diminishing interest in France in her work and in Sartre's. Young people today, she observed, were not much concerned with philosophy and with "the question of what it means to be human"; they were more taken up with health matters, with activities to insure physical well-being, and with "things of the moment." But she added that each spring she received letters from lycée graduates who reported that of all the philosophers they had read, they found Sartre the most meaningful to them. So perhaps someday her ideas and Sartre's might be found relevant again. I was a bit disappointed that, when I asked her what aspects of their work she would like to see further developed in the future, she seemed to be totally at a loss for a reply. Probably I was at fault here. It was unreasonable to expect her to go beyond her own vision.

I brought up a few questions specifically about Sartre. When I asked if she knew what the "insurmountable difficulties" were that had prevented him from completing the book on ethics he had started to work on after *Being and Nothingness*, she said that she did not. Since he never explained them to her, I wonder if he ever spelled them out for himself. Sartre's need for a fresh start, she said, led him to write the *Critique*. His failure to complete the second volume of that, she added, was not due to any philosophical difficulties but to his reluctance to take on the enormous historical research it would have demanded, especially since all that was vitally important to him was in the first volume. In response to my inquiry as to whether Sartre's scenario for John Huston's *Freud* represented any change in his attitude toward Freudian theory, as has been claimed, she responded negatively. Sartre "did it only for the money." But she cautioned that Sartre's profound admiration for Freud should not be underestimated, even though Sartre *never* (her voice underscored) accepted the notion of the Unconscious. She approved of my idea that Sartre did indeed develop the positive dimensions of the Look; she deplored the way that critics saw only the negative aspects of his view of human relations. Yet she warned that he never embraced any notion of an easy union of all humanity as suggested at the end of his last interview with Benny Lévy. Instead, she said, "There will always be both friends and enemies."

Simone de Beauvoir spoke to me enthusiastically about work she had recently been doing on a large television project featuring *The Second Sex*. With respect to the current status of feminism in France, where legally women had attained a full equality they had not yet achieved in the United States (I assume she referred to the failure of the effort to pass the Equal Rights Amendment), all had been done that could be done in the short run. What was required now was reform through the slower process of education. She did not appear discouraged. She did not refer, nor did I, to the division between her and some of the younger French feminists, but she was emphatic in reaffirming her rejection of biologically determining differences between the sexes with respect to intelligence, personality, or values. That women's cultural situation might have led them to develop a different kind of value system, she was willing to accept, but she showed little interest in the subject. I was surprised that she was unacquainted with Carol Gilligan's book *In a Different Voice*, which has been so influential in the discussion of feminine ethics. I promised to send her a copy. Of course, I tried to express to her something of how much her writing and her example had meant to me, and she thanked me warmly for what I had done to promote interest in her writing. That was about it.

Later I learned from her (and my) friend Oreste Pucciani that she had enjoyed seeing me and found me "très sympathique." On my side, I cannot say that I learned anything of great importance that I had not known before, nor can I claim that there occurred between us one of those rare and momentous instances when a sudden sense of intimate understanding seems to dissolve all distance. But the hour was deeply satisfying. I can recall unfortunate instances when the flesh-and-blood presence of an author whose book I had admired made me suspect the existence of a ghostwriter. By contrast, Simone de Beauvoir's demeanor, manner, gestures, facial expression, even her voice, in which Sartre took such delight and which on recordings had sometimes sounded to me unpleasantly shrill, all seemed to express her essential being as I had imagined it. Her presence was a confirmation.

So I had proved the truth of the old saw; a cat can not only look at a queen but talk with her—even make comparisons. We had noted that both of us had been slow to realize the restrictions imposed on us as women and that this was largely due to "parental attitudes." I am sure that each of us had in mind particularly her father's interest in her intellectual development.

I admit that I am one of those persons described by Beauvoir's biographer Deirdre Bair as so "besotted by Sartre and Beauvoir" that they can even read her letters to him with pleasure. Compared with some of Beauvoir's critics, I go very far in the direction of accepting her own view of her life as closer to the truth than the reconstructions offered by a number of later interpreters. I have immense admiration for her personally; I regard her contribution to the century as of the utmost importance. Paradoxically, I know that to some of her followers I have seemed, by giving greater emphasis to Sartre, to have underestimated Beauvoir. In my own mind, my attitude toward her and her achievement is neither uncritical nor condescending. My feelings about her have been an important part of me; even now my reactions to feminism bear indelible traces of my having for a time all but identified it with what she wrote about the situation of women.

While I never consciously modeled myself after Beauvoir, as some women have reported of themselves, she represented for me in many respects the apotheosis of the type of woman I wanted to be—even before I read *The Second Sex*. She had succeeded brilliantly in her career, first as teacher, then as writer. She had written serious novels and even published books in philosophy. Rejecting traditional feminine patterns, she fearlessly claimed her right to sexual freedom outside of marriage. She and Sartre together had designed a lifestyle peculiarly their own. If ever a person created for herself exactly the life she wanted and lived it with relish and integrity, she appeared to be the one. What more could anyone want? *The Second Sex* immeasurably increased her stature and pointed up, perhaps even more than she had intended, how great had been the odds against her having been able to create the woman she became.

The complex pattern of "essential and contingent loves" that Beauvoir and Sartre established did not strike me as a desirable model for most people. I would have been incapable of living with it myself and could not wish for it even in my imagination. I suspect that, maybe to a fault, I have seen Sartre and her relations with him through Beauvoir's eyes. With respect to one another, bizarre as the situation may seem to outsiders, the two did seem to me successful in maintaining a basic fidelity and honesty that never violated the bond between them. Until their deaths, I found no reason to doubt their personal honesty or their good faith toward one another. Their posthumously published letters and Beauvoir's *Journal* forced a reappraisal, at least of their relations with the "contingent" lovers on the periphery. The couple's behavior has been compared to that of the scheming pair in *Les Liaisons dangereuses*. This is going too far. Sartre and Beauvoir were no cold-blooded manipulators; what they sought for themselves and allowed to one another was the opportunity to experience a variety of loves, not empty sexual conquests (though I will not argue that some of Sartre's more casual flings were anything more than that). But they did not have the same scrupulous respect for the contingent lovers that they showed to one another.

The legacy of Beauvoir's letters to Sartre and her *Journal* posed a special problem since they revealed details of her erotic involvement with three young women. In itself this would hardly have been of concern except to her homophobic admirers, if there were any. Indeed, it should have come as no surprise to anyone who had read her autobiographical novel, *She Came to Stay,* and her sympathetic treatment of lesbian love in *The Second Sex.* But Beauvoir had explicitly and emphatically denied, in published interviews and in private conversation with Deirdre Bair, that she had ever had sexual relations with a woman. She had lied. Why? Though wishing she had not done so, I think I can understand why. In writing of love between women, Beauvoir always reserved the noun "lesbian" for a woman whose sexual life was solely with others of the same sex, a designation hardly applicable to herself. I think her reluctance to admit the truth may have been also for the sake of shielding the women whose names such an admission would immediately have brought forth. I have to admit, though, that no such caution deterred her with respect to the posthumous revelations. Perhaps it would be more accurate to say that she wanted to avoid the reproaches of those whose secrets she would have revealed. In any case, it would not have been possible for her or anyone else to suppress the relevant material, which was all pervasive, without preventing or long postponing the publication of her letters and her journal. What disturbed me was not the fact of the relations, but the way that Beauvoir (like Sartre in his affairs with women) failed miserably in maintaining with the others the honesty she and Sartre insisted on for themselves. In a network of lies and deceptions, they used others as objects in a drama as illustrative of bad faith as *No Exit.* Although I did not find these revelations exactly traumatic, they were disturbing. I am glad that I did not know of them before I had my interview with Beauvoir. It seems to me a bit too facile to say that the disclosures simply show that the two were human after all. (I have always had at least as much sympathy for the recalcitrant Alceste as for the easygoing Philinte at the end of *The Misanthrope.*) Yet, finally, these private failures seem to me to be venial sins, not mortal, or—as the couple might prefer to put it—contingent lapses rather than essential, and certainly not things that should be held to undermine the validity of their literary and philosophical works.

I am exasperated by the charge that her *Letters to Sartre* and *Journal* show Beauvoir's personal life to have been in direct contradiction with the ideal of the liberated woman proposed in *The Second Sex.* Absurdly, some have concluded that she was after all only a woman who lived for love and subordinated herself to one man. To support this claim, her detractors quote passages written during the war when Sartre's life was in danger—exclamations to the effect that she could not face life without him, that he meant more to her than anything else in the world, and the like—things that surely must be read in context and seen in proper perspective. Some critics have pointed to specific small instances in which she put his immediate need before hers, something I would hope might happen occasionally between any two close associates. Among other things, Beauvoir has been criticized for devoting the years immediately after Sartre's death to preparing for publication his letters and a series of interviews she had held with him instead of engaging in work of her own. There is no evidence that she had in mind any creative project that she was sacrificing at this time. Her objective accomplishments by themselves refute any suggestion that she neglected her own career in his lifetime. And we should not forget that it was Sartre who first encouraged her to explore in writing the ways in which her woman's situation had been different from that of a man. John Gerassi, the son of one of Beauvoir's closest friends and the man selected by Sartre to be his official biographer, told a group of us at a meeting of the Simone de Beauvoir Society that in most of their later life it was Beauvoir, not Sartre, who regulated the structure of their daily existence, including the pattern of their sexual involvements with others. Gerassi reported a significant exchange. He inquired of Beauvoir why she had not chosen to stay with Nelson Algren when he begged her to do so. She replied, "It was because Sartre did not ask me to choose." I have tried, whenever I had the opportunity, to fight against the tendency to reduce Beauvoir to a submissive woman whose apparent revolt was an empty show, who did not practice what she preached.

Some partisans of Beauvoir, tired of seeing her discussed too often solely in terms of how she utilized Sartre's philosophy in her writing, have gone to the opposite extreme. The most flagrant example is a literally incredible book by Kate and Edward Fullbrook, *Simone de Beauvoir and Jean-Paul Sartre: The Remaking of a Twentieth-Century Legend*. The authors claim that Beauvoir was the creative and rigorous philosopher, that Sartre was incapable of writing philosophy without her help, that he took from her ideas that he passed off as his own, that he finally stopped writing philosophy after the *Critique* because he could not go any further with what she had given him—and that she (the founder of middle-of-the-century feminism) willingly allowed him to do this, so resigned was she to the belief that the world would not accept philosophical theories from a woman, and so devoted to the myth she was creating of the perfect couple. As the main support of this hypothesis, the Fullbrooks purportedly provide evidence that Sartre stole from Beauvoir's *She Came to Stay* the major ideas he presented in *Being in Nothingness*, all of which, they claim, had been fully developed in Beauvoir's novel before he began working on his own study. The so-called points of evidence do not hold up on close examination; the thesis is preposterous. *Being and Nothingness* is demonstrably an outgrowth of philosophical work Sartre had published in the 1930s and of ideas artistically expressed in *Nausea*. During the period of the "Phony War," Sartre was outlining in his *War Diaries* what later became *Being and Nothingness*, and Beauvoir was writing one of several versions of *She Came to Stay*. We know that they read and discussed one another's work; there must have been a degree of cross influence. And undoubtedly Sartre's discussion of human relations and Beauvoir's fictional account must have reflected their shared experience in the intimate trio they established with Olga Kosakievicz in Rouen, the story of which furnishes the plot of Beauvoir's novel. I myself pointed out points of resemblance in the two works, in *The Literature of Possibility*. But the claim that the essential philosophy, in its purest form, is in the novel rather than in *Being and Nothingness* is unsustainable. The truth is that the philosophical significance of some of the examples chosen emerges only when read in light of Sartre's analysis. Moreover, while Beauvoir's philosophical essays (published, we note, under her own name) offer much that is original, they assume as their starting point the fundamental ontology of *Being and Nothingness* exactly in the form that Sartre has given it.

It is not obligatory to try to downgrade Sartre in order to praise Beauvoir, though some of her supporters seem to think that it is. Nor do I want to appear to do the reverse. I accept Beauvoir's own appraisal with respect to philosophy, that for her it was secondary to literature and that Sartre was the truly creative and original philosopher. But this is not to say that what she did in philosophy was of no value. In addition, it is generally agreed that her essays played a large part in influencing Sartre's decision to give greater weight to social conditioning in his later writing. Her novels are in no way imitative of his literary works. Finally, Sartre never attempted to do anything remotely equivalent to *The Second Sex*. Once that work is considered, we must take seriously the claims of those who say that Beauvoir's influence on the course of history in this century is more far-reaching than Sartre's. It is of my early reaction to this book that I want to speak next.

Among those who jubilantly welcomed *The Second Sex* were at least two distinct groups of women, differentiated partly by age, partly by circumstance. Beauvoir spoke *to* women for whom she opened up a new world, and not only those on the threshold of their adult lives. Directly influenced by her, a significant number of married women went back to school, took up promising careers, and sometimes divorced or were divorced by their husbands. She spoke *for* a different group, women whose situations were more like mine. Though almost eight years younger than Beauvoir, I was, in many respects, of her generation. My education was completed before the end of World War II; I entered the postwar era as an adult, single woman already established in a professional career of my own choosing. When I say that Beauvoir spoke *for* us, I mean that she clarified and articulated for us the nature of the choice we had made, the unspoken assumptions that had led us to make it, our secret resentments, and the kind of future we hoped for.

As Betty Friedan pointed out in *The Feminine Mystique* (1963), the experience of girls who became women in the years preceding and during World War II was strikingly different from that of women who were born just a little later. Our generation did not enjoy sexual equality. Interesting job opportunities were limited. It was a rare few who combined professional lives with having a family. Women who chose careers instead of marriage were unusual, but there were enough of them to provide a significant number of role models for girls. It was only after the war that public sentiment returned so fervently to the ideal of wife and mother as the sole and essential goal for women.

At Wilson College in the thirties I found a basic assumption that even if presumably most of us students would marry, we should train ourselves for what would be at least an interesting and worthwhile interim job. The important idea conveyed to us, implied rather than explicitly formulated, was that it was up to each one to determine what sort of future she wanted for herself. Still, while Virginia Woolf's *A Room of One's Own* appealed greatly to many of us, we did not read it as a call to action. Mostly, I believe, we assumed that we would be able to make it even as things were and that the situation was bound to improve in the course of humanity's march on the road of inevitable progress. (We did not, needless to say, realize how privileged we were.) A report of survivors in our class, which I read recently, showed that while only a few had remained unmarried, a very large proportion of the class members had done significant work outside the home during most or part of their lives.

These were the positive things. Away from the shelter of my women's college, especially during my childhood and early teens, there was abundant testimony to the inferiority of women's place in the scheme of things. As a girl, I looked on my situation as posing a clear either/or, crystalized in the contrast between my mother's life and that of my still unmarried teacher-aunts and reinforced by my father's urging Jean and

Paul and me alike to seek to become eagles. I heard the message, "You don't have to be an ordinary woman." What I had in mind was not a feeling that I possessed unordinary abilities. (On the contrary, I have sometimes thought that an appropriate title for my autobiography would be "Memoirs of an Over-Achiever.") I did feel that I could, if I tried, avoid having to submit to the kind of situation most women lived in. I did not wish that I had been born a man. I wanted to be a woman with the freedom of a man to choose my own way of life, to be independent. Like Beauvoir, I assumed that to pursue a serious career necessarily meant rejecting the roles of wife and mother.

Did I think that I would be giving up anything in refusing the traditional pattern for women? No. As for marriage, I recall the dismay I felt when one day at a church camp meeting, I listened to my mother and other women checking as to what had become of various girls they had known. In every instance the question was, "Who did she marry?" I decided that to marry was to become anonymous. Again like Beauvoir, I felt no sense of loss at the prospect of not having children. Beauvoir's refusal of maternity (never, as she herself remarked, Sartre's refusal of paternity) has been judged by some persons to be abnormal or due to an innate defect. But I understood her. The idea that every woman is born with or inevitably develops the wish, acknowledged or repressed, to bear a child is patently false. Given the world's overpopulation, the notion that every woman ought so to wish is absurd, if not wicked. When I was a child, I found babies uninteresting and annoying. If my brother cried in his crib, my sister went to pick him up; I ran out of earshot. I have never wished that somehow children of mine might have been fitted into my life plan. At no time did I want them. I have not come to regret their absence. And I, who have worried and held guilt feelings about almost everything, never for a moment felt guilty over that. Possibly the fact that most of my relatives were teachers led me to see their kind of caring for the young as more important, or more interesting, than maternity. Granted, whether man or woman, one has missed something by choosing not to have children. But whatever choice you make, you have missed both the positive and the negative experiences that another choice would have entailed. At any rate, we have our priorities. Beauvoir dared to live by hers. I have never wished that I had done otherwise. What about love? Though I cannot say that in my girlish daydreaming I ever knowingly resolved to separate sexuality from matrimony, I did not spend time imagining myself forced to choose between them. My erotic fantasies were as consuming as those of the adolescent Emma Bovary, and not much more realistic. Like Emma's, my reveries never ended in a stable marriage. Later, when I developed a tendency to fall in love with inappropriate or unavailable men, it was years before I recognized the existence of a self-imposed pattern in what I had taken to be a series of mishaps.

Among women of my generation, a tiny minority, mostly among the "stars," combined careers and marriages, and I am sure that among un-married working women, there were some who would have preferred, if they had been given the chance, to have stayed at home as wives and mothers. But for the majority of us who had succeeded in winning pro-fessional success, what we wanted was freedom for all women who so chose to pursue an independent career without social stigma and with-out the obstacles that had impeded us, and, almost more important, without the limitations on how far we could hope to go. *The Second Sex*, despite its radical presumption of individual self-determination and its rejection of the idea that mental and personality traits were sexually de-termined and its insistence that so-called "femininity" was a concept conveniently invented by males, essentially demanded only what earlier feminists had asked: women's privilege to define themselves as indi-viduals and to enjoy those human activities and rewards that men had found good and from which women had been excluded. In a sense Beauvoir was still writing in the tradition of the Enlightenment. She ar-gued, on rational grounds, that recognized "human rights" be extended to women—much as marchers in the Civil Rights movement here ap-pealed to the Constitution's guarantee of equal rights against states' racial discrimination. Equality was its keystone. It could not have been otherwise. There is a necessary order even in revolution. You can't send the King and Queen to the guillotine before you take the Bastille. To have attempted to anticipate later theories based on sexual difference would have been to make oneself incomprehensible. If I (like certain present-day French feminists) had tried at that date to speak of inventing a spe-cial language for women, or of enjoying the feminine body and culti-vating *jouissance*, the most sympathetic response I could possibly have hoped for would be, "Well, fine, Hazel, if that's your wish. But why did you want to go to college?"

Many women for whom the book came as a gospel of liberation ac-cepted it uncritically and hailed Beauvoir as their mother. Others, who considered it a breakthrough, nevertheless found, even in the years im-mediately following its publication, that in addition to a few factual er-rors, there were certain built-in limitations and blind spots. Some of these reservations I shared, others not. Naturally I disagreed with one often heard comment, that it would have been better if Beauvoir had not cluttered up her discussion with Sartrean concepts and terminology. Some persons who thus complained may have been motivated by unwillingness to accept Sartre's overall position and regretted Beauvoir's embrace of it. Most, I suspect, had not read Sartre but felt uneasy in the presence of a philosophical position sometimes implied rather than explained. But I think Beauvoir adequately clarified what was essential. To me, her exploration of women's situation in light of a specific view on what it means to be a human being is one of the distinctive, admirable features of her work compared with that of feminists who preceded her (and many who followed her). A feminism without philosophical underpinning risks being purely political. Similarly, I was never bothered by another objection (though I think this was not often voiced until later): the reproach that Beauvoir "blamed the victim." True, she claimed that a sexist society could not have endured for so many centuries if many women had actively resisted it, a fact that seems rather obvious. But her emphasis was on the diabolical way that women were manipulated into believing that their well-being lay in maintaining the status quo. The hope of any revolution rests on convincing the victims that they are not as helpless as they have believed themselves to be. A few limitations are undeniably present. The book is strong as a call to action but weak in specific proposals of steps to be taken. Its point of view is decidedly that of a Parisian intellectual. Beauvoir did seem to try to lift herself above the struggle, to distance herself from other women, to use "they" rather than "we." (In later years, of course, she demonstrated conclusively her solidarity with all women—in militant action more than in her writing and without essentially modifying the fundamental doctrines of *The Second Sex*.) Beauvoir wrote perceptively of the difficulties a woman faced if she wanted to have a professional career without giving up the traditional roles, but her sympathy sounds a bit perfunctory. Clearly she felt it was wiser not to try to do so. Her suggestions for communal care for the children of working mothers are not without merit, but she herself appeared incapable of truly appreciating the positive aspect of being a wife and mother.

Shining through the text of *The Second Sex* is Beauvoir's personal conviction that a success comparable to her own is the best if not the only right goal for women. Anything else is second best, and presumably the species will be carried on by those who do not rise to this vision. She is, of course, not the only one to want to refashion the world in her own image. I once heard Betty Friedan assert rather tactlessly to a group of women deans and counselors that no woman can have a fulfilling life who has not, as she herself had, enjoyed marriage, motherhood, and a career—all three. Both she and Beauvoir, in my opinion, have been a bit narrow and dogmatic in their pronouncements as to what is right for all women. I have always thought that we ought to respect a variety of options as legitimate if the choice is satisfying to the one who makes it and not injurious to others affected by it. I myself would have pity and, I confess, some disdain for a woman who, with other possibilities open to her, would be content to live as a slave to a man or to her children. But women who, within a traditional but not exploitative family structure, lead lives that are personally creative and rewarding and/or valuable to the community should not be labeled failures because they choose not to enter the job market. To be fair, Beauvoir did not intend to redefine exactly what women ought to be. Her great appeal to me was that she fiercely argued that every woman should be free to choose the kind of person she wants to be, and Beauvoir fought for social changes to make this possible. Granted, she sounded at times as if she naively assumed that most women, if enlightened and given the opportunity, would find her style of life the most rewarding. The fact is that many women of my generation did find it so, and we owe her a great debt for encouraging us in so choosing. The right to make a one-sided choice is as precious as the privilege to try everything.

With such small reservations, my own thought, in the fifties and on into the early sixties, was comfortably in harmony with the position set forth in *The Second Sex*. I believed as Beauvoir did that dispelling the sexist myth would liberate men as well as women. Perceiving the book's wide influence and witnessing the increasing political pressure that women were beginning to exert, I assumed that all that remained to be done was to find ways to implement the goals that it laid down: to create a society that would enable both sexes to find better ways to realize themselves as human beings.

MY LATER JOURNEY

I realize now that one of the reasons that I looked on *The Second Sex* as a validation more than an awakening was that I myself was all too ready to see myself joined with Beauvoir in a "we" determined to help "them," the as yet unenlightened women from whom I had been fortunate to dissociate myself.

Two recollections are especially relevant. Once, in the early sixties, a woman I was visiting in a small midwestern city complained to me that she could find no women friends to talk to. Since she lived in a community made up mostly of young executives whose wives were college graduates, I felt that she was exaggerating. We went to a women's lunch given by one of her neighbors. I found out what my friend was facing. Wanting to show myself friendly but not condescending, I tried to interrupt the flow of remarks on baby care, knitting, and cooking by a neutral inquiry as to whether anyone had read Harper Lee's current bestseller, *To Kill a Mockingbird*. No one had. To fill the silence, one person said, "I keep thinking that I'll read a book one day, but something always comes up." I thought then that these women were too sound asleep to feel pain. Later, reading Marilyn French's *The Women's Room*, I felt as if the author must have been present on the occasion. Then I did a double take. French's all too accurate portrait was of a specific stage. Her fictional women were complacent on the outside; there was discontent underneath, and later in the novel there was a bitter awakening. My easy dismissal might have been unjust. Still, at the time the experience strengthened not only my conviction that I had made the right choice but also my sense of detachment. I reacted similarly on the surprisingly frequent occasions when a faculty wife remarked half admiringly and half wistfully on how free and interesting my life seemed to be.

Another memory goes back to my first year of teaching, in Greensboro. It concerns the other side of the choice. I could not hide from myself the fact that not all of my female colleagues felt that a career was enough, some because they genuinely wanted to be wives and mothers, others, I am convinced, because they had unreflectively internalized the prevailing notion that only women who couldn't take husbands didn't, that almost any marriage was better than none. I recall Helen, middle-aged, unmarried, who tried one day to persuade me to accept the marriage proposal of a man she admitted to be not the sort of person I would be likely to choose enthusiastically. She told me a parable about the man who entered a forest to find a stick that was exactly right for a cane. Rejecting first one, then another, he came out the other side empty-handed. "So you see. . . ." I was less surprised at her lack of understanding of me than I was appalled at what she had revealed of herself. In her own eyes, hers was a wasted life. Well, you may say, she had never met the right man for marriage, but was she so unattractive that she couldn't even find a lover? In that small community, as in most other similarly situated women's colleges then, extramarital affairs were usually grounds for dismissal. Mostly they were ventures for the foolhardy. Helen's life was somewhat better than that of a spinster teacher in the nineteenth century, but not sufficiently so for her to be happy. I was sympathetic, but privately I felt impatient with her for not trying harder to make her life worthwhile to herself.

Looking back on both of these instances, I marvel that it took me so long to realize that the central issue was not that women should be free to choose between an either/or, but that they should be expected to make such a choice. I was just beginning to realize this when one day (probably in the mid-sixties) Judy, one of my most brilliant seniors, came to me in tears. Her Honors adviser, a man especially admired by students as genuinely concerned with their academic and personal well-being, had told her that she must confront the fact that she would have to decide between having an academic career and developing her potentialities "as a woman." By that date I was able to assure her that he was wrong, but I still felt it necessary to warn her that she would not always find things easy.

As for myself, by the time I was established in a university in the forties, I felt that I was fully liberated. I believed that I had arrived at this position through willpower and considerable good luck. That, given the circumstances, I had been singularly fortunate I continue to believe. It was not until the end of my graduate school years that I was forced to confront seriously the existence of external limits to my aspirations. I remember calculating exactly what my chances were. It was unthinkable that I could teach at any of the Ivy League or other all male institutions. It was barely possible that I might get something at one of the state or municipal universities. My most likely opportunity would be at a women's college, and indeed my first seven years of teaching were at colleges for women only. This fact may in itself help to explain why I did not personally suffer from discrimination inside academia in those early years. I was well aware that it existed in hiring practices, and I met with one particularly interesting example at the time I was thinking of leaving the University of Toledo. I was under consideration for an appointment at a state university at which Gardner Williams's brother-in-law taught. He reported to Gardner what happened behind closed doors. The all male committee was inclining favorably toward me when one man objected: he agreed that Miss Barnes's qualifications were excellent; he would vote for her if the position were in any subject other than philosophy. But "women simply cannot think philosophically," he said. (Apparently he had never heard of Beauvoir.) Gardner did not pass on this information to me until some years afterward, but I knew there were other coeducational institutions where my application was not or would not have been given consideration, and specifically because of my sex. Though I was troubled by such things, my resentment was mostly smothered by my sense of triumph in getting to where I wanted to go in spite of the obstacles.

Events moved me forward almost providentially. Sometimes the system actually seemed to work not against but for me, including even the infamous "old boys network." My coming to Colorado is a case in point. When things collapsed for me at Ohio State, I sent out letters of application to numerous places where I would have liked to be, whether I had reason to think there was an opening or not. One of them was the University of Colorado, which I included primarily at Doris's suggestion. While she was under no pressure to leave Columbus, where she had won recognition for her unusual success in teaching English (or, more accurately, reading) at a trade school for delinquent high school boys, the job was not inspiring. She had decided to continue graduate work (she had at that time an M.A.) in a location where, we hoped, I could find an appointment. Colorado, she urged, would be an ideal spot. I think that I addressed my letter to the dean of the College of Arts and Sciences, indicating my experience in Classics and philosophy departments and my interest in teaching in either or both. I added that I was enthusiastic about an interdisciplinary course I had been developing ("humanities" in this context was not yet a term familiar to me). Serendipitously there proved to be an opening for a person who would be half-time in Classics and half in a new humanities program, which the university had been one of the first institutions to adopt; the classicist who was being replaced had also taught a course in ancient Greek religions for the Philosophy Department. My qualifications precisely fit the requirement. My final selection and the particularly friendly interest bestowed on me by John Hough, the Classics chair, were helped by a letter of recommendation from Hough's personal friend in the Department of Classics at O.S.U., whom I knew. When Doris and I arrived that summer in her Ford, packed with books, the old vinyl records, and trailing philodendron, John and Eleanor Hough welcomed us both, and John inquired about Doris's plans. Learning she was to be a doctoral candidate in English, he made a phone call to the chair of that department. Within twenty-four hours Doris was offered a teaching associateship. The first two weekends after classes began, the Houghs gave a large sherry party at which Doris and I were introduced to other faculty and administrators, a most propitious beginning. For Doris it proved to be a decisive moment in her career. Before completing her work for the doctorate, she became a teaching associate at what was then still an extension division of the University at Boulder. After receiving the degree, she stayed on and was given a tenured appointment when the greatly enlarged institution was officially made the University of Colorado at Denver.

If I was ever the object of sexual discrimination at the University of Colorado, I was unaware of it. My departmental colleagues pushed my promotion, tenure, etc., with all possible speed and twice elected me chair of the department. One incident was of special significance. With three of my colleagues (all men) I went one day to a meeting of a state Classics association held at the Denver University Club (no academic affiliation). Arriving a bit early, we decided to order drinks at the bar. We were denied entrance on the ground that we were not accompanied by a member of the club, but one of the waiters said that nobody would object if the men went in without me. None of us went in. My companions shared my indignation. When I said angrily that I would leave and not attend the meeting, one of them, Harold Evjen, declared, "If you go, I will leave, too." Because of that offer, I stayed.

There were shadows, of course. Whenever one of us academic women accomplished anything of note, compliments usually included the irritating observation, spoken or implied, that this achievement was especially remarkable for a woman. Clearly we were regarded as exceptions to the general rule about women's ability. An amusing example not only shows how far this attitude could be taken, but illustrates how differently we women responded then. It must have been in about 1962, after I had given a public lecture at Colorado College, that one of the Colorado Springs newspapers carried a report of it in a column called "Personally Yours." In his well-intentioned review, the columnist gave serious praise to what I had said but included such idiotic remarks as "her mind was as sparkling as her eyes," and the opening lines, "The Doctor had lovely legs and the Doctor had a Ph.D. Without doubt a formidable amalgamation for any mere man." A few weeks later my friend and colleague Phyllis Kenevan told me of an amusing follow-up. A man whom she had met at a philosophy conference happened to come to Colorado and tried to locate her. Not sure exactly where she was teaching, he inquired first at Colorado College, saying that he could not remember the name of the woman he had met, but she taught philosophy and had lovely legs. He was told, "Oh, you must mean Hazel Barnes!" Eventually the matter was straightened out. When Phyllis told me about it, she added, "I thought it was a compliment to both of us."

I was aware that my situation was not duplicated everywhere in our university. Some departments seldom or never hired women; unquestionably, women were held to higher standards than men in academic advancement, though male self-deception may have been responsible here more frequently than deliberate discrimination. I had no reason to complain so far as I personally was concerned. Why should I in particular have been so lucky? It was when I began to ask "Why me?," not under Beauvoir's influence, not really until I began to read the more radical feminists in the later sixties and seventies, that the shell began to crack. As the protests and publicized evidence of sexual discrimination increased, the question of why my experience had been atypical became more urgent. The fairness of the male colleagues with whom I was most closely associated, while a contributing factor, was not by itself a sufficient cause. At first I told myself that perhaps it was because I had always taken it for granted that I would be judged as myself, not merely as a woman, and that my confident expectation of respectful acceptance insured it. This explanation crumbled when I considered how many other women claimed to have started out the same way only to have reality crash down upon them. Probing further, I searched to discern what my personal goal had been as an academic woman. I found it: To prove that I could hold my own in all of the professional activities normally carried on by male professors and to do so in such a way that no one could ever find occasion to blame or to excuse me by saying that I had behaved "like a woman." In short, I had never rocked the boat; hardly something to be proud of.

I perceived how far this attitude extended as I thought back on how I had reacted in instances of sexual harassment. Though fortunate, once again, in never encountering it in circumstances in which my academic status depended on how I responded, I had (like every woman, I dare to say) been forced to deal with unwelcome sexual aggression—sometimes amusing, as when I was chased around a table by a retired professor afflicted with what one of my women friends dubbed "senile virility"; most often unpleasant but harmless; once so forceful that I am convinced that it was only my threat to shout for help that prevented what would have been rape, however the perpetrator might have regarded it. In every instance I had flattered myself on being able to handle such matters without creating a disturbance or even, in the long run, making the offender feel uncomfortable. Sometimes I felt enough empathy with the man not to want to afflict him with painful embarrassment; much of the time my purpose was simply to make sure that a woman's presence would not be looked on as disruptive. The truth, I suppose, was that my accommodating behavior was a form of connivance.

Disconcerted at this revelation of how deeply my internal attitudes had been molded, how much less free I had been than I thought, I looked back more carefully at the strictly academic side. Had my controlling purpose paid off here? For the most part it had, but here, too, I found cause for discomfort. I was struck especially by my recollection of an event that took place a year after I had come to Colorado. I presented an hour-long paper at a meeting of the Rocky Mountain and Plains States Philosophical Institute, held in Laramie. Speaking as requested on a topic related to philosophy of education, I elicited a lively discussion to which I had two unusually interesting responses, one immediately afterward, the other of which I learned many years later. Joe Cohen, chair of philosophy at the University of Colorado, who had become my firm supporter, mixed his commendation with a serious reproach. In his view, my defense of the paper had been too "strident." I should have been more conciliatory, more propitiating, more "feminine." Annoyed by what I considered an inappropriate display of male bias, I did not take his advice to heart. At another meeting of the institute, in the seventies, held in Colorado Springs, Sterling McMurrin, professor of philosophy at the University of Utah and for a time national Secretary of Education, publicly reminisced on the history of the association. Recalling the meeting in Laramie, he said that my session had prompted him to a radical change of mind. Until then he had insisted that any woman would join the Utah Philosophy Department "over his dead body." But having heard me present and defend a paper "as well as any man," he decided to withdraw his opposition, and did so. Naturally I was pleased, and I do not see any reason not to be so even now. But retrospectively I realized that with both Cohen and McMurrin I assumed that a traditional male standard of judgment was the just and only one. Some feminists would say today that Cohen's response was perhaps unintentionally the more perceptive.

Although in wanting to win success and recognition in a male-dominated world, I did not then recognize the extent to which I internalized many of what have become known as "male values," I was not so blinded as to want to be considered "just like a man," even professionally. I cherished a mostly hidden resentment against the prevailing assumption that women's experiences as such had nothing of value to contribute to the intellectual world, a feeling that prompted me often to use in class examples from women's interests in contrast to the wornout analogies of men smoking pipes in their studies or fixing their cars. I had mixed feelings when John Hough told me, soon after my arrival, that one of the things predisposing him to want to hire me was the statement by his friend at O.S.U.: "You will like Hazel. She thinks like a man." At the time I recognized that it mingled insult with flattery; knowing John was unaware of that, I took it as the compliment he intended. There was an interesting aftermath. Years afterward, John on his own told me that he had come to see the real implications of his statement, and he thanked me for not pointing out the truth before he was ready to receive it. At about that time some of us demanded that a committee of university women be appointed with authority to investigate the question of salary equity between the sexes. The man who was then president strenuously objected but gave in when outvoted by his executive committee. Some weeks later, at a reception, he confessed to me that observing the quiet efficiency of the committee and the results of its work, he regretted his initial opposition. Wanting to meet him halfway, I assured him that I realized how changes in attitude took time and told him of John's turnabout with respect to "thinking like a man." Totally missing the point, he concluded that I needed to be reassured about my femininity. He put his arm around me and said, in a voice both caressing and condescending, "That's all wrong. You're not at all like a man!" (He had a habit of misunderstanding; he was the only president of our university ever to be fired after a faculty vote of no confidence.)

   The truth is that in that early period before feminism became an active struggle for women's liberation, I was not wholly clear in my own mind as to how I felt about being a woman. I emphatically did not wish that I were a man instead. I felt obscurely that my feminine situation gave me a special point of view on the world that I would not have wanted to give up. Yet I resisted any suggestion of basic difference between men and women. Smug and complacent at having been able to break through, I was also as prickly and insecure inwardly as Dostoyevsky's Underground Man. It must have been this ambivalence that prompted my foolish words on the occasion (about 1954) of my first speaking out in our faculty senate. Clare Small, chair of the Women's Physical Education Department (gym classes were still required for both men and women students in those days), proposed a motion urging that insofar as was possible, every university committee should have one woman member (or something of the sort; my memory is not precise). I stated that while I appreciated the spirit of Miss Small's motion, I would vote against it. We women, I argued, were capable of making our way without help inasmuch as the sexes were equal and the same except for purely biological differences. Some wag inevitably shouted, "Vive la différence!" The innocuous motion passed in spite of my opposition. Yes, I actually did that, and it is one of the things in my life of which I am most deeply ashamed. I can truthfully say that I was not jealously guarding my own elevated status; I would gladly have welcomed more women associates anywhere in the university. I believe that I did feel threatened by what I took as an implicit assumption that some inherent weakness in women necessitated their being given the benefit of a handicap.

At any rate, the event serves as a corrective to any tendency on my part to assume that from the beginning I was a full-fledged feminist according to a minimal consensual definition that would hold today. It also serves for me as a milestone by which to measure how far I have come. Under the influence of writers in what I think of as the middle period of feminism, I changed greatly. I spoke publicly in favor of the need for affirmative action before the term was formally established, during that brief period when some of us used the expression "reverse discrimination" in a nonpejorative sense. When I was approached by students wanting to establish a program in women studies, I gladly promised my support. And, as I have shown, I began to reinterpret the meaning of my own past.

How complete and far-reaching was this slow conversion? As feminist thought has developed in the eighties and nineties, I have sometimes welcomed new theories as illuminating advances. Other ideas and arguments have seemed to me mistaken and regressive. I have wondered, in cases where I resisted, whether this testified to my ability to maintain a balanced point of view or signified that I was, after all, fixated at a certain stage. Probably this is not the proper question. Feminists today are split, if not splintered, on almost every issue except for the basic premise that women must play an active role in determining their own future. From my individual Existentialist position, I find myself moving back and forth between what are generally considered respectively the more conservative and the more radical sides of the controversies.

POSITIONINGS

Sometimes employed as a pejorative even now, "feminist" in some circles is a term one has to prove one's right to apply to oneself. When I speak of feminism, I neither use the noun so loosely as to indicate merely a desire to see women play a more important part in the world's history nor so narrowly as to require adherence to any particular set of doctrines. I suppose that I am with all feminists in wholeheartedly supporting the principle that society must take steps to accommodate women's legitimate needs and interests that for centuries have been overlooked. But even as I say this I recognize that both the remedies and the definitions of these needs and interests are subject to debate. My feminism undoubtedly is peculiarly my own, colored by my generation, by my Existentialist philosophy, and by my individual experiences and personal prejudices. I am, for example, too puritanical (or should I say, too fastidious, or too romantic) to feel comfortable with the idea of sex as entertainment; I am too pedantic to use "their" as a singular possessive or "herstory" since I know that "history" is not a gender-laden word like "wo-man" but a derivative of the neutral Greek *historia* (inquiry). Whether my feminism is internally consistent or merely seems so to me I cannot say. I can most briefly describe *what* it is by showing where I stand with respect to three major theoretical controversies.

These are: (1) Should a feminism be based on the assumption of equality or on the recognition of sexual differences? (2) Is there any significant way in which the term "human" or "humanity" (or "person") is inclusive of "male" and "female" other than as referring to a biological species? (3) Should we view sexual practices and preferences as "essential" or as "socially constructed"? While it may be true that to cling to the extreme view in any one of these issues would lead to a *reductio ad absurdum*, it would be equally foolish, I think, to assume that the ideal feminism would represent a position squarely in the middle of each. Here, then, are my opinions: I do not pretend to offer proof.

Equality of Difference

Both intellectually and emotionally—and unsurprisingly—I incline strongly to the side of equality. I am initially suspicious of any argument stressing innate differences between male and female; this, after all, was the assumption supporting women's oppression. In its strongest form it smacks of the fallacious "separate but equal" claim utilized by segregationists. And I would argue that difference itself can be accommodated under the goal of insuring to everyone equal opportunity for self-making. Clearly we must distinguish between biological and situational differences; my objections are solely to attributing a deterministic force to the former. Some neo-Freudian and Lacanian feminists seem to me to come dangerously close to reinstituting the old Freudian "anatomy is destiny," a view I resist whether it is in the form presented by some of the French feminists or by Camille Paglia. I stubbornly insist that becoming a woman means designing one's place creatively, not building a nest by instinct. That centuries of male dominance have rendered language phallogocentric is undeniable. To claim, following Lacan, that a girl's psychological development differs from that of a boy because of the association of the "word" of the father with the penis is not, in my opinion, an improvement over the infamous "penis envy" ascribed to all females by Freud, even if enfolded in new theories of language.

I do believe there is a legitimate feminist standpoint in discussions of ethics, values, and rationality. A feminism that emphasizes difference seems to me progressive so long as it deals with differences stemming from women's situation. And I would certainly include in that situation the special knowledge derived from having been a mother. (It would be interesting, by the way, to compare the personal values held by men who have lived for years as single parents of young children with those of men who have not.) Nel Noddings, in *Women and Evil*, has stressed the mediation skills that women are likely to develop as the result of being an authority figure for their children while at the same time subordinate to their husbands. If, as Gilligan and others have demonstrated, girls, and the women they become, tend to live by an ethics more relational, empathic, and situational than traditional ethics based on abstract, universal principles, certainly any future ethical thought ought to be concerned with insights derived from this discovery. One might even argue (as Sartre in fact did) that women, like minorities, are in a privileged position to open up new areas of thought because as partial outsiders in the established system of rewards, they are inwardly less imprisoned by it.

If my position here puts me closer to the conservative than to the radical wing of today's feminists, the same is true of my attitude toward rationality. Whereas I was offended by the accusation that women cannot think philosophically, a few feminists today attack abstract reasoning and rationality as a narrow, inadequate, and distinctively male approach to reality. I agree that much of what has passed for rationality has often been no more than biased opinion and demonstrably a male bias. Emotional sensitivity is as essential to our humanity as reason is. Some recent philosophers claim that emotion is so inextricably associated with rational judgment that the two are virtually inseparable. There are many "ways of knowing," and we need to expand our understanding of what does and does not constitute reason as such. But I am not willing to identify rationality with masculinity and hand it over to men for their use only. This would be once again to define women by what they lack. Are women to be saddled with irrationality? Or to be limited solely to intuition and feeling? As the Underground Man reminded us, whatever other adjective you might apply to history, you would not call it rational. I see one of the chief tasks for women as being precisely to take the lead in putting reason where there has been unreason.

There is no hard evidence that psychological qualities, desirable or undesirable, are determined by one's biological sex. Even if it could be proved that some traits are found more often in one sex than in the other, there would still be more difference among members of either sex than between the two groups. A group of women in Northern Ireland won the Nobel Peace Prize, for which I applaud them. Many American women are demanding the right to engage in active combat in war. With my strong inclination toward pacifism, I personally regard this aspiration as misguided; but I emphatically believe that women should have access to the special privileges that service in combat and preparation for it win for men. Even Plato recognized such individual differences among members of the same sex when he argued that gifted women should be allowed to be Philosopher Queens.

To avoid misunderstanding, I should add that it is, of course, necessary to explore and to legislate in areas where biological differences create special problems. That medical research, for instance, should include women subjects and not assume that their susceptibility to heart attacks will be covered by knowledge gleaned from the study of men is as obvious as it is that there should be special provisions for pregnancy. To treat women with the assumption that they _are_ men is not to treat them equally.

Male, Female, and Human

In _An Existentialist Ethics_ I chose as my target for particular attack a sentence from Abraham Maslow's _Toward a Psychology of Being_. Though on the whole I admired Maslow as one of the best of contemporary psychologists, I had always objected to his acceptance of what I think of as the "acorn theory" of personal development. Allowing for a greater degree of self-determination than most psychologists are willing to grant, Maslow nonetheless continued the Aristotelian tradition of viewing each individual as born with a given set of potentialities peculiar to him or her but finally somehow constraining. A glaring example was his statement, "Femalehood is prepotent over personhood." In the mid-sixties this seemed to me not only demonstrably false but emblematic of every-thing that I or any other feminist found most objectionable. I saw in it the equivalent to saying that to be born female (or by extension, to be born African American or Asian or Jewish or Arab or whatever) is to be born with a set of limitations that prevent a given individual from realiz-ing a fully human status. Maslow's choice of "femalehood" rather than "malehood" (echoed in my deliberate exclusion of "Caucasian" in my ex-amples) implied, though he may have not intended it this way, the same hidden identification of human with male that, Beauvoir pointed out, makes woman "the Other." I would gladly have reversed the sentence so as to support Beauvoir's insistence that one is not born but becomes a woman. I agreed with Sartre's claim that our way of living our sexuality reflects what we have chosen to make of ourselves as persons. Such ba-sic truths seemed to me to be beyond challenge. I could not have imag-ined that future feminists (some, at least) would find cogent reasons to support Maslow's formulation.

While I have not changed my opposition to the statement, I have come to realize why one cannot simply reverse it to say, "Personhood is prepotent over femalehood." Even Sartre, who has often been accused of bestowing on consciousness too much power of detachment, insisted that every freedom is situated. Feminists have joined with other propo-nents of "identity politics" in pressing home the fact that no purely hu-man point of view exists, that concepts also are always situated. This probably is technically irrefutable. However objective I try to be, my outlook remains that of a white woman and a retired professor, also that of a longtime resident of Boulder, with a particular past; mine is the out-look of a "singular universal," in short, unique. While identity politics stops short of taking particularity this far, it has reduced the notion of commonality to the point at which the possibility of communication between different groups becomes problematic. Yet we *do* communicate; we *are* capable of empathic concern for persons or groups quite different from ourselves; and we do in fact, every day of our lives, mentally ab-stract the common essence of material objects, of animals, and of a wide variety of feelings, experiences, etc. I am unwilling to acknowledge that the notion of an all-embracing humanity is useless today, though I admit that it can be and often is misused.

Obviously, if "human" is equated with the self-description of a partic-ular group, this is a vicious perversion. Similarly, if "human" is employed as a determining designation, it can be injurious. Sartre, for example, objected to the idea that we have a fixed human nature either in the

sense that there exists some discernible blueprint prescribing what we
all ought to be or that we are so governed by instincts and innate psychological traits that it is futile to hope that human patterns of behavior
can significantly change. I suspect that it is always unwise to assume the
existence of any clear and universally accepted definition of the meaning of human, never more so than when one group feels itself sufficiently
advanced in its understanding of what is good for humans to impose its
prescription on all others. Still, if the notion of humanity is allowed to
function as a sort of regulative idea, it may be helpful, even indispensable. It does so in legal matters, though today we are more aware of
cases in which the law must be a "respecter of persons" if it is to distribute equal justice instead of assuming the situational equality of all those
who stand before it. I myself felt the need of some governing notion of
"human" at the very moment that I recognized the validity of the argument that a woman's point of view on the Western tradition must be included in teaching it.

I never had any problem in making room in the curriculum for courses
devoted specifically to women's issues or to literary works by women
(and similarly with respect to ethnic minorities). I found the question of
a multiple standpoint more complex when it came to teaching the mas-
terpieces of "dead white males." I believe that it is possible for a pacifist
to be thrilled by Homer's *Iliad*. I do not hold that because ancient Athens
was indisputably a phallocracy, a woman should teach Greek literature
solely from the point of view of an outraged feminist. One of my humanities colleagues did exactly this.

Assuming I would approve, she showed me one day her written plan
for introducing Plato's *Symposium* to her freshman class. Starting with the
absurdity of Plato's depicting a discussion of love by men with no women
present (presumably women by themselves would never do the same),
Julia intended to devote the entire class hour to ridiculing the dialogue
and to using it as a basis for an attack on Greek sexism. Philosophical
and literary questions she ignored. Possibly she would get to them on
the second day allotted to the work; it is hard to see how by then any of
the students would feel inclined to find in it anything of value. That my
colleague's approach might be viewed sympathetically as an understandable over-reaction to the one-sided tradition of male-biased critical presentation is true but aside from the point. In my eyes her treatment of
Plato's dialogue would be a travesty and a desecration. I use the word
"desecration" advisedly, fully aware of the sneers directed today at the

idea of a "sacred canon" of works with universal appeal. I grant that membership on the list needs occasional reevaluation and that even authors most securely there should not be exempt from criticism. On innumerable appropriate occasions I have attacked the sexism of Greek society directly; in teaching the *Symposium* I regularly drew attention to the fact that women, on this occasion as always, were excluded from the banquet; I pointed out the infinite condescension implied in the gesture of sending the flute player to entertain the isolated women since the men wanted their talk uninterrupted by music. But to undermine the possibility for a woman to savor the kind of intellectual and aesthetic delight that men have enjoyed in reading the *Symposium* is to deprive a human being of her birthright. It is particularly ironic in this instance in that while Plato goes very far (perhaps too far) in the direction of making of love and of all creative impulses a stepping-stone on the way to a final rational vision, he believed that male and female alike might achieve that goal. He would have been delighted but not amazed to read the sonnet beginning "Euclid alone has looked on beauty bare," written by a woman poet, Edna St. Vincent Millay.

However difficult it may be to abstract from our multi-situated experiences those things that we share simply as humans, I think we do and must live by some such regulating idea. We rely on it implicitly when we expect that in introducing into the curriculum works from cultures formerly alien to us, we can read them with comprehension and empathy. It is assumed in the very efforts we make to transcend ourselves.

In papers that came to light after his death, Sartre chose the expression "integral humanity" with a look to the future, to designate a legitimate goal for an ethics. Here "integral humanity" is neither a restrictive term nor a label for a loosely defined existing condition. Sartre intends it to contrast with the subhumanity that is our present reality. Integral humanity would characterize a society in which communal responsibility would exist in harmony with freedom for individuals to develop to the maximum their unique possibilities for growth. This is, of course, a utopian ideal to be approximated, not a realizable state of perfection. But in the sense that it represents an ideal synthesis in which the right to difference is one of the ingredients of commonality, I think that "integral humanity" as a goal to be achieved may have meaning in feminist discourse. Of course it must be held in constant tension with the knowledge that "humanity" is never a finished thing. What is humanity?, asked James. He answered that we won't know "until the last man has had his last say." How tiresome! We have come far enough to know that the sentence has to be rewritten. "We won't know what humanity will have been until the last humans have had their last say." The time of integral humanity is not yet. But as Dewey pointed out, to believe an ideal is possible is the first and necessary step toward realizing it.

Essentialism and Social Construction

In the controversy over essentialism versus social conditioning the question of biological sexual determination reappears in another form. In this context those committed to the essentialist view are not concerned primarily with innate differences between the sexes but with forms of individual sexuality; that is, with sexual preference. Essentialists argue that we are born, physically made to be heterosexual or homosexual or—I suppose logically one would have to add—bisexual (chemically hermaphroditic?). Social constructionists insist that human sexuality is not reducible to an animal sexuality; that is, it holds that any individual's form of sexuality is the result of a choice (or series of choices) made within a social context. At first thought, the question of sexual preference might seem to be separate from the issue of feminism, but of course it is not. There are historical factors: many, though not all, lesbians have considered their choice to live with women, according to women's values, as a rejection of male sexist society. Lesbians have joined with male homosexuals in the fight for gay rights. Indeed, philosophically it would be hard to conceive of a feminism not concerned with freedom to design one's sexual life as one chooses.

Firmly, though somewhat uneasily (because of practical political implications), I take my stand here with the social constructionists. To be sure, scientific reports appear from time to time suggesting that homosexuality is genetic; they have yet to meet with universal acceptance by other scientists. I am far more persuaded by the arguments and evidence presented in *Dual Attraction: Understanding Bisexuality*, by Weinberg, Williams, and Pryor, who claim that sexual preference is neither fixed nor stable and that it is known to fluctuate radically within an individual's lifetime. What they claim fits my personal observations. I realize that we cannot know absolutely. I believe that in this instance Freud was right: that all of us are born with bisexual potentialities, that we develop as heterosexual, homosexual, or bisexual (ambisextrous, to use my friend Lynn Martin's term) according to a complexity of chance factors and continued personal choices. Many homosexuals (among them some whom I know personally) say that I am totally wrong; they point to themselves as living proof of their being what they are and always have been; they declare that they *know* their preference to be as much something given as the color of their eyes. They may be right. Or they could be mistaking a long-established reaction for one that was always inescapably there. In many instances they may have convinced themselves of the essentialist view because it has become politically expedient. The social constructionist theory, which I myself assume to be a radical one, has been somehow transformed into a trap set by conservatives. If homosexuality is a choice, a lifestyle, the argument goes (or so gays often believe and fear it will go), then a largely homophobic society has the right to declare it culpable and punishable. But on what basis other than sheer caprice? Not with the support of any natural or divine law. Not if all values and ethics are human creations, as social constructionists are not alone in maintaining. I sometimes wonder whether in a few cases, homosexuals' eagerness to look on themselves as ready-made is not an unacknowledged carryover of the old habit of internalizing society's verdict on them as undesirable deviants—as if to say, like the handicapped, "We can't be blamed." In the absence of proof, it seems to me that it would be better to state confidently: "This is our choice—as justified and as unjustified as yours."

Perhaps what I have given as my own view overstates the case. Certainly I would not be so foolish as to hold that by a simple wish or act of will, persons could suddenly find their desires and sexual responses rearranged. Perhaps if we accept Freud's claim that each of us biologically, or psychosomatically, is born with sexual inclinations of both sorts, one kind may initially be more strongly present in one individual than in another. Even so, the question of how or why one or the other preference did or did not develop into a stable sex orientation would remain.

Whether my feminism should be seen as radical or just middle-of-the-road liberal, or merely as a collection of personal prejudices, it is at any rate consistent in putting the emphasis always on the side of allowing for a multiplicity of free choices, both in what I believe to be internal possibilities for self-determination and in what I hold to be a desirable social and political goal. Sartre spoke of the need for "resocialization," a thorough reexamination of all of our traditional ideas with respect to the relations between the sexes, education, family structure, parenthood, and codes of behavior. In actual fact, such changes are coming about more rapidly than he or anyone else could have anticipated. Mostly we see them in the form of new problems for which there are no easy solutions. This occurs in any genuine revolution, and recent cultural change is certainly that.

MAKING PREFERENCES KNOWN

Living in Boulder, Colorado, I have the distinction of being a resident in one of three cities in the state to be among the first in the country to pass a law prohibiting discrimination based on sexual preference; as a result of this action, the voters of my state were the first to pass an amendment to the State Constitution that would have made the municipal regulations illegal. In May 1996 the United States Supreme Court declared this amendment unconstitutional. Among supporters of the amendment, along with those who are overtly homophobic, are the same kind of timid compromisers as have appeared on the national scene; they profess that they would never seek to uncover the perpetrators of "deviant" practices but object to any public avowal of being gay. Needless to say, I find the second position as unacceptable as the first; it is tainted by both self-deception and dishonesty. I do not see why people should be required to keep secret what they have no reason to feel ashamed of. "Coming out" should be one among other individual privileges. Yet here once again I find points where I am out of step with the vanguard.

When coming out is made into a moral imperative, I grow uneasy. In part this may be simply because I feel that personal reticence ought to be respected. Consensual adult sexual practices, like many other personal preferences, should be one's own business. In principle I object to labeling someone as if a designation of sexual preference expressed the whole person. This feeling on my part becomes a philosophical objection whenever "homosexuality" is assumed to carry with it a cluster of assumptions concerning an individual's personality traits, attitudes, and behavior. Social constructionists note that homosexual practices are not the same as "being a homosexual" and that the latter notion first emerged in Europe as late as the seventeenth century (some would say nineteenth). I recall meeting a young man many years ago who, having enthusiastically discovered Sartre, confessed to me that he was worried about how he, with his homosexual preferences, could live authentically when his lifestyle demanded that he conform to a host of expectations, beginning with the dress code. By now such anxieties may be less likely, but the idea that "being a homosexual" demands that one plays a certain role in a certain way has not entirely disappeared. Sartre himself, by the way, although in *Being and Nothingness* he used the idea that homosexuality was a given essence as an example of bad faith, was equally stringent in *Saint Genet* in ascribing bad faith to homophobes, whom he accused of projecting unacknowledged impulses onto a scapegoat Other. In his last interview, one with representatives for the homosexual journal *Le Gai Pied*, he responded sympathetically to the suggestion that at that date, as a temporary measure, some gays might prefer to live withdrawn into a kind of enclave. Whether this solution would be more likely to prove to be a positive step toward freedom or an imposition of a new mode of conformity is debatable.

What I regard as outmoded ideas have a way of reappearing, sometimes in the most unexpected contexts. We all know of homosexual couples who, in the name of sexual freedom, set up relationships that reinstate the fundamental patterns of patriarchal marriages against which feminists initially revolted. This was certainly true of the Stein-Toklas menage. My friend and colleague Donald Sutherland, who was an occasional visitor to the couple's home in Paris, reported a revealing incident. He had brought a bouquet of roses and handed them to Gertrude. Alice, reaching for them, said something like, "Here, I'll take the flowers Donald got for me." Obviously, she was instructing him: one gives flowers to the equivalent of the writer's wife, not to the writer. I suppose that almost any companion would perforce have stood in the shadow when Gertrude Stein was present, but Alice's subordination to Gertrude seems excessive.

Even the seemingly most radical of recent demands for freedom to determine the nature of one's sexual life sometimes reveal an ultraconservative position as their basis. Take transsexuality, for example. I suppose that to have one's body redesigned so that it has the physical characteristics of the opposite sex might be taken to stand for the ultimate exemplification of Sartrean self-making—or remaking. While I think there may be more imaginative ways than surgery to design a sex life uniquely suited to one's taste, I should certainly not favor any law or coercive sanction against change of sex operations for those who want them. On closer examination, however, the reason so often quoted for the transsexual choice ("I was born a male in a female body," or the opposite) points to a biological and psychological essentialism that is quite foreign to Existentialism. It repeats exactly the ancient conviction that a male or a female personality is fixed, defined, and clearly recognizable even if in this instance it has found itself in the wrong body. I continue to maintain that in reality we define our sexuality as we define ourselves and that society should allow us to do so—publicly or privately, as we choose.

AFTERWORD

It is easy to see that my commitment to Existentialist philosophy, working closely with the same factors that had led me to embrace that position, has determined my reaction to feminism in both its earlier and its later phases. I have always been aware that my personal life evolved in response to my situation as a woman at a particular time and place. Should I attempt the fruitless task of trying to determine points at which limiting circumstances in the past may have impeded my growth in directions I have not chosen to go? Obviously I am not the same person I would have been if I had lived in a world more like today's. But I cannot honestly say that I wish I had enjoyed the freedom to make myself other than what I have become. With respect to myself I am content to side with Sartre who, in one of his more expansive optimistic moods, concluded that chance is opportunity, obstacles are the ingredients out of which a freedom makes itself.

SEVEN

Teaching for a Living

CLASSROOM AND OFFICE

I have a recurrent dream, one that verges on a nightmare: over and over again, on into the years since my retirement, I have dreamed that I lost my job. Evidently, whenever I feel threatened in any way, losing my job is the form the menace assumes in my dream. I do not think this means that underlying and surpassing all other anxieties in my existence is the ultimate terror of economic insecurity, even though I did grow up in the Great Depression when finding a livelihood was never assured. Rather I believe that the dream testifies to something I have been fully aware of in my waking life: the inextricability of my work and my way of being. I cannot remember a time when I did not want to be a teacher. Being a professor has been for me, not primarily a means to support myself, but a way of life; and teaching, while not the whole of it, has always been at the heart of it, its raison d'être.

Occasionally, students of mine whom I have seen years after their graduation have spoken of how they had tried to imagine what it would have been like to devote one's life to teaching. Three instances stand out: Ersi Hadjopoulou, from my Pierce College period, I met again in Athens when we were both visiting there. Happily married and living in Beirut (before that country collapsed into Civil War), Ersi enjoyed a measure of fame as a leading dress designer for a sophisticated clientele. From her present pinnacle, school days in postwar Greece seemed very far away, but she remembered them as something precious. She told me that things I had said had stayed with her and that when she thought of how I had influenced her formative years and how over a career span I had "gone on and on" in contributing to young people's lives, she felt there must be something especially wonderful in being a teacher. I shared her view though I was a bit frightened by the thought as she expressed it. Linda Donnelly, one of my students from the University of Colorado, now a lawyer in Denver, spoke appreciatively of her classes with me, but her judgment on teaching as such was quite different. How could I endure the repetitiveness of teaching? How could I stand it to go over the same material year after year? Then there was Harvey Averch, a distinguished economist, *not* a professor, who returned one day to Boulder to speak at a conference at his alma mater. Looking at me as if I were a survivor, he remarked that it must be strange for us professors, and it would certainly not be satisfying to him, to spend our existence preparing others to live rather than living ourselves—his version of the cynicism, "Those who can, do; those who can't, teach."

It apparently did not occur to any of the three that they themselves were visible symbols of one of the rewards teachers strive for. I do not, of course, mean that I myself could take credit for what they had each achieved. But to discern, to watch, sometimes to help in developing potentialities in individual students and to receive from time to time confirmation that one's hopes have been realized is profoundly gratifying. The supposed negative aspects of teaching mentioned by Linda and Harvey seemed to me off the mark. In the humanities at least, new courses or different materials for the same course are always an option. It is not all repetition. Scholarly and creative writing are tangible results of "doing" as much as the products of any other career. Even what seemed to the two objectors to be limitations can be seen in a positive light. To have the opportunity to return more than once to the landmarks of human achievement is not only to find more to learn from them every time but also to measure one's own growth and to learn from the ever changing response of students reflecting what their world has made of them. To meet continually with persons undertaking something new to them gives one the feeling of making fresh starts oneself. For me this sense of perpetual renewal that the cyclical academic calendar provides compensated for the undeniable downside of teaching. Along with such necessary drudgery as correcting examinations and the anguish of determining borderline grades, disappointment and frustration were constants: discontent with my own performance for a given day or course, the realization of how small a minority of students came close to mastering all that was offered them, the ever present reminders that communication seldom hits its mark exactly. Yet while the goal of teaching may be more obviously an unattainable perfection than it is for the average profession, I think there cannot be many that offer more built-in occasions for reflecting back on positive accomplishments and planning a future that can be counted on to produce other as yet unpredictable rewards. Now and then a student would effectively challenge a basic assumption of mine and make me rethink it; occasionally a question or comment would open up new vistas I might not otherwise have perceived. On the best of occasions in the classroom, a genuine "we" emerged that included all of us. It was not only a few superior minds that made the enterprise worthwhile. "C" students would sometimes come up with provocative insights, original points of view, owing perhaps to the very fact that they were less academically conformist than the "A" students. They were every bit as likely to take our subject matter to their own account, to try to make a place for it in their private lives. A particularly touching testimony came to me in a letter from Gail D. A freshman in my yearlong humanities class, she had begun as a "D+" student and gradually pulled herself up a full grade point. But she was memorable for her serious, idiosyncratic response to each new work. Writing to me a year after she graduated, she explained that she was married now and since her husband was often away on long military assignments, she had a lot of time at her disposal. She decided to enlarge her reading. "You know my limitations," she said. "Can you suggest some books that I can read without frustration?"

Teaching is at once the most egoistic and the most altruistic of pursuits. It gives you infinite opportunity to express yourself and to talk about what most interests you. I think most of us who teach would have to admit that this narcissistic reward is a significant factor. It is a joy, too, when your vocation actually requires that you engage in a ceaseless pursuit of greater understanding in a field you have yourself chosen to explore. But teaching is also a unique kind of sharing, an activity in which giving and receiving are inextricable. You give of yourself as well as of your knowledge; the reward is the pleasure of seeing others learn, grow, and create. To teach is always to be engaged in a common project. It is also to take on many roles: information provider, actor, guide, counselor, and—yes, inevitably—preacher.

I believe I must have been a good teacher. My class evaluations and an abundance of positive comment volunteered by students throughout the years seem to indicate it. Most of all, the reason I think I must have been good at teaching is that I loved it so. Surely that would not have been possible if I had done badly. When I listen to formal discussions of what constitutes effective teaching, I feel that I should never have passed the test. I was not especially innovative. I did a lot of lecturing. I seldom

let even smaller classes carry the full weight of the period without intervening at all. I demanded a lot from my students, perhaps too much.
Accustomed to being hard in judging myself, I graded them overseverely.
(I take this opportunity to make public apology to them.) Yet somehow
it all worked. Recently when the *Colorado Alumnus* invited its readers to
send in evaluative recollections of professors they especially remembered, one person wrote that my "overarching goal was wanting people
to learn"; another said she was grateful to me for giving her permission
to explore her own ideas. Seen in their fullest implications, these two
modest appraisals may be a clue to my measure of success.

Walter Veazie, a former member of our Philosophy Department, who
had been a student of John Dewey, once described the difference between Dewey the Preacher, who in a host of publications attacked the
traditional emphasis on rote memory, the accumulation of information,
etc., as a substitute for developing free and creative thought, and Dewey
the Teacher, who insisted that his own students achieve precise understanding of the text before them. In this respect I was a bit like him.
Though I designed each course in terms of what I thought would be ultimately significant for the students either as preparation for their chosen
careers or in their overall intellectual development, I was convinced that
thorough mastery of the material at hand was essential. I aimed above
all at lucidity in my own presentation. I insisted on everyone's obligation
to pay attention to details. Granted, twenty years from now most of
these would be forgotten; the general recollection later would be valid
only if there were precise understanding now. My students would find
no scene rewarding, I believed, if they moved about like nearsighted
persons without glasses. I never allowed myself to give to the class any
explanation or interpretation until I felt that I clearly understood it myself. Or if I felt compelled to do so, I confessed my confusion, saying in
effect, "This is the best I can do, but it's not altogether clear to me. Does
anyone have a suggestion to help?" Occasionally someone did.

Concentration on details and clarity can easily become pedantry.
Here I was helped by my own all but pathological intolerance for wasted
time and boredom. Admittedly not all material is immediately fascinating. I tried to help my students discover that to understand something
completely can be satisfying in itself. When feasible, I pointed to the relevance of the subject under discussion to their understanding of themselves and others or to contemporary social issues. In short, I was always
on the alert to make things meaningful. In order to bring things alive,
some degree of dramatization was demanded; and I suppose it could be

said that, if "all the world's a stage," the teacher is the biggest ham. Another parallel between professor and actor strikes me as more interesting—the degree to which each one must be aware of the response of the audience. A successful stage performance is impossible without some sign that communication is taking place. In the case of the teacher, a warning signal on a face expressing confusion or doubt is all important. Like any halfway effective teacher, I encouraged students to ask questions whether or not I stopped to invite them. (Incidentally, one of the hardest tasks for a professor is to convince students that an honest question or confession of ignorance may be at least as helpful both to the class and to the instructor as the insightful comment of someone who has gone beyond the rest of the class—though this, too, is welcome.)

It was in the papers my students wrote, whether graduate or undergraduate, that I allowed the maximum latitude for developing ideas that went beyond or apart from our immediate concern in class. If I erred in my supervision of theses and dissertations, it was because I gave too little advice rather than too much. I approached the work of a doctoral candidate in the same way that I read the manuscript of a colleague who sought my opinion. I have often thought that the intelligent directing of another's writing project exemplifies perfectly the kind of empathy Sartre (in *Notebooks for an Ethics*) says we must cultivate if one is to shelter the Other's freedom in one's own without trying to possess it. It is possible to be a guide without being a leader. The aim is to point out the pitfalls and traps the Other has not seen, but in light of the Other's end and within the Other's network of means. Undergraduates need more in the way of help and suggestion than graduate students, but here, too, I hoped they would know they had not only my permission but my encouragement to explore their own ideas. Once I overshot the mark. Assigning a written report apropos of some aspect of Sartre's theory of relations with self and others, I stressed that I wanted the students, in a short paper, to illustrate, to extend, or to challenge his views on the basis of their own observation. To my dismay, I received accounts so personal and so confessional that I found it impossible to assign grades to them.

That students should be free to hold and to express their own ideas is obvious. A more delicate question arises with respect to the professor. Many parents and some of my professional colleagues, fearful of indoctrination, argue that teachers should never commit themselves on controversial issues and should maintain a position of total impartiality. I have never gone along with this. In the first place, it is impossible. We cannot be inwardly neutral on matters of concern to us; even with the

firmest resolve to be noncommittal, we will inevitably reveal our bias—
in the examples we choose, in the connotations of the words we use, in
our voice, gestures, body language. This conviction was reinforced for
me when, still early in my career, I took over in mid-semester a course in
psychology of religion from a colleague who fell ill. One of the members of the class, who was planning to be a minister, told me how much
he appreciated my making my own commitment known. This way, he
said, he knew where he stood, he was in a better position to judge for
himself how to respond to the material as I presented it, and, since I encouraged open disagreement, he felt free to express it. The other professor, he told me, while proclaiming that his stance was one of tolerance of all points of view, subtly pressured everyone to accept what he
himself defined as impartiality, allowing for no divergence. In the name
of his own noncommitment, he blocked others' commitments.

It goes without saying, I hope, that I tried to present fairly ideas with
which I was not personally in agreement. My approach was always to
try first to understand a work on its own terms (that is, as the author
seemed to want it to be taken) and to find in it whatever positive insight,
truth, or value it might hold, then to allow its weaknesses to emerge naturally in discussion or at the end. On one occasion my attempt to enter
imaginatively into the author's world produced an explosion. (This was
decades before the advent of political correctness.) My humanities class
and I had descended with Dante into Hell as far as the circle of Lethe,
where the poet allowed the virtuous pagans, ancient Greeks and Romans
and other admirable non-Christians, to enjoy a second-best existence,
delighting in each other's company but denied entrance into Paradise.
(Privately, I felt this to be the most interesting place of residence that
Dante's real estate offered.) Fred Smith erupted in sudden protest, so angry that he stood up and banged his chair for emphasis. As a Jew, he objected that we seemed to be reading with admiration a work based on
the exclusionary doctrine that was responsible for centuries of anti-
Semitism and ultimately the Holocaust. Grateful that he had raised the
point but disturbed by his vehemence, I assured him that I myself as a
non-Catholic (philosophically even anti-Catholic) could not accept the
literal doctrine either but that I found in the poem a wealth of insight
and metaphorical truth that I could appreciate without forswearing my
own convictions. And I brought in all the obvious points that teachers
make in helping students confront the *Inferno* as an imaginative vision
and not as a religious tract using poetic devices to spread propaganda.
Fred was assuaged but not convinced. Years later, on a return visit to the

university, he came to my office to assure me that he had gradually come to see that I was right. I assured him that both of us had been right.

Classroom indoctrination seems to me usually a false issue, at least in this country and in the second half of this century. If it does occur, it is most likely to be in small, narrowly denominational colleges where nobody objects to it. Or, perhaps I should add, in an occasional course in something like feminism or African American studies for which an entering student is prepared in advance for a one-sided approach. At secular colleges and universities the range of offerings and consequent competition of ideas will be the preventive. If in spite of my best efforts at objectivity, I overstressed the positive aspects of Sartre's philosophy and too easily dismissed objections to it, even if I showed myself openly as an advocate of Existentialism, there was no lack of professors ready with antidotes or alternative prescriptions.

I doubt that it is possible to teach anything, even basic science or a skill, without transmitting something of one's own values. In philosophy and literature courses, criticism, interpretation, and personal commitment are virtually inseparable. (This is most evidently true in the case of those who would deny it.) Since I was anxiously concerned to avoid imposing my own prejudices, I was greatly reassured when a student said to me in approximately, if not precisely, these words, "My value system is not all the same as yours, but what I owe to you is that you made me feel it was necessary to create *a* value system I was willing to live by. It had never occurred to me that anyone should do this."

Other experiences were the very opposite of reassuring. As is well known, students often show themselves capable of distorting what is offered them or deviating it into unexpected, not always desirable directions. The history of Sartrean Existentialism provides all too many examples. Authenticity might be equated with willful caprice or individual responsibility for what one made of one's life, divorced from the recognition of the interdependency of consciousnesses. Spontaneity could be exalted at the expense of commitment. In seeking to avoid the narrowness of life inside the cocoon of the "serious world," a few persons seemed to want to turn themselves into weather vanes. Whereas Sartre claimed that each of us is "an always future project," some of his self-proclaimed followers chose to demonstrate their freedom by acknowledging only the appeal of the present moment. I saw little of such extreme manifestations among my own students, but there were times when I felt uneasy at what appeared to be transformation of Sartre's teaching into a device in bad faith when it came to applications of theory to practice. While, of course, it was Sartre whose ideas were twisted, I felt responsible as the one who had presented them. But then there is a long tradition of teachers' having their words perverted; Socrates and Nietzsche are only two outstanding examples. As Sartre said, the world has a way of "stealing my action from me."

Although my goal in teaching, in both classroom and office, was to guide, not to lead or overdirect, I must admit that the line between academic guide and personal counselor was sometimes thin. Indeed, a role occasionally thrust upon me was that of therapist. This I found to be at once challenging, perilous, and chastening. I did not seek it out. Compared with some of my colleagues, I maintained fairly formal relations with my students. Though I was easily accessible at the university, it was only rarely that I invited them to my home. I did not intrude into their private lives. Yet every now and then, directly or under the guise of an academic inquiry, they would consult me about their psychological problems or specific dilemmas they faced. For the most part, I served as a nondirective sounding board, sympathizing, helping them to clarify their feelings so as to recognize what they would find best for themselves. Sometimes the underlying malaise was philosophical in nature; counseling was merely another form of teaching. On a few occasions I was shocked to learn what skeletons in the closet my students lived with. At Ohio State a returned G.I. confided to me that he was still tormented by the memory of an incident in which he had been involved in the Pacific theater of the war. An officer had led him and a few other men into a situation where he was needlessly exposing them to almost certain death. When they could not dissuade him, they maneuvered him into a position where he was immediately shot by the enemy; the rest escaped. My student still believed that he had done the right thing, but he felt the need to justify it—emotionally as well as rationally. In the fifties one of my undergraduates confessed to me with horrified self-reproach that he had virtually committed murder. While still in high school in a city on the West Coast, he and his companions would go down to the local skid row along the wharf and push sleeping, dead-drunk derelicts into the water. I do not know what finally happened to either of the troubled young men. Presumably they learned to live with their burden.

In some disturbed cases, the thought of possible suicide was always in the back of my mind, particularly when it was never mentioned. In instances when it was, I felt that it figured mostly as an abstraction and that I was consulted chiefly as a source for more arguments against it.

Fortunately I was never proved wrong. Twice I had reason for serious anxiety. In the case of each of the men concerned, a girl friend called me ahead of time to say that he was coming to me as a last resort, that he was resolved to kill himself unless I could provide convincing arguments to dissuade him. While I did not flatter myself that I could change either of them by simple persuasion, I feared that too glaring inadequacy on my part might be enough to push him over to a negative decision. For though some degree of self-deception and dramatization may have been involved, neither of the students was knowingly playing games. At each meeting I kept everything low-keyed, using what I think of as the "Wait till Wednesday" approach. Since the time after the irrevocable act was so long, there was no rush. Why not take a couple of days so as to be sure to look at every angle? Meanwhile, there were other people it would be worthwhile to consult. . . . Here and in certain other encounters I realized acutely the limitations I had to work with. Not only did I lack any formal training as a therapist; even if I had wished to do so, the situation did not allow me to ask the intimate questions and to expect the full disclosure that would have been appropriate in a psychotherapist's office. In both of the instances I mentioned, it was obvious that personal conflicts were at the root of the troubles, but each man insisted that it was on general philosophical grounds that he had decided that life was not worth living further. One of them, who struck me as a character halfway between Goethe's Young Werther and a Dostoyevsky hero, insisted that he wanted to die now when he was at the peak of his power and in control, "like Hemingway" (an inexact comparison, I thought) rather than to submit to any diminishment. Since he was invoking literary examples that he felt showed suicide to be a heroic act under some circumstances, I reminded him of Gide's adolescent hero (in *The Counterfeiters*), who turned on the gas after his first perfect night of love but was rescued in time to be grateful that he could enjoy many more. The student was able to smile at this. But when finally I suggested gently to him that his eagerness to leave life was possibly not because he could not hope to equal his present exalted state but that he did not find in himself adequate strength to confront an unknown future and that he should explore the reasons why, he grew pale. He did not protest but fell silent and soon afterward left.

Though I avoided disaster on these two occasions, I acutely felt my inadequacy. I was entirely helpless when I found myself faced with more serious psychic disorders. One such confrontation occurred without warning; the student concerned had never come to see me outside of class. At my invitation, Robert Hawkins, a professor of fine arts, was giving a guest lecture to my class in myth in the arts. Suddenly we were interrupted by the crash of a heavy object (it turned out to be a metal wastebasket) being repeatedly hurled at the door. Going out, I found a male student whose absence from class I had noticed. Giving as an excuse only that he wasn't interested in hearing this lecture, he agreed to desist. He did not. While our visitor continued to speak, I left the room by another door and phoned for help. Meanwhile two women members of the class, who, without my knowing it, were on the campus police force, went out to talk with the young man; he consented to go with them to the student health center. Some months later, after a stay in a psychiatric unit, he appeared at my office. Apparently cured, he talked with dispassionate interest of what had occurred. In the days preceding the incident, I had been lecturing on O'Neill's *Mourning Becomes Electra*. He told me that I had seemed to him to be addressing coded messages to him; he identified me with Christine, the Clytemnestra figure in the play. He could not say that Professor Hawkins represented any other specific character, but clearly he was, in the student's mind, an intruder, if not a threat, to him and to me—hence the attempt to disrupt. Given the plot of O'Neill's tragedy, we were both grateful that the imagined identification had not gone any further.

A second episode I remember more painfully. Graham, a first-year graduate student with excellent training in Classics, good undergraduate grades, and favorable letters of recommendation, enrolled in my seminar in the Greek pre-Socratic philosophers. He said little in class but came frequently to my office, chiefly to discuss Existentialism, in which he had developed a special interest. I found him bright though a bit erratic. All went well until the day he gave an oral report on Heraclitus. Beginning appropriately, he soon abandoned Heraclitus and went on into pseudo-intellectual jargon and wild statements that made no sense at all. I finally stopped him, saying that he had exceeded his time. After class I told him briefly that his paper had been impossible for his audience to follow. "Ah, that is the problem," he said resignedly. Over the next day or two he kept out of sight but sent me a series of bizarre notes, some of them not in any recognizable language, some not even legible. At my office door he left a heaped-up assortment of evergreen branches, a pair of scissors, and other utility articles purchased at the bookstore. I learned later that campus police had found him wandering around at midnight near our locked building; he claimed to have an appointment with me. Afterward he phoned the hospital to report that he was suffering a heart attack. An ambulance brought him to the emergency room, where the personnel, taking his statement literally, told him there was nothing wrong with his heart and dismissed him. Meanwhile my department chair had got in touch with Graham's parents, who revealed that he had been under the care of various psychotherapists and had been institutionalized for a time. Before taking him home, his parents brought Graham to my office so that he and I might talk privately. With seeming rationality, he reproached me bitterly. He had come to the University of Colorado because he believed that I would understand him whereas others had not. He knew that if I would, he and I together might do significant work to improve the world. He had trusted me to be able to read the mnemonic messages in the collection of items at my door. Now I had not only failed but betrayed him. "This is the worst sort of treachery!" I will never forget his distress—or my own.

A third story had a happier ending. Carole, an undergraduate who continued to come regularly to talk with me long after her course with me was completed, was, on the surface, a happy-go-lucky person, with a brilliant wit, directed primarily against herself; a refreshingly original individual. I enjoyed seeing her though I worried a little that she seemed to be growing somewhat overdependent. She never spoke of any psychological problems, though she did confide in me that she had vague recollections of a troubled childhood in the Soviet Union and that at the end of World War II an American had brought her, an abandoned child, to this country. A farmer in Pennsylvania had adopted her. Dubbing herself "the Mad Russian," Carole appeared to look back on all this as a confusion safely past. One evening she asked me to have dinner with her, something that had not happened before. After the meal she became very serious, and I realized that here was an exceedingly vulnerable young woman. Revealing how much my approval and understanding meant to her, she asked rather dramatically whether, if she were dying and sent for me, I would come. Uncomfortably I dismissed the event as unlikely but assured her that I probably would. In the middle of the night I had a phone call from the person she lived with. Carole was having some sort of strange attack and had said at its outset that, if anything went wrong, I should be called. I found her lying feverishly flushed, distraught, muttering in what seemed to be Russian, unresponsive to what anybody said. When she saw me, she did not recognize me as myself; but her face lit up and she called me by a Russian name. She gripped and held on to my hand so hard that even the next day I could hardly move my fingers normally. As Carole continued to address me in Russian, I steadily spoke to her in English, repeating who I was and where we were. At last, as if she could barely utter the words, she slowly, hoarsely, asked in English, "Who are you?" Without quite grasping the meaning of my response, she calmed down, guided my hand, passing it above herself, making a cross as if of someone blessing and saying goodnight to a child. Then closing her eyes, she fell into a deep sleep. After a short interval she awoke, seemed perfectly normal, and asked with great embarrassment what she had done to bring the department chair (that was then my position) there in the middle of the night. I learned that she had suffered earlier a few such attacks in which I had not figured. This one was the last, no thanks to anything I had done. A new psychiatrist decided that Carole had something wrong beyond psychological trauma, a physical abnormality in the brain, one which could be corrected by medication. She went on to a successful career as a psychological counselor. For thirty some years we have been fast friends.

Carole's case in particular led me to reflect on Sartre's Existentialist challenge to Freudian psychology. (The fact that the discovery of a physiological cause effectively cured her does not justify the reductionist view that all mental troubles are bodily in origin and psychoanalysis a waste of time.) The particular form of the psychic episode I witnessed might seem to reinforce the Freudian concept of the Unconscious. Certainly Carole was regressing to an earlier stage; clearly she was casting me in the role of an adult who had been present in her child's world and was capable of giving her a security she desperately missed and wanted, none of which could have happened if she had not been able to banish from her immediate awareness all active realization of her real, present situation. But the hidden plan behind it all is equally striking and vividly illustrates Sartre's theory that emotional conduct is a purposeful recourse to the magical as a way of altering one's relations with the world in an unacceptable situation—in extreme cases, creating a magical world as a temporary replacement for the real one. This was what Carole had done.

GROWING WITH AND APART

I am often asked whether and how students and my relations with them changed in the course of my forty-five years of teaching. Of course the students changed, and so did I, as the world changed. The question of how our ways of relating to one another may have altered is more complex.

To be constantly associated with young people, while it cannot insure that one will remain young in spirit, does tend to keep the moss from growing too fast and too thick. For quite a while I felt that my students and I were growing together with the times. At the start I was in fact closer to their generation than to that of their parents; a little later, during my years in Ohio, the presence of World War II veterans helped to blur the dividing line. Then, for a time, the growing distance between the students' average age and mine still did not seem to figure significantly. At most I gradually perceived that in their attitude toward me a tinge of camaraderie was subtly replaced by deference. On my side I continued to assume, perhaps fatuously, that my students were more recent versions of what my friends and I had been at their age. The sixties put an end to all that. In spite of my feelings of sympathy, even of empathy for many of the activists in the student movement, I knew that we communicated by long distance, across the generation gap. I regretted the fact and did all that I could to keep the lines open. In this and in the ensuing decades my students and I were able to bridge the gulf in richly rewarding encounters; we no longer lived on the same side of it. Since it was at the University of Colorado that I became fully aware of changes in successive generations of students, I will be speaking here of the years I spent at this institution, the major portion of my career.

Reflecting back on the fifties is likely to evoke two dominant images: Joseph McCarthy leading the hunt for Communists—under the bed or in the pumpkin patch—and Jack Kerouac's fictional heroes careening across the country in search of drugs and nirvana. Indeed, it is possible to see the hippies of the sixties as the more gentle but equally irresponsible descendants of the Beat Generation and to view the revolutionaries as the angry activist respondents to the excesses of the political reactionaries of ten years before. What the two images omit is the group of tired but still voluble liberals, persecuted by the McCarthyites, disdained by the Beats. It was they who typified the outlook of the majority of us working within the university and their views that were radicalized and put into action by the Civil Rights marchers and the student militants. It was not only I, with Existentialism and Beauvoir's early feminism, who found students ready to respond to new visions. Riesman, Denney, and Glazer, in *The Lonely Crowd* (1950), had been entirely accurate in depicting Americans generally as anxiously "other-directed"; we professors used this and other comparable critiques as a means of awakening our students to individual self-questioning. On the surface, and especially compared with the next decade, the student body in the fifties was indeed apathetic, as it has usually been described. Intellectual talk may have remained at the level of Sartre's Electra's rebellious daydreams, not of

Oreste's blueprint for action. I still believe this was an interval of ferment.
I recall that I myself lived in expectation of a genuine breakthrough even
if that feeling was based on nothing more than the illusion common to
many intellectuals—that what appears to be clearly true and just is
bound in time to be seen as so by enough others and will prevail.

What I remember especially about the undergraduates of that period
is their earnestness and serious purpose. Obviously I do not mean that
these qualities were present in all. There were many of the kind who had
earlier given the University of Colorado the reputation of being a "party
school," those who apparently never felt a pang of loneliness amidst the
other-directed crowd. But the bright ones, the *students*, were singularly
thoughtful, searching for authenticity and ready to take responsibility
for their own self-making even before they met these ideas in the work
of Sartre. The old Jamesian notion of self-improvement had not yet become for them synonymous with upward mobility.

I noticed this, for instance, in their concern with religion. Both individually and in groups, students wrestled with the question of whether
traditional religious doctrine needed rethinking. A freshman girl came
to me one day with a list of reasons for believing or not believing in the
existence of God. It seemed to her that the balance tilted toward the negative side, and she wanted to discuss with me what consequences this
might have for her. (It was this same student who once confessed to me
that she was afraid she had "no moral fiber," a worry brought on by her
inability to force herself to work the whole of a previous Saturday, without a break, on a paper she was writing. As a fellow sinner, I was able to
offer comfort.) At that time the university sponsored an annual "Religion
in Life Week." This did not involve religious services, either denominational or ecumenical. Instead there was offered a series of discussions on
religious themes with panels set up to insure debate. One of them, the
exact title of which I have forgotten, raised the question of whether organized religion was helpful or injurious. I was asked to take the negative side. Somehow I must have managed to be emphatic and forthright
without being offensive. The local Pillar of Fire radio station had someone preach against me. His remarks were, however, a condemnation of
what I had said, not a personal attack on me or on the university as
might have been later on. I was told that the Episcopalian bishop from
Denver, who was also on the panel, was greatly shocked. My informant,
himself a priest who worked with college students, added that the experience had been good for the bishop, perhaps now he might realize
what life was like in the real world. The most surprising comment came

from the dean of the College of Arts and Sciences, Jacob Van Ek, a man I greatly admired. He actually attended the panel and confided in me afterward that he wished he could have spoken out like this but that fears instilled in him in his childhood would have inhibited him even in his thoughts. The committee in charge liked my presentation because they felt it was serious and honest and offered something the students should hear. They did not accord the same approval to my colleague Donald Sutherland, who on another occasion gave a flippant account of his personal relations with the Holy Ghost. But I suspect that Donald's remarks, which delighted many in his audience to the point of near hysteria, were remembered much longer than mine.

One odd episode in connection with students' attitudes toward religion I still do not know how to interpret. One of the texts we used in the beginning humanities course in the fifties was James's essay on "The Will to Believe." This is the one in which James argued that if faced with questions that could not be settled by scientific evidence, a person had as much right to affirm belief as to withhold it. In particular James insisted that religious belief fell under this heading since it was a "genuine option"; that is, the hypothesis was living (not dead), momentous (not trivial), and forced (not avoidable). By "forced" James meant that no middle position was possible, that to suspend belief was to reject the possibilities that belief had to offer. It was this point over which my students argued, on both sides, with all the fervor of James's contemporaries. In the late sixties, or perhaps it was the early seventies, I decided to use the essay again in a different class and after a long lapse. To my surprise the class was willing to grant that the option was living and forced but insisted virtually unanimously that it was not momentous. Religious belief was to most of them a purely private predilection of no great consequence. I was shocked, feeling like a Don Quixote with nary a windmill. How to explain this reaction? At first it seems out of harmony with what was going on. A number of Christian ministers, prompted by their religious convictions, had joined the forces of Martin Luther King, Jr., Eastern religions were still winning proselytes. But perhaps these manifestations were part of the answer. Not all church leaders approved their brethren's active involvement; many of the marchers came prompted by other than religious motives; some were radical Marxists. Eastern teachings seemed primarily to address individuals in their solitude. Possibly my students were beginning to perceive that ethical concerns and personal lifestyle were as likely to determine as to be determined by religious commitments. Perhaps the concept of religion was being used so loosely that it no longer meant much of anything. Tillich had already defined it as whatever is one's ultimate concern, which seems to consign the atheist to oblivion. I had even heard religious belief identified with the spirit of poetry. At any rate, the attitude of my class was as different from that of students in the fifties as it was from that of today's Religious Right.

Unless my memory deludes me, beginning students in those earlier years, compared with those in the last decade and a half of my career, were less sophisticated, less well informed about contemporary events, but better prepared academically. They could read far more intelligently, and a significant number of them had already cultivated the habit of reading for pleasure. While the university still found it necessary to offer what was in essence remedial English, most of my freshmen could adequately express their ideas in writing, and with proper spelling, at least well enough to be intelligible if not always logical, something which could not be assumed to be true of later entering freshmen. Outside academic concerns, there was a certain amount of anxiety over the nuclear threat and distrust of the government's ability to cope with the problem. On the whole, however, I remember that students then were generally optimistic and self-confident with regard to their individual futures. They were ready for change but not impatient for it.

Then came the sixties. My reflections on the crisis in the university in this decade of progress, violence, and overall turmoil I have recorded in my book *The University as the New Church*. In this I tried to clarify the position of both the traditionalists and the radical students, to suggest ways of meeting the latter's demands without confirming the worst fears of the former, and to discuss how the university might best acknowledge and fulfill its role as a moral leader in the contemporary world. As an attempt to influence thinking on the subject, the book was wholly inefficacious—misplaced and mistimed. I had been requested by an editor at C. A. Watts in England to write something for *The New Thinker's Library* series. I don't know what he and I could have been thinking of in settling on this topic. Published in London in 1970, the book dealt specifically with the university as it was in the United States; its analysis of the conflict so much reflected the just-passed sixties that it was beginning to seem anachronistic by the time it appeared on the market. Sections dealing more generally with questions of philosophy of education still seem to me to have some merit. Basically, it was an "occasional" piece that missed its season. Royal Stokes, a visiting colleague who was an active sponsor of the ultra-leftist Students for a Democratic

Society, told me, speaking not just of the book but of my overall outlook, that I was a good liberal who tried to be a radical but never quite made it. I was not as successful as Sartre in thinking against myself.

Still, for the most part, my sympathies were with the rebellious students, whether the issue was social and political (antiracist, against the war in Vietnam) or reform within the university (curricular matters, student representation, or the institution's role *in loco parentis*). Partly this was because my own convictions were in harmony with what the protesters were asking for. Partly I was repelled by the excessive hostility of those who opposed them. Too many of the latter, unwilling even to listen to what the students had to say, took the position that they had no right to protest against authority in any case. The critics fell back on the old line that those who questioned actions of the government or of the university administration were anarchists or, worse yet, Communists. Even unconventional appearance—long hair, beards, and torn jeans—was taken as visible proof of subversion.

At our university, action never reached the level of violence that elsewhere alienated even faculty who had been initially supportive. There were noisy demonstrations, attempts to disrupt lecturers by conservative speakers, "sit-ins" at the entrances of buildings in which CIA recruiters were interviewing applicants. In freezing weather, day and night, antiwar protesters sat and slept on the library steps to express their sense of urgency; they did not try to prevent anyone from entering. The closest to actual violence occurred when someone threw a chair in the general direction of S. I. Hayakawa (the future U.S. senator who was at that time an outspoken, ultraconservative professor from San Francisco State College), who was speaking on campus. There was not the remotest chance of the chair reaching its target, and Hayakawa was deliberately baiting his hecklers in language matching their own.

The most notorious episode of the decade, the one that generated the most adverse publicity for the university, the one that nevertheless evoked what some believe to be the university's finest hour, and the one that had lasting disastrous effects was the "Carl Mitcham business," as we still refer to it. Although there was never any reason for my name to be mentioned in this connection, I am still haunted by the possibility that I may, in all innocence, have served as a catalyst in initiating what happened. If so, the story begins in the spring semester of 1962. On March 2, Senator Barry Goldwater, two years before he ran for President, came to lecture, sponsored by the Young Republicans. Editorials in the student newspaper, the *Colorado Daily*, had opposed his coming, and the Young

People's Socialist League had held demonstrations against his conservative policies. On the day of the lecture everyone was tense, expecting
some dramatic development. Knowing there would be a crowd, I decided
to watch the event on television. I never did hear all of Goldwater's
speech: After a rather long introduction by a professor who scolded the
students for their earlier disrespectful behavior, the time scheduled was
running short; the program's producers cut the coverage before the
Senator had finished. (Rumor reported that he was more angered by this
than by anything said or done by the students.) The Senator's presentation was not interrupted; the discussion that followed was heated but
within normal limits. At the end of the program, however, the Young
People's Socialist League displayed a banner reading "Tippecanoe and
Goldwater too." Afterward the American Legion Post in Denver rebuked
the students for "abuse and vilification" of the Senator and publicly rep-
rimanded the university for harboring un-American organizations. Fall-
out from the flurry continued until the end of the term.

In mid-September I arrived a few minutes early for the first meeting
of my honors seminar in "Schopenhauer and the Eastern Tradition." As
always before a new class, I felt a bit ill at ease. I imagine that then, as on
many other occasions, I reminded myself of what Eugene O'Neill Jr. had
told me at Yale when I expressed the fear that I would be struck with
stage fright on the day when I finally came to teach. "You will always be
afraid and anxious on the first day of class," he said. "If you're not, you will
be through as a teacher; it will mean that you no longer care." Nervously
searching for something to say to those already present while we waited
for the others, I made a banal comment to the effect that the previous
year had indeed been a memorable one, for better or for worse, and I
wondered what sort of unusual events and burning issues the year ahead
would produce. One of the senior philosophy majors sitting at our table
was Carl Mitcham. I had not known or heard of him before. Within the
context of the seminar, he was mild-mannered and reserved, intelligently
perceptive, ready to join in our discussion but showing no tendency to
try to dominate. Whether or not my bland remark secreted a spark, I have
never known. But within a week or so, an article, "Riding the Whale,"
written by Mitcham and published in the "Gadfly" section of the Colorado Daily, ignited a chain of explosive reactions with far-reaching consequences. Decidedly not on a par with Mitcham's academic work, the
piece was discursive and at times a bit incoherent. Part 1 presented a
reasonably fair summary of Goldwater's policies as set forth in his
books, The Conscience of a Conservative and Why Not Victory? Part 2 offered

a rapid, idiosyncratic survey of how the intentions and processes of democracy in the United States had departed from the ideals of the Founding Fathers, along with a diatribe against the tyranny of "the organization man" in a "world of objects" and the "glorified nationalistic slaughter of the nuclear bombs"—all familiar themes in the protest literature of the period but hardly inflammatory. In the last section Mitcham worked somewhat cumbersomely with an image borrowed from Orwell. In a 1940 review of Henry Miller's *The Tropic of Cancer*, Orwell had compared Miller to a Jonah who preferred to stay inside the whale. While not approving of this retreat from the world, Orwell wrote sympathetically of it as an understandable rejection of a contemptible society. Mitcham contrasted Miller's choice to remain in the whale's belly with that of Goldwater, who chose to ride on its back—to Goldwater's disparagement, of course. Though singling out the Senator for his most specific reproach, Mitcham linked him with all other "politicians." (Kennedy, surprisingly in light of today's retrospective view of him, was viewed as "a dangerous man" and strongly criticized for failing to match his acts with his rhetoric.) To underscore that he was using Goldwater only as an example, Mitcham added, "For my consideration, he does not differ essentially from Eisenhower, or Kennedy, or the Fascists. They are all politicians." Then returning to the militaristic theme of the Senator's book *Why Not Victory?*, he said, "Barry Goldwater is a fool, a mountebank, a murderer, no better than a common criminal." It was these two ill-considered sentences that brought on enemy fire. Condensed in the charge that Mitcham had declared Goldwater to be a Fascist and a criminal, it was offensive even in the eyes of the most ardent defenders of the right to free speech. Formal apologies were sent to the Senator by the editor of the *Colorado Daily*, by the board of regents, and by the president of the university, Quigg Newton. President Newton, after extending his "sincere apologies," stated, "The words in question were obviously irresponsible and defamatory, and the University of Colorado disavows them unqualifiedly." The Senator was not placated. In his reply, after remarking that the University of Colorado was the only school he had encountered in which "socialists, or whatever you call them, seem to have the ability to do what they want without censure," he added these inexcusable words:

> I must because of this, then, come to the conclusion that you either do not know what is going on in the University, or you don't care, and in charity, I will presume the former. To put it briefly, I

doubt that you have the interest or the concern to be in the position you hold.

In his response Newton, ignoring the personal attack on himself, wrote a letter in defense of freedom of thought in the university. The Senator had now, Newton said, made it clear what the real issue was: not "the bad manners of a handful of students whose violent expressions of opinion only embarrass their friends and strengthen their enemies," but "the question of academic democracy."

> We have a genuine democracy of ideas on our campus. We have fought long and hard to achieve it, and the fight has been against those who—like yourself—believe the function of a university is to indoctrinate rather than educate, to control thought, rather than to stimulate it. The cry you raise has a very familiar ring to us. . . . It is always the same. "Our way is the only American way. All others are un-American and subversive. You must silence those who do not agree with us."
>
> Senator, I shall not silence them.

This last sentence is still quoted on our campus, virtually every time that the issue of freedom of speech arises. Even among those most vociferous in condemning Mitcham, many were outraged at Goldwater's effrontery, and proud of Newton's ringing defense of academic freedom.

Unfortunately, on the very date that this letter was written, October 3, the *Daily* carried another piece by Mitcham. In this he explained that he had not intended the terms he had applied to Goldwater to be taken literally and that the attack was directed at him only insofar as he embodied what Mitcham regarded as the mistaken policies of our recent governmental representatives. Then, as if incited by some ancient demon of madness, in an effort to "spread the guilt," Mitcham spoke disparagingly of Eisenhower, whom, he claimed, nobody could take seriously. "With Ike, it was hard to keep from laughing at the old futzer's grammar." I am reasonably sure that Mitcham did not know the real meaning of "futzer" and used the word—as some of the rest of us did—as the equivalent of "fuddy-duddy." But some enterprising person located a dictionary that included it (most do not) and learned that "futzer" was a crude synonym for "fornicator" or, as it would appear today, Mitcham had called Eisenhower "an old fucker." That did it! This time Newton, by executive order, fired the editor of the *Colorado Daily* for "editorial irresponsibility"; he actually succeeded in persuading an initially hostile student body to support his action. Carl Mitcham had to appear before the university disciplinary committee. In the face of considerable pressure from both outside and inside the university administration, he was acquitted of the charge of improper conduct on the grounds that despite his use of injudicious language, the committee upheld his and all students' right to "engage in free and open discussion."

I think the decision was a just one if Mitcham's actions should be judged by his intentions and by what he thought he was doing. What he wrote, though a radical denunciation of national policies, was not incendiary; it did not advocate violence of any sort. Nor did Mitcham wish to harm the university; in the midst of the uproar, he telegraphed to Goldwater a futile request that he alone be held responsible for what he had written. If judged in the light of consequences to the university, Mitcham probably wreaked more havoc than any other student in its history. Neither he nor anyone else could have foreseen the train of events. Attacks on the university, and especially on its president, intensified, becoming more and more political. In December Quigg Newton announced his resignation, to become effective at the end of the academic year. Although he claimed that he was leaving because of the opportunities offered by a new position (he became president of the Commonwealth Fund of New York), I cannot believe that this was the sole or most compelling cause. In private conversation he told me that one reason for his decision was his belief that he was serving as a lightning rod for attacks on the university, partly because he was still the focus of political enmity he had incurred during his previous term as the Democratic mayor of Denver. For this reason he felt that his departure would help the university. Most of us on campus regarded it as a disaster. It was Quigg Newton, in his eight years of office, who, more than anyone else, was responsible for putting the university on a level commensurate with that of other leading state universities. When he left, most of the outstanding administrators he had appointed went, too—the provost, the dean of Arts and Sciences, and other heads of schools. Whether these developments might have come to pass without the "Mitcham business," nobody can prove. Certainly those two essays of his triggered it all.

I am brought to wonder once again if my retrospective-prospective remark on the opening day of class played any accidental but significant part. *I doubt it, but I cannot be sure.* I cannot really feel guilty. I was not intending to suggest anything at all. But then Carl Mitcham would probably not write those manifestos if he had it to do over again. It is not surprising that the omnipresence of chance as a determining factor in human history has been interpreted by some as the workings of Fate.

Within the university itself, though there were tensions, we avoided the extreme polarization and hostile confrontations that plagued some institutions. This was probably due in large part to the good judgment and diplomatic skills of university officials. Newton's successor, President Joseph Smiley, for example, allowed the Students for a Democratic Society to hold its national convention on campus. I went to one of the sessions; it was so dull in its procedural arguments that it made faculty meetings seem like spirited entertainment. There was one ironic consequence: The SDS refused to allow representatives of the electronic media to attend, even forcibly ejecting them from the room. When one of the university regents insisted that the media ought to be permitted to be present, SDS members pointed out that the board of regents excluded electronic media from their meetings. One result of the public uproar was that the board itself was obliged to change its policy. Other significant steps on campus were taken quite peacefully. Gradually the university yielded to the new demand that it abandon its role *in loco parentis*. Roland Rautenstraus, who followed Joseph Smiley, quietly managed to please students and parents alike by adopting, for a transitional period, a plan whereby students could choose between unisexual and sex-segregated dormitories.

Meanwhile, in the College of Arts and Sciences we tinkered, mostly constructively, with the curriculum. As on other campuses, we introduced courses in ethnic and women studies. I supported all this and was active in furthering other liberalizing modifications—such as granting permission to undergraduates to take a few pass/fail courses outside their major fields and setting up, with faculty supervision, an individually structured major. I cannot say that my own teaching was much affected by the student revolution. One futile attempt I never repeated. Impressed by an article I had read suggesting that professors "contract" with students as to the amount of work they would like to do in order to guarantee a certain grade, I announced such an arrangement as optional. The idea was that the students would select special projects beyond the minimum requirement and that those would be of a kind suited to their particular talents and interests. The better ones did not avail themselves of the option. Some of the weaker ones, glad to oblige and to profit, did indeed write extra papers—at the same level or below that of their usual work. I could not see that anyone much benefited.

Only a very few professors undertook radical action to express their solidarity with the militant students. Royal Stokes, at the end of his year as visiting assistant professor, posted one night a list of final grades for his huge class in ancient history: all A's. At 7:30 A.M. the department secretary phoned me as chair to inform me of the fact and to suggest that I try at once to catch him and discuss the matter since he was planning to leave that same morning. Getting no reply by phone, I went to his rented cottage in Chautauqua Park. All the blinds were drawn. I tried to peek under the edge of the one on the front door to see if I could discern any signs of occupancy. My eye met that of Royal Stokes, peeping out to see who was there. This double illustration of Sartre's famous keyhole example, in which the Peeping Tom perceives himself seen, made both of us laugh. Opening the door, Royal insisted that he would not take back his gesture of protest against the academic establishment. Dean William Briggs, to whom I reported the matter, withheld his last paycheck. Royal returned to campus to complain that this was unjust and illegal, that the natural and appropriate rebuke could be administered by means of later unfavorable recommendations, a punishment he was willing to accept. Dean Briggs later conceded. Though not supporting Stokes's action, which seemed to me unfair to the students who had actually earned an A, I—separately and along with the local chapter of the American Federation of Teachers—had urged the dean to yield. Some time later the chapter's president, ungraciously and, I hope, owing to faulty memory, listed as one of the A.F.T.'s accomplishments its having been able to pressure the Classics Department into allowing the payment to be made. This was in no way the fault of Royal Stokes. The one thing for which I was not prepared to forgive him was the fact that he secretly took with him our best graduate student! Their marriage still endured as of a couple of years ago. An enthusiast for rock music when he was here, Stokes became well known as a free-lance writer of jazz history and criticism.

The occasion that here brought faculty and students closest together in that troubled period came almost at the end, in 1970; it was a meeting of the university senate, held just after the report of the disaster at Kent State when four of the students were killed by the National Guard. We debated whether or not we should, as a group, adopt some unusual action as a sign of protest. We met in our vast Macky auditorium, the students filling the balconies, not participating directly, though their reactions were made plain. After motions ranging from the proposal that we do nothing at all to the suggestion that we shut down the college before the imminent examination period, we passed a compromise: faculty members, preferably in consultation with their classes, should make their own decision, which would be honored by the college office. Results

varied. Some faculty, of course, simply carried on as usual. My own procedure, worked out with my students, was fairly typical. In my smaller,
advanced class, we decided to skip the final examination, but we held an
extra meeting so that one student could present a special report. In a
large class, I gave to all a choice between taking the examination or accepting the grade their current average would give them. A sizeable minority took the exam, probably the ones most eager to raise their standing, though a few of those who refrained may well have done so on
moral principle. An empty gesture it seems in retrospect. At the time the
sense of outrage felt by most of us compelled us to adopt some kind of
symbolic act in preference to passive acceptance. Any of us who wished
could, of course, have opted for some additional, more radical action.
We might, for instance, following the example of earlier antiwar protesters, have held an all-night vigil on the library steps, which would
have attracted more public attention as well as providing more of masochistic balm to our guilt feelings. Nobody proposed this, and in the long
run it would hardly have made any difference. In any case, the crowd
would have been considerably smaller than the assembly in the auditorium. Would I have been there? Let's change the subject.

As I have said, my mostly sympathetic, often admiring attitude toward the student movement in the sixties did not mean that I felt we
were, in spirit, of the same generation. I was alienated from those who
succumbed to the drug culture, I was unattracted to the casual use of obscene language, torn jeans, and general grubbiness. Try as I would, I
could not develop an appreciation of rock music, though I regarded this
as a lack in myself, not a sign of my superiority.

In the seventies and eighties, my enthusiasm for teaching remained
high. From one point of view, since I was teaching more of my own specialty, I found my class work and contact with individual students, both
graduate and undergraduate, more rewarding than ever. But there was a
difference, perceptible especially in the large introductory courses I still
occasionally taught. I recall my dismay when, happening to run across
some old tests I had given, I realized that I could not fairly use them
now. Evidently my standards of expectation had changed without my
knowing it. I mentioned earlier the progressive deterioration in reading
and writing skills. Like most college professors, I was all too ready to put
the blame on high school educators; an unexpected encounter gave me
wider insight. One afternoon a student, not one of my own, walked into
my office and asked if I would be his guru. Despite his odd request, I

found him unusually bright, self-knowledgeable, also profoundly unhappy. He himself analyzed his malaise in sociological terms, seeing himself as typical of "the TV generation," except in his discontent with the
situation. As he expressed it, he was so accustomed to the quick, summary pictures of television and film that he found reading just too slow;
he could not force himself to adjust to the tedious unfolding of a written
text. At the same time he felt that most of his experience was perforce
all on the surface, empty and unrewarding because of its lack of depth. I
do not claim that this young man had fully grasped either the roots of
his own problems or that of his peers. I did think that his perception of
the negative aspects of the new world described by Marshall McLuhan
had a certain validity and relevance in explaining an uneasiness I felt
with respect to some of my students, the kind of concern that must be
quadrupled for today's professors confronting the infinite possibilities
and dangers still to be revealed in the computer age.

Since my retirement in 1986, some of my former colleagues have told
me that I am lucky to be no longer teaching, that they themselves are
finding it less rewarding than in the past because of the change in the
undergraduates themselves, whom they judge to be not only less idealistic than in the past but without much intellectual interest. It is hard for
me to believe that I would ever find teaching not enjoyable. Not long
ago, however, I read with horror a report of one state university (not
mine) in which low esteem for education and disrespect for instructors
had made some classrooms into an only somewhat subdued version of
what we hear concerning many public schools in the inner city. So perhaps my friends have a point. I would describe my own experiences in
the last half dozen years of my career as something like this:

Students in general seemed to me to come into class out of a different
world. Their notion of entertainment and sense of humor, their values,
their lifestyles were foreign to me. Even in the sixties I occasionally had
a wistful, fleeting moment of yearning to be able to come closer to them,
to be capable of being more like them. Now I felt no incentive to
struggle to go along with them in the way they seemed to have chosen.
In thinking of students as a whole, I am afraid that I tended to view them
chiefly in terms of what they lacked as compared with their predecessors.
When it came to particular students in my own classes, the case was different. Partly, I suppose, my finding so many exceptions to the general
rule was simply because in meeting individuals you discover that stereo-
types never hold. But beyond this I found, as I always had, persons with
whom I enjoyed a mutual congeniality, no matter how different our

backgrounds. With pleasure I remember developing, after the course was over, a close friendship with three Iranian students of mine. At dinner in one of their apartments, or in our home, Doris and I enjoyed hours of pleasure based equally on a shared commonality and on the discovery of interesting differences. Less obviously but just as surely, I felt a close bond with other students with whom shared basic values overshadowed specific radical dissimilarities. In time I began to think it challenging to try to see in these undergraduates forerunners of a future society so different in its way of life that even the greatest effort of self-transcendence on my part could not let me grasp its inner flavor. I realized that it was all too easy to see differences only as privation.

I took a particular interest in observing one exceptionally bright student—Harris, who showed himself exemplary in first mastering an author's point of view, then trying to extend its relevance in an effort to apply it to resolving contemporary problems. Since he took at least two courses with me, plus an independent study project, I saw a lot of him. Without his being aware of it, I thought of him as representative of the best of the young people who would in all probability help to design—radically, perhaps, but constructively—a new style of living. After graduation Harris traveled for a year or two in what I picture as backpack-style and wrote to me from India, where he stayed for a fair length of time. In letters invariably beginning "Dear Professor Barnes" and signed "Your friend, Harris," he set down his impressions from a point of view that was vaguely, undogmatically Marxist, always alert to what was needed to improve things. Returning to the United States, he enrolled in a graduate school, finally deciding on a program in which he could work both in philosophy and psychology. For a long time I heard nothing more from him. Then I learned that he had more or less begun over again: he had earned a Ph.D. in economics and was placed in a tenure-track position at a university with considerable prestige. Soon afterward, on a visit to Boulder, Harris came to see me. I scarcely recognized in the handsome, well-groomed young man with a Brooks Brothers–style suit the shaggy-haired hippylike student I remembered. He seemed nervous as he explained that he had changed his career plans as a matter of economic expedience, that he was pleased with his professional situation and liked teaching. Sensing that he was a bit anxious as to my response, I gave him a hug as he departed and told him I was happy that all had turned out so well for him. This was true, though I recalled how different my expectations had been. It was not the end of the story. After a year or so, I received a long letter from him telling me that self-reflection, initiated by his father's sudden life-threatening illness, had led him to re-orient his existence. He had succeeded in moving both his research and his teaching into areas where he could deal with environmental and other social issues; he was finding ways to use philosophy in courses dealing with business ethics. He wrote as one exhilarated by the discovery of new direction and existential meaning. In my reply I finally told him of how I had looked on him as a sort of symbol in his undergraduate years. I'm not sure what the moral of all this is, but I know it was a happy ending to the chapter.

In the beginning of my career I was happy to feel that I was growing along with my students. It has been even more satisfying to keep in touch with those who have gone beyond what I was able to give them.

SPECIAL VENTURES AND FRINGE BENEFITS

If I were forced to choose between two descriptions of myself, I think that I should say that I am a teacher who writes rather than a scholar who teaches. I have sometimes wondered whether whatever influence I have had may have been more via the oral than the written word, especially if I were to count as teaching what I have said and taught outside my own classroom. However that may be, I have always found happily that the two pursuits have reinforced one another rather than conflicted. Of course, they have sometimes competed. In general, I always gave priority to the imminent class, but I had to learn to judge which claim was more urgent on any given date. On one day, I might decide that a lecture I had already used was good enough to serve once again and allow me to concentrate on meeting a publishing deadline; on another, my need to prepare something new led me to let the editor wait. That I was able to find teaching and research mutually nourishing was due in large part to the fact that the departments with which I was concerned and the higher levels of the administration, too, encouraged my inter-disciplinary interests. At Colorado I gave my first seminar in Sartre while I was still rostered in Classics. Later the dean granted my request to move to the Center for Interdisciplinary Studies, of which I was director for three years. Finally, a few years before retiring, when I accepted the Philosophy Department's invitation to join it on a full-time basis, I still retained the right to offer my course on myth in the arts every other year for Classics and humanities students. Thus the university provided me with the maximum opportunity to develop my work along the lines of my particular interests. In 1991, it rewarded me for having done so.

Chancellor James Corbridge, anxious to show that the university valued both teaching and research, established in my name an award of twenty thousand dollars to be given annually to a faculty member recognized to be outstanding in both areas. As often happens in such circumstances, the recipients have surpassed the one in whose name the award was bestowed.

Teaching and research, as everyone knows, are not the only areas of academic activity. On those occasions when university faculty come up for evaluation (for salaries, promotion, etc.), the formal criteria are demonstrated ability in research (or creative work), teaching, and service; the last—its nature and its status—is the most loosely defined. "Service" includes committee work inside the university, participation in community projects and in professional societies, consultation for government offices—all those things other than teaching or creative and scholarly work that one would not do if one were not an academic. Much of service can be described as useful drudgery; intramural committee work, for example. I did my share of this, with the same ambivalent feelings entertained by most of my colleagues. Faculty governance is a sacred ideal; its implementation is devastatingly time-consuming. "I could have taught a new course or written a major portion of a book in the time I spent on that committee" is a familiar complaint and one that is often not exaggerated. An assignment such as setting up a new structure for the honors program was demonstrably worthwhile; the job of deciding who should receive a fellowship or other award was interesting; work on review committees for promotion and tenure was painful but self-evidently important. Some task forces might have been better employed in cleaning blackboards. The committee on which I felt myself least qualified to serve was one set up to investigate whether there was racial discrimination in the management of men's sports. After weeks of work, we concluded that there had been some in the past, that there was no evidence of such in present official policy, and that steps were being taken to insure it would not be found in the future. I note that this was precisely the conclusion reached by subsequent committees. One of the positive rewards of this kind of activity was that I came to know people from other academic disciplines and to feel that I was living in a large circle of more or less kindred spirits.

This sense of community was further extended in professional meetings with colleagues in my field from other places. I rarely attended the national conferences with their inhibiting crowds. Even when I was a department chair, I cravenly arranged that other willing members of the

department would undertake the interviews at the "slave markets" for re-
cruits. But I have enjoyed some of the regional convocations and those of
the smaller, more specialized organizations. The meetings of the Sartre
Society of North America and the Simone de Beauvoir Society have
come to seem like family reunions except that similarity of interests and
the chances of meeting exciting new members are greater. I was not
among those who originally got the idea and worked to establish the
Sartre Society: Thomas Flynn, William McBride, Phyllis Morris, Ronald
Aronson, and Joseph Catalano deserve credit for that. They honored me
by asking me to present the keynote address at the society's first meeting
in New York in October 1985. I spoke on Sartre's *War Diaries*, using also
some material from his letters to Beauvoir. I was happy not only to meet
established Sartre scholars (both philosophers and people in French literature), but to observe the large group of impressive younger ones. I recall with particular pleasure a meeting in Chicago at which five of us
Sartre translators had an interchange: Carol Cosman, who translated
The Family Idiot; David Pellauer, who did *Notebooks for an Ethics;* Vincent von
Wroblesky, who rendered *L'Etre et le néant* into German; Yvanka Raynova,
who put it into Bulgarian. Strangely, the *Chicago Tribune* did not report
this momentous event. The Beauvoir Society held the first of its bian-
nual conferences at Palo Alto in January 1991. This was arranged almost
single-handedly by Yolanda Patterson. She, too, invited me to deliver
the keynote paper. This time I talked about Beauvoir's *Journal* and her
Letters to Sartre, in coincidental symmetry with my other presentation. The
Beauvoir Society, though its membership overlaps somewhat with that
of the Sartre group, includes more persons interested primarily in feminism; its offerings are—if anything—even more varied. In both associations, friendships developed that went far deeper than the sharing of
a hobby.

With other associations and national committees, because they were
not concerned with my particular areas, I strengthened my sense of the
university as a structure transcending disciplinary boundaries. On the
American Council for Learned Societies' faculty fellowship committee,
on the Charlotte Newcombe Committee (administered by the Woodrow Wilson Foundation), which gave financial aid to outstanding doctoral candidates, and on others less well known, we struggled to help
each other in evaluating proposals outside our immediate expertise. I was
impressed by the members' effort to be unprejudiced and fair, to recognize the merit of offbeat proposals as well as those that fit the mold. I
was also disturbed at the extent to which chance entered into the selec-

tion process. I know that the sheer happenstance of my presence served to block or to salvage certain proposals in connection with which I had special insight. I always advise colleagues whose work I respect to apply again, if rejected the first time, in the hope that changes in committee personnel will favor them.

Sometimes professors who engage temporarily in off-campus occupations end up accepting permanent appointments other than teaching. This did not happen to me, though there were two occasions when I was offered the opportunity to leave the world of the university. To the first, wildly inappropriate as I look at it now, I gave serious consideration, though it never advanced beyond a possibility on paper. While I was at the University of Toledo, I received a letter from Jerry Sperling, for whom I had corrected papers in my graduate days at Yale. Now holding what sounded like an important post in the Central Intelligence Agency, he asked if I would be interested in working for the CIA. At that time, like most people, I knew very little of the peacetime activities of the agency. Its job, which I vaguely assumed to be that of insuring the nation's security against malevolent conspiracies of foreign origin, sounded intriguing and important. Talking it over with Doris, I agreed with her that "it might be fun to be part of that Washington mess." I wrote to Jerry that I was interested and provided a list of references. Subsequently, I learned that some of my acquaintances had been consulted regarding me. As time passed and nothing more happened, I concluded that the matter was closed. I had almost forgotten about it when Sperling wrote that I had been approved so far. He wanted to know, before the final background check was undertaken, whether I was still seriously committed to the prospect. I was not sure. I wrote to ask just what sort of thing I would be doing, whether I was likely to find it sufficiently rewarding so that I would not soon be wishing that I were still teaching. His response, though vague as to what the nature of my work would be, made my decision easy. Not only was he overemphatic in saying he could not guarantee my not regretting teaching; he added that he himself would probably return to it after a few years. Fortunately for the CIA and for me, I told him to drop proceedings. I have only one regret: It would be interesting to know how the agency would have reacted to my police record on the island of Santorini.

The second opportunity is interesting chiefly because of its extreme contrast with the first. In October 1969, I accepted an invitation to spend a month at the Institute for Policy Studies in Washington. I was free to do so since I was currently on leave with a faculty fellowship. I could not have had a more fitting environment in which to work on my study of student protest for *The University as the New Church*. While I was there, two hostile articles appeared in *Barron's* attacking the IPS as "a radical think-tank" leading "the radical thrust for social change." To some extent, the description was one that its directors and fellows would have accepted. The two co-directors, Marcus Raskin, formerly an aide to McGeorge Bundy, and Richard Barnet, author of *The Economy of Death*, had been active in urging disarmament at a date when the United States was building its strategy of nuclear deterrence. Among the fellows of the institute, Arthur Waskow had argued the merits of "creative disorder"; Milton Kotler, in advocating new forms of neighborhood self-government, explicitly recognized that organized demonstrations and even riots sometimes produced positive results. Most of those connected with IPS looked with sympathy on activist supporters of Eugene McCarthy at the 1968 Democratic Convention in Chicago. But charges that the organization was subversive and un-American were absurd—save in the eyes of, say, a Strom Thurmond or a Jesse Helms. Participants in its activities included such persons as Paul Goodman, David Riesman, Christopher Jencks. It maintained formal associations with several colleges and universities, which sent their students to study and do research at the institute's headquarters. Among its financial backers were the Ford Foundation and the National Board of Missions of the Presbyterian Church. A few of the people at the institute would go further than I in lip-service support of such dangerous groups as the Weathermen. For the most part, I found in IPS a unique and exhilarating blend of theoretical exploration of ideas and social planning, the quintessence of what was most positive in the sixties, albeit occasionally skirting the outer edge. Still, I did not feel that this was quite my natural orbit; I considered that my own contribution was so negligible that it would never be remembered. I was surprised when some time later Marcus Raskin wrote to tell me that the institute was enlarging its teaching program and invited me to take on a full-time job there. I rejected the offer but was pleased to be asked.

During my month in Washington, it was a joy to become acquainted with the city, its physical layout as well as its historical sites and museums. I dropped in to listen to one of the House committee sessions (I forget which one). My sole visit to the White House was on the evening of my arrival, when I went along with one of the IPS staff members to take part in a candlelight peace march. At the end each one of us deposited a candle stub by the fence. Two things stand out in my memory of that night: One is the depth of my feelings as I joined in the half-songs, half-chants adapted from the Civil Rights marchers—"We shall overcome" and "All we are saying is 'Give Peace a Chance.'" The other was a trivial incident. At the counter in the Mayflower Coffee Shop, where my new acquaintance and I went afterward, an elderly man struck up a conversation with us. Seeming a bit puzzled, but by no means disapproving, on learning what we had just been doing, he tried to pay for our food, almost as if he wanted to make a gesture of appreciation. This kind of half-complicity on the part of persons unwilling to engage themselves openly in action that seemed to them futile, if not misguided, was typical of many persons in that period.

Regrettably, my month's stay in the nation's capital was typical of visitors' experience then in another way: I was "mugged," not literally but close to it. On the weekend that Doris came to visit me, we were walking back from a restaurant in the area where I was staying, near Dupont Circle, rather early in the evening and on a well-lit but not heavily frequented street. Suddenly three youths appeared. One broke through between us, a second stood by as lookout, the third took hold of my purse, which I involuntarily and foolishly held on to. Luckily the leather strap broke, the clasp opening as the purse fell. The thief grabbed the wallet as I picked myself up from the sidewalk where I had fallen in the scuffle. My shock at the violence was worse than my bruises or the loss of quite a bit of money. There was a cheering footnote to this episode. A man who lived nearby, finding my wallet, emptied of cash but with credit cards and everything else intact, took the trouble to mail it to me at my address in Boulder. He enclosed a note of sympathy, expressing his distress that a visitor had obviously been subjected to much inconvenience.

In spite of this mishap, I was happy when, in the late seventies and eighties, I found myself in a position requiring me to go to Washington two or three times a year. In walking each day from my apartment to the IPS building, I had passed, on Q Street N.W., the national headquarters of Phi Beta Kappa. As one among thousands of Phi Beta Kappa members, I saw no reason to make my presence known. Five years later this address was central to the most interesting and deeply satisfying of all my ventures into the farther reaches of Academe. For 1974–75, and again for 1977–78, I served as one of the Phi Beta Kappa visiting scholars. Though I had attended lectures by scholars who had come to our campus, I knew little about the program until I became part of it. Selected by a committee of the national Phi Beta Kappa Senate, thirteen scholars make eight to ten two-day visits to a college or university campus, giving at least one public lecture, speaking to classes and other student or faculty groups, etc. Theoretically, we had four formal engagements; in practice, usually more than that. The original intention had been that the scholars would enrich the intellectual experience of institutions with limited resources or those off the beaten track for travelers. By my time, these specifications were mostly ignored, although smaller places may still have received some special consideration and leading universities in the East were less likely to want to add more speakers to their already crowded schedule. I thoroughly enjoyed these visits, which took me into virtually every region of the United States. They differed from my customary ones in the length of my stay. Also, though one department might be officially my sponsor, local chapters (only institutions with Phi Beta Kappa were included) made an effort to appeal to as many disciplines as possible. Hence I found myself speaking with students in all the fields with which I had any connection and some where I had none; for example, I spoke on Sartre's political views to a class in political science and on aspects of Greek myth to a variety of literature classes. On a couple of occasions I was assigned to sit in a room for an hour or two and respond to whatever questions anybody came to ask. The topics brought up ranged from technical details of Sartre's ontology to Aeschylus' view of justice, to inquiries about my own personal philosophy. The first time this happened, I felt extremely tense. Then, reminding myself nobody could be expected to be the Delphic Oracle, I relaxed and found it fun.

These visits, along with being stimulating to my own scholarly pursuits, were immensely informative about the state of higher education in this country. I felt reassured, particularly with regard to the quality of smaller, less well-known colleges. With schedules of often four or five courses a semester, their faculty did not publish as much as in large universities, though some of them miraculously did produce significant work. What particularly impressed me was that most of those who did not publish nevertheless kept up with what was going on in their fields and were offering to students original approaches and insights that deserved a greater audience. I will not say that I never encountered a single individual whose tenure might be questioned, but these rare exceptions were fairly evenly distributed among places with greater or lesser prestige. The kind of complaints and frictions that I had encountered at the various schools at which I myself had taught recurred so universally as to be almost amusing. It is one of the points I bring up when trying to dissuade a discontented colleague from leaving in order to find peace and harmony elsewhere.

A year after my second stint as visiting scholar, I was elected by the United Chapters of Phi Beta Kappa (the name was later changed to the Phi Beta Kappa Society) to their twenty-four-member national senate. My two six-year terms (1979–91) as senator provided all sorts of privileged opportunities; I look back on them with unalloyed pleasure as one of the most valuable peripheral rewards of my academic career. There was a certain irony in my being in the senate at all, let alone the fact that for three of those years I was on the executive committee. When I was at Wilson College, it did not have a Phi Beta Kappa chapter; in 1952, shortly after it was granted one, I was named an alumna member. The tenuous nature of my standing was underscored when, during my tenure in the senate, a financial crisis at the college resulted in its losing many of its best faculty and having its chapter suspended.

Before I became a visiting scholar, my involvement on our local level was slight. Now I began to realize how much the society did beyond issuing certificates and keys to the brightest of liberal arts graduates—its fellowships and awards, its support of publications (*The American Scholar* as well as *The Key Reporter*), establishing and maintaining high standards in the nation's colleges and universities. Its sphere is self-limited, of course, since the focus is on the liberal arts. The society is regarded by some as elitist. In a sense the charge is just; its primary concern is with the intellectual life of the country, and much of its activity consists in selecting those persons and institutions of demonstrated excellence. Yet it might be argued that this area is as legitimate a concern as a host of others. Moreover, the scholars it supports are engaged in disseminating knowledge of all sorts of matters relevant to the well-being of our culture. All of these things remain true today, though I have read that students in the nineties are often less eager to accept Phi Beta Kappa's invitation to membership.

It was appropriate that I should be assigned to the committee that selected the visiting scholars. Mina Rees, the distinguished mathematician and former president of the Graduate School and University Center at C.C.N.Y., was chair for my first term. I succeeded her for my second six years. From this perspective I discovered how much the presence of the scholars meant to the schools they visited. Small though our committee was (six of us at first, then nine—most of us members of the senate, a few from outside), we tried valiantly and succeeded reasonably well in pinpointing leaders in the three fields of natural and social science and the humanities. In the process I developed at least a superficial awareness of who was doing what in research and criticism. (We occasionally included a creative artist, once a television commentator, but mostly the scholars were suitably so named.) Our committee functioned so informally that I sometimes wondered how we performed so efficiently. Charles Blitzer, formerly with the Smithsonian, later director of the Woodrow Wilson International Center for Scholars, declared it the most enjoyable of the dozens, if not hundreds, of committees on which he had served. In part, Mina Rees deserved credit for this; she created such a climate of collegiality and mutual respect that even after she left, we arrived at all our decisions by consensus. Responsible for the successful implementation of the program were the two secretaries who administered it: Frances Robb, who played a key role in setting up the program in the mid-fifties, and Kathy Navascués, who took charge when Frances chose to work only part-time. From both ends of the program, I had reason to admire these women's extraordinary skill. When I started coming regularly to Washington, we three became close friends, always arranging to meet for a long dinner for which they and I alternated in the roles of hostess and guest.

The opportunity to meet and to work with eminent persons whom I would never otherwise have encountered was one of the supererogatory graces of being at the center of the Phi Beta Kappa Society—not only the senators and my associates on the committees, but the authors and their editors (or publishers) who came for the annual banquet at which the book awards were presented: the Christian Gauss Prize, the Ralph Waldo Emerson Award, and the Phi Beta Kappa Award in Science. Dislike of name-dropping prevents my listing all whose presence I valued, but I cannot let pass unmentioned a few whom I came to know well, since we worked closely together all those dozen years, and for whom I feel a special bond of friendship. Along with those whom I have already named there were: Kenneth Greene, who, as secretary (in the British sense of that term) seemed to many Phi Beta Kappa members the living personification of the ideals of the society (he and I delighted in sharing our enthusiasm for the novels of Trollope); Catherine Sims, who perhaps did more than any of the others of its presidents to guard the society's vision without allowing it to ossify; Virginia Ferris, professor of entomology from Purdue University; Norman Ramsey, the Nobel Prize—winning physicist. The chance to know Norman Ramsey still better came when he spent a year as visiting professor at our university. When

Norman and his wife came up to our mountain cabin, they helped us stack logs for the fire. Norman, born in the same year as I, put me to shame in claims of youthfulness. For his birthday (it was one that came after his seventieth), his wife presented him with tickets to take both of them skydiving near Boulder.

Phi Beta Kappa's triennial meetings with delegates from all of the United Chapters, held in various cities across the country, intensified my sense of being a member of a unique, close-knit community, though our differences were as pronounced as in any large body of people representing local concerns. These sessions were sometimes quite contentious, particularly when the question arose as to which new institutions should be given chapters, or whether we should, as a group, issue a public statement with political implications. By contrast, our small senate meetings maintained an atmosphere of extreme courtesy and never (during my years there) became personally acrimonious, however sharply divided the final vote proved to be. Procedure was ultra-formal. With amusement I heard us refer to each other as "Senator so-and-so," a practice that reminded me of the embarrassment I had felt long ago at the use of "Brother" and "Sister" in the Free Methodist Church and later on in my brief term as representative of the University Teachers' Union at the Toledo Central Labor Union. A central task of ours was to insure that rules for admitting new members into Phi Beta Kappa remained appropriate to the changing educational scene and that chapters were abiding by the rules. An unusual problem came up at my first meeting, one which coincidentally touched on an experience of my own. It appeared that a Midwest chapter had listed as one of its initiates a man whose course work for the Bachelor of Arts degree had been done partly in extension classes offered in a prison. One of the criteria originally laid down for a Phi Beta Kappa initiate was that he/she should be a person of "sound moral character." This quaint phrase was seldom invoked; still, the case did appear to represent a flagrant violation of the rule. As I recall, the person in question was finally disqualified because his work had been done as part of an outreach program and not within the university's regular program. In our discussion, however, someone proposed that anyone who had spent time in prison should be automatically excluded from initiation into the society. I objected, observing that we should not forget the names of such distinguished prisoners as Socrates, John Bunyan, and a host of others, including recent conscientious objectors and Civil Rights protesters. The proposer of the motion withdrew it. I agreed, however, that such cases as the one before us should be carefully scrutinized. I had myself been badly misled by what appeared to be a virtual guarantee of worth and promise in a prison inmate, leading me not to a fringe benefit, like the Phi Beta Kappa experience, but a most unusual special venture.

One day (it must have been in the second half of the sixties), I received a letter from Larry M., a prisoner at Leavenworth. He told me that he had been reading in my translation of *Being and Nothingness* and that Sartre's message of responsible freedom had come to him like an awakening. The text itself he had found formidable, but my introduction to it had been useful. He asked if I could suggest further reading to help him understand Sartre better. I sent him information and some of my own books and articles. Soon we were corresponding regularly. He wrote much as one of my eager students might have done. I soon discovered that he was taking extension courses offered through Highland (Kansas) Community Junior College. In August 1968 he received a degree, Associate in Arts, and he sent a photograph of himself in cap and gown. Larry, now in his mid-thirties, told me that he had been imprisoned for stealing, writing bad checks, and forgery. I learned later that his criminal record included an escape from jail in Arizona, during which he and some others had overpowered a sheriff and left him locked in the trunk of a car, which they abandoned in the desert heat. (By a strange coincidence, the sheriff was shortly afterward rescued by the father of my friend and colleague Hal Evjen.) Larry's and my letters at first discussed chiefly philosophical questions. Gradually he wrote more personally of himself and his hopes of leading a new kind of life once he was paroled. This he hoped to accomplish through continuing his education. He attributed his changed outlook to the classes he had already taken, and particularly to the reading he had been doing in Existentialism. I believed in the genuineness of this conversion. I had no illusion that Larry was a Jean Genet. His letters, though not brilliant, seemed to testify to his being well qualified to do college-level work and to show a high degree of intellectual curiosity and interest in what was going on in the outside world. Some of his observations showed remarkable insight. I undertook to see if I could help him in getting parole and in being admitted to the University of Colorado. I even visited him once at Leavenworth. All went well there, although I recall a moment of claustrophobic panic when I found myself between locked doors in the passage between outer hallways and the visiting room.

I still marvel at the way that all persons concerned worked to make the plan succeed. Letters of recommendation from Larry's vocational trainer in computer use and from his instructors in college courses praised him highly; one compared him favorably with undergraduates taught on a university campus. His grade point average, 3.8 out of 4.00, supported these evaluations. At my university I got cooperation every-where. William Douglas, the dean of admissions—though he confessed to me afterward that it had not been without reservation—cleared the way for Larry's admission, waived the application fee, and advised me how to arrange for part-time employment so that Larry could be granted the status of a Colorado nonresident for tuition purposes. A vice presi-dent, the college dean, a departmental colleague, and one of the local ministers whom I knew all wrote to the chairman of the U.S. Board of Parole, both to promise to lend their support to the project and to confirm that I myself was a person whose judgment could be trusted. A Denver parole officer, Robert Walker, agreed to take Larry in his charge and to serve as liaison for all parties. I have seen copies of the remark-able letters he wrote, advising and counseling Larry, offering help wher-ever possible. Walker was under no illusion that a happy outcome was assured, but he was willing to give Larry the benefit of any doubt. Concretely, he arranged for Larry to receive a small monthly stipend from the Colorado Division of Rehabilitation. He also spoke seriously with me, telling me that, while the chance was worth taking, I should re-member that Larry had been diagnosed as a sociopath. "If he runs true to form, he will get everything out of you he can and then toss you away like a squeezed orange."

In the spring of 1969 Larry's parole was approved. (I learned from Walker that an official at Leavenworth had expressed great surprise.) In July, Doris and I drove to Kansas and picked up Larry at the prison gate. We had brought with us a box of clothes that his mother had sent to me to give to him. She and I had been in touch by letter and phone. In ex-pressing her appreciation, she assured me that I need have no fear of Larry, that his record showed no signs of anything but gentlemanly be-havior toward women. It was only later that I reflected on what she did *not* say; at no time did she express her conviction that the enterprise would succeed.

In Boulder, my friends all joined in helping out, inviting Larry along with Doris and me to dinner parties, volunteering to aid him in finding his way about, introducing him to other students. As Hal Evjen put it, we were all engaged in a project of applied Existentialist ethics, con-fident that Larry would remake himself. All did not go well. Almost from the start, Doris and I began to have qualms. Larry's obvious disdain for the modest housing arrangements we had made for him and his unrealistic expectations as to the style of living he could manage were disturbing. He frequently fancied himself insulted when there was no good reason. We caught him in several lies. What bothered us most was that we learned he had been boasting to others (entirely falsely) of sexual conquests he had made of women he had met through us.

When classes began, things seemed to improve. Larry claimed to be enjoying them. He was holding down a job at the computer center, and Desmond Cartwright, professor of psychology, was pleased to have Larry as his student research assistant. I felt sufficiently at ease to go off for my month with the Institute for Policy Studies. Then Doris wrote me with surprising news. Larry had chanced to meet one of Doris' graduate students, Marilyn, an older woman whose ability had so impressed Doris that she had provided the equivalent of a scholarship for her. She and Larry, who had both been divorced at least twice, started an affair and were married before my return from Washington. Needless to say, they did not consult either of us as to the wisdom of this step. After Larry's predictable departure, Marilyn confessed to me that she had married him because he was our protégé and she had hoped through him to gain entrance into our circle.

Back in Boulder, I found things collapsing on all sides. Larry was failing in class or wasn't bothering to attend. Before long, he had abandoned the university and was staying at an unknown address in Denver. (Whether he deserted Marilyn or she threw him out, I was never quite sure.) One night, he got drunk and drove his car (procured by what means I don't know) into a parked police vehicle. Informed of this by a call in the middle of the night from Denver police headquarters, I declined to intervene. As it turned out, I wasn't needed. The next morning Larry showed his student ID card, said he had never been arrested before, and was released on his own recognizance. His parole officer happened to be in court that day, heard Larry's name called but decided he must have been mistaken, and left without checking. Larry soon disappeared from our area, leaving a wake of unpaid bills and bad checks. A few months later, I learned that he had been picked up for armed robbery in Michigan.

In February 1972, a letter came to me from a counselor in the Division of Vocational Rehabilitation, who worked with the State Prison of Southern Michigan. He reported that he was helping Larry "to define a practical and realistic rehabilitation plan," that Larry "alleged" that he had been enrolled at Colorado, where I had befriended him, and that he

wanted to continue his education after his next release. Did I, the letter
asked, feel that Larry had "the discipline, motivation and perseverance
needed in pursuing a Bachelor's degree"? I sent back a brief description
of what had happened here. I concluded, "It is a painful task to write
such a letter, and I am asking you, please not to communicate to [Larry]
what I have said. I do not want to hurt him, but unless you have witnessed demonstrably effective results of psychotherapy, I see little reason to hope for a change in him." The counselor promptly showed my
reply to Larry, who wrote me reproachfully. I did not answer this nor the
couple of other letters he wrote in the obvious hope of resuming correspondence as though there had been no interruption. I decided that
aside from its being a waste of time and no pleasure for me, it would not
be a kindness to him to confirm his belief that he could avoid the consequences of breaking trust. Before long he was back at Leavenworth. I
have heard nothing of him since.

Looking back on this fiasco, I reflect on two things: In the one interview I had with Larry after the truth came out with respect to his situation in the university and before he left Boulder, he told me that he tried
but had been unable to bring himself to talk to me about "the real
things"—that he had wanted to smash the whole facade and ask me
to help him understand why he felt the compulsion to lie, sometimes
"simply for conversation," why he knew that he would never change his
way of life though he wished that he could. I think that this was not the
sociopath speaking, and it makes me wish that I had been more perceptive, able either to help him myself at this deeper level or to bring him
to someone who could. On a practical level, it was probably too late. I
doubt that anyone, any more than he himself, could say what had gone
wrong. Nothing in his comfortable middle-class background stands out
as probable cause. His mother, in an after-the-event phone call told me
that Larry had been in trouble off and on since high school. Just before
his first incarceration at Leavenworth, his parents had sought the help of
a famous lawyer (Percy Forman, I believe it was). He had defended Larry
before. He said now that he could probably get Larry off but asked what
good it would do since he would continue on the same path; he advised
them to leave Larry on his own, which they did. When she heard of my
endeavor, his mother said, she hoped there would be success this time,
but she would believe it when she saw it.

The second thing, something to be wondered at, is the fact that nobody so much as hinted to me that I should have acted otherwise. Not
one of my friends reproached me—not those whom, without my

knowledge, Larry had tried to enlist in improbable money-making schemes, nor those whom he slandered. University administrators extended their sympathy, withheld any criticism. Dean William Briggs not only assured me that I had been right in making the attempt, but added that if ever a similar opportunity should arise, I should respond the same way. Though agreeing with him in theory, I did not follow his advice in practice. In 1971 I received a letter from a prisoner in Florida State Prison. Having come across *Being and Nothingness*, he wanted to know if I could aid him in his study of Sartre. Not knowing for certain that this was a copycat strategy, I replied courteously but did not encourage further correspondence. Whatever tale there might have been remains untold.

Another unusual venture for which I received administrative support had more positive results, though this, too, produced some unexpected consequences. In the summer of 1962, Doris and I took one of several trips that we made to Greece. As always, I looked up former colleagues at Pierce College, who introduced me to its new president, Margaret Steward. From her I heard the surprising news that when a recently passed regulation required that the college be formally associated with one of the states, she had arranged to have it registered with Colorado. This was partly because she had personal ties with this state and partly because it was not already encumbered by a large number of such involvements, as were some of the Eastern states. Both because I still maintained a warm interest in the college and because, as a member of the Classics Department, I thought it would be beneficial for us to establish a relation with an institution in Greece, I saw in this chance affiliation with Colorado a great opportunity. I persuaded our president, Joseph Smiley, to establish a "formal bond of friendship" between the University of Colorado and Pierce College. Margaret Steward visited here as an official guest; a program was initiated that brought about many good things. Over the years a number of Pierce College faculty and students came here on fellowships or scholarships; the university used the college building for its Hellenic Institute, a summer study abroad program; and several people from Colorado took on various jobs at Pierce College.

It was the first of our Greek visitors who opened up the most startling of unforeseen possibilities. Clio, as I will call her here, was one of the teachers I had known during my first sojourn in Greece. (President Steward wisely wanted to reward some of her established faculty for their service and to provide them with further training.) Clio proved her academic ability in the two years she spent with us. She enthralled everyone with tales of her early experiences; she had been among those forced to leave Turkey at the time of the Greek exodus in the twenties. From time to time she spoke of treasured possessions that her family had left behind. One day in her last semester, when Hal Evjen and I were talking with her, she revealed to us something of extraordinary importance. She told us that in the original home in Istanbul, her family had kept hidden some ancient manuscripts, stored in a secret place behind or underneath false walls or flooring. One of her relatives had managed to gain repossession of the house and still lived there. She went on to say that she thought these manuscripts ought now to be brought to public light and that in return for what it had done for her, she wanted to bestow them on the University of Colorado. She did not ask much in return, only that financial assistance might be given to her two granddaughters when they were ready for their higher education, also a guarantee that the manuscripts would be properly protected. Clio said that she could effectively prove to the present owner of the house her right to the ancient items. The question was how to get them here without attracting attention to them prematurely.

Hal and I perceived that we were on the verge of one of those rare but not unprecedented paleographical discoveries. When we questioned further, Clio said that the family had always held the manuscripts to be from the sixth century, that one of them was a legal code, the others (she was unsure how many) literary. It was hard for Hal and me to keep our imaginations under any sort of control. Though at this period I was heavily committed to my work with Existentialism, this epitome of every classicist's dream gripped me completely. If Clio was right, we might be privileged to touch the oldest extant copy of the Justinian Code. The literary manuscripts could be lost works of the Byzantine period. More likely they were copies of older writings. If there was nothing comparable to the discovery of Aristotle's lost treatise on comedy, as Eco imagined happening in *The Name of the Rose*, a manuscript of that date was a major discovery even if of a work long familiar to us. And if these were not actually as early as the sixth century, any pre-printing manuscript was of utmost significance.

I made an immediate appointment for Hal and me with President Smiley, merely indicating that it concerned a matter of great importance. He asked Provost Manning to be present as well. Both responded enthusiastically to our report; they assured us that adequate facilities in the library would be provided, with temperature and humidity control, and they promised to find a way to have the treasures safely removed and transported. They seemed to revel in the drama of it all as much as we did. As Hal and I walked down the stairs, Ted Manning called to us in a stage whisper, "Come with me to the Casbah!" At a second meeting Smiley told us that he had made an arrangement with a senior naval captain, the head of the campus naval ROTC. This man would be able, during the summer, to go freely in and out of Turkey, our NATO ally, and would not have to undergo customs scrutiny.

Exultantly we reported all this to Clio, who provided the Istanbul address and said she would now send instructions to the relative living there. Hal and I and Doris, the only other person in whom we confided, passed a few days of pure anticipatory gloating. Then one Saturday morning Clio phoned; almost unable to speak, she stammered that something terrible had happened, she would come by to tell me. She brought a letter from another relative, one living in Greece; the writer said that the resident of the house in Istanbul had died within the last year and that just a few weeks ago the house itself had caught fire and burned to the ground. I reported this tragedy, more Hardyesque than Greek, to Hal, later to Manning. Meanwhile, for our mutual consolation, Doris and I invited Clio to spend the weekend with us. For hours, as we talked, she sat and sewed, first mending things of her own, then whatever Doris and I could dredge up of ours. For a while we lamented what had happened, then by tacit consent laid it away as unbearable to mention. Gradually, as I looked at Clio, her attitude seemed to me to express primarily a great relief. Reluctantly, the conviction grew in me that the news of the fire was her invention to free herself from a situation in which she had trapped herself, that the coveted manuscripts never existed. When I compared notes with Doris, I found that she had reached that same conclusion. We said nothing of this to Clio, who herself did not bring the matter up again. We did speak of it to Hal, who agreed with us. That our suspicion was correct was later supported, then confirmed by two things that happened afterward: Not long after these events, Clio, having earned her graduate degree, returned home. When I took care of her phone bill, which came after her departure, I noted a call to a number in Greece, made a day or two before the date of the fateful letter. (Clio almost never made overseas calls.) Then a few years later when Hal was in Istanbul, he looked up the address Clio had given us. Not finding it, he inquired of a woman living close to where it should have been. She replied, "There is no building with this address. If it existed, it would be there." She pointed to a vacant space. But in response to Hal's question, she said that there had been no fire there, no house within present memory.

It is easy to laugh at our credulity. I do not believe Clio deliberately set out to deceive. I had never before known her to lie though she tended to overdramatize in her reports of what had happened to her. I think that probably she began with exaggerating in her own mind something that stemmed from a vague family tale, then let her imagination take over until for a time she may have been convinced herself that something valuable lay hidden in the house—though she could not sustain belief in light of realistic planning.

As I reflect on this episode, what bothers me is not my gullibility but my lack of ethical scruples. We would not have been stealing antiquities, but it would not have been legal or exactly honorable to smuggle them out. I have always protested against the removal of archaeological treasures from their country of origin. I was never willing to excuse Lord Elgin for transporting the marbles from the Acropolis even in light of all the so-called proof that this was the best way to preserve them. Were manuscripts different? Or did I simply surrender to the overpowering nature of the temptation, just as Clio let herself slip into mythomania? I have never known for sure whether Smiley and Manning genuinely believed in the probable success of our venture. Perhaps they were skeptical but decided not to stand in the way of our following up on a remote possibility worth the gamble. As in the case of the Larry fiasco, the administrators responded to our unusual appeal and did not remonstrate when the enterprise collapsed—a tribute to them, I believe, though perhaps not everyone would agree.

I am afraid that in my portrayal of academic life, I may appear to have given too bright a picture as if there were never any dark spots. My own personal history has indeed been a story of fulfillment, but it would not be truthful to imply that there were never any conflicts around me or that I myself was not involved in any of them. From my present vantage point, I am tempted to view these upheavals as unnecessary squabbles, "trouble in the bird cage," but this would be to do violence to the lived experience. While I do not think it important to record the details of particular disputes, their existence has to be acknowledged. Sometimes they grew out of opposing outlooks with respect to educational issues or ideological disagreement over the approach appropriate to a particular discipline. Sometimes the struggle was over faculty versus administrative authority. On one occasion I recall that faculty members took sides in a confrontation between administrators—President Newton versus Graduate Dean Dayton McKean. (A faculty vote gave overwhelming support to Newton.) This one entailed a laughable incident in which I was concerned. The provost, Oswald Tippo, wanted to enlist my support but did not want to be seen or heard trying to influence me. By phone he asked me to walk on a certain pathway between his building and mine. The temperature was well below zero. When we met midway, Tippo casually tipped his hat as if surprised to see me; then we talked for a bit. I fear this dramatic performance was lost on the two or three students walking as fast as they could to keep warm.

The most frequent and bitter battles were intradepartmental and were usually based on personal interest, sometimes sheer power struggles, sometimes the outgrowth of personality conflicts. A split in the Classics Department was the catalyst that led me to choose to sever my association with it in 1977 after nearly twenty-five years. I did not leave without acute unhappiness, but at least those on the opposing side joined with me in rebuilding bridges so far as personal relations were concerned. This happy outcome was not exactly typical. Too often resentments smoulder for years, flaring into open conflict from time to time until departures or retirements change the personnel roster. And the best do not always win, not any more here than in any other arena.

Admitted, then, that I did not live in Arcadia, I will switch metaphors and make a quite different point. In sharp contrast with what was true earlier in the century, the particular location of our university as "a marketplace of ideas" did not mean isolation. I do not refer merely to the ease of transportation that has largely canceled out the significance of geographical space, but rather to the network of visitations—by lecturers invited for a day or two, by visiting professors coming for a semester or more. In a few cases I established lasting friendships with scholars I would otherwise have known only in their books or by their widespread reputations. Among these I think especially of two classicists, Zeph Stewart from Harvard and Hugh Lloyd-Jones from Oxford; Keith Guthrie from Cambridge, who wrote the multi-volume *History of Greek Philosophy*; David Daube, professor of law, first at Oxford, later at the University of California at Berkeley; Herbert Schneider, whom I knew after he retired from the Department of Philosophy at Columbia; Nel Noddings at Stanford, who combined philosophy of education and work on a feminist approach to ethics; Leonard Pronko, at Pomona College, who far surpassed me in the range of interdisciplinary activities (he is a recognized authority in both French literature and Japanese kabuki).

Of brief encounters with famous visitors, the most memorable of all came about long before I was established at Colorado. In my first semester at the Woman's College of North Carolina in Greensboro, I learned that Thomas Mann was coming to lecture. At that stage I allotted to Mann an exalted station above all other living authors. In an aggressive manner quite unbecoming to a newly appointed instructor, I went to the man in charge of arrangements and declared that I simply had to talk with Thomas Mann and could not be content with a few words exchanged in a reception line. My fervor must have impressed him, for he told me that though he could not arrange for private interviews, I could plan lunch for Mann and a small group of appropriate people for which the college would pay. As "hostess" I sat with Thomas Mann on my right. He talked freely, especially about the "imperial responsibility" the United States would have to assume after the close of the war (this was fall 1941, before Pearl Harbor). Then he drifted on to philosophical reflections on good and evil in humankind. I remember verbatim his words: "Poor little Man! He walks with his eyes on the stars and one foot in the gutter, no wonder he limps. Poor little Man!" That moment marked the high point of my feelings for Mann. His lecture was anticlimactic. I was even put off a bit by his complacent assumption that he himself was the appointed incarnation of the Artist about whose obligations he was speaking. I read his later books with appreciation but not adoration.

Before concluding, I want to mention one other fringe benefit—the opportunity to take up residence myself on other campuses. This I did on four occasions—once for just three weeks in the summer, each of the others for a semester. Doris went with me for all of these sojourns; twice she had a sabbatical that came up just at the right time, once she simply asked for leave. Her presence added greatly to my feeling that I was living at home even though away. The summer venture (1985) was at the University of Idaho in connection with a grant that this university had received from the National Endowment for the Humanities. At the suggestion of Galen Rowe, professor of Classics and dean of the Arts College, I conducted a seminar with Idaho faculty from various disciplines, taking as our subject the Orpheus myth. (I had lectured once earlier at Idaho on Greek mythology and had brought up the subject of the

Orpheus myth as it was connected with a popular religious movement in ancient Greece and reflected in Greek philosophy.) We studied various treatments of the story in literature, art, music, and film. Each member of the group contributed appropriately according to his/her specialty. Doris volunteered to produce for us a modern English version of Robert Henryson's fifteenth-century poem "Orpheus and Eurydice," written in Middle Scot. It was exhilarating for all of us to be teaching each other.

It was as a classicist also that I was invited to spend the fall term of 1982 at San Diego State University. The Department of Classics there is unique, I believe, in that a volunteer community group, "Friends of Classics," established itself for the sole purpose of thinking up ways to promote the department and its subject matter with financial assistance and considerable time and effort on the part of its members. It owes its existence to a remarkable woman, Gail Burnett, now in her nineties. One of the early Ph.D.s, she taught at S.D.S.U. in Classics and comparative literature some decades ago. She so enthralled some of her women students that after her retirement they refused to say good-bye, setting up a Tuesday Club which still meets weekly with Gail for literary discussions and presentations by herself as well as by others in the group. Through Gail we became acquainted with townspeople in San Diego. After our return to Boulder, Doris and I both admitted having considered, though finally rejecting, the possibility of moving to San Diego after retirement since we would have a built-in circle of friends in an extremely attractive city.

My other two visiting appointments were in philosophy. Fall semester 1984 I held a Mellon Professorship at Tulane University in New Orleans. Along with teaching one class, I was responsible for another interdisciplinary project—a series of weekly public discussions in which a small group of faculty and I presented our views on various aspects of imagination. It was another richly rewarding term, and one which, thanks to our having earlier acquaintance with people living there, was another "town and gown" experience—if that fascinating city can be called a town.

Most significant of all for me professionally was my position as a visiting professor of philosophy at Yale; this was earlier, in spring 1974. My first return to Yale had been the previous year when I was invited by the Philosophy Department to come for a lecture. Being on the spot had seemed to renew all my happiest associations and to dispel the negative ones. Sentimentally, I went to the Yale Co-op and bought glasses with the Yale seal, something quite out of character for me. I loved being at Yale for the semester. It was, of course, very strange to see women undergraduates. (Yale had first admitted them only in 1969.) And I was in a different department now. In addition to association with my colleagues in philosophy, I became acquainted with several professors in the French Department and enjoyed attending Classics events in my old haunts, in Phelps Hall. I was taken in as a guest fellow at Timothy Dwight College. That semester Senator Sam Ervin, who was appearing on television regularly in connection with the Watergate hearings, and Elliot Richardson, of the Saturday Night Massacre fame, both visited Dwight as Chubb Fellows. It was exciting to meet them, though I cannot claim to have held any sustained conversation with either one. The students and I seemed to get along extremely well. In May, I felt downright sad at the thought that I probably would never return to Yale, at least not as one belonging there.

Actually, I *might* have done so. Later that year a letter came from Yale asking if I would be willing to be considered as a candidate for a professorship in philosophy. After much thought and not without some feeling of anguish, I said no. It was the right decision. In my reply I explained that I thought that the ten or so years I had remaining in my career ought to be spent in the place where I would retire. And I wanted this to be in Boulder. I had put down roots there, it was my natural environment.

Being and Nothingness

An Essay on
Phenomenological Ontology

by
Jean-Paul Sartre

Translated and with an introduction by

HAZEL E. BARNES
University of Colorado

PHILOSOPHICAL LIBRARY
NEW YORK

Pl. 9. The title page for the first edition of her translation
of *Being and Nothingness.*

Pl. 10. On the set for television series *Self-Encounter*, 1961.

Pl. 11. Scene from Beauvoir's "The Blood of Others" (from *Self-Encounter* series).

Pl. 12. In her study, about 1970.

Pl. 13 *(top)*. With Doris at hotel on the Isle of Wight, 1989.

Pl. 14 *(bottom)*. With John Gerassi at meeting of the Sartre Society. Boulder, 1990.

Pl. 15 (*top*). Corner of residence in Boulder.

Pl. 16 (*bottom*). Hazel outside Boulder residence, mid-1990s.

Pl. 17 *(top)*. The Barnes-Schwalbe cabin at Dory Lakes, Colorado.

Pl. 18 *(bottom)*. Doris Schwalbe fishing at Dory Lakes, mid-1990s.

Pl. 19. Hazel at breakfast table in the cabin, mid-1990s.

EIGHT

Living in the Rockies

THE PEOPLE'S REPUBLIC OF BOULDER

The sign at the north entrance read, "Stay a while, play a while. You'll like Boulder." I did, though my reasons for cherishing the small town I found here in 1953 and my affectionate appreciation of the city it has become in the mid-nineties have little in common beyond the fact of its location in the shadow of the Rocky Mountains. That is quite a bit in itself. What other city can boast of having its picnic park five miles from the center of town and nearly fifteen hundred feet up at the top of a mountain? Plus two exit roads leading within minutes into spectacular canyons? When Doris and I arrived, there were a couple of movie houses, a choice of two full-scale restaurants—no alcoholic drinks, since Boulder was dry by local option. (A liquor store stood just outside the city limits on each main thoroughfare.) Technically it was possible to clothe yourself and furnish a house reasonably well without going thirty-some miles to Denver, but not if you wanted much choice. We did not then, as everyone must now, think of ourselves as living in a suburb of Denver, since so much open space, grazing fields, and truck farms separated us from it. Along with the natural beauty of the site, Boulder had a unique charm. Individualism and idiosyncrasy were positive values for most of its inhabitants. Even the physical layout of its houses was democratic. Though there were areas where most of the homes were very modest, there was nothing that could properly be called a slum. On the older streets, old-fashioned mansions sat next to cottage types. And it was a lively place, both in the progressive civic-mindedness of its city officials and in the passionate partisanship of its citizenry as a whole on any and all issues, making the letters in the *Daily Camera* must reading for everyone. I remember that adaptations of Swift's ironic approach in *A Modest Proposal* were a favorite device to express outrage until overuse made it ineffective. These debates were not always political nor were they necessarily representative of a clash between university employees and other residents, though the latter on the whole tended to be more conservative.

Townspeople not connected with the university were sharply divided in their attitude toward it. Supporters were eager to engage in its activities insofar as was possible. They formed a good part of the audience at all events open to the public, especially during the annual Conference on World Affairs when close to a hundred visitors from outside came for a week of panel discussions and lectures on a wide variety of topics. This same program served as a focus for the university's hostile critics. In the fifties, McCarthy-style criticisms were not uncommon. As polarization intensified in the sixties, attacks on the university as a nest of radicals began to appear, some of them virulent. The owner of a local loan company, Mrs. E. C. Pickett, wrote so many and such vitriolic letters to the *Camera* that the editor at last announced that he would print nothing more from her. Resorting to paid advertisements, she entertained us with a series of little boxed pronouncements. Some of these were direct attacks on Howard Higman, who was primarily responsible for planning the Conference on World Affairs; some condemned the university as a whole; some reached beyond the local scene. I still have copies of a few of these. Typical are:

One after another, universities—Berkeley, Champaign-Urbana, Madison—are becoming narcotics and crime centers. Boulder will be next unless C.U.'s cancerous growth is halted immediately.

Extremist professors are now substituting revolution for learning in our universities in the same way radical theologians have substituted "humanism" for faith in God.

America's and Boulder's hard-left "liberals" are the ideological descendants of the French Revolution's Jacobins, who sent thousands of innocent men, women and children to the guillotine during the reign of Terror.

There must have been a few Boulderites in whose eyes Mrs. Pickett's messages were not ridiculous in their extremism. She did not speak for many. The predominantly conservative outlook of the earlier city had greatly changed. By this time Boulder outran Denver in its support of liberal candidates and causes and was sharply at variance with most of Colorado.

I am told that it was in reflection of this state of affairs that other Coloradans began to speak of "The People's Republic of Boulder." Whether used sarcastically or affectionately, this appellation connotes more than voting habits. I have heard it said that Boulder is so independent it has its own foreign policy. This remark may have referred to the fact the city was quick to announce that it would support the economic boycott of South Africa by divestment, a policy rarely adopted by municipal officials. Or perhaps it reflects the fact that Boulder has established a number of "sister city" bonds with communities from Tajikistan to Tibet. More generally, the epithet surely points to the city's idiosyncratic independence, its insistence on going its own way, and its sublime assurance that its way is the right way for everyone to follow.

Molly Ivins, when she came to the Conference on World Affairs, on a return visit, wrote in her syndicated column (April 6, 1994):

> Back in the Alfalfa Sprout capital of the Universe, standing here at the ground zero of political correctness, I am reminded of my old fondness for these dear and fuzzy folk. . . . Here they are, saving water, saving whales, saving dolphins and generally trying to bring humankind up to a level of perfection that is in almost lunatic defiance of everybody else's tendency to let things go to hell in a handbasket.

Recognition of this same moral earnestness was expressed a bit more sardonically in a statement quoted to me by my nephew, David Barnes, who, as a professor in the University of Denver Law School, has an outsider's view: "Boulderites think they have a solution for every problem in the world while having none of the world's problems." Given a broad enough perspective, there is a modicum of truth in this judgment. More to the point is a remark I heard from Ruth Correll, a former mayor. She observed that somehow, whenever a gap in social services is recognized, either the city or private groups will quickly provide what is needed: Attention Homes for sheltering young people who get into trouble with the law and do not have a supportive family; People's Clinic for drug problems; Parenting Center for the fathers and mothers of newborns; a plan for helping with teen pregnancy, one that won a national award. To take care of the needy transients who regularly show up here, a scheme was worked out whereby generously inclined citizens might buy coupons redeemable only in groceries and distribute these in lieu of money.

It is easy to find and poke fun at the absurdities and inconsistencies of some of Boulder's activities. Typical as an example was a notice I received from the Rocky Mountain Peace Center, which was collecting clothes for victims of some disaster somewhere. It closed with the words, "Only natural fabrics, please." This organization provided another interesting example: A few young people from here who were participating in a protest demonstration against bomb testing in Nevada trespassed on government land and were sent to jail. At the center's suggestion, many of us wrote to the presiding judge to ask him to shorten the sentence, which he did, significantly. Meanwhile the center's newsletter described life in prison for our local group. They had just one complaint—no vegetarian meals were provided. After protesting to the authorities, the complainers were put in charge of the kitchen detail and planned meals for everyone. (Whether nonvegetarians were now satisfied, the report did not say.) I wonder whether the Nevada officials were unusually humane or simply cowed by the confident self-righteousness of the Boulder contingent.

The city offers a strange mixture of permissiveness and Puritanism, displaying both extreme reverence for individual freedom and a willingness to coerce people into doing what is viewed as good for them and for the community. Sometimes called the "Berkeley of the Rockies," at one time it was considered to be a place where hard drugs were easily procurable. Almost every year sees a so far abortive attempt to decriminalize marijuana. But in 1995 voters, by a large majority, passed a law to prohibit smoking in all public indoor locations, including restaurants and bars, unless in closed, specially ventilated rooms designated solely for smoking; in a sense this was the equivalent of the earlier ban on alcohol, long since rescinded. I once picked up a paper reporting that the City Council had passed an ordinance stipulating that no white bread should be served in restaurants in the downtown mall. I quickly realized that I was reading a column meant to be humorous; the fact remains that I had been able for a moment to consider the measure extreme but not beyond belief. In the social sphere, laws are strictly enforced to protect racial or ethnic minorities. Molly Ivins noted that Hooters, the restaurant with its scantily clad waitresses, was forced to close, not by women's protest groups but for lack of customers. As I mentioned earlier, Boulder was quick to pass a law forbidding any kind of discrimination on the basis of sexual preference. One would expect that the city would be predominantly pro-choice, and it is. This did not prevent an attack on a clinic where abortions were known to be performed; someone shot at Dr. Warren Hern, its director. Boulderites like to blame this violence on outsiders. But though Dr. Hern, who has been a leading speaker at world conferences in defending the pro-choice position, is said to be listed as a target by antiabortion extremists, the fact is that some citizens have publicly supported the action of groups who tried physically to prevent access to the clinic. (Warren Hern, by the way, is a former student of mine; I think it is doubtful that my presentation of beginning Greek exerted much influence on the development of his social philosophy.) Not only liberal movements have had their beginnings here. The chief founder of the Promise Keepers was Bill McCartney, the C.U. football coach, who held his annual men-only meetings in the stadium until it proved to be too small to hold the vast numbers of men who came here to participate. Boulder is not homogeneous. Still, the reformist tendency prevails—that and the conviction that quality of life can be improved if we work at it.

When the *Camera* advertised that a Renaissance festival would be held in a downtown park, Doris and I went to it expecting it to be a historical reconstruction—like the medieval fête in Larkspur, Colorado. What we found was a celebration of "rebirth," as the name would have told us if we had not been led astray by the historical connotations. Instead of looking backward, it hailed the New Age. Exhibits and sales tables displayed products and advertised methods to rejuvenate our health, clear our minds, adjust our psyches. Suggestions for protecting the environment were there, too. Although this particular set of offerings did not enlist our interest, I noted that it depicted three major aspects of the Boulder scene: preoccupation with self-help health care, interest in nontraditional approaches to psychic and spiritual well-being, and vigilant environmental concern.

On virtually every block of commercial areas, you can find a grocery selling only organic produce and "natural" foods or a "health store" specializing in herbal remedies and food supplements. Bee pollen, myrrh, burdock, nettles, kelp, primrose oil, goldenseal root, bread made of spelt, and innumerable other products selected from nature by humans to keep the body in shape are readily available. Practitioners in alternative medicine also find a haven here, utilizing methods some of which have earned worldwide respect and been imported; a few, I suspect, are unique to Boulder. Doris believes that some of the proffered items and services have noticeably helped her in coping with diabetes and a variety of allergies. I tend to stand aloof. But I go regularly to a chiropractor in neighboring Longmont who cured my back pains and keeps me in shape by using meridian therapy (like acupuncture but using a cold laser).

To take care of mental, psychic, and spiritual concerns, there is a wider spread between the crackbrained and the intellectually respectable. Psychotherapists of every kind flourish. I suspect the ease with which they find a clientele is due, not to a higher incidence of psychic ailments, but to the population's devotion to the ideal of self-improvement. For the most part, I believe the counsel they receive is, for better or worse, on a par with what they would find elsewhere. There is also a fringe of New Age orientations relying on the more airy forms of transcendentalism. In the context of Eastern thought, again one must differentiate. Various popular cults have members here, though I know little about them. On another level entirely is Naropa Institute. Describing itself as a "Buddhist inspired nonsectarian liberal arts college," it offers both undergraduate and graduate degrees in the arts, sciences, and humanities. The Buddhist background is reflected in its inclusion of contemplative meditation and its offerings in Eastern philosophy and relevant languages. Even before Naropa became a college, it was recognized as an important center for Buddhist studies. In *Turning East* (1977) Harvey Cox wrote at length of his experience here. Graduate students who had studied at Naropa occasionally showed up in classes of mine; they added considerably to the depth and breadth of our discussions.

As for the third aspect, nobody in Boulder would admit openly to not being pro-environment, though debates over specific questions as to how much open space and environmentalist restrictions are commensurate with economic well-being are frequent and heated. Recently confrontations between opposing sides became so bitter that a new group formally organized itself under the name "Citizens for Civility" and initiated action to remedy this new problem.

My nephew told me that when he asked a Boulder friend what she considered to be the city's most serious problem, the woman replied that nobody had found a way to prevent the marauding deer (protected, of course) from eating the flowers and shrubs in private yards. Such ostrichlike complacency is rare. The city's more difficult problems stem from a situation nobody ever intended to create. Boulder has won the reputation of being elitist in that the income and the educational level of its inhabitants are well above the national average. By itself no cause for anxiety, this is the natural result of the lack of heavy industry and the presence of a large number of government and private research centers.

This factor combined with the resolve to restrict population growth for environmental reasons has brought about a situation in which land is so scarce and property values so high that only the comparatively wealthy and old-timers, like Doris and me, can afford to own homes within the city limits. (The sign inviting visitors to stay disappeared years ago.) Junior faculty settle in the nearby towns that are fast becoming a new satellite suburb. It is reported that Boulder's population in the daytime working hours is two hundred thousand; double that of domiciled residents at night. Some people genuinely worry about this factual exclusiveness, not enough of them, however, to pass a proposal on the ballot in a recent election that would have provided for more affordable housing, hence greater economic diversity.

Though not blind to its ironies and its shortcomings, I must plead guilty to chauvinistic complacency if that is taken to equal content—no, absolute delight—in living in Boulder. To be sure, I do not take advantage of what many would consider to be among its chief attractions. I do not ski in the winter or run in the Bolder Boulder races on Memorial Day or join the annual Ride the Rockies bicycle procession across the mountain peaks. But Doris and I enjoy the mountains in other ways. We find Boulder itself an inexhaustible source of interest, its optimistic activism exhilarating and endearing. From the first day we have felt that we belong here.

Our house, small and unpretentious but designed by a student of Frank Lloyd Wright, gives us the feeling of always being in touch with the outdoors. It sits next to an irrigation ditch that can easily pass for a stream, one that dries up in the winter months; we look up at the Flatirons, the distinctive feature of Boulder's mountain range. So close to the campus that a ten-minute walk will take me to my former office or the library, I have always been willing to overlook the fact that we live near two fraternities and in the midst of buildings occupied mostly by students. Over the years, population density has increased to the point where Doris declares alternately that we live in a giant parking lot or that we inhabit a ghetto; she has never, however, proposed that we move. I have to admit that students are neither the quietest nor the neatest of neighbors. But they keep the place alive and are often fascinating to watch. They are sometimes helpful when they see us struggling to carry something heavy; on the few occasions when we have shamelessly asked for their aid, they have cheerfully obliged. Mostly we have so little contact with them that we hardly feel we reside in a neighborhood. The exception comes at breaks between semester when we meet via the dumpsters that line the alley next to us. These become a center for exchange of goods as the outgoing students clean out their apartments and the incoming settle into them. Doris rescued for us an abandoned toaster oven so much better than later models that we have had parts of it replaced, also a typewriter, a pair of almost new pillowcases, and a lot of lumber useful for shelving. Whenever I want to get rid of a piece of clothing, I drape it over the edge of the containers; it soon disappears. As a reminder that not everyone lives in prodigal affluence, we often see shabbily dressed men come by to search for redeemable bottles in the trash bins or in the boxes put out for Ecocycle. One man comes by regularly for a different purpose. He carefully smashes each beer or wine bottle and throws it back into the container. When I asked him what he was doing, he explained that he was trying to prevent students from drinking. The only way to do it, he explained, was to break all the bottles so that the supply would be used up. "No more bottles, no more alcohol!"

While I do not believe that Boulder has more of the harmless mentally impaired wandering its streets than other places, its tolerance, if not encouragement, of any kind of eccentricity has always been remarkable. Strong individualism is manifested in more than character traits. At its best it is expressed in creativity in arts and crafts and in unusual inventions. The most bizarre example of the latter that I can recall was a specially designed tank, filled with a warm saline solution and large enough to hold a person lying down. The idea was that a paying customer could rest floating on the surface of the liquid with the lid closed down but enough air provided to prevent suffocation. There in the darkness he or she was supposed to reexperience the sensation of lying safely rocked in the womb. I never tried it myself, fearing an attack of acute claustrophobia. Though some hardy experimenters reported total relaxation and psychic refreshment, this invention never really caught on. Another more conventional business enterprise succeeded far beyond the limits of Colorado. Inspired by the local interest in herbal beverages, Moe Siegel launched his Celestial Seasonings tea company, which still has its headquarters in the city's environs.

Far from being inhabited exclusively by WASPS, Boulder has more diversity than one might expect, given its restrictions on population growth. Research centers attract scientists from all over the world, many of whom live here for extended periods if they do not settle permanently. They and the numerous foreign students and the university's moderately diverse faculty and staff give the place a cosmopolitan flavor.

You can see this reflected even in the chain grocery stores, which offered a wide variety of ingredients for ethnic cooking long before they were available elsewhere except in the largest cities. At the same time, the small-town flavor has not been wholly lost. Boulder is still little enough so that we usually run into acquaintances in the supermarkets and entertain friendly relations with clerks in most of the shops we frequent. Former students turn up in unexpected places—as restaurant manager, as owner of a boutique, as receptionist in a doctor's office, as newspaper reporter come for an interview, or as passersby on the streets who manage to recognize me and after many years stop to exchange news. (Students often are reluctant to leave here when they graduate.) Acquaintances turn up on the City Council. By chance I have had a personal connection with three of our mayors: Linda Jorgensen, once a student in my class in Greek philosophy; Ruth Correll, wife of my colleague in the Program of Interdisciplinary Studies; Leslie Durgin, who, as an alumna from Wilson College, joined me in entertaining the president of the college when she came to visit.

As a gateway to other spots of beauty, interest, and enjoyment, Boulder is hard to surpass. A few hours' drive brings you to the inexhaustible wonders and tripartite culture of the Southwest (Anglo, Hispanic, Native American). Over the years Doris and I have been enthusiastic amateurs in learning to know something of Native American history and culture in southern Colorado, New Mexico, and Arizona: its history, as we view the ancient remains of cliff dwellings in Mesa Verde and Bandelier and the amazing condolike multistoried brick structures left from the prehistoric village in Chaco Canyon; its contemporary culture as we see it in the pueblos, whose festivals and ritualistic dances used to be open to the public, and in the magnificent arts and crafts—jewelry, pottery, rugs, paintings, and carvings. Early on, especially, we visited Taos and Santa Fe at the drop of a long weekend. We still go there often, though we deplore the too great presence of people we look down on as only tourists and the growing tendency in both places to be "upscale" or frankly "yuppie."

The Southwest, for us, is mostly for holidays; Colorado's Rocky Mountains belong to our everyday life. These too, of course, provide sites for special visits, to be reached by a drive of anywhere from an hour to half a day. Doris and I have explored most of them. We have gone countless times to Rocky Mountain National Park to see the Rocky Mountain bighorn sheep, to hear the elk bugle in the fall. Occasionally we drop in on the ski villages, among them Vail and Beaver Creek, places

of extraordinary beauty but so dominated by the accoutrements of the
affluent that the natural world is almost submerged. We feel more at home
in the small, less developed communities such as nearby Georgetown
and Gold Hill.

Our cabin—more accurately, our small brown wooden rectangular
cottage—has been our Querencia since we had it built in 1972. At an al-
titude of 9,200 feet, a scant hour's drive from Boulder (at 5,400 feet), it is
located near but not too close to the old goldmining towns of Central
City and Black Hawk. Surrounded by woods, it stands facing a little
meadow, which we keep clear of trees so that we can look out from our
deck directly at the mountain range known as The Sleeping Bear. A tiny
stream flows at the bottom of the slope before us. For twenty years we
could not see another house from ours; now there are three, but at a
kindly distance. If weather permits, we go there at all seasons of the
year. Our cabin has been inestimably valuable to us, both as a place for
uninterrupted academic work and as a wellspring of physical and psychic nourishment. Doris fishes at a lake close by; I talk long walks; we
both work hard and happily at the neverending task of taking care of
our woods. Sometimes with the aid of obliging friends to help with the
heaviest work, more often by ourselves, we fell dead trees, carry, cut, and
stock the logs we burn in the Franklin stove, our main source of warmth
when we are there though we have backup electric heat to prevent pipes
from freezing when we are absent.

A possible threat to this idyllic existence appeared in 1991 when
Colorado voted to permit limited gambling in Central City and Black
Hawk. So far as those towns are concerned, our worst fears have been
realized. Wall-to-wall casinos have replaced the original shops and many
of the old houses; surrounding mountains are being literally hollowed
out to make room for new casino hotels. Traffic in the narrow canyon
leading out from the area is sometimes bumper-to-bumper. Economically, this development has been pronounced a great success, though
those who continue to profit are, with very few exceptions, not the original residents; *they* sold their property at a high price and moved elsewhere to seek a lifestyle they valued. I suppose that the thousands who
come to enjoy the fun of putting expendable dollars into the slot machines are grateful to have this miniature Las Vegas as a recreation spot.
That feeling is probably not shared by those who put on an opera reper-
tory each summer in the nineteenth-century opera house. Because of
the congestion, most patrons now either come by specially arranged
buses or park some distance away in the surrounding hills and take a

shuttle down. I wondered whether there was a cynical intent behind the recent choice to produce Tchaikovsky's seldom played *The Queen of Spades*, the tale of a compulsive gambler who, because of his obsession, destroys himself and those close to him. I would be a hypocrite if I pretended that my objection to gambling as such is the sole or chief reason for my disapproval of the scarring transformation of the two towns. I have enough taste for vulgarity, if it is sufficiently lavish, to have enjoyed a few short visits to Las Vegas. On occasion I have even put some quarters into the Colorado slot machines, though, unlike Doris, I quickly grow bored. Doris, after losing or (very seldom) increasing the pittance she allows herself, can enjoy watching others play. But though she goes fairly often to spend a morning or afternoon at one of the casinos, she regrets as much as I do the profanation of the natural setting and is even more pessimistic than I in fearing its effects on our cabin area.

Being six miles away and not on the main road, we have so far seen only slight changes, but some have been noticeable. A few more houses have been built for yearlong residence for persons connected with the gaming industry; some of these are the outsized structures of the sort that has led Doris to predict that this site, like Boulder, is in danger of being "Aspenized." That they reflect a different attitude on the part of the newcomers was made clear a year ago at the annual meeting of the property owners of our district. Several of them wanted to establish new building regulations designed, as was openly stated, to prevent our area from becoming a "cabin community." Apparently they wanted to live in something more nearly resembling a suburban subdivision. This time we and other early settlers forced a reasonable compromise. For how long?

Though clearly we have cause for worry, we hope that our six and a half acres and the "greenbelt" that lies on the other side of our stream will prevent our being seriously encroached upon in the years we can reasonably hope to keep coming to our cabin. Meanwhile we continue to relish the delights furnished by the wild creatures. Chipmunks, chickarees, ground squirrels, too many varieties of birds to list provide us with a floor show on the deck where we put out food for them. We watch the rabbits who live under our tiny barn, get a glimpse of the bobcat who tries to catch them, occasionally see deer, raccoons, porcupines, coyotes, weasels (brown fur in the summer, ermine in the winter). Once Doris saw a moose. We have not caught sight of our resident bear, though it left its pawprint on our glass door the time it knocked down the hanging hummingbird-nectar and birdseed feeders. (Now we take them inside each night.) Our meadow in the summer looks like a Monet canvas—

mariposa lilies, spotted coralroot, wandflowers, pink elephant heads, shooting stars, purple columbine—to mention only a few of my favorites. In the woods early in the spring come the uncommon Calypso orchids (also called fairy slippers). These are not golden orchids; they are lavender pink, exquisitely beautiful. But in my mind they stand for the rare flower my Aunt Jennie, so long ago at Beach Lake, hoped I would someday find.

AT HOME IN BOULDER

I have been resident in Boulder for more than half my life. For all of that time and for a couple of years earlier (since 1950), "home" for me has meant a life shared with Doris Schwalbe, a "We" that each of us and all who know us have come to take for granted as a given. That it was something never planned for nor ever seriously put into question is as remarkable as its long duration. We never saw this relationship as fitting into an established pattern or as constrained by one of our own invention. It did, of course, develop its own internal structure, which is perceptible in retrospect, but it has been self-created, self-regulating. This is doubtless one of the chief reasons it has been at once nurturing and liberating.

Both Doris and I have a certain reticence (more natural to yesterday's generation than to today's) when it comes to public discussion of private matters, and it is not my intention to subject to vivisection a vital, ongoing relationship. But while my choice to write an autobiography requires willingness to self-disclosure but does not grant license to bring all the household goods outdoors for a yard sale, still it would not only leave my narrative incomplete but be unfair to Doris if I were not to offer some reflection on the large part she and our association have played in my life.

In trying to convey the quality of what our life together has been, I inevitably think of how it resembles and how it differs from other close partnerships and ways of being a couple. Neither of us, when we met, had ever wanted to play the traditional role of wife and mother. (Though Doris is seven years younger than I, we had been subjected to essentially the same general conditioning with respect to gender roles.) Therefore neither had any sense of having failed in not achieving a recognized social status in marriage, feelings that might have undermined any satisfaction in the companionship we did enjoy. If I had married, I might or might not have found it possible to maintain a position of equality and to assign central importance to my academic career. At the very least, there would have been a problem to be solved. For better or for worse (and who would presume to say which?), there would have been prescribed roles in a myriad of social conducts. As Doris and I worked out a lifestyle, we literally had no models; at least they were not ready at hand, and we did not search for them. At no time did we ever fall into the pattern of dominance and submission which had been accepted as the normal structure for marital and parent-child relations and which has often been built into that of other dual associations, whether based on sexual attraction or long-lasting friendship. We met as adults. That Doris was my student when we first knew each other might have been expected to introduce a basic psychological inequality; somehow it did not. Or, if at the beginning it was there, it was so inessential that we never noticed either its presence or its departure. Nothing but strict equality would have been workable for two strong-willed persons who regarded individual freedom as the fundamental indispensable value on which all other goods are based.

Our dividing up of household duties is perhaps illustrative of deeper accommodations. Without setting up rules, we fell into a division of labor, based on the principle of letting each one do what she could do best or disliked least. Thus Doris, who excelled in cooking, making of it almost a hobby, took over preparation of meals. I clean up afterward. Being more mechanically inclined than I and more dexterous, she usually sees to repairs and "fixing up." But I manage most of the details of keeping the house in order. She does almost all the driving. I take care of desk work connected with shared expenses for the house, keep up with social correspondence in matters in which we are both concerned. And so on. This kind of habitual procedure saves time and bother; we have found it easy to adjust and modify it if necessity arises; for instance, a bout of ill health for one of us or temporary increase in the pressure of outside obligations.

One of the interesting aspects of our life in common has been the way that we have, separately and together, enveloped ourselves in a wider network of other social relations. For traditional married couples, there is an all but written provision for certain segregated activities—"the night out with the boys," meetings of women's groups, luncheon engagements assumed to be the occasion for "men's talk" or women's "gossip." I have often wondered if the underlying reason was the need to recognize those supposed basic differences between male and female personalities and interests (whether genetic or cultural in origin) or whether there was another, more hidden cause—a protective device for individual separateness. I think here of Freud's claim that the conflict between libido directed toward others and narcissism is expressed in the edge of hostility and resentment that accompany even the most tender and close-knit unions. In recent years I have noticed in some same sex couples (whether overtly gay or not) a conscious effort to separate their sets of friends so as to guarantee for each of the pair an independent life alongside the one they shared in common. For that matter, I remember that Sartre and Beauvoir so jealously guarded their respective freedoms that they agreed that if either of them was engaged in conversation with another person in a public place, the other would pretend not to see them. (I am not speaking here of "contingent loves" but merely of friends and acquaintances.) This pattern would have seemed to Doris and me quite artificial and not desirable. This is not to say that we never enjoyed acquaintances or experiences apart from one another. Quite the contrary. We have maintained separate professional contacts. We do not do everything together even on everyday social occasions. Doris has her fishing and stamp-collecting companions. My greater interest in films often takes me off to the movies with someone else—or by myself. But for the most part, we have wanted to share the friendships developed with others. Whether or not the others are glad to know us primarily *en pair* I cannot say. We ourselves have found it enriching. Over the years we have gradually become the equivalent of relatives of one another's relatives, close friends of friends one or the other of us knew first. Jointly entertaining our invited guests (professional or purely social) and being asked to come together for return visits, we have long been accepted as a nuclear social unit.

My inclination would be to say that the distinctive quality of the relationship that Doris and I have built resulted solely from the interplay of our unique and complex personalities, but that would be true only in the way that Sartre claimed that every individual is a "singular universal." Any dual or group relationship reflects and affects its particular social setting. In earlier periods it was rare indeed for two professional women (or women with independent means) to choose to set up a home together—viewed by others if not by themselves as at best an accommodation *faute de mieux*. More recently, unless strictly pro tem, a pair of women would be assumed to be making a political statement. In the nineteen-forties and -fifties, arrangements such as ours became more common as women, for divers reasons and in various fashions, established themselves in more or less permanent associations.

I suppose that the things that brought us together held us together and that in essence they are little different from the kinds of bonds that figure in any long-lasting attachment. Here I could quote Montaigne's reply when he was asked the reasons for his intense friendship with La Boétie, "Because it was he, because it was I." Or I could say tritely that Doris and I had similar interests and held the same fundamental values. On the surface we arrived at these quite differently. Doris came from a somewhat higher economic background. Her father was a glass engineer who owned his own company. Her parents were not religious; she was allowed to satisfy her curiosity about Sunday School by trying it out and to drop it when she found it unrewarding. One could say that she had achieved naturally and easily the humanistic outlook that I struggled so long and hard to attain. While it was I who introduced Doris to Sartre's and Beauvoir's Existentialism, she did not embrace it because of regard for me. Rather, our shared enthusiasm for their philosophy was a cornerstone in the foundation of our early friendship, and, in the broadest sense, it has continued to play a major part in our common outlook. Those of our values that had been established in childhood were less dissimilar than might first appear. Doris's father, without reference to church teachings, inculcated in his children a brand of ethical instruction comparable to that which my father gave to me in his personal admixture of Christianity, William James, and the ideals prevalent in the moral *Zeitgeist* of middle-class Americans in the first half of the century: independence, self-sufficiency, individualism, but also personal responsibility, empathic concern for others, the importance of justice, and, above all, accountability, absolute honesty and integrity: all those old-fashioned virtues that sound so dreary but turn out to be life-sustaining in a relationship. This part of our fathers' teaching survived in us whereas their political conservatism did not. Compatibility in this area was something we developed on our own—in general, before we knew one another and, more particularly, afterward. Happily Doris and I have the same basic attitude toward money, something the practical-minded (or cynical) might say is the necessary cause in any successful cooperative venture. We both have a depression psychology; that is, a close to pathological aversion to debt, accompanied not by miserliness but a willingness to enjoy the good things money can buy provided only that a secure base is established first. Maintaining a small household account side by side with our strictly separate personal funds, we never had difficulty in arriving at major financial decisions such as buying jointly a house or a car. Our arrangement could not be more unlike that which Sartre and

Beauvoir adopted for themselves and their "family." I am compelled, almost ashamed, to admit that our pattern is ultra bourgeois, but so it has been.

Our career interests were similar but not competitive. In the English Department at the University of Colorado in Denver, Doris gradually began to teach more classes in her special field of the English novel and introduced a course on women in the novel before the feminist movement was well under way. In addition to our similar involvement in the academic life, and to our shared devotion to literature and interest in the other arts (especially opera for which we are rabid enthusiasts), we have a common bond in our love of the wild things in nature and in our delight in travel. There have always been less tangible affinities. In each of us, our high regard for individualism has led us not only to tolerate differences and idiosyncracies in one another and in our mutual acquaintances, but to prize them, finding them endlessly fascinating, and to enjoy the company of persons whose views often are opposed to our own rather than to associate solely with the like-minded. Yet, despite the high premium each places on self-fulfillment and alongside our common resolve to keep ourselves open to new points of view (as Sartre might put it, to remember that self-making is a never-ending process), both of us have felt a strong need to put down roots, to maintain a stable center, to relate present and future coherently with the past without being enslaved to it. Hence we have grown, together and separately, without growing apart.

I hasten to add that I am not claiming that this relation has been or is one of absolute serenity and seamless harmony, either in appearance or in reality. The illusion of such perfection, I am convinced, could be achieved only if one person so dominated the other that both lived in total bad faith. Believing that ours has been a relation in good faith, I think this is because of the particular way in which we have lived out all three of the dimensions in the metaphor of the Look.

The Look-as-exchange (to use my term), the empathic response of subject to subject that Sartre discusses so movingly in *Notebooks for an Ethics*, has been an underlying constant. This continued interest in, and concern for, each other has manifested itself visibly in the continuous psychological, intellectual, and practical support on which each could unfailingly rely. We furthered one another's projects, tried to help the other understand and discover her own best solution to her specific problems, professional or personal. We have discussed, listened to, and read one another's work, sympathetically and critically. I cannot express adequately just how much this has meant to me. We have unswervingly been loyal to one another.

But what about the negative and most familiar aspect of the Sartrean Look, the Other's hostile, objectifying stare, the "Hell is Others"? Need I even bother to admit that I would be a liar if I claimed that this has never been present? Especially since I have publicly declared that to experience this aspect of the Look, at least fleetingly, is universal for all but the most ephemeral of human relations? Doris's and my disagreements have been numerous and not left unexpressed—overarticulated, if anything. Argumentative we were and are, but even our most angry exchanges have remained disputations, not quarrels. We never clashed over anything of real significance, but occasionally over detailed points of difference deriving from a position agreed upon, most often over absurd trifles in the daily routine. Solutions to conflict have varied with circumstances. Sometimes when we could not agree on a decision, we have done or bought two things. (Our shelves are crowded with similar items of different brands); or else whoever felt more strongly was the one to decide. Altercations based on opinions were rarely resolved; they continually recur, anticipated, if not quite welcomed, as from time to time we fall into our own version of Sartre's subject-object conflict, in our case closer to a game than a battle. Neither of us is free from the compulsion to prove herself right—even and especially when it does not matter. What might be called temperamental differences certainly exist and express themselves resonantly, especially if one of us is feeling under par or is facing a difficult external problem. Overall, however, like the hedgehogs in Schopenhauer's parable, we have learned to leave room for one another's quills without imposing a chilling distance.

In the long term, the third dimension of the Look has counted for the most: looking-at-the-world-together. I have in mind not only our common projects, houses to be bought, trips taken, a shared circle of friends and acquaintances, and the like, but also and especially our mutual memories of all the experiences, the web woven by our responses to them. I feel sure that anyone who has lived in close association with another for several decades will have noted the way in which oft trod paths of associations facilitate a kind of shorthand, an elliptical reference to a cluster of events or ideas, communicated as a unit without any spelling out. Sometimes, too, there is a startling simultaneity of new insight, owing to the similarity of the reflections that have led to them. Using very strictly Sartre's definition of the ego as an objective structure of habits, self-image, and thought patterns imposed by a consciousness reflecting on its own past states of consciousness, I think that it would not be an exaggeration to say that Doris and I have created a common ego that exists all but tangibly alongside each one's personal ego. Of course, there is no merging of consciousnesses. The unexpected continues to arise, whether in the form of "Hell is Others" or in the unpredictable rewards that continue to remind us that any Other is an invitation to growth, not a means to completion.

Some might want to explain the particular quality of Doris's and my life together as related primarily to our gender. My predilection for nominalism leads me to be more interested in the particulars of our personalities. To have had as my closest associate for all these years a man instead of a woman would indeed have been different but not necessarily more radically so than if Doris had been an altogether other type of woman. To say how things would have been if she and I had never met is as impossible as to give an answer to any other far-reaching "What if . . ." I am deeply glad for what has been and grateful for her presence as we approach the border of our allotted time.

NINE

Making an Ending

HAVE I OUTLIVED MYSELF?

The question that he frames in all but words
Is what to make of a diminished thing.
from "The Oven Bird" by Robert Frost

Retirement

I taught until I was seventy; that is, until I reached the university's im-posed age limit. Optional retirement at sixty-five I never considered; I was grateful for the five years of grace before the dreaded inevitability. While I cannot say that I ever looked forward pleasurably to retiring, I did hold to the principle that there ought to be a stipulated date at which it was compulsory. As May 1986 grew close, I was even glad that I had no choice in the matter. This was not because of any fear (reasonable though it would have been) that, no matter what was said to me overtly, my colleagues might feel that a new face would be welcome. Nor was it that teaching had become less satisfying. My classes in the last two years were particularly enjoyable. I was teaching exclusively my own special-ties, and I suspect that a large proportion of my students were there be-cause they knew I would soon be leaving; hence they were especially well disposed. At any rate, I recall thinking that the best of those studying Sartre with me, including even a couple of undergraduate majors, could hold their own in discussions with recognized scholars in the field. I had never felt more at home with my lower division classes in philosophy and psychology and in Existentialist literature. I thought that this pleas-ant feeling was in itself a reason to stop, to leave before I might begin to sense or, worst yet, fail to perceive that I had noticeably slipped. Then, too, while I was not tired of teaching, I was tired. It was more of a strain to juggle my varied activities so as not to cheat on any of the demands made on me. And although theoretically I should by then have felt relaxed about my ability to teach, I found myself overanxious in trying to raise my standards for each individual class hour and less able to tolerate my own shortcomings. For all these reasons, when the time did come, I made the break complete; I discontinued thesis directing and rejected the invitations to teach part-time that were extended by the several departments with which I had been associated. It seemed to me fitting and (though this may sound absurd) almost an aesthetic necessity to bring down the curtain at the end of the act—the fourth one, not the final fifth.

Formal observances made the occasion of my retirement as happy a one as anybody could ask for. At a large birthday dinner the previous December, I was presented with a *Festschrift* titled *Hypatia*. The implied comparison of me with the Greek woman philosopher living in the fourth and fifth centuries was gracefully flattering if a bit high-flown; it was sobering to reflect that Hypatia was murdered by a band of monks hostile to her pagan teachings. (Their precise motivation remains obscure.) The editors of the *Festschrift* arranged for Professor Oreste Pucciani from U.C.L.A. to come and present a lecture in connection with the event. Besides being a friend of mine (and, incidentally, of Beauvoir's), Oreste was the first French scholar in this country to offer a seminar in Sartre's philosophical work. My seventieth birthday was a peak experience. In May, the Philosophy Department, recognizing that nothing pleases philosophers more than the opportunity to speak themselves, followed its normal practice and had me give the lecture before the farewell reception. The overflow crowd, the mixture of my recent and former students, of university and townspeople, made me feel gratefully glad. Again, I did not feel sad on the day of my last class, which was lovely but low-keyed. One of my departmental colleagues had asked if he and some other members of the department might follow the German custom of accompanying me to the classroom and sitting in for my last lecture. I asked that they not do so, chiefly because I wanted to use that hour as a question period for the students in preparation for their final examination. All proceeded routinely except that some unidentified person or persons had put flowers on my desk and the closing round of applause was longer than in other years. In the evening, two of my closest friends, Phyllis Kenevan and Betty Cannon, took Doris and me to dinner at the Red Lion Inn in Boulder Canyon; we indulged in happy reminiscences untainted by nostalgia. It was appropriate to be with these two special friends with whom I had shared so many academic pursuits and hours of leisure as well. Phyllis, for many years, had been my closest associate in the Department of Philosophy. Like me, she had taught and written on Sartre, though gradually her interest shifted more toward Jungian psychology. Betty, once a student of mine, was presently teaching in Golden at the Colorado School of Mines. A part-time practicing therapist as well, she was working to integrate her study of Sartre with her clinical experience. The result was her well-received book *Sartre and Psychoanalysis*, published in 1991.

So it was a pleasing closure, and various things have happened since then to confirm my feeling that these years of teaching had not been misspent. The university established the award in my name that I mentioned earlier. Former students wrote or came to see me. Climactic was a letter printed in the *Colorado Alumnus*. I will quote it here, immodestly, though I recognize it to be exaggerated and a reflection of one exuberant student's momentary impulse rather than a considered objective appraisal.

> It was with the greatest pleasure that I saw Hazel Barnes' picture among the "Favorite Faculty" in your July 1994 issue. I had the privilege of being her pupil both as an undergraduate and a graduate student. Each of her lectures was absolutely breathtaking, and each class hour always passed far too quickly. The contents of her lectures were fascinating and presented brilliantly. To my mind, she embodies the entire concept of a university in her very own person. The only thing which could compete with her profound intellectual magnitude was her kindliness. Wearing the mantle of her brilliance lightly, she was always very approachable and interested in assisting students with their individual concerns. Sometimes only once in a lifetime does any one have the sensation of being in the presence of true greatness. In Dr. Barnes' presence, I had that feeling. I wish to remain anonymous as I know that I speak for many of Dr. Barnes' students. It was through her inspiration that I was best able to realize the enduring value of the humane letters.
>
> "Student X"

Who "Student X" is I cannot even guess. But he/she has given me a precious antidote against ills that have or will come.

The transition was not altogether serene. On a day in July, I went over to Ketchum Hall to finish cleaning out my office. I had too much to do to indulge in sentiment. I packed my books, except for duplicates and unwanted volumes that I stacked on a table in the hall with a sign saying, "Help yourself!" I put in boxes all the accumulated papers that could not be discarded and I labeled them appropriately. A little after noon I closed the office door for the last time and started to walk home. I was hungry and exhausted. After walking for about half a block I began to feel strange. My ears were ringing, I was trembling. Suddenly it seemed to me that the ground was shaking, so much so that I looked to see if others showed signs of noting anything unusual. They did not. I half staggered over to the steps of the music building and sat down. After a few minutes all was back to normal, and I went on home. I believe that this transparently psychosomatic reaction reflected an underlying short-term anxiety and a deeper one: how to live my retirement, and "what to make of a diminished thing," life in old age.

My problems in adjusting to retirement were wholly internal and self-created; I might even call them gratuitous. Directly or indirectly they derived from my having been so strongly achievement oriented. I realize that I am far from unique in this reaction. But I foolishly carried things to excess, and I did so in a situation that did not in fact represent so sharp a break as retiring does for many people. During the summer and early fall, living with a sense of crisis, I entertained two sets of worries: First, I wondered whether, while there was still time, I ought to attempt a work of larger dimension, to produce something quite beyond what I had done up till now. But I looked in vain for this embryonic vision. I felt a bit like the character Ulrik Brendel in Ibsen's *Rosmersholm*, who hires a hall so that he may deliver the earthshaking speech he has dreamed of all his life and finds that he has nothing worth saying. Chastened, I resigned myself to continuing along lines already laid down. Here I met a difficulty of another sort. After so many years of writing enthusiastically on Sartre, Beauvoir, and related topics, I felt that I had had enough of it. There were other subjects that interested me, but they would require a long period of research before I could handle them adequately. Did I really want to start from scratch like a graduate student? And in the midst of scolding myself for a reluctance to take the bit in my teeth and run into new pastures, I did a *volte-face*. Didn't I have the courage, I asked myself, to try for a while what it would be like to indulge in laziness or to do things that did not lead anywhere? I despised myself because I could not find it in me. Then I thought that a compromise solution might be to take up a learning project just for the fun of it. I had always resolved, for example, that someday I would take a class in beginning Spanish and concurrently listen to lectures on pre-Columbian art and archaeology; thus I would at least be in a better position to appreciate more fully my visits to Mexico. This I resolved to do, but I never found time!

That is what cured me of my self-imposed ills. Gradually I perceived that my life had not changed so drastically after all. I still had outstanding commitments for writing and speaking, not to mention the inevitable requests for letters of recommendation, reviewing of manuscripts, and the like. I found myself still serving on a couple of special university committees, though I would gladly have done without those. My work with Phi Beta Kappa would continue for another five years. I allowed one exception to my rule against taking further teaching assignments and met once a week for five weeks with a small group of doctoral students at the C.U. School of Nursing, which was seeking to provide a stronger philosophical foundation for its doctrine of nursing as a science of caring. I hope they learned as much as I did. Finally I realized that I was, as it were, enjoying a faculty leave or a typical professor's vacation—busy but without the usual pressure. I was able to use time instead of being dominated by it. I discovered, too, that I did after all have a number of scholarly postscripts that I wanted to write. I was forced to choose which tasks I wanted to undertake. Gradually I abandoned the ludicrous role of a fretful septuagenarian expecting to grow a new set of teeth and settled down. An unexpected event helped to crystalize my sense of resituating myself. In 1989 I was named "Woman of the Year in Philosophy" by the Society for Women in Philosophy, a subdivision of the American Philosophical Association. In connection with the award, which was formally announced at the time of the annual APA meeting in December, I read a paper on "Sartre and Sexism" for which Linda Bell and Judith Butler were commentators. Clearly I was being recognized for what I had done in the past (stress was laid on how early I had worked as a woman in philosophy). I certainly was not being hailed as a new leader. All the same, I gained a better understanding of the degree to which I was still actively engaged—and respected.

Retirement has not been just a prolongation. New friends have appeared, new experiences, new travels, too; it has been a pleasant novelty to be able to take trips at times other than in the summer. Among the more interesting ventures was a journey to China some months before the tragedy in Tiananmen Square and a vacation in Yugoslavia the last year that it was possible to travel there. (Doris and I began to wonder if we were bearers of the Evil Eye.) We have gone several times to Greece, for which Doris has developed an affection rivaling my own. Our most recent expeditions there have been under the guidance of our archaeological friend Haroula Tzavella-Evjen. With her in charge, we and her husband, Hal, have explored ancient sites the existence of which I had never suspected, even scaling the partially fallen walls of ancient Plevron, a town so remote that nobody had bothered to set up an admission gate. In Denver we recently joined as charter members of the Hellenic-American Cultural Association of Colorado, designed to foster knowledge and appreciation of their history and culture in the generation of young Greek Americans and, incidentally, to give their elders opportunities to enjoy contemporary Hellenic festivities along with them.

In things of this sort, aging has not been a deterrent. Neither has it been something that I could totally ignore.

Aging

To "accept the universe" and to accept old age are alike in allowing only one and the same alternative, and you have to make compromises with both. Growing old and retiring (whether this means withdrawal from employment or from the task of raising a family or sustaining a working spouse) are often confused because they are linked in time. Existentially and practically they are not at all the same. Retirement as such has brought good things to many and, for my generation, not only to people in the highest economic bracket. Members of the middle class as well enjoy the freedom to travel or to indulge in other pleasures available to the self-styled WOOFS (well-off older folks). Though it would be shockingly unfair to say that those who are not among them are left out because they chose to live as grasshoppers rather than as industrious ants, it is usually not retirement per se that has taken from them any chance of well-being. Old age is different. At best it offers only relative goods, and the supply is bound to dwindle. There is no other existential situation in which sheer luck plays a larger part—whether or not you get Alzheimer's, whether the maladies you develop are curable or not, whether weakening bodily parts and functions can or cannot be replaced or reinforced by available props. The cliché "You are only as old as you feel" is less reassuring as you reflect on it. And if we are to shift to the question of attitude, it may be equally true that you are as old as others make you feel. We hear frequently of the vulnerability of the very young; for the old the equivalent is an ever increasing consciousness of dependency on factors your will cannot control. Yet, even as I write this, common sense, as well as my Existentialist habits of thought, prompts me to add that what is important here, as at any other stage of our existence, is how we live our given situation. Everyone's observation will testify to the infinite variety of adaptations even when external circumstances are roughly the same.

At the moment I am not concerned with the extreme limits that aging may impose. Nor will I attempt either a phenomenological description of aging as such or the sort of portrayal of the aged-in-situation within our society that Beauvoir so effectively and grimly provided in *The Coming of Age*. Still, in conscious confrontation with a universal experience, one is bound to reflect on its underlying meaning as well as on the way one has uniquely lived it oneself.

Sartre, and Beauvoir, too, insisted that age is an "unrealizable"; that is, I am old for others, not for myself. I think they are mostly right. To be sure, I cannot grasp my total situation objectively. What I am overflows the category of being an old person just as my being is never wholly expressed or confined in being a woman or an American. With respect to age as with any other aspect of my facticity, my understanding of it is colored by the reactions of others. But there is another sense in which I can and must be old for myself. Growing old compels new adjustment to every aspect of our existential situation: the way we "exist our bodies" (to use Sartre's awkward but vivid terminology), our position with respect to the three dimensions of time (perhaps also to space), and the all too realizable change in our relations with particular others and with the larger world. Even the old existential questions of life and death and their meaning take on an increased urgency.

We often hear someone remark that "So and so has grown old gracefully." I suspect that the intended meaning of this sentence varies with the speaker. Often it might be translated as "Fortunately X handed over authority easily and did not make a nuisance of him/herself." Or "Realizing that he/she was no longer young, X behaves as you expect the old to do." Or "X never disturbs us with complaints about the troubles that come with growing older." But sometimes surely it means "X has been able to find that 'a diminished thing' has use and value." I like to think that this is true of me.

Favored by fortune in being among those who have been allowed to cope with the problems of old age without serious physical or mental impairment, I respond with sympathetic understanding to two contradictory statements often voiced by my peers (sometimes at different times by the same person): "Really I have no reason to complain" and "Growing old is no fun!" If sentimental talk of "the golden years" is nauseating, I find it equally offensive to describe our closing decades as un-mitigated decline. Most of the possible attitudes toward aging I myself have held at one time or another in the process of taking it to my own account. Only one have I totally rejected—resignation. I do not take this as a synonym for acceptance, which is quite another thing, some-thing every one of us in our own way ought either to begin or end with. What I object to is resignation that amounts to submission. I have in mind those persons who do not enjoy this new phase of their existence but who embrace the negative limitations of old age as an excuse not to struggle to find what good may still be attainable, preferring to settle for self-pity in place of self-realization. I do not set up my own solution—to continue to pursue actively for as long as is feasible goals I had cho-sen earlier—as the best for everyone. To change one's course completely may be the greater achievement, whether for personal satisfaction or as a gift to others. Nor do I regard the Calvinist work ethic as a necessary premise for a satisfying conclusion. Deliberately to abandon that may be a reasonable and justifiable choice for anyone at any time but espe-cially for the elderly. What I am stressing is that accepting old age ought to mean accepting the fact that you are working or playing under new conditions but still choosing what the task or game is to be—and in a way still playing to win whatever stakes there are. Perhaps at this stage the giant jackpot is some form of self-content, whatever kind we choose—a new career or the role of healthy couch potato—if that is not an impermissible oxymoron.

For me acceptance was always tinged with revolt (not to be confused with resentment), and I cannot claim that my effort to achieve it was ex-emplary. As in the classic stages of confrontation with one's imminent death, I began with denial. Because my appearance had not altered grossly, I pretended to myself that it had not changed much at all. For some years I did not take advantage of senior rates at the theater or on the bus. This device did not work, of course. Not all mirrors were as dimly lit as the one in my bedroom. Sometimes the ticket seller would take it for granted that I should get a discount. (I accepted it but did not say thank you.) I soon dropped these futile efforts to confront inevi-table changes and faced them head-on. I learned that where prevention was impossible, accommodation was less painful than expected. This was nowhere more obvious than in bodily appearance. Women writers, Beauvoir among them, have described bitterly their anguished resent-ment at the onset of wrinkles and brown spots, thinning hair or facial hairs, excess flesh and double chins or ropelike neck chords and sharp collarbones. Never having been noted for beauty at any stage, I tend to find all this lamentation a bit exaggerated, but I cannot deny having felt pangs in the diminution of what few assets I had. At any rate, I perceived that among other women who were no longer young, there was a level of aesthetic attractiveness still worth trying to reach. Instead of concluding that it no longer mattered what I wore, I took extra pains in trying to look presentable, at least "in the dusk with the light behind me."

It is strangers rather than friends and relatives who bring home what it means to have entered a new category. Everyone, except for those who die young, will ultimately know what it is like to belong to a group looked down on as inferior and will experience the indignity of being viewed without differentiation as simply "one of them." There is a particular pseudo-affectionate, patronizing intonation adopted by a secretary, a salesperson, or a restaurant employee toward a senior woman that makes me seethe; it frequently accompanies the practice of calling one "dear" and giving an indulgent chuckle at whatever little whims one may express in making requests. I recall one example so egregious that I was too stunned to protest. I had gone to consult an ear doctor, a man so appallingly young and inexperienced that, especially in view of my complaint of loss of hearing and with my age written on the paper he held in his hand, he could be pardoned for considering that at sixty-six I was ancient. But along with giving me medical instructions, in exactly the offensive tone of voice I have described, he kept referring to what I could "tell the other ladies." Clearly he took me to be one of a group of women residing in some sort of retirement or nursing home, presumed to have no subject of conversation other than physical ailments and their remedies. At this, the busiest stage of my life, I was surprised at his presumption that I had withdrawn from any active life. What truly shocked me was the stereotype he entertained of older women as such, whether living in retirement or not. I was more irritated than wounded, but I can imagine how traumatic repeated contacts of this sort might be to a woman less sure of herself.

The changes in external appearance that aging brings are at best unwelcome and may in some circumstances be as bitter and restrictive in affecting quality of life as they are inevitable. I do not dismiss them lightly. Yet, as we all know, they do not prohibit meaningful relations with others, not even in the erotic and sexual spheres. In any case, one's own attitude plays a major part. Physical ailments threaten more seriously your belief that you are still your own project. Even those of us who have avoided major disruptions in contact with others and the

world—such as blindness or total deafness or some form of paralysis—
have had to make concessions. I have been remarkably lucky in avoiding
the greater afflictions, but emphatically not immune to the lesser ones.
In growing old, I have appreciated more keenly the truth of Sartre's
statement that we both are and are not our bodies. We speak of *having* a
headache or pain in the back or fatigue; it would be more accurate to say
that we *are* the headache or the back pain—or, perhaps better, that we
are *in* them as we are in a room or on a hill and that whatever view we
take has them as background. When you seldom or never enjoy the triumph of sleeping straight through the night, when assorted discomforts
are the norm and not the exception, when you have to force yourself to
set to work in spite of "being too tired," the body takes on the quality of
being more of an obstacle than a means. Yet the very fact that we can
look at it in that fashion shows that we can go beyond it, that we are *not*
it. Just as we learn that activity is the cure for the physical lethargy that
makes us reluctant to move, so we discover that consciousness is capable
of keeping the body as ground and not focus. (Again I remind you that I
am not speaking of extreme situations but of the various forms of debil-
itation that aging normally brings to most of us.) Although on occasion
I have been guilty of participating in the elderly's favorite pastime of
chronicling the progress of ailments, taking my turn in inflicting and
suffering the boredom of such recitals, I think that I have succeeded reasonably well in making my life in the last couple of decades a recognizable if somewhat subdued facsimile of what it was before. The body demands its due, of course. I generally go to bed early and ration my
nights out. But then, as my friend Lynn Martin lamented for himself, I
never did have the constitution for depravity.

Whether wisely or foolishly, I keep a vigilant watch over myself to
discern (since there is no way of preventing) signs of change in my mental activity. There are some, unmistakably, and I have worked to find
ways of coping with them. I suppose my solutions are the same as countless others have discovered. Names of people and the precise word I want
will frequently not come when summoned. Time will usually dredge
them up, but later is often no better than never. I try to be alert ahead of
time to the danger ahead. If I fear that a blank is going to occur, I may
suppress what I was about to say. If pressed, I seek a synonym or a de-
scriptive phrase. And if I have to admit that I have forgotten, I confess it
without overwhelming distress. Distrust of my short time memory leads
me to write a plethora of notes to myself. It seems to me sometimes that
I think more slowly and that I have to make a greater effort to master

serious reading. But then I have more time at my disposal. All of this, though a nuisance, is manageable. If some of the connections in my brain have become loosened or worn-out, still the apparatus as a whole supports me—just as I can maintain a rapid pace in walking even on days when my right ankle hurts.

Though most of the time I make the effort to keep up with what I have defined as essential to my psychological well-being and to fulfilling what I regard as my obligations, honesty compels me to recognize that I have allowed my horizons to shrink a little. Is it because of narrowing interest due to diminishing energy? Does the inevitable repetition of old arguments in new contexts too easily breed boredom? Or have I arbitrarily lowered my standards for myself? Whatever is the cause, my guilt and regret are minimal and perfunctory. I still feel passionately about many issues in the world beyond my private sphere, and I find it worthwhile to try to maintain a nodding acquaintance with major intellectual trends and literary currents. I do not work very long at what I find difficult and not intrinsically interesting to me. Some articles in *The New York Review of Books* I cut out and save for rereading, but now there are more of them that I skip. If I dislike a book, I no longer, as used to be my absurd practice, make myself continue through to the end so as to be sure I am right in declaring it not worth reading. This may be a step forward. In some contexts, I suspect I have cut myself off too quickly from following through on what might have been rewarding for me to develop. I cannot boast that age has taught me patience. Such things bother me a bit when I reflect on them but not very much. Letting go, in moderation, can be a pleasure. I know it is also dangerous, but so are a lot of good things if you don't keep them in check.

Our anchorage in time is most severely shaken as the years advance. Sartre says that to be a human being is to be an "always future project." Does the human condition itself need to be redefined for the old? At first thought it might seem so. If we have lived intensively in and for the future, we may suddenly feel homeless. The past is a storehouse but not a dwelling place, the present a moving sidewalk. Yet I have come to think that, as we grow older, we realize our temporal situation more acutely. As always we live in all three dimensions simultaneously. I like Heidegger's poetic way of putting it: "Our past comes to meet us out of the future." Or, as Sartre explained it more prosaically: We must not deprive the present of its due even as we define the present as being only the flight from what we have made of ourselves toward what we want to be—and we should realize that we choose the future self toward which

we are fleeing. Even so, our position with respect to each of the three dimensions undeniably changes, since the nature of the possibilities they
offer is different.

I have little patience with the sentimental notion that the old can live
happily on their memories alone; no past provides sufficient nutriment
for that. Nevertheless, active reflection on the meaning of what has been
can be immensely rewarding; old age is conducive to this, for the obvious reasons that it usually brings more leisure and that there is more to
reflect on. To perceive a previously hidden chain of cause and effect, to
reveal a pattern hitherto undiscerned, whether in one's own past or in
that of others one has known—such illuminations may sometimes lead
one to take some sort of action; most often the closure is purely psychological. In either case it satisfies in the same way that the solution of
a fictional mystery does. Fortunately most of us do not have to do our
remembering alone. It is in the exchange of recollections or even in one's
own telling of them that new insight most often comes. I myself have
taken special pleasure in rereading books that I have not looked at for
decades. It has been as enlightening of myself as it is intrinsically rewarding. With Proust, for example, his psychological analysis, for which
I had extravagantly admired him formerly, struck me later as somewhat
thin and contrived. I was now impatient rather than empathically fascinated by his hero's morbidity. But I had a better appreciation of the social satire, of the humor, which I had almost forgotten, and of the picto-
rial quality of Proust's prose—as in the quiet loveliness of his painting of
Mme. Swann walking with her parasol in Maytime on the Avenue du
Bois. Trollope, on the other hand, seems to me now (after reading almost
the entire corpus) to possess a much deeper understanding than I had
given him credit for and to grasp the true pathos of women's condition
even in his formulaic plots.

When memories come unbidden, they are as likely to be distressing
as delightful. Possibly even more likely. A friend of mine in her mid-
eighties, a woman comfortably situated, who still lives creatively and
mostly contentedly in the present, writes to me that it is chiefly the negative things, the small failures, the missed opportunities, the deficiencies
that keep coming back to haunt her although, in tangible accomplishments, her past life has been one that many would envy. How universal
this experience is I do not know. I understand what she means, for I have
noted the same thing in myself. It is not, at least with me, connected
with any conscious attempt to make an inventory of my past. The unwelcome intrusion is not often of unhappy events already examined;

more frequently it is a trivial thing which suddenly seems to have a negative aspect I had not noticed before—or had not let myself acknowledge. Now and then it is one of the "Could I actually have said or done *that?*" variety. And I cringe with shame. Such moments are medicinal. They remind me that my self-portrait needs to be re-examined. Though disconcerting, they are also reassuring in that in the act of wishing I could disavow the self I was, I go beyond it. Vanity over our self-image and the actuality of our growth beyond what we have been both play a part in these painful reminders.

If circumstances are favorable, *carpe diem*, the injunction to make the most of the present, though it is usually addressed to youth, has a poignant relevance for the aged. This is indeed the time to indulge oneself, to take time to savor, or to do finally the thing one has always resolved to do "someday" so that whatever else my happen, at least one will have had that. Suddenly I note that even in writing that sentence, I have slipped out of the present tense, invoking not only the past but the future and the future perfect! Pleasurable sensations and a few aesthetic delights may seem to be so confined to the immediate as to be suspended in time. Only a quibbling philosopher, it seems, would insist that the movement from past to future is still there in the present. On a practical level, immersion in the present means simply that one's personal relation to the other dimensions of time has been reduced to insignificance. Other satisfactions that the present may bring derive precisely from awareness of its bond with the other dimensions—as when the lasting consequence of past action stands there before you or when the value of what you have done is affirmed by someone else; then something out of the past becomes, as it were, a tangible possession in the present.

Most important of all is the present expectation of future activities, and of goals, whether these represent novelty and growth or only desired repetitions. If the present is to be worthwhile, I believe that we who are older, differently but just as certainly, need to work self-consciously at structuring the future. Evelyn, my friend from Wilson College days, expressed this well in a recent letter to me: "I'm convinced we must always direct our energies to the processes of being reborn lest we spend our energies in the processes of dying."

Writing now when I have just turned eighty, I cannot say I find that my life from day to day is as fully satisfying as in the years when old age was only an abstract probability. But its intrinsic value remains high inasmuch as I still, mostly nonreflectively, look on it as filled with possibilities. In this sense I have not outlived myself. But there are other questions that need to be raised. Changes have been taking place outside, not only within.

Where in the World?

Even in the most everyday sense of the words, the question of what it means to outlive oneself varies according to its context. It may, as in my speaking of my attitude toward aging, ask whether one still feels oneself to be "an always future project." At the opposite extreme we might say that persons who, as organisms, lie irrecoverably in a coma have outlived their human selves. Or those might be said to have outlived themselves who have lost all reliable connection with the continuity of past and present or the distinction between the world of imagination and what the general consensus declares to be reality. In one of its most interesting usages, the query, "Have I outlived myself?" inquires how I see myself positioned in the present world. On this level the self in question is the network of habits, attitudes, personality traits, accumulated knowledge, everything that comes into play as an embodied consciousness relates itself to the external environment of things and other living beings. But if this is simply what I *am*, then is there any sense at all in asking whether I have outlived myself? Or is this self *not* the whole of my being?

In a venture in Existentialist autobiography, the question of what Sartre (and I, following him) considers the self to be and whether or how anyone might rightly be said to have outlived it cannot be ignored; it calls for a short expository digression in this story I tell of myself.

Sartre uses the word "self" in several ways, but he differentiates clearly among them. He would say that the personal self to which I referred a moment ago (the personality, etc.) is my ego and that it is not the same as my consciousness. The idea that the whole self or psyche includes more than consciousness and ego has long been familiar to us, as is the all but inextricability of ego and consciousness. For Freud the ego is the reservoir of everything that is or may become conscious; it is the ego that establishes our relations with external reality. Jung adds the concept of the persona, which serves as a mediator between the ego and the world; the persona is the ordered pattern of conduct we exhibit to others as contrasted with our inner landscape. For both psychologists the ego is the subjective "I"; each also holds that while the ego is the active agent, its seeming freedom is an illusion. It is governed in large part by irruptions from the unconscious, messages sometimes disguised, often obeyed without the ego's fully understanding them for what they are.

Sartre effectively turns all of this upside down. Consciousness, instead of being the subordinate part of a larger self, is the creator of the personalized self, which Sartre calls the ego. The ego is never a part of consciousness but separated from it as a book is separate from its author. It is consciousness, not the ego, that is the active agent; the ego is a passive structure. To put it more simply, a consciousness is individual but not personal. It is a pure, ordering awareness. Sartre calls it a self-consciousness, but by this he means only that to be aware of an object is to be simultaneously aware that the object is not the same as the awareness itself. If I perceive a butterfly, I establish the butterfly as being *out there*, the object of my consciousness, not a part or aspect of my consciousness. Sartre's view of how a consciousness creates a self from which it always stands aloof is neither so bizarre nor so difficult as it may at first appear. As a consciousness directs its attention (as James would say) or intention (to use the Phenomenologists' term) on external objects, it reflects as well their ground, their forming a world. Similarly, each consciousness "intends" its own successive awarenesses, ordering them into an inner world, unifying them as a self. It is here that the personal "I" comes into being. For Sartre, this "I" is a dependent structure, just as it is for Freud and Jung, but for different reasons. For them it is the agent that acts in response to both the external environment and the hidden depths of a larger unconscious (personal or collective). For Sartre, it is consciousness which determines actions and which is always capable of taking a new point of view on the psychic structures, or self—on the "I" that it has created. This self, the ego, is what Sartre refers to in the famous pronouncement "Man makes himself." My consciousness does not make itself. It makes a self for itself as it reflects on my interactions with the material world and others. Creating a self is the unavoidable task for a consciousness that must make itself be. To choose not to make the self would be to choose insanity. And while Sartre has placed his emphasis on the capacity of consciousness to modify the ego, to the point of virtually remaking it rather than being imprisoned by it, the fact is that finally it is the self each consciousness has made that, along with the body, differentiates us as persons.

Though Sartre never precisely said so, I think that consciousness both is and is not its ego in much the same way that it is and is not its body. Both body and ego are not only the inevitable accompaniment to consciousness's presence in the world; together they are the means by which it can interact with the world. Yet, consciousness in a certain sense always transcends or goes beyond both of them, determines how to place them in the world.

To return to my initial question: Have I outlived myself? What can this mean from a Sartrean perspective? Since by definition human consciousness is self-consciousness, this impersonal self cannot be consciously outlived. Only the no longer conscious body can be said to outlive it, and we may question in what sense this existence is still life; certainly it is not human life. But if we use the word "self" to denote the personal ego, then to outlive oneself is both the description and the moral imperative for a human being. To be conscious is to be, in fact, always remaking or making oneself anew. Metaphorically, I might be said to have outlived myself if my consciousness were to cease to work actively at making the self grow, either because of bodily affliction or because of a psychological retreat that takes refuge in the dying process before it is necessary. In this case to outlive myself would mean only that consciousness chose to do nothing but contemplate its own product and label it "finished."

To tell the truth, Sartre's concept of the ego is a bit slippery. At one point in *The Transcendence of the Ego* he suggests that the ego is so evanescent as a mental (more accurately, a psychic) construct that you can grasp it only as a peripheral presence; if you look at it directly, it vanishes—like Eurydice. I think of this aspect of the ego as comparable to my self-image, intangible, unstable, but real; an underlying unity of past and present and projected future, presented as an enduring self. But Sartre says elsewhere in this same essay that my ego exists as an object out there, "in the world," like yours or like that of anyone else, and he says it is equally accessible to all. As it stands, the statement exaggerates. There is certainly much in my ego that is available to my scrutiny and not to yours. But Sartre's essential point is that both our egos exist as potential objects of consciousness, not part of a consciousness. My ego is the history of my past states of consciousness as my consciousness has reflected and continues to reflect on them. You might liken it to the plot that consciousness imposes on its experiences so as to make them into a coherent story. And it is true, of course, that someone might interpret this plot differently than I do or demonstrate that a significant subplot is revealed without my having recognized it—as psychotherapists do routinely.

Whatever image best describes it, my ego has become by now my

personality, my character, the accumulated patterns of conduct, preference, and attitudes that I carry with me as the ground for every new encounter. Though Sartre insists that the ego can be expanded or restruc-
tured, its components cannot be magically made to disappear as though
they had never been. Somehow the existing ego must be accommodated.

In light of these considerations, I find a special meaning in the feelings that sometimes sweep over us, those which might be verbalized
by such declarations as "I am tired of myself," "I am discouraged with
myself," or "I am proud of myself." Only, strictly speaking, if they are
authentic and spontaneous, we ought to say, "My consciousness is tired,
discouraged, proud of myself." Finally, what about "Have I outlived myself?" What, I wonder, would be the Sartrean implications of this relatively common form of self-questioning? Flaubert, for example, must
have asked it of himself when he wrote that he was a fossil in his contemporary world—or as someone today would say, a dinosaur—though
not of the kind the children love. This question is less a matter of self-
judgment than an attempt to place the self with respect to the outside
world. Does the apparatus I have constructed for dealing with the world
still work? Are the changes that others have brought about "out there"
challenges to further self-growth? Or do they make demands my self is
not equipped to deal with? To put it another way: My evolving self has
lived in *the* world as if it were *my* world. Of course, changes were always
taking place outside my neighborhood, but they did not seem to threaten
my movement, whatever direction I might choose to go. Gradually,
passing time has led me to wonder whether I have moved from the status of full citizen to that of resident alien in this world that used to be
mine. In Sartrean parlance, my consciousness looks at my self out there
in the world and asks how or if it fits in. In everyday language, "Have I
outlived myself?" means, do I feel myself at home in the world? Or better, in what part of the world do I live? At its center or in an enclave? Are
there areas in it for which I have no passport? And finally, do I want to
move or to stay where I am?

Recognizing the validity of two often heard, opposite but not contradictory generalizations—(1) that at least since Homer, in Western
history, the older generation always tends to view change in terms of
what has been lost, and (2) that in actual fact my generation has witnessed more major changes in every corner of the globe and in the re-
cesses of private lives than that of any preceding century—here I do not

set out to prove or to take exception to either of them. Rather I will try
to avoid the trap of the first (though surely I will not wholly succeed)
and to describe briefly how I react to the second.

In trivial matters I not only acknowledge but indulge myself in a certain crotchetiness. My tastes are not contemporary, not even in foods. I
do not like yoghurt or alfalfa sprouts or mashed potatoes with the skins
left in them. I hate having what I expect to be "real" tea turn out to be
mango or Red Hot Zinger. Though appreciative of a variety of ethnic
cuisines, I am not pleased with the way chefs now mix them together
in unpalatable combinations. I resent having other people's ideas of a
proper diet circumscribe my own choices. Recent styles in women's
clothing do not appeal to me—skirts so short that most should know
enough not to wear them, or so long they impede walking, and glitter
slopped on everything. I complain a lot: As traffic has become more
dense, drivers seem to grow ruder and more reckless; even when walking, I am in danger of being run down by joggers, if not by bicyclists.
Crowds clutter up any site worth visiting. Mail service deteriorates in
direct proportion to what we pay for it. Packaged goods can't be opened
without instruments suitable for a carpenter or a plumber. Concern for
correct grammar is disappearing. Politicians and TV news commentators alike say "between you and I," use "like" as a conjunction, and follow
their own whim in pronouncing anything. In both speaking and writing,
obscene terms are so overused that even invective has become trite. . . .
At last I put an end to this listing and not only because it is tiresome and
because for much of it, it is I who am out of joint and not the times. The
truth is that while my frequent feeling of being out of step is discomfiting
and sometimes I can't even hear the beat, my cantankerous impulses are
minimal in the overall.

I do not need to make a mental inventory in order to realize how
overwhelming are the compensations. To stay on the same quotidian
level, I am more than willing to have kiwis and avocados (neither of
which I ever tasted as a child) in exchange for the bother of avoiding
tofu. It is a pleasure to be able to watch a film in the quiet of our living
room (that is my only use of the VCR; its other functions are beyond
me) and to take advantage of all the timesaving gadgets my mother
never knew. I am delighted that women can enjoy the free comfort of
slacks on any occasion. If I miss the old "downtown," the fact is that I
prefer a choice of shopping malls. How I would love to take my mother
to a factory outlet! On balance, I see that I have not outlived myself as a

consumer. My enjoyment of what I have found good is not poisoned by my occasional perception that I have worn the wrong clothes to a party. I can always take refuge in the thought that the others have forgotten how to dress.

I will not spell out the obvious benefits of more significant gifts that scientific and technological advances have bestowed on me and for which I am profoundly grateful. I will mention only one example; in my mind it is emblematic of the way that many earlier evils have been ameliorated. Taking a walk one day with my parents (I must have been still in grade school), I was horrified when we saw Mr. Anderson, our cheerful paperhanger, sitting as a beggar, totally blind, his little daughter attending him. We learned that because of cataracts he had been forced to abandon his work until these had "ripened" to the point at which he could have an operation. Some months later we saw him again. The surgery had been successful; the thick glasses he wore enabled him to see normally, but his story of what he had endured in having to be for a long time motionless, surrounded by sandbags while the eyes healed, gave me nightmares. Even for a long time as an adult, I thought of cataracts as an affliction greater than I would be able to bear; I feared them more than any terminal disease. When my time came, there was no problem. With no waiting, with less distress than I have sometimes suffered from a trip to the dentist, I was given a lens implant first in the right eye, a little later in the left. My 20/20 vision was restored as quickly as it was in need of help. I am not forgetting today's negatives. Complacency over medical progress has to be balanced by new threats— AIDS, increased incidence of cancer, the emergence of new forms of tuberculosis once considered conquered. But I would not want to return to the situation of earlier decades unmodified.

I think I can be objective in concluding that some undeniably bad aspects of life today were not as flagrantly present in the first and middle part of the century. I have in mind only the obvious things: the violence that has made streets and schools unsafe and the growing presence of gangs and drug dealers often associated with it; the increase of alcoholism and suicide among the young; the bitter incivility in public life; the disappearance of loyalty on the side of both institutions and employees; the gradual erosion of the middle class and widening gap between the wealthy and the poverty stricken; the large number of homeless. (I do not include the wars of the present and recent past, for war regrettably seems to be a constant.) These particular problems of our time and

other lamentable ills that should be added to this partial litany are developments that I recognize as alien to what I knew formerly. If, dreadful as they are, they do not make me feel a stranger, this is because these
things have happened to *us*. I have plenty of company, old and young, in
deploring them. I feel a sense of solidarity with all the others who,
whether they suffer from or are working to overcome the problems, see
the wrongs for what they are and want to right them. These last may
not be in the majority. There is obvious divergence between persons
who try to cure social ills by more oppressive legislation and those who
seek to attack the causes. I have no assurance that justice will prevail. I
am as frightened as anyone by the rightist militia, whether they are
racists or not. But I remember the Ku Klux Klan when it was far more of
a menace than it is now. Fear and worry are not the same as alienation.

There are two important areas in which I do indeed feel that if I have
not exactly outlived myself, I no longer know how to keep up with the
world. Since I can't quite give a name to the first, I will approach it indirectly: I have never found reason to want to abandon the premises of the
Existentialist philosophy I have made my own. No proposals by psychologists or biologists have convinced me that I should abandon what I
have believed to be true of human consciousness. Recent claims concerning the bringing to light of repressed memories, for instance, have
not persuaded me to grant greater validity to the hypothesis of the unconscious but have thrown still more suspicion on the way psychologists have used it. I do not find that the framework of thought which I
have adopted is inadequate when put to the test. What is put into question is the relation between this outlook that I have taken to be a liberating philosophy and the particular turns of recent radical theory, this
and the status of corollary assumptions that had seemed to me to be so
self-evident as to be part of the very definition of "human." I touched on
this subject in relation to feminism, but the issue is broader than that.

Just how topsy-turvy things have become was brought home to me
when one day I had occasion to make specific comparison between matters at stake in the student protests of three decades ago and the disputes
that take place on university campuses today. In making such comparisons I situate myself on ground most familiar to me although the questions are not solely academic and the debates not confined to the campus.

To mention only the most notable: Concerted struggle for equal
status and equal opportunity, first racial, then gender, has been replaced
by conflict centered on the concept of multiculturalism and identity pol-

itics. Thirty years ago the demand was to provide *for everyone* access to the traditional course of study from which many were excluded. At present the "sacred canon" and the Western tradition itself are under attack; some argue that there is *no* tradition that everyone should be required to know. The demand for freedom of speech, which *then* concentrated on the privilege of expressing one's opinion and, along with that, the right to use four-letter words, has given way to insistence on the importance of advocacy courses and political correctness (viewed by some as repression of freedom of speech). At that time a common complaint was that the university had become fragmented, that instead of a university it had made itself a multiversity. Today, in a complete reversal, the multiversity is held up as the ideal. In the sixties, students opposing the military-industrial establishment pleaded for more "humanization" of education. They flocked to courses in the humanities and social sciences to the neglect of others. In the nineties, eagerness for full utilization of the technological resources of our computer age—the information superhighway, the internet, and all the rest—leads some to question the validity of printed books as the central tool of education. Practically, if not by logical necessity, this view tends to denigrate the relevance of our literary heritage. Finally, the early student revolution was based on the notion that humanizing the university, making it relevant, would be a means of liberation, if not a salvation. In the present decade we confront a new and serious anti-intellectualism, mostly outside the university itself, though friends who are still teaching tell me that many incoming students share this point of view and are interested only in the professional training essential to their future careers.

In the midst of all this, I mostly stand bewildered; or perhaps it would be better to say that I don't know where to stand. To use the word in its meliorative sense for once, I do not know what is liberal and what is not, what is progressive and what is retrogressive, and the middle ground is hard to find. My dislike for the excesses and absurdities committed by some upholders of political correctness is matched by my disgust with their insensitive opponents who deny that there is a problem to be solved. If we adopt a Hegelian stance, it is easy to see that the "melting pot" image was a disguised WASP thesis; but is multiculturalism a healing synthesis or only the antithesis, the American equivalent of Balkanization? The meaning of terms can no longer be taken for granted. To me "cultural relativism" has always referred to a factual condition: the divergent points of view that have to be taken into account by anyone seeking to establish self-evident truths or to make generalizations about humanity. As such it was a starting point for increasing our under-standing. In dominant circles today, the term stands for the impossibil-ity of attaining knowledge that transcends one's own culture as though both synchronically and diachronically we live in encapsulated, noncom-municating spheres. It is in this context that I feel least at home. I would gladly revise the Canon, require study of cultures hitherto ignored, ex-plore new points of view on accepted interpretations and re-evaluations of factual and cultural history. But I would do so in the name of allowing individuals to comprehend more fully and more meaningfully their affiliation with all of the human species and to have access to its accu-mulated treasures. I realize that from the point of view of most recent currents of thought, this is to live by a naive, sentimental illusion. But I will not forswear this part of myself even if the world has passed me by.

I have merely hinted at the clearly defined area in which I have to rec-ognize that I am unmistakably a fossil. Partly by choice and partly by negligence, I am a computer illiterate. It is only within the last couple of years that I have come to realize the degree to which this denotes some-thing more than ignorance of a particular skill (like not knowing how to fly a plane). The label applies to me even on the most literal level. Like Jocasta, in Cocteau's *The Infernal Machine,* I have sometimes felt that "I am surrounded by objects that hate me." I have never effectively de-fended myself against Doris's charge that I am "a mechanical idiot." When personal computers and word processors appeared in the studies of my acquaintances, I considered whether or not, with my manual inept-ness, it was worth the trouble to learn to use them; I made the momen-tous decision that it was not—despite many attempts to persuade me otherwise. On a practical level I have managed fairly well, thanks to my being in a position to have someone else type manuscripts and long re-ports for me, though I grow increasingly ashamed of the professional letters I dare to send out after mistyping them on my outdated electric typewriter.

As for the larger vision, I do not think that those exaggerate who claim that the computer and corollary applications will transform the face of the world more radically than the industrial revolution. Some-times I try to reassure myself by assuming a bird's-eye view, reminding myself of how a new device has always provided solutions to the prob-lems it creates. Machines introduced in the nineteenth century, though they represented a genuine threat, ultimately raised the standard of living for workers and for a long time increased their political power. I think of Plato expressing doubts as to whether the written word was truly a benefit to humankind or whether it would make the spread of information easier but diminish the power of memory and habits of reflection essential to wisdom. Although his other fear, that without the author's presence the intent of his book would be distorted by its readers, has been amply justified, I suspect that Plato, if we could consult him, would be reconciled even to the later discovery of printing. By analogy, I like to imagine that today's dislocation of employees (white collared as well as blue) *could* lead (as has been suggested) to a new kind of community in which citizens' roles are no longer defined by their job and income. It is possible, I suppose, that the chatter on the internet might educate instead of reinforcing prejudices as talk shows tend to do. It would be nice to see, in the threat to privacy that computers pose, a move toward the society based on transparent trust, with no need for secrecy, that Sartre dreamed of in his millennial fantasies. Abstractly, I can grant the possibility that what I consider the essential ingredients of a satisfying life might be provided in new and better ways than I can now imagine. For someone else, not for me. When as a child, still committed to the myth of inevitable progress, I used to envy later generations for the still to be invented keys to enjoyment they would possess; somehow I pictured these future men and women as just like me but with more opportunities. In my imagination I moved among them with wonder and delight. It never occurred to me that I would be Tarzan brought into the city.

Whether life in the fully developed computer age will be psychologically richer or poorer I do not even try to guess. The only thing of which I am sure is that I cannot fit into it the self that I carry with me now, not even in my thoughts. The more pressing question is whether I should attempt to modify my self so as not to be pushed even farther from the mainstream. On a practical level, it is too late to put myself abreast with those who live close to "the cutting edge." I could, if I wished, learn enough of the new language to "get around"—like those conscientious travelers who take time to learn ahead the everyday phrases used in the foreign countries they plan to visit. At the moment I know only that "Windows" are not panes to look through and that not to be "on-line" is a mark of disgrace. Perhaps when I am caught up on other commitments and have time to do so, I will learn to utilize the word processor. I could take one of those introductory classes especially advertised for seniors. Or, when that leisured day arrives, I might prefer to audit those classes I have always wanted to attend in Spanish and in pre-Columbian art.

Extreme Limits

My father used to say, perhaps a little too often, that fainting and death are nature's greatest gifts to humankind. Western society, most of the time, seems bent on treating death as the ultimate evil to be combatted to the bitter end. I can acknowledge a relative truth in each of these views. What disturbs me is the unwillingness of the majority to allow the person who is going to die to determine which one is applicable and under what circumstances.

We have come a long way toward providing the elderly with more in-dividual choice as to how they will spend their closing years until death is clearly imminent. I view with suspicion the rosy painting of a former era when parents died in the homes of their grown children, who grate-fully cherished and revered them till the end. For every such ideal ex-ample I am sure there were many more families in which the parents were in fact a burden, and often knew themselves to be so, while their offspring fretted under a duty they assumed perforce. I recall one of my former colleagues, back in the forties, telling me ruefully that because of the presence of his ailing mother-in-law, he and his wife had been un-able to go away for a true vacation during almost the whole of their married life and not until his retirement. Another familiar pattern was for the last unmarried daughter to be expected to return as household manager in the parental home, especially when the father was the lone survivor. Despite the problems, even scandals, that surface in nursing homes, they and retirement centers have been, on the whole, a blessing, not a curse. What is especially encouraging to me is the recent tendency in offices of social services to find ways to enable even nearly helpless older persons, including those below the poverty line, to stay in their own homes or apartments when this is possible. My senior acquain-tances have been about equally divided between those who moved to retirement dwellings and the ones who chose to stay at home until they died. Although most of the former seem to be content with their choice, Doris and I have chosen to follow the example of the latter. We plan to stay where we are until . . .

Until what? I want to say, "until we die." But while I hold absolutely to the principle that if the body and circumstances permit, every person should have the right to choose death as a preferable alternative to an abhorrent existence, control over one's own death is a freedom very seldom granted. Not death itself but the possibility that it might come too late is what I fear most. Recent legislation has helped to assuage some anxieties. A living will, though not always accepted without challenge, could, I think, in my case and in Boulder, guarantee my not being kept alive by artificial means if I were irremediably in a vegetative state. It does not protect against other nightmarish contingencies. To put it bluntly, what I want is freedom to choose suicide or assisted suicide or to arrange for documents guaranteed to provide what would amount to benign euthanasia should a predefined situation arise. Nobody at the present moment is assured of such freedom. Derek Humphry and Jack Kevorkian have done what they could to provide some measure of it. In spite of their efforts, we remain in the position of the women before the Roe vs. Wade decision who, if they carried an unwanted child, had to resort to back-alley abortionists. And just as abortion, while never an intrinsic good to be sought for its own sake, is frequently the best thing in a given situation, so death, without ceasing to be a negative, may be demonstrably better than life under some circumstances. I am pro-choice with respect to both.

If at present I am as eager as ever to postpone death, this is because I still find reason to prolong existence as I enjoy it now. If its eventual inevitability is less an abstraction and the thought of it something easier to accept, this is because the increasing difficulties and discomforts that come with aging make me realize more keenly that life on *any* terms is not something to be valued. Even fundamentalist Christians recognize this truth implicitly when they utter such remarks as "It's a blessing that he died" or "I hope that God will see fit to take her away soon." These same people would vehemently oppose allowing the death to be hastened by human intervention, whether by the dying person or by a loving relative, least of all by a physician.

For many the way we look at death is inseparable from the question of an afterlife. I remember one of my devout Christian cousins, when we met at a funeral, saying to me in tones of naive wonder that she could not imagine how nonreligious believers could bear the death of a loved one without the assurance of meeting again in the other world. Though I do not have such faith myself, I can see that it brings genuine consolation to the bereaved—although the conditions of such meetings defy my powers of imagination. I do not see that the reluctance or eagerness to leave *this* life oneself is greatly affected by whether one views it as an absolute ending or as a transition into the unknown. What one's life has become now is the determinant. To view death as a hated curfew makes sense when it is pleasurable to stay abroad. I myself have no difficulty in imagining that I might come someday to look on it as a liberation.

Belief in immortality—that is, in some sort of personal consciousness after death—I have never held since I was a child. Nor have I even wished for it, chiefly because it seems to me such a meaningless concept, so inherently self-contradictory. To exist forever as the limited being I am now would be as undesirable as it is scientifically impossible. To be a different consciousness or part of another consciousness would not be for *my* consciousness to endure. Reincarnation? Once the chain of memory is broken, as Lucretius said, there would be no significance in the fact that "I" was once Helen of Troy or the traitor Ephialtes even if it could be proved. In this respect humanistic Existentialism did nothing to alter my basic attitude. Indeed I have been struck by the fact that Sartre's comments on death have been singularly close to those of the ancient Epicureans. His basic assumption is the same as theirs: that death is evil only in that it puts an end to consciousness, but there is no self-awareness of the deprivation. Others will live my death, not I, and it is they who henceforth will assign meaning to my dead life. Sartre did allot to us a kind of metaphorical immortality. We *are* our projects, and our projects will live on in the consciousness of others. Cold comfort? Not really. When I realize how the dead, those close to me, live now in my mind, not only as they were but even helping to shape my thoughts, I do not hold as of no account that kind of immortality as something to hope for myself.

Apropos of somber considerations about the meaning of death, I once had an amusing revelatory dream. It came on the night after I had finished reading Ernest Becker's book, *The Denial of Death*. While I have never been comfortable with the idea that fear of death is the motivation (largely unconscious) for most human achievement, and though I resist resorting to semimystical hypotheses, much of what Becker had to say resonated in me, particularly his moving portrayal of our futile quest for final, all inclusive answers, our thirst to impose meaning on life and to make our own lives something meaningful in the whole of things. The book was implicitly present in my dream, though comically trivialized. It seemed that I was about to be executed by electrocution, having been found guilty of having publicly expressed my approval of a subversive Roumanian poet named Enesco (Ionesco, I wonder?). Terrified, I stood fitted with electrodes as someone reached for the switch. The shock came. It was quickly over and hurt no more than the short jolt I felt once as a child when I accidentally stuck a metallic pencil into an electric socket. If this was all, I thought, I had been needlessly fearful. With other dead persons, I walked to a waiting elevator. On the way down, they told me that at the bottom we would find an ordinary, populated landscape in which we dead would find ways to keep ourselves busy, much as in our former life. In great relief, I shouted, "Oh, we must find a way to go back and tell them up above that there is nothing for them to worry about!" To which one of my companions sneered, "Well, if *you* aren't the little do-gooder!" In spite of this jeer, I awoke with a sense of release and reassurance. This silly dream, considered, was not very flattering to my self-esteem; even my dream self condemned my false heroics. The influence of Sartre's *No Exit* is obvious, but the play's everyday Hell was stripped of everything negative. That connection and the juxtaposition of the dream with my reading of Becker prevented me from being content with the sort of sexual interpretation that Freudians would find obvious. I took the dream as confirming that my perhaps shallow, easy acceptance of death as not my essential concern was the one I was content to live with and that what truly mattered was what kind of life I was making and hoping to share with others. At any rate, my lightweight advice to any aged person wondering if it is important to reflect on death as such would be something like this: Think about whether it demands any change in your way of living now or any action to be taken, and act accordingly. Otherwise let the thought of it come if it will; do not repress it and do not dwell on it. Then you will find that you can quite comfortably forget about it.

I am both unable and unwilling to forget what I see as the necessity for legislation to insure to whoever wishes it freedom to choose death for oneself as preferable to a greater evil. (In referring to this kind of extreme situation, I am thinking primarily of the aged; but on very rare occasions a younger person, one in great pain, helpless and without hope of cure, might deservedly ask for the same compassionate release. Though admittedly it is a tautology, I think it would help to consider the choice of death squarely for what it is: the refusal of a life that is unacceptable. I hold strongly to the belief that self-killing—either in the form of active suicide or of the rejection of available measures to prolong life—is always a right and never a duty. That it should never be seen as a duty seems to me obvious to any member of a society sufficiently compassionate and just to honor the basic right of an individual to strive for a significant life. A command, persuasion, or even subtle pressure to make the aged feel that they *ought* to die, whether for others' sake or for their own, is murder. I would not condone it anymore than I approve of medical experiments being conducted on human subjects without their knowledge and not in their interest. That self-killing is also a right seems to me equally evident. An individual who finds good reason to choose self-administered or assisted suicide should not be looked on as guilty of criminal intent nor should those who respect his/her wishes be condemned.

What the majority opinion in this country is, nobody really knows. The 1994 vote in Oregon and some private polls suggest that the general public is more receptive to the notion of legalizing assistance in dying under clearly defined conditions than timid lawmakers believe—though I am sure I myself would go farther than most in the latitude of choice I would be willing to grant. I cannot see that resistance to any attempt to relax current restrictions is either logical or humane. We should hardly speak of a duty owed to society in the case of one who will no longer enjoy its services. There is, of course, the problem of people's religious beliefs. Many persons hold that self-killing is a sin because it is contrary to the will of God, an argument patently illogical in the context of almost everyone's eagerness to take all positive steps to prevent deaths that would naturally take place if not combatted. It is not only the Judaeo-Christian tradition in Western society that has opposed suicide. Plato's Socrates argued that we are, as it were, slaves of the gods, hence should not cheat our masters of our services, an idea that has always struck me as singularly unappealing. The ancient Stoics, on the other hand, in spite of their belief that this is a rationally controlled universe, approved as exemplary the sage who chose to kill himself rather than to submit to extreme physical or mental pain. Among theologies and philosophies, one may take one's pick. What I cannot accept is the idea that anyone's personal conviction in this matter should be allowed to control those of a different persuasion. And I believe that the burden of proof should be on those who would deny the right to die, not those who lay claim to it.

Many physicians, though not all, are willing to refrain from the use of heroic measures to stave off death in hopeless situations. Most, understandably in light of prevalent attitudes, oppose any effort to allow doctors openly to bring death deliberately under any circumstances. The argument they usually give is that their training, their mission, is solely to preserve life. Once again life itself is taken as intrinsically an absolute good at whatever cost, and death is denied the status of ever being the lesser of two evils. At a meeting of our local chapter of the

Hemlock Society, of which I am a member, a doctor talked with compassionate frankness of the physician's responsibility to ease pain and to recognize when a situation called for noninterference; that is, when death was not the worst thing. He was adamant in opposing any action to hasten the death of persons who wanted it, no matter how intolerable they found their present existence. In defense of his position, along with invoking his own reluctance deliberately to cut off life, he reproached his audience for a kind of cowardice and failure of our human responsibility. Why, he asked, should we want to have only the desirable things offered by life and to reject the negative? Moreover, he argued, the supposed sufferer in extreme situations might with medication be protected from acute pain; the victim of a stroke did not necessarily feel the frustration of paralysis in the way that we outsiders imagined it; many an Alzheimer's patient was blissfully content, far more than the average "normal" person. Even granting the speaker's claims with regard to the state of the sufferers (though I am not convinced that all are self-evidently true), I cannot accept his secular equivalent of the religious claim that it is our duty to endure whatever God sends to us. To choose not to live through to the end the natural course of Alzheimer's or cancer or any other affliction one finds intolerable does not seem to me unworthy of a human being. Above all, people ought to be allowed to make such moral decisions for themselves and to count on the willingness of others to help them when their wish has been clearly expressed.

I know that opponents of my position, including those not motivated solely by religious scruples, offer two objections that merit consideration; that is, they claim that two negative possibilities exist, sufficiently dreadful to forbid any challenge to the status quo. One is that if the right to die were extended, interested relatives and acquaintances might pressure older persons to remove themselves from the scene; the other is the chance that those assisting in bringing about a requested death might unknowingly do so when the victim had changed his/her mind or would do so if given further opportunity. I would agree that everything possible must be done to avert both of these contingencies, but the task does not seem to me insurmountably difficult. Undue influence on the elderly is already a reality of which we are aware, and steps have been taken to detect and to prevent it. As for the unpredictable change of intention on the patient's part, this risk must be measured against the alternative probability of prolonging an existence that he/she has already declared unacceptable. Speaking for myself, I find the latter to be the greater hazard. I admit that there is a special sort of consideration that enters in when a person is neither terminally ill (in the short term) nor in extreme pain; for example, one who is rendered almost helpless by paralysis or one who is faced with a diagnosis of Alzheimer's. The argument here is that since it is impossible to know what one's future attitude will be until one has lived through the situation, to refuse it in advance is to act in ignorance. This would be, it is claimed, to liken the person in question to a man or woman who, bereft of a loved one, would rather die than to wait for time to heal if it cannot cure. This seems to me to be a false parallel. In instances in which the outcome is predictable, one ought to have the freedom to choose whether to learn to endure it or to reject it. People vary in their tolerance of humiliation and frustration as they do in their thresholds for pain—or in the value they attach to bare existence at any cost. The fact that the body may at the last moment rebel at what the mind has decreed is no reason for disregarding the conscious decision that remains fixed—as some who have attempted to follow Humphry's prescription in *Final Exit* have attested.

At the end of his novel *After Many a Summer Dies the Swan*, Aldous Huxley imagines that the secret to immortality has been discovered. The catch is that the price to be paid for living indefinitely is willingness to descend in the evolutionary scale. After the first gasp of horror at the sight of the former human couple now living as a pair of apes, one of the onlookers concludes that perhaps the price may after all not be too high. The two creatures looked as if they were "having a pretty good time . . . in their own way, of course." Most of us would uphold the idea that for one to choose to close off any possibility of one's becoming willing to settle for this kind of existence is defensible even though we are *not* judging the situation from within.

Someone might argue that special circumstances could arise that would make self-chosen death no longer a right—because of duty toward others. I can readily imagine a situation in which my wish to die for what seemed to me to be valid reasons would seem less weighty when balanced against the need of someone else for me to live. Such ethical dilemmas always arise when rights and moral obligations conflict. Individuals trapped in such a situation will and should decide in light of the personal ethics by which they have lived—though in such cases they should not make the decision all alone. Indeed, one of the most important advantages of openly permitting assisted suicide is that then it would be possible to insist on full discussion of all aspects of the question so that the one wishing to die may examine whether the personal decision is harmonious with an objective appraisal of the situation.

Truth bids me confess that I would probably be the first to resent the necessity of such discussions. But if one wants to have public assistance, one must be prepared to pay a price.

Conversely, some (Richard Lamm, former governor of Colorado, most notoriously) have argued that sometimes members of the older generation have the "duty to die." What Lamm referred to was the fact that in a society where medical equipment and procedures are not available for all, the aged do not have the right to claim privilege at the expense of the newborn, children, or other youthful members. I believe that the old are neither privileged nor expendable. I myself would not feel justified in asking for an organ transplant in the present context of scarcity of donors, but I would not go so far as to hold that age should be the sole or dominant consideration in every decision as to who is to be helped when not all can be. Again we are speaking of competing rights. That nobody has a duty to choose death still seems to me to hold as a basic principle in the same way that we declare murder to be wrong, even though, in exceptional circumstances, killing a particular person might be justified as the lesser of two evils.

On the comparatively rare occasions when I discuss these matters with persons other than associates in the Hemlock Society, someone will usually remark that persons seriously bent on killing themselves will surely find a way to do it and that there are many instances in which family members have helped them with no feelings of guilt and without public disclosure. Would it not be better to leave such matters in the private realm where they effectively are now? I emphatically disagree. To begin with, they are not securely in the private realm. Compassionate, well-intentioned relatives sometimes find themselves charged with murder, in a very public court of law. If the would-be suicide does not want to implicate another, a very painful form of death may be the only sure thing, or there may, for the helplessly bedridden, be simply no saving solution. For a person in full consciousness, chosen death with dignity and innocence is all but impossible today. I would hope that anyone caring for me in such a situation, one who sympathized with my wish but did not want to risk being legally prosecuted, would find some workable means midway between leaving the requisite pills by the glass of water on the bedside table and hiding them in a spot inaccessible to me. But why should deceptive scheming be necessary and any open sharing prohibited?

I speak only for myself, of course. I have no desire to initiate any effort to encourage people generally to turn their attention to the advantages of departing sooner rather than later. I honor as heroic the choice to continue to be of service as long as it is possible even when the physical toll is enormous. I respect the wish to experience till the end whatever is offered, whether sweet or bitter. Nor would I deliberately try to undermine people's religious conviction that it is wrong to hasten for themselves what God or nature has delayed—not so long as such persons do not try forcibly to make others live or die in accordance with this opinion. I insist that all should be permitted to choose which role they prefer in this final act. I suspect that I represent a minority view, but it is that of a sizable group, one that deserves to be given attention.

I think that the time will inevitably come, in the not very far future, when the State will distinguish between murder and aiding people to die by their own choice. It is not my task here to try to specify exactly how permissiveness and safeguards against abuse should be combined. I do not believe that making it legal to choose death will suddenly make people long for it. On my eightieth birthday, friends presented me with a cushion bearing the slogan, "Despite the high cost of living, it's still popular." It is with me. But I would cling to it more serenely if I knew that the way to the exit would be unblocked when I am ready to leave.

Discussion of the hazard of dying strikes most people as depressing, morbid, in bad taste. I do not often inflict it on my acquaintances. Personally, I find it intensely interesting, probably because I stand at just the right distance with respect to it. Still thriving but by definition moribund, I am remote enough so that I am not yet caught up in any particular private conflict for which I must struggle to find an immediate solution; yet I am close enough to be involved in a matter of deep concern. It is exhilarating in a way to witness or to take part in the fight for this ultimate freedom which, in the West and in the Christian era, only Holland has seen fit to recognize. Though not a leader in the "right to die" movement, I feel here that I am once more with the avant-garde. In assuming this position I am claiming the right not to be forced to outlive myself.

REFLECTING ON THE STORY

When I was a girl, we had a mail order catalogue that pictured on its cover a woman looking at a catalogue that pictured on its cover a woman looking at a catalogue that. . . . As I looked at it, I wondered where the series ended. Did it become so tiny that it just disappeared? Or did it come in a circle back to the first woman? Or to me looking at her? Feeling dizzy, I ran outside and twisted myself tightly in my rope swing for as long as it would twist and then suddenly let go.

Sartre says that consciousness can take its self as its object; that is, it can reflect on its previous conscious acts and on its past attempts to impose a unity upon them, to constitute them as a person, an ego. At the same time, it is implicitly aware that the reflecting consciousness is not identical with the ego it is reflecting on. It can pass judgment on that self, but this judgment itself becomes part of the self that consciousness will next reflect on.

Let's twist again. One of today's established truths is the assertion that any verbal account of an event is a fiction as compared with the event itself. The story a consciousness tells and makes into its self is a fiction; thus the self as such is a fiction though as a fiction its existence is real. If I tell this story to others, is my tale a fictionalized version of a fiction?

You are your acts, Sartre's Inez tells Garcin. True, but the acts taken by themselves do not yet tell a story. They stand there like those dots in children's puzzles, which are formed into shapes only as the child, following the given numbers, draws the lines that connect them. Were the shapes there all the time? Of course. Are there other shapes that could be disclosed? Probably, but they would never have existed in the mind that planned *this* shape. If *that* is what you want, you have to go by the numbers.

In turning my lived history into a written autobiography, I have tried to connect the dots in such a way that the shape of the story that emerges is a faithful copy of the "I" that my consciousness formed. As Gerald Edelman has pointed out, memory is a re-creation, not a playback. We know that the borderline between remembering and imagining is sometimes blurred. But just as there are degrees of certainty (I recall here Gardner Williams's "Ivory soap theory of truth"), so what is intended as an objective eyewitness account is different from a fairy tale. At the very least, the picture of what my life is and has been is what I take to be the truth of myself; it is the reality I live with. Today we are forbidden to raise the question of the author's intention. Even if known, it is said to be irrelevant, since the text must be judged by what others (an infinity of others) perceive in it. But even if my own judgment on my life is to be given no privilege, the way I look at and feel about it is part of the story.

Having long since abandoned my childhood practice of assigning a
grade to myself at the end of each day, I will not be so foolish as to
try now to appraise the objective worth of my life. Even by my own
standards, that would be impossible, and what would such a judgment
mean anyway? One thing I *can* do is to compare my early expectations
with my tangible achievement, and I find the result interesting. I did not
become the creative writer I once dreamed of being; I never achieved
dizzying pinnacles of fame. While I think I have flown higher than the
barnyard chickens, I cannot claim to have soared with the eagles. But I
have enjoyed a greater degree of happiness and contentment, of conscious satisfaction with the actuality, than I would have believed possible. Without being so arrogant as to feel that others should envy my
life or that everyone would pronounce it good, I realize how extraordinarily fortunate my circumstances have been. I am grateful though not
smug. Within reasonable limits, I have done what I wanted to do. There
have been disappointments and failures. My overall self-acceptance has
had to accommodate a considerable measure of self-dislike. I find less
merit than I used to see in what I regarded as my positive accomplishments. But I have learned not to take any of these things or myself quite
so seriously.

It is hard to imagine the point of view from which I would now be
reflecting back on my life if on that day when a student asked me about
Existentialism, I had not taken up the challenge to pursue the matter further. The decision led to a turning point in my career. The very framework of my thought was profoundly affected. Yet I never think of my
encounter with the Existentialist writers as a *bouleversement*, an upheaval
that uprooted all I had taken for granted and put something new in its
place. It was more like the opening of a door I had been struggling to
unlock or like a sudden illumination of an area in which I had been
stumbling over hidden obstacles. This raises a question: If I consider my
engagement with humanistic Existentialism as the natural outcome of
the direction I was taking, is that to say that given my earlier history, it
was inevitable that I would do as I did? And would that be to introduce
precisely the claim of deterministic conditioning that is the antithesis of
the responsible freedom and self-making which Existentialism presup-
poses to be the existing core of every individual? To put the question
differently: I have always believed that I was freely determining what I
made of my life. So do many, if not most, other people. The question is
whether the feeling was an illusion. Nothing can be proved one way or
the other. But reflecting on this story I have told of myself, the hypoth-

esis that it developed as a series of self-choosings rather than as the unfolding of a ready-made self or a self continually processed by others seems to me best to describe the lived experience. Two sets of observations are relevant:

First, the probabilities of my turning out to be quite different from the person I became seem overwhelming in retrospect. I could, for instance, have modeled myself more closely after the pattern of my beloved aunts. True, my father once remarked that I was born rebelling. I appeared from the beginning to want to remake whatever situation I found myself in. Someone might see a genetic factor here, I suppose. But the precise way in which genetic and environmental elements and sheer chance interplay is either a mystery or what Sartre refers to as a freedom making itself be. When, still quite little, I learned of Elizabeth, my stillborn older sister, I wondered if, having missed this first chance, she had waited to be born in me, if she and I were really the same. Now I sometimes like to imagine a novel written of her life, one in which, starting from almost the same point, she might have become one of the Hazels I might have been. Of course, and this is relevant to my second point, it is possible to trace familiar patterns embedded in products radically dissimilar. That I was conditioned to teach I willingly admit—though in fantasy I can see an Elizabeth who carried rebellion still further or who, alternatively, opted for a service occupation within the church. Someone might say that in embracing and in working to promote Existentialism, I was obeying the call to conversion and earnest commitment to belief that I had resisted as a child. Or that my later talk of responsible freedom and self-making was only in response to the Free Methodist teaching of personal accountability to God. Or that my zeal for liberation of the oppressed was in obedience to the Church's commandment to serve others. The grain of truth contained in such assertions is of very slight significance compared with the radical divergence between what was there at the start and what is here, near the finish. My Aunt Grace's decision in the early 1900s to go as a missionary to India and my resolve to go to Greece after World War II were more dissimilar than comparable, both in motivation and in what each of us made of the experience. The presence in a Byzantine church of a lintel lifted from the ruins of a temple to Apollo did not determine the nature of the new architectural style. That Paul devoted the same sort of energy to spreading Christianity as Saul had shown in persecuting it does not mean that in his choice to be Paul rather than Saul, nothing significant had changed or that the choice had not been freely made.

Two constants in my life, unrelated to the question of philosophical orientation, have contributed to my continuing sense of the inexhaustible riches of existence. One of these is the miracle of friendship, and I would include here those relations that are reinforced by kinship while not dependent on it. Though I would not dispute Sartre's assertion that ultimately each of us is solitary in that there is no getting inside the subjectivity of another or escaping our own, that there is no merging of selves, I have found that empathy is more than an exercise of the imagination as community is more than an armistice (Sartre, of course, would agree in spite of his "Hell is Others"). I have, for most of my life, had the happy feeling of living in the middle of concentric circles of friends, more and less closely interwoven in my life. With varying circumstances their position relative to me would change; especially gratifying was the not infrequent experience of suddenly feeling that one at the periphery had the potentiality of holding a place near the center. Advancing years inevitably introduced a verticality, so much so that I have sometimes exclaimed with King Lear that the world "smells of mortality." Whether still living or not, my close friends have indeed become a part of my self, not by merging of subjectivities but by the kind of commingling and sharing expressed in the notion of the Look as an exchange and Looking-at-the-world-together. Camus said that he was in all of his characters. Reversing this, my friends are reflected in me; we have been each other's mutual concern. Friends draw us out of ourselves without uprooting us. In saying all this, I do not lay claim to anything more than the personal discovery of a universal truth. But in ordering my recollections, I have been aware that my own story could have been told as a history of friendships. The varied and intricate forms of the "we" that I have been privileged to enjoy have prevented me from confusing solitude with loneliness, from seeing existence as barren or monotonous. I have found in others a source of riches, an embellishment of the world itself.

Whether or not this story I tell myself has at least the status of what Sartre called a "true novel," the feeling of the interpenetration of life and literature has been another constant in my way of being. I am not speaking here merely of the delight in the imaginary that seems to be one of the most basic characteristics in all humans but specifically of books and primarily of the text as read rather than as enacted on stage or screen— of fiction, in prose or in poetry. (You may include auto/biography here, too, if you like.) I suppose that when I read a mystery story for distraction (my generational bias is shown in my preference for Agatha Christie and Ellis Peters over Sara Paretsky and Sue Grafton), I am satisfying the same need that brings viewers to soap operas and situation comedies. As for defending the relative value of the content, *de gustibus.* Even in this context, reading broadens the view. It is interesting that what Flaubert condemned in Emma Bovary was not the impulse to take refuge in trashy romances but her belief that she could transform everyday reality into the imaginary.

The process of reading is, I understand, a left brain activity. So apparently is the response to it so far as most of today's literary theorists are concerned—unless they indulge in secret bouts of empathy in their solitude. In trying to help students to appreciate a literary work as fully as possible, I have drawn heavily on rational analysis and the attempt to discern the objective means by which authors got their effects—explanations, in short. But it was with the assumption that these were devices to facilitate the student's own subjective encounter. When I am reading for myself, whether the author is Homer or Kazantzakis, Virginia Woolf or Tom Wolfe, the fictional beings and their stories (like living people I have met) become real as memories, as sources for new feelings about the world and myself. They are part of my lived experience; they color all future meetings. My self has changed in letting them enter, and they have changed the environment I live in. Once I have deciphered the printed words, their content resides in the right side of my brain. The world of a novel which I am currently reading or have just read is part of the texture of my day. Hopelessly out of fashion (and not only in my solitude), I stand by the old clichés: that literature breaks down the barriers of time and space, that it enlarges our understanding, that it develops our capacity for empathy, that it awakens us to possibilities in ourselves we had not suspected, that it literally expands the horizons of the self. I have been especially aware of the way that, under its influence, all of our lived experience is metamorphosed. It is not that the line between reality and imagination is blurred in a semipathological sense. Rather the imagined becomes part of the immaterial real that adds new dimensions to all of our actions and encounters: connotations, resonances, meanings, awareness. In reflective introspection, we realize connections that before had not been apparent. Life becomes more than its denotative description. Or so it has been for me.

By contrast, and paradoxically, I think that my approach to questions of religion has been largely from the left brain (using the term very loosely and not technically), though by general consensus such matters fall naturally to the provenance of the right. The narrowness of the religion that dominated my childhood may be chiefly responsible for my preference for dry rationality in dealing with religious phenomena, at least with respect to my personal beliefs. I have tended to be more concerned with the explanatory hypotheses employed to justify a faith or a vision than with the impulses that led to it, and interested in its effects on the believers' behavior in the world more than in what they claim to be an inward state of being. I ask myself now whether, looking at religious phenomena more broadly, I still view them so negatively.

With all due respect to others' right to commit themselves differently than I, my attitude toward fundamentalist Christian denominations has not changed. News of movements initiated by Pentecostal Protestants and charismatic Catholics sounds to my ears like replays of what I long ago found reason to reject. Those religious leaders who work in the name of liberation theology have won my intense admiration, but I look on them as having substituted active empathic compassion for human beings in place of the Church's authoritarian teaching of the duties of an abstraction called Love. Ardently supportive of the principle of freedom of religious belief, for individuals and for groups, I am unwilling to extend blanket approval to all religious practices. The circumcision of female children, to take one extreme example, whether it is defended as a religious ritual or merely as a corollary tradition attached to a particular religion, seems to me indefensible for two reasons: that it is patently a cruel and blatant manifestation of male thirst for total domination and that it violates the most basic human right to self-determination. While I acknowledge the great value that many derive from the supportive community within their chosen church, in looking at religions worldwide, I am inclined to conclude that sectarian fervor is more divisive than reconciliatory, more oppressive than liberating.

These are still left brain reactions and directed at religious institutions and belief systems rather than toward what are variously referred to as spiritual impulses, awe in the presence of the sacred, the thirst to go beyond the everyday self toward a greater reality, pursuit of expanded forms of consciousness, or simply the search for "something more" of which James spoke. To dismiss all these things as nothing but examples of illusory wish-fulfillment would be the worst sort of reductionist psychologism. I find no difficulty in accepting the possibility that extrasensory perception or even some form of telekinesis might someday be part of ordinary human experience or that the mental limitations we take as fixed might someday be dissolved. Whether these revolutionary developments could be assimilated in the same manner as other leaps—that is, as communication techniques or technological developments—or whether they would redefine what "humanity" is, we can only speculate. To try to live by them now would be to live by metaphysical hypotheses or science fiction rather than by knowledge—as Sartre said apropos of the suggestion that there might ultimately prove to be intelligible dialectical connections in nature. Still, if the future is to be open, we have to open ourselves to it.

Claims of other than rational insights (rational by present criteria) and revelations are not limited to future possibilities. I have described my reactions to conversions and semimystical experiences of my own at an earlier period of my life, and I spoke then of how I would look at them from my later Sartrean perspective. Should that be my final word? Not quite. I have had no late life conversions, mystical or otherwise, that have led me to throw into question the conclusions at which I arrived then. But now, questioning myself closely, I try to discover whether perhaps certain impulses, feelings, emotional responses to moments of closeness to nature, to which I have declined to give the adjective "religious," would properly be called so by others.

Once I came close, at least, to what Zen writers name the "little satori." On one of my adult visits to Beach Lake, I was swimming in the lake that gives the village its name. Suddenly I felt, not just a continuity with the "I" who used to swim there, but a oneness and the simultaneous presence of whoever (I or others) would swim there in the future. It seemed that this moment alone was real and that in it all other moments were contained—a sort of eternal present. Nothing of this was conceptual, only overwhelming feeling, profoundly though fleetingly satisfying, numinous in its own way. It was also ineffable, so much so that the attempt to remember it, by describing it to myself in words, distorted whatever message I might hope to find in it. This happening did not *mean* or *reveal;* it *was.* It had no perceptible effect on my subsequent conduct or my everyday happiness or my overall outlook, nor did I have any uneasy sense that it ought to do so. As I thought about it afterward, it seemed to me to have associations with accounts I had read in discussion of Zen teachings but not to fit with them exactly. I thought rather of Nietzsche, not of his doctrine of eternal recurrence, which I have never felt that I understood, but of a passage in *The Birth of Tragedy* in which he describes how the artist's imagination can momentarily so completely assume the point of view of cosmic becoming that the artist, so to speak, coalesces with it. The individual self is not so much lost as put in parentheses. Nietzsche was interested in searching for the "eter-

nal essence of art." I did not consider my transient exultancy as primarily aesthetic but rather as proof that our consciousness is capable of rising above its preoccupation with the self it has created and of contem-
plating external reality as a whole for what it is in itself, in such a way as
to include us without keeping ourselves as central. Someone else may
prefer to say that such moments of nonconceptual insight represent a
contact with the basic energy that supports all things, living and lifeless.
To me the experience was one of transcendence, not of immanence.

For some people the religious is inseparable from, often almost indistinguishable from, a feeling that there remains at the heart of things an
ultimate mystery, not to be confused with the sort of problem for which
one may expect or wish for a solution. Back of this belief, I think, lies an
unarticulated feeling that may range from the conviction that only an
answer incommensurate with what we think of as scientific knowledge
would befit the question, to the vague hope that things are somehow
more signifying than they appear to be on the surface. I have sympathetic
vibrations here. I feel them, not only in thinking about possible future
evolvements in human capacities but in certain psychological explorations. Though my habit of searching for cognitive, rational meanings
in interpreting my dreams and conversions may strike psychoanalysts as
naive and self-deluding, I do not think of the experiences themselves as
a shallow interplay of received ideas. I feel a more than intellectual excitement when, for the first time, I believe I am able to grasp the underlying significance of a myth. I do not remember or reflect on even my
most chaotic and apparently nonsignifying dreams without a quicken-
ing of the pulse and a sense of being on the edge of something inexplicable but mysteriously signifying. There are times also when I feel as
if "I" were appealing to resources beyond my everyday self. The appeal
is not a prayer addressed to an external power. I do not feel compelled
to conclude that I am pounding at the door of an Unconscious. Perhaps
on these occasions my consciousness is most urgently at work to refashion its self. Sartre never claimed to understand how consciousness does
all that it does. He shared with most Phenomenologists the view that
human consciousness is not to be studied and understood in the same
way that objects of science normally are. There is a qualitative difference, not only a quantitative one. Although John Searle might be surprised to be invoked in support of Existentialism, I think he states
the case well in arguing that even if we can discern the origins of self-
consciousness in the processes of biological evolution, we are not yet

able to say exactly what self-consciousness *is*. And, I would add, might become.

In my case, though I would not quite go so far as to join with Nietzsche in declaring that the world can be justified aesthetically and in no other way, I think it has been more through literature than in religion (even stretching the meaning of the word to its limits) that I have been able to live with a sense of being surrounded by an infinity of significations, nuances of meanings, dimly heard resonances, hidden harmonies waiting to be discovered; and through literature, too, that I came to know the real effects of the imaginary in myself and in the world. On second thought, though, what else is the religious impulse if not the thrust toward something beyond what is known now, the hope for personal life enhancement, for seeing with new eyes, for opening the self? Perhaps I was too quick in refusing to say that religion is poetry. But if I were to say it, I would be speaking in metaphor.

Sartre claimed that the aim of the biographer is to uncover the subject's fundamental project. At times he wrote as if it should be possible to abstract and condense in a single totalizing sentence the essential motif of a life. Indeed, we can quite easily make such summary statements concerning the subjects of the biographies he published. We can say that (as Sartre saw them): Baudelaire "lived his life backward" as if it were a long fall from an earlier Paradise; Genet sought to make himself the creator of the Being that Society had thrust upon him and to infect Society with his own nonBeing; Flaubert chose the imaginary over the real in a vain attempt to emerge as victor in the game of "loser wins." True as these insights may be, I think they are after the event summary judgments imposed by Sartre. Yes, we understand how each life could be described as having that overall shape. We can hardly see these summations as regulating principles of the evolving lives as the subjects lived them. It is neither realistic nor helpful to reduce the fundamental project to a single overgeneralized motif. What Sartre actually does in his biographical studies (except for *Baudelaire*, which is really more of a critical essay than a biography) is to show us the fundamental project as a gradually evolving unity; a crystalizing moment in childhood indicates a specific orientation that in turn is modified in later critical choices, unfolding, not in a determined linear direction, but as in a spiral. Reflecting on my own life, I can certainly not arrive at any one all embracing declaration of what essentially constituted my choice of how to make myself be. I do feel that my life has been a unity, a unity as I lived it, I mean, not just as I have recorded it.

In old-fashioned biographies, the author often concluded with a chapter summarizing the qualities that together made up the character of the subject. Often, as I recall, these took the form of "On the one hand this . . . but on the other hand, that." Such clumsy efforts never struck me as resulting in anything but failures. The distinctive character of the life, if it was revealed anywhere, was displayed in the pages preceding, not in the biographer's critical abstractions from it. I will not attempt anything of the sort here. In so declining, I fly in the face of my overcultivated tendency perpetually to hunt for networks of meaning and unifying motifs in what I have been and to pass judgment on myself. Suddenly I wonder: Is *THAT* my fundamental project? And have I not just condemned such encapsulating formulas? To pursue this point would be to reflect on a reflection on a reflection on. . . . I have had enough of twisting. It's time to swing free.

Index